PRINCIPLES

OF

CONTRACT LAW

By

Robert A. Hillman
Edwin H. Woodruff Professor of Law,
Cornell Law School

CONCISE HORNBOOK SERIES®

THOMSON

———✦———™

WEST

Mat #40083736

Concise Hornbook Series, WESTLAW and West Group are trademarks registered in the U.S. Patent and Trademark Office.

© 2004 West, a Thomson business
        610 Opperman Drive
        P.O. Box 64526
        St. Paul, MN 55164–0526
        1–800–328–9352

Printed in the United States of America

ISBN 0–314–14365–3

TEXT IS PRINTED ON 10% POST
CONSUMER RECYCLED PAPER

1st Reprint — 2006

FOR THE MEMBERS OF THE R B J & H CLUB
WITH MUCH LOVE AND APPRECIATION

*

Preface

I have written this book to help students understand and apply the greatest of law subjects, namely contract law. But it is not a substitute for hard work. I strongly recommend that you read and study the cases in your casebook, take feverish notes in class, and synthesize the material in your own outline of the course. You should use this book to review concepts, to clarify issues that give you trouble even after all your diligent work, and to help you understand how everything fits together. The book should also prepare you well for contracts questions on the bar exam (so keep it in good shape).

To get a feel for the nature and scope of this book, please take a look at Chapter 1, which is an introduction. Here I simply want to list some of the book's attributes that will facilitate your understanding of contract law:

1. I have tried to explain concepts clearly and concisely. The writing is informal, and I even have attempted to be humorous at times (you, of course, will be the judge of whether I succeeded).

2. The book contains numerous examples and illustrations of rules and principles. Often, I have taken the liberty of assigning you a role in a problem, on the theory that you will be most interested and attentive if you can envision having something at stake. (For example, Chapter 1 asks whether you have any legal rights to a 2001 Ferrari after you see an advertisement in the newspaper listing the car for sale for $30,000 and you call the owner and say you want to buy the car.)

3. For ease of reading and understanding, the book omits annoying textual footnotes that often confuse the reader or make issues more difficult and complex than necessary. Instead, the footnotes cite cases, articles, and treatises, with most including short quotations to substantiate positions taken in the text. But for a straightforward explanation of rules and principles, you don't have to look at the footnotes at all.

4. The book contains lots of cross references in case you want to review concepts that are building blocks for the current material you are reading.

5. The book covers all of the major issues of contract law and discusses in text most of the leading contracts cases that appear widely in the various contracts casebooks.

6. The book covers timely issues such as amended Article 2 of the Uniform Commercial Code and electronic contracting.

Many people helped me in this endeavor. Thanks to April Anderson, Phil Cummins, Imri Eisner, Eric Franklin, Courtney Herz, Heather Hillman, Jessica Hillman, Emily Paavola, Brad Wilson, and Nathaniel Yale for excellent research assistance, extensive work on the footnotes, and editorial suggestions. Thanks also to Professor James Henderson for reading early chapters, and Karen Wilson for her general assistance. As always, Betsy Hillman supplied encouragement and support.

Enough said. Hope you enjoy contract law and this book!

ROBERT A. HILLMAN

Ithaca, New York
January 15, 2004

Summary of Contents

Table of Contents

*

PRINCIPLES
OF
CONTRACT LAW

*

Chapter One

INTRODUCTION

Congratulations! Because you are reading this book (or at least perusing it), you must be interested in contract law, and, most likely, you are a first-year law student studying the subject. I extend my congratulations because your study of contract law is time well spent—contract law is the most interesting legal field and, by far, the best law school subject. You don't believe me? Here's what two law professors have to say about the issue:

> For lots of reasons, contract law is by far the best law school subject to teach and to learn. What other subject contains such a wealth of theory, doctrine, and substantive reasoning? What other subject focuses so clearly on essential components of economic and other organization in our society, namely private agreements and exchange transactions? What subject better exemplifies the power of general theory, the functions and limits of the common law, the rise of statutory law, the interaction of right and remedy, and the role of various legal actors in our system (including transactors, lawyers in their various roles, judges, and lawmakers)?[1]

O.k., if you looked at footnote 1, you know that I am one of the authors of this quotation. And the quotation is pretty abstract. But I still think I can convince you that contract law is a great subject and that you will enjoy learning it and even enjoy reading this book.

At its core, contract law answers two basic, but immensely interesting and important, questions (see, I told you): What promises does society enforce, and why does it enforce them? By enforcement, I mean that society will devote its resources to ensuring that a promisor performs or pays damages to the promisee for failing to perform. (Throughout this book, the promisor is the party who makes the promise at issue and the promisee is the party who receives the promise.) For example, suppose you (the promisor) promise to give your piano to your neighbor, Alice (the promisee). You will learn that if you break your promise before Alice reasonably has relied on the promise, she has no legal recourse against

1. Robert A. Hillman and Robert S. Summers, The Best Law School Subject, 21 Seattle U. L. Rev. 735, 735 (1998).

1

you, although she legitimately may be very disappointed in you. On the other hand, if you promise to give Alice the piano in exchange for her promise to give you $400, both of your promises would be legally enforceable even without any reliance on them. You could go to court and recover money damages if you were ready to perform but Alice broke her promise to pay (and she could recover from you if you broke your promise and Alice did not). Of course, the issue of promise enforcement does not relate only to simple promises and exchanges for small amounts between neighbors. Contract law also applies to mammoth deals between huge companies in the business world, and everything in between. By studying contract law, you will learn how to determine what promises contract law enforces, and understand why society enforces them.

Such questions are not insignificant. By enforcing people's private promises and agreements, contract law recognizes the power of parties to order their own affairs without the intrusion of the government. Contract law allows you and Alice to create your own private law, every bit as legal and significant as pronouncements of a legislature, such as traffic regulations and the determination of criminal conduct. This recognition of "freedom of contract" constitutes one of the core principles of our free-market economy and is a fundamental precept of our political philosophy. Ironically, contract law marshals the resources of government to enforce contracts against contract breakers in order to facilitate parties' *private* lawmaking.

Moreover, contract law's enforcement of private agreements, such as the exchange of the piano for the $400, benefits both parties—you valued the $400 more than the piano and Alice valued the piano more than $400. Otherwise, neither of you would have made the agreement. Because both of you have improved your position, society benefits as well by getting the most out of its resources. Of course, it is another story if you were aware that the piano was seriously defective and therefore worthless and Alice were reasonably unaware of this. The study of contract law also includes a consideration of the many factors that may lead to non-enforcement of defective private exchanges.

A. Scope of this Book

The scope of this book is easy to describe. The book covers the main topics of contract law typically treated in a first-year course on the subject. A short synopsis of each chapter follows (at the risk of raising more questions than can be answered at this point). By reading this short summary, you will get a flavor for contract law's response to the questions of what promises society enforces and why it enforces them.

Chapter 2: Bargain Theory for Enforcing Promises and the Requirement of an Agreement. This chapter first covers the principal ground for the enforcement of promises, known as a "bargained-for exchange." You will learn in detail about the difference between a bargained-for exchange, such as an agreement for the exchange of your piano for $400, which is legally enforceable, and a simple promise to make a gift of the piano, which is not enforceable (in the absence of reasonable reliance on the promise). In a bargained-for exchange, a promise is said to be "supported by consideration" because the promisor gets something in exchange for her promise. You will also read about the reasons contract law settled on this distinction between enforceable bargained-for exchanges and unenforceable gift promises.

Chapter 2 also covers the equally important concept of "agreement." A party seeking the enforcement of a bargained-for exchange must show that the parties actually reached an agreement for the exchange. Suppose you casually mentioned to Alice that you were thinking of selling your piano for $400 and, before you could utter another word, she announced that she accepted your offer and would pick up the piano immediately (she's very strong). Obviously, if you refused to give up your piano and she sued you for breach of contract, you would hope to be able to defeat her claim by insisting that you hadn't offered to sell in the first place. Although this may be an easy example, the law of agreement enforcement requires difficult line drawing as well. Consider newspaper advertisements. When should contract law treat these as offers that, without more, can be accepted by the reading public to form enforceable agreements and when should contract law consider advertisements as mere invitations to the public to negotiate further? (In other words, if you see an advertisement for a 2001 Ferrari for $30,000, can you call the owner and accept, thereby forming a legally enforceable agreement? Stay tuned.)

Chapter 3: Additional Theories for Enforcing Promises. Chapter 3 covers theories for enforcing promises in addition to a bargained-for exchange. The chapter first takes up the doctrine of promissory estoppel, which boils down to the legal enforcement of promises when the promisor reasonably should understand that her promise will induce the promisee to rely and the promisee does rely. For example, suppose you promise to give Alice your piano as a gift with full knowledge that, induced by your promise, she will forego an opportunity to purchase another piano for half its market value. In fact, Alice does pass up that opportunity. If you fail to keep your promise you will be liable to Alice on the basis of promissory estoppel.

Many analysts support promissory estoppel because of the perceived injustice of failing to enforce promises that induce reasonable detrimental reliance (reliance that injures the promisee). On the other hand, promissory estoppel was bound to be controversial because it expanded promissory liability beyond the traditional theory of bargained-for exchange. Nevertheless, promissory estoppel is now a well-established theory for enforcing promises. Moreover, promissory estoppel no longer is restricted to gift-promise situations. Courts have applied it to statements made during pre-contract negotiations and to agreements that are unenforceable because of some defense, such as a failure to put the agreement in writing. (Some, but not all, agreements must be in writing to be enforceable under what is called the "statute of frauds." See Chapter 4.) Although the scope of application of promissory estoppel is broad and some analysts predicted that it would "swallow up" the bargained-for exchange theory, promissory estoppel has met with only limited success in the courts.[2]

Chapter 3 also takes up the theory of unjust enrichment. This theory has lots of uses and names in various contexts, but, in general, it applies when a party confers a benefit on another party and it would be unjust for the recipient to retain the benefit without paying for it. Unjust enrichment law imposes an obligation on the recipient to pay or return the benefit. Unjust enrichment issues arises in promissory situations in at least three distinct ways. You are probably thinking "pianos" right now, but put that aside and think of another deal between you and Alice: You and Alice agree to an arrangement in which you will care for her lawn for monetary compensation, but you fail to specify either orally or in writing how often you will work for her, the amount she will pay you, or the duration of the arrangement. Contract law may decline to enforce such an agreement because it is too uncertain—how would a court determine the appropriate measure of damages for a breach when the parties have not specified the amount of compensation or duration? However, suppose you have already worked for Alice for a total of three days. You have conferred a benefit on Alice that would be unjust for her to keep without compensation. Courts allow you to recover the fair market value of your services under the doctrine of unjust enrichment.

Unjust enrichment issues also arise after a breach of an enforceable contract. Contract law generally allows an injured promisee to sue either for breach of contract or for unjust enrichment. If you and Alice had agreed to the amount of compensation for, and the duration of, the yard work, say $20 per hour for the total hours

2. Grant Gilmore predicted that promissory estoppel would "swallow up" the bargain theory in his great book, The Death of Contract (Ronald K. L. Collins ed., 2d ed. 1995). For a recent work (not quite as great) questioning Gilmore's thesis, see Robert A. Hillman, Questioning the "New Consensus" on Promissory Estoppel: An Empirical and Theoretical Study, 98 Colum. L. Rev. 580 (1998).

worked, and Alice wrongfully refused to pay for ten hours of work, you could recover $200 for breach of contract. In the alternative, you could sue for unjust enrichment based on the fair market value of the ten hours of work performed (which may be the same amount as the contract price, $20 per hour, or, if one of you was a good bargainer, may be larger or smaller than $20). Obviously, you would want to use the unjust enrichment theory when the benefit you conferred was greater than $20 per hour.

A third use of unjust enrichment in the realm of promissory activity involves a party who confers a benefit in a business setting, not intended as a gift, but the conferral is not pursuant to a formal contract. Such a situation arises, for example, when someone, whom we'll imaginatively call X, helps arrange a lucrative business transaction for two other parties and then seeks a "finders fee" for putting the parties together. If neither X nor the business parties had discussed compensation for X, the question is whether the business parties are unjustly enriched by X's services. After all, the business context suggests that X was not donating his services. The term "quasi contract" is especially relevant here, because, as the name suggests, the parties did not enter an actual contract with X, but the relationship was "like" a contract.

Chapter 3 also covers warranties for the sale of goods. These warranties are found in the Uniform Commercial Code, which has been adopted by the state legislatures as state law. (I introduce the UCC in Part B of this chapter.) When you go to Wal–Mart and purchase an air conditioner, your rights, should the air conditioner prove to be defective, depend in large part on your sales contract and the warranty provisions of the UCC. So you'll want to pay attention to this part of Chapter 3.

Chapter 4: The Statute of Frauds. Certain agreements must be in be in writing to be enforceable under what is called the "statute of frauds." The idea is that the writing requirement deters people from fraudulently asserting that the parties made an enforceable oral agreement. Chapter 4 takes up the categories of agreements that must be in writing to be enforceable. The chapter also considers what kind of writings satisfy the statute of frauds and exceptions to the writing requirement when the statute of frauds otherwise applies. Perhaps the most interesting question we consider is whether the statute of frauds induces more fraud than it discourages because it sometimes enables a promisor who has made an otherwise enforceable oral agreement to avoid her obligation.

Chapter 5: Remedies. Chapter 5 covers the remedies for breach of contract, promissory estoppel, and unjust enrichment. Although these remedies sometimes overlap, they also can differ significantly. The most important remedy for breach of contract is called "expectancy damages," designed to put the injured party in as good a position as if the contract had been performed. Assume an enforceable contract, in which you have performed ten hours of yard work for Alice for $20 per hour. You can recover $200 for breach of contract if Alice fails to pay you anything because that would put you in the position you would have been in had Alice performed. Imaginative readers might wonder whether you can recover damages for the delay in payment or for other adverse consequences of Alice's breach. (O.k., maybe you are imaginative even if you didn't think of this.) We will see that, with certain limitations, courts do award such "consequential damages" because they are necessary to put you in the same position as if Alice had performed.

In some cases, an injured party may be granted the remedy of "specific performance" instead of expectancy damages. Specific performance is a court order requiring the breaching party to perform the contract. If Alice has an enforceable contract to purchase your piano, for example, specific performance would constitute a judicial decree ordering you to deliver the piano to her. If you fail to obey the order, believe it or not, the court can fine you or throw you in jail. So give her the damn piano.

Some contracts include a "liquidated" (also called an "agreed") damages provision. Such a provision spells out in the contract the amount of damages upon a breach. Agreed damages provisions are not always enforceable, with enforcement generally depending on, at the time of contracting, how accurately the provision approximates a promisee's potential damages and how difficult actual damages would be to measure. We will investigate the not-always clear application of these principles as part of a broader discussion of the wisdom of enforcing or striking liquidated damages clauses.

Chapter 5 also takes up the measure of damages in promissory estoppel cases. This topic is controversial. Some analysts believe that damages should compensate the relying party only for the detriment she suffers. After all, the crux of the theory is that a promise induced detrimental reliance. For example, you promise to give Alice your piano (worth $500) as a gift, with full knowledge that your promise will induce Alice to forego an opportunity to purchase an equivalent piano (also worth $500) from a music store for $250. You should be liable to Alice for the difference between the market value and purchase price of the other piano ($250) because that is what she lost by relying on your promise. Another possible measure, one endorsed by other analysts, is to compensate Alice for the full value of your promise. After all, you broke your promise to give Alice your piano. The value of your promise to Alice, of course, was $500.

I already have touched upon the remedial goal in unjust enrichment cases, mainly to give the injured party the fair value of the benefit conferred. This is also challenging because courts must decide precisely what constitutes a benefit and how to measure it. For example, a court could measure the benefit based on its market value, its value to the party receiving it, or the cost of the benefit to the party conferring it (or some variation of these). Chapter 5 considers these issues too.

Chapter 6: Policing Contracts. This chapter discusses various "policing" doctrines, which are rules and principles that focus on the fairness of the contracting process and of the resulting terms. Policing doctrines include duress, fraud, unconscionability, and more. The challenge for courts applying these doctrines is to sort out fair bargaining from unfair overreaching and reasonable terms from "unconscionable" ones. Put another way, courts engaged in policing contracts must determine when "freedom of contract" ends and appropriate regulation of contracts begins. Moreover, the problem extends over a wide range of transactions, from important business deals that included lots of negotiation, to standard-form contracts between businesses and consumers, to simple contracts between neighbors.

In fact, drawing the line between enforceable and unenforceable agreements constitutes a daunting challenge for lawmakers and, therefore, an interesting subject matter for you. For example, suppose you and Alice are negotiating the sale of your piano. Alice is a piano teacher and you know that she needs your piano to give lessons and cannot get another piano in time. You insist on a price of $600, even though the market value of the piano is only $200. Should contract law enforce the $600 deal if Alice promises to pay $600? You will see that decisions on this and similar issues are not always consistent. In fact, cases dealing with policing issues help illustrate the reality that in hard cases the rules of contract law may not produce definitive results. Judges must rely on the equities of the case and policy objectives in combination with contract principles in order to reach a desirable result.

Chapter 7: The Parol Evidence Rule and Contract Interpretation. Please note the spelling of "parol" in the parol evidence rule. You will score high marks with your professors and with partners in law firms if you spell parol correctly (yes, there is no "e" at the end—when you write "parole" you are talking about what an inmate in a correctional facility sometimes gets at the end of a prison term). "Parol" means "expressed or evidenced by speech only; not expressed by writing."[3] The parol evidence rule

---

3. Blacks Law Dictionary 1273 (rev. 4th ed. 1968). Of course, there are more recent legal dictionaries, but, for senti- mental reasons, I wanted to cite the dictionary I used in law school (just this once).

bars the admissibility of evidence of prior or contemporaneous oral agreements or promises that vary or contradict a written term that the parties intended to be complete with respect to that term. A simple example may clarify this mouthful. Suppose you and Alice make a written contract for the sale of your piano and you include all of the pertinent terms, including a price of $500. Alice refuses to pay any more than $300, and claims that, prior to signing the written contract, you orally agreed to accept $300 for the piano. She explains that you listed the purchase price as $500 only because you thought that your mother would be angry with you for selling the piano for as little as $300. You go to trial and Alice seeks to introduce this evidence. The traditional parol evidence rule bars the evidence because it contradicts the signed writing. In this way, the rule is supposed to protect written contracts from untruthful attacks on their veracity. People who sign written contracts intended as complete and comprehensive are bound to the terms.

For now, only two additional caveats about the parol evidence rule. First, we will see that it is full of exceptions. Courts created these exceptions in cases where they strongly suspected that the parties did agree to terms that contradict a writing. For example, perhaps you really did tell Alice that you would accept $300 and you both forgot to change a previously typed $500 price term. Judges who believe this understandably are reluctant to enforce the contract as written. Second, the parol evidence rule usually applies to prior *written* drafts as well as oral agreements. So why call the rule the parol (oral) evidence rule? Whatever the reason, the wisdom of treating prior written drafts the same way as prior oral agreements makes sense if one believes that the parol evidence rule performs a service by protecting the *final* written product.

Chapter 7 also treats the law of contract interpretation. Once we decide what evidence is admissible (by applying the parol evidence rule), we next must apply rules to ascertain the meaning of the language in the contract. This is the process of contract interpretation. For example, we will see that contract law utilizes an "objective" approach to interpretation, meaning that the law enforces a reasonable interpretation of language, not what one party may have subjectively and secretly meant by the language. ($500 means just that, not $300.)

Chapter 7 also takes up how courts fill gaps in incomplete contracts. (But note that if a contract leaves too many gaps, it will be unenforceable.) Contracts may be incomplete for many reasons. The parties may not foresee an event that affects performance. Alternatively, the parties may choose not to deal with a particularly thorny issue or with a problem that is unlikely to occur. We will discuss the various sources of rules to fill gaps that arise in these and other ways. For example, one judicial strategy is to fill gaps with the term the parties would have wanted had they contracted concerning the issue. Champions of freedom of contract approve of this approach because it is consistent with the idea that parties, and not courts, should be the principal drafters of contracts. Further, lawyer-economists see this strategy of gap filling as the best way to reduce the costs of bargaining over terms. Parties can omit terms if drafting them is too costly (for example, in time and lawyers' fees) because courts will fill gaps with the terms they would have wanted anyway. Obviously, the wisdom of this judicial gap-filling strategy depends on the reliability of the judicial process of determining what the parties would have wanted. We will see that courts also resort to other gap-filling strategies, sometimes because they cannot confidently predict what the parties would have wanted.

Chapter 8: Conditions and Breach. After parties make an agreement, usually everything goes smoothly. You promise to mow Alice's lawn on Saturday and Alice promises to pay you $40 on condition that you do the job. You mow, she pays. Unfortunately, sometimes things don't go so well. You fail to mow, or complete only part of the job. She refuses to pay all or some of the $40. You dispute whether you are supposed to mow first, or she is supposed to pay before you mow, or if you have a duty to mow even if it is raining.

Chapter 8 discusses how courts resolve these issues using the rules of conditions and breach. The chapter also shows how good drafters can avoid disputes and litigation. For example, you and Alice did a fine job drafting a term with respect to the order of performance. You promised to mow and Alice promised to pay you $40 *on condition* that you mow. You have expressly set the order of performance in the contract. We will see that contract law calls your promise to mow an "express promissory condition precedent" to Alice's duty to pay. The order of performance is so clear that a reasonable person would not go to court to dispute the issue.

But now let's suppose you and Alice simply agreed that you would mow and she would pay and your contract omits any express conditions. Things are not so clear-cut if you dispute who must perform first. Further, if you cannot resolve the dispute amicably, a court cannot simply enforce the contract as written. Courts must use the tools of interpretation and gap filling presented in Chapter 7 to determine the "implied" or "constructive" conditions in your contract. Do the circumstances show that you agreed to mow on condition that Alice pays you first, or is it the other way around? If the circumstances shed little light on the issue, what gap filler with respect to the order of performance does contract law supply? Chapter 8 discusses how courts resolve such issues.

Chapter 8 does not deal only with order-of-performance problems. Another frequent dispute involves the quality of performance. Suppose Alice promises to pay you for mowing on condition that she is satisfied with the quality of your performance. Unfortunately, your mower drips gasoline on several areas of Alice's lawn, which kills the grass in those areas. You may have little to quarrel about if Alice doesn't pay you because of the express satisfaction clause in your contract. Suppose, however, that your contract omits any express reference to the quality of performance, but she still refuses to pay you. A court resolving this dispute must determine the content of any implied conditions precedent to Alice's duty to pay you. We will see that contract law's usual answer is that Alice must pay you if you have "substantially performed" (or if you have not "materially breached," which means the same thing). The challenge, of course, is determining just what constitutes substantial performance in a particular situation.

Chapter 9: Grounds for Excusing Performance. Chapter 9 covers various grounds for excusing performance of a contract because the circumstances turn out to be very different from what both parties supposed at the time of contracting (called the mistake doctrine) or because the circumstances materially change after contracting (impossibility, impracticability, and frustration of purpose). These doctrines are controversial because they excuse parties from otherwise enforceable contracts. Obviously, if too generous, the excuse doctrines threaten the institution of contracting. Will you want to make contracts if contract law excuses the other party simply because the circumstances change? So, Alice cannot assert a defense to the piano contract based on a simple change of mind for the very reason that contracts would not be worth the paper they are written on if she could. Instead, contract law assumes that once Alice promises to take and pay for the piano, she must perform the contract.

On the other hand, if parties reasonably did not contemplate certain important facts or did not foresee a change of circumstances that dramatically increases the cost of performance, one can argue that they did not allocate the risk of the new circumstances. Suppose an energy supplier promises to deliver oil to an electric utility under a long-term supply contract for $15 per barrel. Prices then skyrocket to ten times that amount because of an unforeseeable world crisis. The energy supplier will soon go bankrupt if forced to honor the contract. Contract law must consider whether the energy supplier is entitled to relief under the impracticability doctrine because performance is so different from what the parties contemplated.

Consider another example involving the mistake doctrine. Suppose both parties to a sale of jewelry reasonably thought the seller was selling a worthless stone for $1, but the "stone" turns out to be a diamond worth $50,000. Clearly, the parties did not contract for the sale of a diamond and the buyer will receive what is arguably a windfall if the court enforces the sale. The challenge, of course, is to draw the difficult line between enforcing contracts freely made and overturning contracts that create a forfeiture for one party and a windfall for the other. No challenge is too great for us and we'll take up all of this in Chapter 9.

Chapter 10: Third Parties. Up to this point in this introductory chapter, virtually all of the discussion of the legal rights of parties involves just two parties, namely the contracting parties themselves. But contracts can affect third parties in many ways. A contract between a city and a manufacturer can regulate the amount of pollution raining (literally) down on the citizenry. A husband and wife can contract for the inclusion of terms in the husband's will that will benefit a family member. A small local hardware store can sell to a national chain, such as True–Value, the hardware store's contract right to the delivery of inventory from a wholesaler. Chapter 10 investigates the rights of these and other third parties. For example, in the first example, can the citizens group sue the manufacturer directly if it is exceeding the pollution limits set in the contract or must the group wait until the city itself sues? In the second example, what are the rights of the family member if the husband breaks the contract and does not include the family member in his will? In these first two examples, the citizens group and the family member are called third–party beneficiaries of the contract and the issue is whether they should have the right to sue directly. We will see that the answer depends in large part on whether the contracting parties intended to confer on these third parties the right to sue in case of a breach of contract. Without such intent, contract law bars third parties from suing and therefore avoids the flood of litigation that would result from another approach. (Imagine, for example, if contract law allowed you to sue a television network for cancelling your favorite show, "Ed," in violation, you thought, of the network's contract with the show's producer.)

The third example is different because True–Value actually purchased the local hardware store's contract right to the delivery of hardware by the wholesaler. The sale of the contract right by the hardware store is called an "assignment of rights," and issues arise, among other things, over whether the wholesaler must sell to True–Value instead of the hardware store. You may think that the wholesaler should not care who it sells to and who pays it. But suppose the wholesaler had promised the local hardware store to supply all of its needs for one year and the hardware store assigned this right to True–Value. Does the wholesaler have to honor this obligation by delivering to True–Value all of its needs? After all, the needs of the local hardware store may be very different from the needs of True–Value.

We will see in Chapter 10 how contract law sorts out the various rights of all of these third parties.

B. Sources of Contract Law

The contract law you will study in this book comes from the common law and statutory law. Restatements, treatises, and law review articles play a role too. Common law is judge-made law arising from judicial opinions that resolve disputes. Suppose Alice brings an action against you to get her money back because she has decided that your piano is too large for her living room. A judge deciding this case might look at previous opinions dealing with the issue of "change of mind" and write an opinion stating that this is not an adequate reason for refusing to enforce an otherwise enforceable contract. Lawyers and judges in subsequent cases could look to this new "precedent" too in deciding that similar changes of mind do not constitute sufficient reasons for overturning enforceable agreements.

Although contract law is predominantly judge-made, statutory law (law enacted by legislatures) also plays a role. For example, Article 2 of the Uniform Commercial Code ("UCC" throughout this book) governs "transactions in goods."[4] Goods are "all things * * * which are movable at the time of identification to the contract for sale * * *."[5] Because this definition of goods and many other sections of Article 2 refer specifically to sales of goods, the scope of Article 2 is mainly sales of goods, such as the sale of your piano to Alice.

The UCC was a joint project of the American Law Institute and the National Conference of Commissioners on Uniform State Laws (at the risk of anesthetizing you with too many acronyms, ALI and NCCUSL, respectively). These bodies sought to unify and improve commercial law in all of the states by drafting the UCC and by urging each state to enact it. They were highly successful and now all fifty states' legislatures have enacted at least portions of the UCC (with only some non-uniform amendments). As of this writing, ALI and NCCUSL have promulgated amendments to Article 2. These have not yet been adopted by any states, but adoption in at least some states is likely in the next few years. Accordingly, when pertinent, I will discuss current Article 2 throughout the book, but

---

4. UCC § 2–102 (1989).   **5.** UCC § 2–105(1).

I will also mention the amendments when they will have an important impact on the analysis.

One further caveat about Article 2. As mentioned, Article 2 governs the sale of goods and we will be referring to it throughout this book. However, the book does not cover Article 2 exhaustively because many of its provisions are treated in upperclass commercial law courses. For now, understand that when an issue arises with respect to a contract for the sale of goods, Article 2 applies. However, if the specific rules of Article 2 fail to govern an issue, common law contracts principles still apply.[6] For example, a judge would refer to the common law to decide the validity of the defense to a claim of breach of contract that a seller or buyer has changed his mind, because Article 2 does not address the point. In addition, judges interpret the express rules of Article 2, which may be vague or ambiguous as applied in a particular context. These judicial decisions that interpret the provisions of Article 2 help us to understand its meaning.

As I mentioned, Restatements, treatises, and law review articles also influence contract law. ALI published the Restatement of Contracts in 1932 and followed this up with the Restatement (Second) of Contracts in 1981. Each of the restatements sets forth a series of rules and comments that synthesize the learning of existing case law and, to some extent, present the drafters' views of what the law should be. The Restatements are not state law in that they have not been enacted by any state legislature. However, if a court pronounces that it is following a restatement section, the rule of that section becomes part of the common law of that state.

Lawyers sometimes rely on and cite treatises and law review articles as persuasive authority for points they wish to make in litigation. We will cite and discuss a wealth of material from these sources too.

C. Contract Lawyers' Various Roles

You will learn lots of rules and principles of contract law in this book and in your contracts course. You will also learn the reasons behind these rules and you will be asked to evaluate these reasons. Equally important, you should begin to form a sense of how lawyers actually use the rules and principles you encounter. For example, lawyers do more than go to court and try to recover money for an injured client, although this is an important role. Lawyers also apply contract law when they advise clients about the wisdom of entering a contract and about appropriate terms. Lawyers also draft contracts, after taking into account the goals and circumstances of their clients. Lawyers also negotiate with the other side

---

6.   UCC § 1–103.

about appropriate terms, and, after the contract has been completed and is being performed, about rights and obligations when something goes wrong, or circumstances change, or a dispute arises. Because the rules and principles of contract law guide the lawyer in all of these roles, it is helpful to ask yourself how you would use a particular rule to plan, draft, or negotiate a contract, as well how you would use the rule in a lawsuit.

D. Conclusion

Now that you have had a taste of what follows, it is time to dig in and learn the details of the best law school subject. One last thought before you proceed: This book is entitled "Principles of Contract Law," and its goal is to help you learn this fabulous subject. Based on the philosophy that learning should be fun and interesting, indeed with the view that learning is enhanced by these attributes, I will make every effort to explain the principles clearly and succinctly, to offer many clarifying illustrations, and even to make you laugh once in a while.

Chapter Two

BARGAIN THEORY FOR ENFORCING PROMISES AND THE REQUIREMENT OF AN AGREEMENT

The principal ground for the enforcement of promises is called a "bargained-for exchange." A bargained-for exchange, such as an agreement for the exchange of a piano for $400, is legally enforceable, whereas a simple promise to make a gift of the piano is not enforceable. In a bargained-for exchange, a promise is said to be "supported by consideration" because the promisor gets something in exchange for (or as the price of) his or her promise. Part A of this chapter covers the bargained-for-exchange theory for enforcing promises (also called "the bargain theory of consideration").

A party seeking the enforcement of a bargained-for exchange must also show that the parties actually agreed to the exchange. Chapter 1 presents the example in which you casually mention to your neighbor, Alice, that you are thinking of selling your piano for $400 and Alice instantly announces that she accepts your offer and insists that you have a contract. It does not take much knowledge of contract law to believe that Alice is not entitled to the piano because you did not reach an agreement. But suppose you used language that Alice reasonably believed demonstrated your intent to contract, such as "I would like to sell," even though you were still not sure that you actually wanted to sell. Does Alice's acceptance of your "offer" form an enforceable agreement? Part B of this chapter illustrates how contract law sorts out mere talk and negotiations from the formation of enforceable agreements.

A. The Bargain Theory of Consideration

1. Bargained-for exchange versus gift promise. As already mentioned, a bargained-for exchange is legally enforceable, whereas a simple gift promise is not enforceable.[1] In a bargained-for exchange, the promisor requires something from the promisee in return for the promise. We can think of what the promisor gets in return as the price of the promise. The price of the promise is called "consideration." You promise to sell the piano to Alice, but only in

---

1. For the definitions of promise and bargain, see Restatement (Second) of Contracts § 2(1) (1981) ("A promise is a manifestation of intention to act or

15

exchange for Alice's promise of $400. Contract law says your promise is "supported by consideration," namely the promise of $400, and is therefore enforceable.[2] A simple gift promise of the piano is not supported by consideration and therefore unenforceable. If the donor of the gift actually delivered the gift, however, the donor cannot get it back.[3]

To make a promise enforceable, the promisor must "bargain for" or request the consideration supplied by the promisee in exchange for the promise.[4] Suppose a "benevolent" person, Ron D. Jockefeller, promises to buy clothes for a homeless person if the homeless person walks to a clothing store a few blocks away. If the homeless person walks to the store, is Jockefeller's promise of the clothes enforceable?[5] Only if Jockefeller bargained for the homeless person to walk to the store, which in turn depends on whether Jockefeller's motive was to extract the walk as the price of the promise of clothes. But in order to understand Jockefeller's motive, we need more facts. Suppose Jockefeller owned a restaurant and the homeless person had camped out in front of the restaurant. These facts support a finding that Jockefeller's motive for his promise was to remove the homeless person from the vicinity of the restaurant and we can therefore say that Jockefeller bargained for the homeless person's walk to the clothing store. But if Jockefeller did not own a restaurant and made the promise, not because he would get something in return, but simply because he is a wonderful person, the promise would constitute a gift promise and would be unenforceable. The homeless person still must walk to the store to pick up the gift. But those in the know say that the trip to the store is a condition necessary to pick up a gift, not consideration to support Jockefeller's promise.[6]

refrain from acting in a specified way, so made as to justify a promisee in understanding that a commitment has been made.") and § 3 ("A bargain is an agreement to exchange promises or to exchange a promise for a performance or to exchange performances.").

2. See Restatement (First) of Contracts § 75 (1932) (consideration is something "bargained for and given in exchange for the promise.").

3. Maughs v. Porter, 161 S.E. 242, 243 (Va. 1931) ("A gift is a contract without consideration, and, to be valid, must be executed.... Delivery of possession of the thing given or the means of

obtaining it so as to make the disposal of it irrevocable, is indispensable to a valid gift.").

4. See Restatement (Second) of Contracts § 71(2) ("A performance or return promise is bargained for if it is sought by the promisor in exchange for his promise and is given by the promisee in exchange for that promise.").

5. This example was inspired by a similar problem posed by Williston in 1 Samuel Williston, The Law of Contracts 232–33 (1924), quoted in Maughs v. Porter, 161 S.E. 242, 243 (Va. 1931).

6. See Williston, supra note 5, at 232–33; see also Plowman v. Indian Re-

Of course, determining whether something is a condition necessary to receive a gift or consideration to support a promise is often no easy task. Consider Judge Benjamin Cardozo's famous opinion in *Allegheny College v. National Chautauqua County Bank of Jamestown.*[7] In a writing, Mary Yates Johnston promised Allegheny College $5000. The writing stated that the money "shall be known as the Mary Yates Johnston memorial fund."[8] Johnston contributed $1000 of the gift, with the rest to be paid after her death, but then she repudiated the promise. After Johnston's death, the college sued her estate to enforce her promise. Judge Cardozo held that when the college accepted the $1000 it assumed the duty "to perpetuate the name of the founder of the memorial" and that was "sufficient in itself to give validity to the subscription within the rules that define consideration for a promise of that order."[9] An alternative interpretation strongly urged by the dissent was that "[t]he sum offered was termed a 'gift' by [Johnston]. Consequently, I can see no reason why we should strain ourselves to make it, not a gift, but a trade."[10] The correct interpretation of Johnston's language naming the fund after her depends on Johnston's motive—was she extracting a promise to use her name as the price of her promise of the money, or did she want to make a gift, with the hope or suggestion that the college would use her name. Obviously, reasonable minds can (and did) differ on this factual question.

A promisor's gratitude for the promisee's past good conduct or services does not constitute consideration because the promisor is not extracting and the promisee is not supplying anything *as the price* of the promisor's promise. In the well-known case of *Dougherty v. Salt,*[11] for example, the promisor, Helena Dougherty, gave her eight-year-old nephew, Charley, a $3000 promissory note (a written promise to pay the money). This came about after Helena remarked to Charley's guardian that she wanted to "take care" of Charley, and the guardian told Helena not to "take it out in talk." Helena then gave Charley the note, which included the notation for "value received." As she handed her nephew the note, Helena added: "[y]ou have always done for me, and I have signed this note for you. Now, do not lose it. Some day it will be valuable."[12]

---

fining Co., 20 F.Supp. 1, 5 (E.D. Ill. 1937) (requirement that retired employees come to employer's office to pick up their checks merely a condition necessary to receive a gift).

7. 159 N.E. 173 (N.Y. 1927).

8. Id. at 174.

9. Id. at 176.

10. Id. at 177.

11. 125 N.E. 94 (N.Y. 1919).

12. Id. at 94–95.

Of course, it is difficult to see what an eight-year-old could have "done" for his aunt, but even if he had performed services for her or otherwise benefitted her, Helena's subsequent promise would not have been enforceable. Helena did not make her promise with the motive of extracting something from her nephew in return, and therefore the court held that her promise was an unenforceable gift promise.

2. The promisor's motive. You can see that a lot turns on the promisor's motive for making the promise. For your promise of a piano to be enforceable, your motive must be to obtain Alice's promise of $400. For the promise of new clothes to be enforceable, the promisor's motive must be to remove the homeless person from the premises. The focus on motive, however, is misleading without considering two caveats. First, although few courts address the issue clearly, contract law measures the promisor's motive objectively, meaning that a *reasonable person* must believe that your motive for making the promise of the piano was to obtain a return promise of $400.[13] A promisor's *actual* motive is irrelevant. We will see in Part B of this chapter that this focus on apparent rather than actual motive is consistent with contract law's focus on apparent rather than subjective meaning of the language of negotiation. (So when you ask for $400 for your piano, you cannot enforce your secret, inner intention to sell for $500.) But much more on this in Part B.

The second caveat on the issue of motive is that a promisor's motive of obtaining something in return for the promise (as determined objectively) does not have to be the primary or even a substantial reason for making the promise, it simply has to be one of the reasons.[14] This insight will help you understand this challenging bit of Restatement (Second) of Contracts jargon in Section 81: "The fact that what is bargained for does not of itself induce the making of a promise does not prevent it from being consideration for the promise."[15] *"Of itself "*is the key phrase here. What the promisor bargains to receive may be only one of many motives for making the promise, and even an insignificant motive.

---

13. See Williston, supra note 5, at 232; see also Restatement (Second) of Contracts § 81, cmt. a: "[T]he promisor must *manifest* an intention to induce the performance or return promise and to be induced by it, and ... the promisee must *manifest* an intention to induce the making of the promise and to be induced by it." (Emphasis added).

14. See Allegheny College v. National Chautauqua County Bank of Jamestown, 159 N.E. 173 (N.Y. 1927).

15. Restatement (Second) of Contracts § 81(1).

Not only must a reasonable person believe that one of the promisor's motives was to extract consideration from the promisee, but a reasonable person must believe that the promise actually induces the promisee to deliver that consideration.[16] If it appears that the promisee had a completely different motive for promising or performing what seems to be consideration for a promise, the promise is unenforceable. Suppose for example, Uncle strongly desires Nephew to quit smoking and therefore promises Nephew $2000 if he quits. Nephew quits smoking and demands the $2000. Without more, you might conclude with some confidence that Uncle's promise is enforceable. However, suppose Nephew had seen a doctor two months before Uncle's promise and the doctor strongly advised Nephew to quit smoking. In light of this news, Nephew did quit, unbeknownst to Uncle. Uncle's promise of the $2000 would be unenforceable because of the absence of consideration to support his promise. Uncle's promise did not induce any action on the part of Nephew. (Nephew should not be too sad about losing the $2000. He will gain immeasurably by having quit smoking.)

3. What must be extracted. To constitute consideration, the promisor must bargain for *either* a return promise or a performance.[17] First, with respect to a return promise as consideration: In a purely "executory bilateral exchange" (meaning that both parties have made promises, but neither party has performed theirs yet) of a piano for $400, the seller extracts a promise from the buyer of $400 in exchange for the seller's promise to sell the piano and the buyer extracts a promise from the seller to sell the piano in exchange for the buyer's promise to pay $400. Each party's consideration is a return promise (the seller's promise of the piano and the buyer's promise of the $400).

You can see that in an executory bilateral exchange *each* party is both a promisor and a promisee. (The seller is a promisor with respect to his promise to sell the piano and a promisee with respect to the buyer's promise to pay $400. Conversely, the buyer is a promisor with respect to her promise to pay $400 and a promisee with respect to the seller's promise to deliver the piano.) This seems to confuse some students because in most cases the court refers only to one of the parties as a promisor and one of the parties as a promisee. Usually only one of the parties has breached the contract and the other party has sued for damages. The court focuses on the broken promise and the party who made that promise, namely, the promisor.

Now, with respect to a *performance* as consideration, the seller could have promised to deliver the piano in exchange for the buyer

---

16. See Baehr v. Penn–O–Tex Oil Corp., 104 N.W.2d 661 (1960).

17. See Restatement (Second) of Contracts § 71(1).

actually paying (not promising to pay) the seller $400. If the buyer pays the money, the seller's promise is enforceable because it is supported by consideration, namely the $400. The point is that consideration does not have to consist of a return promise. A promisor can extract a performance as consideration for the promise.[18]

The Restatement (Second) of Contracts sets forth the kinds of performances that constitute consideration. These include "acts" and "forbearances."[19] Actually paying the $400 for the piano is the kind of "act" the Restatement has in mind. Forbearances include desisting from exercising one's legal rights, such as the right to smoke or drink when one is at the age of majority.[20] In other words, if your parents promise to pay for your law school education if you do not smoke or drink for those three heavenly years, contract law would enforce their promise. Your forbearance to exercise your right to smoke or drink is good consideration to support your parents promise.

Courts often state that the consideration extracted by the promisor from the promisee (either a performance or a promise) may be a benefit to the promisor *or* a detriment to the promisee.[21] This language suggests that the promisor need not benefit from the consideration she receives. However, it is difficult to discern what a promisor's motive for extracting the consideration would be if she does not benefit in some sense.

Hamer v. Sidway[22] illustrates the fogginess of the benefit-detriment principle. In *Hamer*, Uncle promised Nephew $5000 if Nephew "would refrain from drinking, using tobacco, swearing, and playing cards or billiards for money until he should become twenty-one years of age."[23] Nephew forbore to engage in those pleasures until the age of twenty-one, and sought the $5000 from Uncle's estate. When the estate would not pay, Nephew sued. The issue was whether Nephew's forbearance constituted consideration to support Uncle's promise.

The court, citing an early treatise, stated that " '[c]onsideration' means not so much that one party is profiting as that the other abandons some legal right in the present, or limits his legal freedom of action in the future, as an inducement for the promise

---

18. See Restatement (Second) of Contracts § 71(1) & (2).

19. See id. § 71(3).

20. See Hamer v. Sidway, 27 N.E. 256, 257 (N.Y. 1891) (finding that a promisee who "restricted his lawful freedom of action" gave good consideration to support a promise); Restatement (Second) of Contracts § 71, cmt. d, illus. 9.

21. See, e.g., Hardesty v. Smith, 3 Ind. 39, 39 (1851) ("The doing of an act by one at the request of another, which may be a detriment or inconvenience, however slight, to the party doing it . . . is a legal consideration for a promise by such requesting party.").

22. 27 N.E. 256 (N.Y. 1891).

23. Id. at 257.

of the first."[24] Based on this definition, the court held that Nephew's forbearance constituted consideration regardless of whether it benefitted Uncle. Still, as a member of Nephew's family, Uncle very well may have benefitted from Nephew's forbearance, which Uncle apparently believed would do his nephew good. This benefit supports the determination that Uncle's motive was to extract the forbearance. Some discussion in the case, however, appears to suggest that Uncle's motive was irrelevant and that Nephew's detriment was enough ("It is sufficient that [Nephew] restricted his lawful freedom of action * * * upon the faith of his uncle's agreement"[25]), leading two luminaries of contract law to criticize the *Hamer* opinion.[26]

In fact, it is hard to think of a case where forbearance would be consideration (*i.e.*, "bargained for") if it did not benefit the promisor at least psychically. Of course, if psychic benefit to the promisor is enough to establish that a detriment is consideration, every gift promise could be enforceable. The promisor enjoys making the gift and the promisee forbears from asserting her right not to accept the gift. Contract law has not gone this far, probably mindful of Lon Fuller's admonition that gift promises are not important enough to enforce legally.[27] Perhaps all that can be said is that benefit to the promisor is "[a]n aid, though not a conclusive test" of consideration,[28] and that courts rule out as consideration a benefit that is too ephemeral.

4. Forbearance to sue as consideration. Suppose Alice has wrongfully trespassed on your property and cut down some trees. (Neighbors can be a real pain, can't they?) You approach Alice and complain, but get no satisfaction. You therefore mention that you "will have to go to court." Alice now reconsiders and states that she promises to pay you $500 for the lumber if you do not sue her. You don't sue. Is her promise enforceable?

Note that in this example Alice's promise is supported by consideration, namely your forbearance to sue on a valid claim. Her promise is therefore enforceable.[29] But suppose you knew the trees

---

24. Id. (quoting Frederick Pollock, Principles of Contract 167 (2d ed. 1885)).

25. Id.

26. See Allegheny College v. National Chautauqua County Bank of Jamestown, 159 N.E. 173, 174 (N.Y. 1927) (Cardozo, J.) ("The promise and the consideration must purport to be the motive each for the other. . . ."); Grant Gilmore, The Death of Contract 111 n. 34 (1974) ("Hamer v. Sidway . . . reject-

ed the so-called bargain theory of consideration.").

27. See infra notes 44–45, and accompanying text.

28. Maughs v. Porter, 161 S.E. 242, 243 (Va. 1931) (quoting Williston, supra note 5, at 233).

29. See Springstead v. Nees, 109 N.Y.S. 148 (N.Y. App. Div. 1908) (discussing the grounds for enforcing promises in exchange for a forbearance of bringing a legal action).

Alice cut down were on Alice's property, and you still threatened to sue, with the same response from Alice, namely a promise of $500. In this example, you and Alice agreed to an exchange—a promise of $500 in exchange for your forbearance to sue. Moreover, your forbearance to sue may be very beneficial to Alice. She doesn't have to pay a lawyer or spend time in legal wrangling. But contract law will not enforce this exchange on grounds of public policy. We do not want people going around extorting promises in exchange for forbearing to sue on claims they know are invalid.[30]

The two examples constitute the bookends of problems that can develop with respect to forbearance to sue. In the first example, your claim was valid—Alice trespassed and you were damaged. Alice's promise to pay was enforceable because it was supported by consideration, namely your forbearance. In the second example, you are a nefarious extorter because you knew your claim was not valid. Alice's promise therefore was not enforceable on public policy grounds. Extreme facts lead to easy decisions. Now the harder stuff.

Suppose you reasonably and honestly thought the trees were yours, but they were not. Perhaps you had never learned the precise location of the property line. (Reasonable people may not know the precise boundaries of their property. I don't and I'm very reasonable.) Contract law calls your claim "colorable" or "doubtful" and treats your forbearance to sue as good consideration.[31] After all, your motive was not to extort Alice and you were both honest and reasonable in your beliefs. In fact, according to the Restatement (Second) of Contracts, you only have to be reasonable *or* honest about your beliefs about the trees—you don't need both.[32] So, for example, if you are honest but unreasonable—the trees are in the middle of Alice's property but you honestly (but unreasonably) believe they are yours—and Alice offers you $500 to avoid litigation, the Restatement treats your forbearance as consideration. Perhaps this approach is too favorable to negligent people— public policy should discourage negligence as well as extortion. In addition, it is hard to see why the Restatement enforces a promise of $500 for your forbearance to sue when you actually knew the trees were not yours even though a reasonable person might believe they were yours. Your dishonesty is exactly the kind of conduct the law should try to discourage.

30. 2 Arthur L. Corbin, Corbin on Contracts 420–24 (3d ed. 1995).

31. See Springstead, 109 N.Y.S. 148.

32. Restatement (Second) of Contracts § 74(1).

5. The policies behind enforcing bargained-for exchanges. The previous section introduces public policy into the analysis of promise enforceability. But we haven't yet evaluated the policy choices made in distinguishing unenforceable gift promises from enforceable bargained-for exchanges.

Hopefully you are gaining a solid understanding of the rules of promise enforcement. Knowledge of the reasons behind the rules should help hone your comprehension. Nevertheless, as you read the following discussion you should understand that it mostly summarizes the work of Lon Fuller, a leading contract law scholar of the last century. As such, you should not take the discussion as gospel. Try to understand the strengths and weakness of the explanations. Most of all, evaluate whether you believe contract law should have drawn the line between enforceable bargained-for exchanges and unenforceable gift promises.

Probably the most famous article positing the reasons for the bargain theory of consideration, at least to contracts professors and their students, is Fuller's *Consideration and Form*.[33] Boiled down to its essence (which cannot possibly do it justice), Fuller posited both formal and substantive grounds for enforcing bargained-for exchanges. Formal grounds, which have to do with the "circumstances surrounding" the making of a promise,[34] include the "evidentiary," "cautionary," and "channeling" functions of consideration. Let's look at these first.

By enforcing bargained-for exchanges, Fuller posited that contract law satisfies "[t]he need for evidentiary security,"[35] meaning that a bargained-for exchange tends to produce evidence that a promise was really made. The bargained-for exchange requirement certainly is not the only method of generating evidence of promises, however. For example, contract law could have required all contracts to be in writing. Perhaps contract law settled on the bargained-for exchange requirement because exchanges are likely to generate sufficient evidence of the existence of a contract without unduly impeding parties who want to make enforceable promises. Of course, contract law also could have enforced written gift promises, which approach obviously would have satisfied the "evidentiary function." The evidentiary function alone therefore cannot explain the distinction between unenforceable gift promises and enforceable bargained-for exchanges.

A bargained-for exchange also cautions the parties about the seriousness of what they are doing. Fuller reasoned that an exchange would more likely alert the parties to the legal ramifications

33. 41 Colum. L. Rev. 799 (1941).   **35.** Id.
34. Id. at 800.

of their acts and promises than a gift promise.[36] His view was that people make gift promises all of the time, often without thinking through what they are doing. (I certainly have made my share of such promises. Come on, admit it. So have you.) Recall, for example, our discussion of *Dougherty v. Salt*,[37] where Helena Dougherty made her nephew, Charley, a promise of $3000 because she wanted to "take care" of him. Remember how Charley's guardian goaded Helena into making her promise by telling her not to "take it out in talk."[38] One suspects that at least one of the reasons contract law does not enforce promises such as Helena's is to protect promisors from such ill-advised and thoughtless promises. A party entering an exchange transaction has to jump through more hoops and therefore is more likely to be forewarned about the legal ramifications of what she is doing. Requiring a writing also cautions parties, but perhaps not as effectively as the formal requirement of a bargained-for exchange.

Finally, Fuller thought that the bargain theory satisfied the channeling function. Reading Fuller on the channeling function is a bit of a challenge, but the gist is that the bargained-for exchange requirement offers parties a recognizable method of entering an enforceable obligation. In other words, the bargained-for exchange requirement constitutes a distinct set of instructions for parties who want to enter an enforceable exchange. (I told you this one was tough.) According to Fuller, the context of gift promising is too amorphous to constitute clear instructions for creating a legal obligation.[39] For example, Fuller thought that it would be very difficult for a gift promisor to show the requisite intention to be bound, as opposed to a "tentative" intention to confer a gift.[40] This reasoning does not seem very persuasive, especially when one considers the possibility of enforcing written gift promises.

Fuller also accounted for the "substantive bases of contract liability," which have to do with the characteristics and importance of exchanges, not how they were made.[41] For example, he observed that enforcing bargained-for exchanges supports the principle of "private autonomy" because people can create their own legal

---

36. Id. at 816–17 ("[T]he fact that the transaction is an exchange and not a gift ... does offer some guaranty so far as the cautionary and channeling functions of form are concerned.").

37. 125 N.E. 94 (N.Y. 1919). See supra notes 11–12, and accompanying text.

38. 125 N.E. at 94.

39. See Fuller, supra note 33, at 815 ("As to the channeling function ... the [gift] promise is made in a field where intention is not naturally canal-ized. There is nothing ... to effect a neat division between tentative and exploratory expressions of intention, on the one hand, and legally effective transactions, on the other.").

40. Id.

41. Id. at 799–800 (substantive bases of contract liability relate to "the significance of the promise made and not merely the circumstances surrounding the making of it"); see also id. at 806–14.

relations through their exchange transactions.[42] In addition, enforcing bargained-for exchanges protects people who rely on their agreements. Further, Fuller noted that when such reliance benefits the other party as in "half-completed exchanges" (for example, suppose Alice pays for your piano before you deliver it—she has relied, you have benefitted), the reason for enforcing promises is strongest because one party has detrimentally relied and the other has been unjustly enriched.[43]

These substantive reasons for enforcing promises are not much help in explaining the distinction between gift promises and bargained-for exchanges. After all, enforcement of gift promises supports a promisor's freedom to make a gift. Enforcement also protects a promisee who relies on a gift promise, which reliance can benefit the promisor (such as when a promisee reciprocates for a gift promise by conferring a benefit on the promisor). Fuller has one more argument, however. Fuller's further explanation for the distinction between gift promises and bargained-for exchanges is that gift promises are more likely than bargained-for exchanges to constitute "sterile transmissions,"[44] meaning that gift promises do not contribute to the "production of wealth and the division of labor," nearly as much as exchange transactions.[45] In sum, exchange transactions are more important than gift promises and therefore require all of the resources of the law.

As you might guess, many others have spilled lots of ink discussing the reasons contract law enforces bargains, but not gift promises.[46] The explanations vary, but one of the more interesting ideas is that contract law fails to enforce gift promises, not because they are relatively unimportant, as posited by Fuller, but for precisely the opposite reason.[47] Gift promises would lose their symbolic meaning if they were legally enforceable:

> The world of gift is a world of our better selves, in which affective values like love friendship, affection, gratitude, and comradeship are the prime motivating forces. These values are too important to be enforced by law and would be undermined if the enforcement of simple, affective donative promises were to be mandated by the law.[48]

42. Id. at 806–08.

43. Id. at 815–16.

44. Id. at 815 (quoting Bufnoir, Propriété et Contrat 487 (2d ed. 1924)).

45. Id. at 815.

46. See, e.g., Charles Fried, Contract as Promise: A Theory of Contractual Obligation (Harvard University Press 1981); Melvin Aron Eisenberg, Donative Promises, 47 U. Chi. L. Rev. 1 (1979); Charles Goetz & Robert E. Scott,

Enforcing Promises, An Examination of the Basis of Contract, 89 Yale L. J. 1261 (1980); Richard A. Posner, Gratuitous Promises in Economics and Law, 6 J. Legal Stud. 411 (1977).

47. Melvin Aron Eisenberg, The World of Contract and the World of Gift, 85 Calif. L. Rev. 821, 849 (1997).

48. Id.

6. Adequacy of consideration. If you are with me up to this point, you now understand that contract law enforces bargained-for exchanges and you have been exposed to several explanations for this approach. But we cannot leave this subject without introducing several additional rules and principles governing the enforcement of bargained-for exchanges.

One of the "principles" of contract law that you will read over and over again in judicial opinions is that courts are not supposed to weigh the adequacy of consideration.[49] The parties should decide what something is worth and third parties (i.e., government officials such as judges) should not interfere with their decision. In this way, private parties create their own law to govern their private transactions. As early as 1851, a court, considering whether a worthless invention was good consideration for a promise to pay for it, captured this principle in the following way:

> [W]here one person examines an invention to the use of which another has the exclusive right, and, upon his own judgment, uninfluenced by fraud or warranty, or mistake of facts, agrees to give a certain sum for the conveyance of that right to him, such conveyance forms a valid consideration for such agreement. The judgment of the purchaser is the best arbiter of whether the thing is of any value, and how great, to him.[50]

The Restatement (Second) of Contracts adopts this position on adequacy of consideration in section 79: "If the requirement of consideration is met, there is no additional requirement of * * * equivalence in the values exchanged * * *."[51]

As with all rules, even long-standing, well-accepted ones, we will see in Chapter 6 that the adequacy rule is subject to several exceptions. As a general matter, for now, understand that many courts feel uncomfortable enforcing imbalanced exchanges, especially when the imbalance is severe. In fact, inadequacy of consideration may serve as a red flag that one party unfairly took advantage of the other at the formation stage and that the exchange should not be enforced. Doctrines such as unconscionability, duress, and misrepresentation, authorize courts to strike contracts made unfairly and often at least part of the evidence of unfairness derives

---

49. See, e.g., Pope v. Savings Bank of Puget Sound, 850 F.2d 1345, 1356 (9th Cir. 1988) (referring to this principle as "the first lesson in contracts"); Carroll v. Lee, 712 P.2d 923, 926–27 (Ariz. 1986); see also 3 Samuel Williston and Richard A. Lord, A Treatise on the Law of Contracts § 7.21, at 383 (4th ed. 1995) ("[T]he law will not inquire into the adequacy of consideration so long as the consideration is otherwise valid to support a promise.").

50. Hardesty v. Smith, 3 Ind. 39, 39 (1851); see also Haigh v. Brooks, 113 Eng. Rep. 119 (Q.B. 1839) (surrendering a worthless paper constituted consideration for a guarantee), aff'd, 113 Eng. Rep. 124 (Ex. 1840).

51. Restatement (Second) of Contracts § 79(b).

from the inadequacy of consideration.[52] Contract law thus includes both an admonishment to courts to keep out of the parties' private exchange and an invitation to courts to police agreements for unfairness. For now, the best I can offer to harmonize these contradictory tendencies of contract law is to say that a promisor usually is fighting an uphill battle when she urges the lack of enforceability of a promise *solely* because of the inadequacy of the exchange.[53]

   7. Mutuality of obligation and illusory promises. Recall our discussion of the "bilateral executory exchange."[54] You saw that this is an exotic name for the simple concept of when an agreement consists of promises by both sides that the parties have not yet performed. Such an agreement is enforceable because both promises are supported by consideration, namely the return promises.[55] But suppose your "agreement" consists of a promise by Alice to pay you $400 for your piano in exchange for your statement that you will sell the piano "if you want to." Contract law treats your statement as an illusory promise, meaning no promise at all, and finds the "agreement" unenforceable for lack of "mutuality of obligation."[56] The agreement lacks an obligation on your part because you haven't promised to do anything. You have reserved the right not to deliver the piano.

   Some of the cases on mutuality of obligation are not as straightforward as the above example, but they all boil down to the question of whether a promise is real or illusory. For example, in *De Los Santos v. Great Western Sugar Company*,[57] De Los Santos was a trucking company that "agreed" to transport in its trucks "such tonnage of beets as may be loaded" by Great Western from Great Western's supply of beets. De Los Santos's compensation depended on how many beets it carried for Great Western. At the time of the agreement, De Los Santos knew that Great Western had entered identical agreements with other carriers. When Great Western terminated the arrangement with De Los Santos, the latter claimed that Great Western had broken the agreement. Great Western insisted that it had the right under the agreement to use other transporters and to exclude De Los Santos.

   The court concluded that Great Western "made no promises at all other than the promise to pay for the transportation of those

---

52. See infra Chapter 6.

53. Restatement (Second) of Contracts § 79(b).

54. See supra notes 17–18, and accompanying text.

55. See Restatement (First) of Contracts § 75(1)(d).

56. See, e.g., Mattei v. Hopper, 330 P.2d 625, 626 (Cal. 1958) ("Whether [a problem is] couched in terms of mutuality of obligation or the illusory nature of a promise, the underlying issue is the same—consideration.").

57. 348 N.W.2d 842 (Neb. 1984).

beets which were in fact loaded by [Great Western] onto the trucks of [De Los Santos] * * *."[58] In other words, Great Western had no obligation to De Los Santos to load any beets, so Great Western had the right to terminate De Los Santos. In the parlance of contract law, the parties' arrangement was void for lack of mutuality of obligation (Great Western was not obligated to do anything), so De Los Santos had no rights.

Although not discussed in the opinion, you should realize that an arrangement that is unenforceable for lack of mutuality of obligation is not enforceable by *either* party. Thus, Great Western could not recover from De Los Santos if the latter repudiated the agreement before Great Western had loaded any beets. De Los Santos's promise to transport beets was an unenforceable gift promise precisely because Great Western had not committed itself to do anything in return. On the other hand, once Great Western loaded some beets a contract would be formed, but only for that quantity of beets.

Sometimes language appears to be an illusory promise, but the circumstances demonstrate that the promisor really did intend to commit itself. Courts often interpret such language as a binding promise even though in form there is no promise. For example, in the famous case of *Wood v. Lucy, Lady Duff–Gordon*,[59] Wood had the exclusive right to place Lucy's indorsements of fashion designs on clothing and to place Lucy's own designs on sale. The parties agreed to split the profits. After Lucy placed her indorsement on fabrics herself and kept the profits, Wood sued her for breach of contract.

Lucy's defense was that Wood had not obligated himself to do anything (just as Great Western had not bound itself), so their agreement was unenforceable. Although Judge Cardozo saw that Wood had not "promise[d] in so many words that he [would] use reasonable efforts to place the defendant's indorsements and market her designs," the judge implied just that promise.[60] In a well-known passage, Judge Cardozo stated "[a] promise may be lacking, and yet the whole writing may be 'instinct with an obligation,' imperfectly expressed. If that is so, there is a contract."[61]

What circumstances proved that the arrangement was "instinct with an obligation" on Wood's part?[62] Cardozo observed that Lucy would not have granted an exclusive right to Wood if he

---

58. Id. at 845.

59. 118 N.E. 214 (N.Y. 1917).

60. Id. at 214.

61. Id. at 214 (quoting McCall Co. v. Wright, 117 N.Y.S. 775, 779 (N.Y. App. Div. 1909)).

62. See Robert A. Hillman, "Instinct with an Obligation" and the "Normative Ambiguity of Rhetorical Power," 56 Ohio St. L.J. 775 (1995).

hadn't committed himself to do something. Lucy would receive no profits unless Wood made some effort. In addition, Wood was obliged to "account monthly" in order to determine how much he owed Lucy. Therefore, "[w]ithout an implied promise, the transaction cannot have such business 'efficacy as both parties must have intended * * *.' "[63] The court therefore found an implied promise that Wood use "reasonable efforts to bring profits and revenues into existence."[64] This commitment by Wood meant that the contract was not unenforceable for lack of mutuality of obligation because both parties were bound. Therefore, Wood could recover for Lucy's breach.

"Reasonable efforts" is not the only implied promise courts employ to find a commitment so that an agreement is not void for lack of mutuality of obligation. For example, some cases involve what are called "satisfaction" clauses. Suppose you promise to purchase a water-color picture of your house "if you are satisfied with the picture." Strictly speaking, you could argue that you had not entered an enforceable contract at all because you could arbitrarily decline to be satisfied with the painting. However, many courts interpret satisfaction clauses to require "good faith" on the part of the promisor (the party who must be satisfied).[65]

The good faith obligation means that your decision about whether you are satisfied with the picture must be reasonable or honest.[66] A court applying a reasonableness standard of good faith would compare your picture with comparable pictures at similar prices. You could not decline the picture if it compared favorably to the other pictures. A court applying an honesty standard of good faith satisfaction would determine whether you truly were dissatisfied or whether you had some ulterior motive for refusing to take the picture. For example, if you said you were dissatisfied with the quality of the picture, but actually declined to accept it because you disagreed with the painter's politics, a court would find you in bad faith for being dishonest—you said one thing about your reasons for declining the picture when you meant another.

How do courts determine which standard of good faith satisfaction to follow? Generally, if the satisfaction clause deals with "commercial value or quality, operative fitness, or mechanical utility" courts generally apply the reasonableness test.[67] Satisfaction can easily be compared with other market alternatives. When satisfaction involves "fancy, taste, or judgment," courts apply the

---

63. Wood, 118 N.E. at 214–15 (quoting The Moorcock, 14 P.D. 64, 68 (1889)).

64. Id. at 215.

65. See, e.g., Brack v. Brownlee, 273 S.E.2d 390 (Ga. 1980); Mattei v. Hopper, 330 P.2d 625 (Cal. 1958).

66. Mattei, 330 P.2d at 626–27.

67. Id. at 626–27.

honesty test.[68] In the picture contract, where satisfaction depends on how much you like the picture, courts would therefore likely apply the honesty test.[69]

Courts find mutuality of obligation in "satisfaction clause" cases by implying an obligation of "good faith" satisfaction for the same reason that Judge Cardozo found the Wood–Lucy contract "instinct with an obligation," namely because courts believe the parties probably intended these results. Further, the particular gap-filling approach in satisfaction clause cases—honesty or reasonableness—also depends on finding the likely intentions of the parties. You and the painter probably believed that you would decide whether you were satisfied based on your view of the quality of the picture and not based on some petty complaint about the painter's politics. Nothing would stop you from insisting on a provision allowing you to refuse the painting for the latter or other arbitrary reason, but a court would then probably find the agreement unenforceable for lack of mutuality of obligation. In the absence of such a provision, however, a court would find that you and the painter intended to make an enforceable contract in which you would determine your satisfaction honestly.

This section on mutuality of obligation began with a brief discussion of when the problem arises, namely when the contract at issue is an executory bilateral exchange. In other contexts, the mutuality requirement simply doesn't apply. For example, suppose an employer promises an employee $60,000 per year if the employee quits another job and comes to work for the employer. The employer also promises not to fire the employee for at least one year. Suppose further, that the employee does quit the other job and begins to work for the employer, but the employee does not bind herself to stay in the new job for any particular period of time. As you can guess, this story ends unhappily when the employer fires the employee within a year and claims the promise of one-year of employment was void for lack of mutuality of obligation. The employer asserts that the employee can quit at any time and therefore has no obligation to the employer.[70]

The employer correctly asserts that the employment arrangement lacks mutuality of obligation, but the employer should still be liable to the employee. This is because the employee has already supplied the consideration to support the employer's promise of one-year employment. Remember, the employee quit her other job

---

68. Id. at 627.

69. See Gibson v. Cranage, 39 Mich. 49, 50 (1878) ("Artists or third parties might consider a portrait an excellent one, and yet it prove very unsatisfactory to the person who had ordered it and who might be unable to point out with clearness or certainty the defects or objections.")

70. See Weiner v. McGraw–Hill, Inc., 443 N.E.2d 441 (N.Y. 1982).

and came to work for the employer as the price of the employer's promise of one-year of employment. Quitting the job and working for the employer was therefore consideration to support the employer's promise even though the employee could quit at any time.[71]

8. Preexisting duty doctrine. Suppose you and Alice enter a contract for the sale of your piano for $400. (Sound familiar?) You then realize that the fair market value of the piano is $500, so you ask Alice to split the difference by agreeing to a price increase of $50. She agrees and you deliver the piano. She then says she will pay you only $400, "according to the contract." Are you entitled to the additional $50?

Contract law's traditional answer to this question was no. You had already promised to sell the piano for $400, so you had the "preexisting duty" to deliver at that price. Alice's promise to pay $50 more therefore was not supported by consideration and was a mere gift promise.[72]

This result caused trouble whenever a court believed that the parties made their modification agreement voluntarily and fairly, such as above. After all, contract law is supposed to enforce parties' freely-made agreements, so why shouldn't the law enforce their freely-made modification agreements? In addition, the cautionary role of consideration appears to be satisfied, without the need for new consideration to support the modification. You and Alice already negotiated a contract for the sale of your piano, so you should understand the seriousness of what you are doing.[73]

Courts therefore began to devise ingenious methods of avoiding the preexisting duty rule. For example, in *Schwartzreich v. Bauman–Basch, Inc.*,[74] Schwartzreich agreed to a one-year employment contract with Bauman–Basch for $90 per week. After another employer offered Schwartzreich more money, Schwartzreich and Bauman–Basch wrote a new contract in which Schwartzreich's compensation was $100 per week. Bauman–Basch then fired

---

71. See id. at 444 (referring to the "not uncommon analytical error of engaging in a search for 'mutuality', which is not always essential to a binding contract, rather than of seeking to determine the presence of consideration, which is a fundamental requisite.").

72. See, e.g., International Paper Co. v. Suwyn, 951 F.Supp. 445, 448 (S.D.N.Y. 1997) ("[A] promise to perform an existing legal or contractual obligation is, without more, insufficient consideration to form a new contract."); Schwartzreich v. Bauman–Basch, Inc., 131 N.E. 887, 889 (N.Y. 1921) ("Any

change in an existing contract, such as a modification of the rate of compensation, or a supplemental agreement, must have a new consideration to support it.").

73. See United States v. Stump Home Specialties Mfg., Inc., 905 F.2d 1117, 1121 (7th Cir. 1990) ("By hypothesis the parties already have a contract, so that the danger of mistaking casual promissory language for an intention to be legally bound is slight....").

74. Schwartzreich, 131 N.E. 887.

Schwartzreich, who brought an action seeking compensation based on the $100 per week salary.

Although the court recognized the problem of the preexisting duty rule—Schwartzreich already had promised to perform for $90 per week, so Bauman–Basch's promise of an additional $10 per week was not supported by consideration—the court affirmed a jury verdict enforcing Bauman–Basch's promise of $100 per week. The court approved the trial judge's instruction to the jury that, if the parties had rescinded the original contract before or at the same time they made the new contract, Schwartzreich did not have a preexisting duty to perform for $90 and his promise to work was good consideration for the promise of $100 per week.[75]

Of course, the court's method of avoiding the preexisting duty doctrine goes too far. In reality, in every case that contracting parties modify their agreement, they have implicitly agreed to rescind the original contract. After all, they are trying to change that contract and certainly do not intend for it to trump the new agreement. It is true that both parties in *Schwartzreich* testified that they wrote a formal new contract and surrendered the old one,[76] but contract law should not and does not depend on such formalisms.

What really seemed to motivate the court was its acceptance of Schwartzreich's testimony that Bauman–Basch voluntarily agreed to the increased compensation after learning that Schwartzreich had received a better offer from a third party and after Schwartzreich asked Mr. Bauman, an officer of Bauman–Basch, what he should do.[77] One suspects that if the court had accepted Bauman's alternative explanation that Schwartzreich wanted to leave because "someone offered him more money" at a time when Schwartzreich's services were crucial to Bauman–Basch's business, the court might have found a way to decide in favor of Bauman–Basch.[78] In such a case, the court would have been concerned that Schwartzreich had extorted Bauman–Basch's promise.

If courts manipulate the preexisting duty rule to reach decisions based on whether the modification agreement appears to be

---

75. Id. at 890 ("There is no reason that we can see why the parties to a contract may not come together and agree to cancel and rescind an existing contract, making a new one in its place."); see also Int'l Paper, 951 F.Supp. at 448 (party who signed a non-competition agreement during the course of his at-will employment, without receiving new consideration, "effectively assented to [that] modification and commenced employment under new terms.").

76. 131 N.E. at 888–89.

77. Id. at 888–90.

78. See id. at 888, 890; see also Alaska Packers' Assn. v. Domenico, 117 F. 99 (9th Cir. 1902) (finding coercion); Recker v. Gustafson, 279 N.W.2d 744 (Iowa 1979) (applying the preexisting duty doctrine to a land sale modification agreement that appeared to have been coerced).

voluntary, contract law should move to a new rule that focuses on the voluntariness question. In fact, contract law has answered the call. For example, in sale-of-goods cases, Article 2 of the UCC provides that "[a]n agreement modifying a contract within this Article needs no consideration to be binding."[79] An "official comment" to the section imposes a test of good faith on the party benefitting from the modification. If that party's conduct constitutes "the extortion of a 'modification' without legitimate commercial reason * * *," the modification will not be enforceable.[80]

In our example of the sale of the piano, for example, Alice's promise to pay the extra $50 would be enforceable only if you negotiated the additional compensation in good faith. Because you learned that the fair market value was greater than you thought and asked whether Alice would split the difference, you do not appear to be extorting a modification. But suppose you learned, after contracting for $400, that Alice was a concert pianist who needed the piano for practice for a major performance and could not get one in time elsewhere. (Law school hypos don't have to be realistic, right?) Knowing Alice's plight, you demand $900 for your piano, even though its market value is only $500. Under section 2–209(1), Alice's agreement to pay the extra $500 ($900 minus $400) would be unenforceable because of your bad faith.

In cases that do not involve the sale of goods, the common law applies. Although some courts still apply the preexisting duty rule,[81] many have followed the Restatement (Second) of Contracts, which provides: "A promise modifying a duty under a contract not fully performed on either side is binding (a) if the modification is fair and equitable in view of circumstances not anticipated by the parties when the contract was made * * *."[82] This approach improves the preexisting duty rule by removing the focus on consideration. However, by requiring "circumstances not anticipated," the rule discourages enforcement of many voluntary modification agreements. For example, Alice's promise to pay $50 more after you realize the true market value of your piano is $500 or Bauman–Basch's promise to pay an extra $10 per week may not be enforceable under the Restatement's standard because those modification agreements arguably did not arise because of unanticipated circumstances.[83]

79. UCC § 2–209(1) (1989).

80. UCC § 2–209, cmt. 2.

81. See, e.g., Yerkovich v. AAA, 610 N.W.2d 542 (Mich. 2000); Johnson v. Maki & Assoc., Inc., 682 N.E.2d 1196 (Ill. App. Ct. 1997); Jaynes v. Strong–Thorne Mortuary, Inc., 954 P.2d 45 (N.M. 1997).

82. Restatement (Second) of Contracts § 89(a).

83. See generally Robert A. Hillman, Contract Modification Under the Restatement (Second) of Contracts, 67 Cornell L. Rev. 680 (1982).

9. Promise for benefit received. Think back (for the second time) to our discussion of *Dougherty v. Salt*,[84] where Helena Dougherty promised her nephew, Charley, $3000 because he "ha[d] always done" for her.[85] We said that even if he had performed services for her or otherwise benefitted her, Helena's promise after she received the benefit would not be enforceable. At the time Helena made her promise, she had already received the benefit from Charley so she could not have made her promise to extract that benefit. Contract law declines to enforce such promises based on the promise-for-benefit-received theory (also called the "past consideration" doctrine).[86]

Harrington v. Taylor[87] presents a particularly dramatic example of the promise-for-benefit-received bar to enforcing promises. Husband assaults Wife who runs to Neighbor's house. Husband begins assaulting Wife again in Neighbor's house. Wife knocks Husband down with an ax and launches a final blow to decapitate him. Neighbor intervenes and takes the blow intended for Husband on her hand, mutilating it. Later, Husband promises to pay Neighbor's damages. It is not hard to predict that, after paying a small amount, this despicable moron of a husband breaks his promise. Is his promise legally enforceable?

One might hope that the court would find a way to enforce Husband's promise. But in a very short legal opinion, the court had no trouble dismissing Neighbor's lawsuit. Characterizing Neighbor's act as "humanitarian" and "voluntary," the court stated that it was "not such consideration as would entitle her to recover at law."[88] The court could have added that Husband made the promise after he had already received the benefit, so he did not extract anything from Neighbor in return for his promise, meaning that there was no consideration to support his promise.[89]

Another promisor also avoided liability based on the past consideration theory in *Mills v. Wyman*.[90] Mills cared for Wyman's 25-year-old son, Levi, who was ill in Hartford, while Wyman was some distance away in Shrewsbury. Apparently the care administered included hiring two guards because Levi was " 'in [a] derang'd state' " and had " 'leaped out of a chamber window.' "[91] After

---

84. 125 N.E. 94 (N.Y. 1919). See supra notes 11–12, 37–38, and accompanying text.

85. 125 N.E. at 95.

86. See, e.g., In re Estate of Lovekamp, 24 P.3d 894 (Okla. Civ. App. 2001); Carlisle v. T & R Excavating, Inc., 704 N.E.2d 39 (Ohio Ct. App. 1997); Montana Pub. Employee's Ass'n v. Office of Governor, 898 P.2d 675 (Mont. 1995).

87. 36 S.E.2d 227 (N.C. 1945).

88. Id. at 227.

89. See Mills v. Wyman, 20 Mass. (3 Pick.) 207 (1825).

90. Id.

91. Geoffrey R. Watson, In the Tribunal of Conscience: Mills v. Wyman Reconsidered, 71 Tul. L. Rev. 1749, 1755 (1997) (quoting court records).

Mills had incurred all of the expenses, Wyman promised in a letter to Mills to pay Mill's expenses.[92] Although the court remarked that "in good conscience" Wyman should keep his promise, the court declined to enforce the promise legally because of the lack of consideration to support it.[93]

Perhaps you are outraged by these results. But proponents of legal rules assert that any judicial deviation from them based on a court's sense of fairness creates ambiguity and uncertainty in the law.[94] In fact, the *Mills* court wrestled with just such a concern. The court saw that contract law had already enforced promises for benefit received in three distinct situations involving promises to pay debts barred by bankruptcy, the statute of limitations, or infancy. For example, a debtor may be insulated from legal liability based on bankruptcy, the passage of time, or her age when she incurred the debt, but then make a new promise to pay the debt. Contract law enforced such promises even before the *Mills* case. But the *Mills* court saw that in all of those instances, the parties had a contract that had become unenforceable (so that the reasons for enforcing exchange agreements applied) and that enforcing Wyman's promise, where there had been no previous bargained-for exchange, would be a serious expansion of promissory liability. In fact, the logical extension of enforcing Wyman's promise, the court believed, was to enforce all moral obligations, whether a promise was made or not:

> If moral obligation * * * is a good substratum for an express promise, it is not easy to perceive why it is not equally good to support an implied promise. What a man ought to do, generally he ought to be made to do whether he promise or refuse * * *. Without doubt there are great interests of society which justify withholding the coercive arm of the law from these duties of imperfect obligation, as they are called; imperfect, not because they are less binding upon the conscience than those which are called perfect, but because the wisdom of the social law does not impose sanctions upon them.[95]

The Mills court plainly did not want to contradict this "wisdom of the social law."[96]

Whether enforcing the promises of Wyman and Taylor would have created too much ambiguity in the law is debatable. After all, Wyman's promise was in writing and Taylor had begun making

---

92. Strangely, a recent law review article reports that Levi Wyman didn't die, despite the court opinion reporting his death. See id. at 1756.

93. Mills, 20 Mass. (3 Pick.) at 209.

94. See Frederick Schauer, Playing by the Rules: A Philosophical Examina-

tion of Rule–Based Decision–Making in Law and in Life 95–96 (1991).

95. Mills, 20 Mass. (3 Pick.) at 228–29.

96. Id. at 229.

payments before he reneged. These acts could have served as distinct grounds for an extension of liability. Some courts have made this leap, but not based on clear reasoning. For example, in *Webb v. McGowin*,[97] Webb saved McGowin from a falling pine block in the employer's mill by directing the block away from McGowin and falling with it. Webb sustained serious injuries and McGowin promised to "care for and maintain" Webb for the rest of his life. McGowin paid $15 every two weeks as per the agreement for more than eight years, but McGowin's testator (the party representing his estate) refused to pay any longer after McGowin's death.

The court held that a complaint alleging these facts was legally sufficient. The court held that Webb had materially benefitted McGowin and that the latter was "morally bound to compensate" Webb.[98] So far, so good. Next, ignoring reality, the court claimed that the material benefit was "sufficient consideration for [McGowin's] subsequent agreement to pay for the services * * *."[99] The court reasoned that the "subsequent promise" by McGowin was "equivalent to a previous request."[100] Finally, the court wrote that McGowin's promise "rais[ed] the presumption that the services had been rendered at McGowin's request."[101]

Webb v. McGowin may have reached the right result, but for the wrong reason. Instead of muddying up the works by creating legal fictions about implied previous requests in order to satisfy the requirement of consideration, the court could have more directly declared that promises for benefit received are enforceable as a distinct obligation (separate from bargained-for-exchange) whenever a promisee materially benefits a promisor, not intending a gift, and the promisor then makes a promise to pay for the benefit. The complaint alleged that Webb had not conferred the benefit gratuitously (apparently because Webb performed his services in the workplace), which the court had to accept as true for purposes of the motion to dismiss.

The Restatement (Second) of Contracts declares directly that a promise "made in recognition of a benefit previously received by the promisor from the promisee is binding to the extent necessary to prevent injustice."[102] Promises are not binding under the Restatement approach if the promisee intended to make a gift of the benefit or the promisor "has not been unjustly enriched."[103] In

---

97. 168 So. 196 (Ala. Ct. App. 1935).

98. Id. at 197.

99. Id.; see also Edson v. Poppe, 124 N.W. 441 (S.D. 1910).

100. Webb, 168 So. at 197 (discussing Boothe v. Fitzpatrick, 36 Vt. 681 (1864)).

101. Id. at 198; see also Boothe v. Fitzpatrick, 36 Vt. 681 (1864).

102. Restatement (Second) of Contracts § 86(1).

103. Id. § 86(2)(a).

addition, if the value of the promise is "disproportionate to the benefit"[104] the promise is enforceable only up to the value of the benefit.[105] For an example of the latter point, if you mow Alice's lawn, expecting compensation, and she is so grateful that she promises you $1000 for your work, her promise will only be enforceable up to the fair value of the benefit.

B.   The Requirement of an Agreement

Part A dealt with the concept of a "bargained-for exchange." A bargained-for exchange is one kind of agreement.[106] (People can make agreements that do not constitute a bargained-for exchange. For example, you and Alice can agree that you will give her your piano as a gift.) Part B illustrates how contract law distinguishes mere talk, negotiations, and preliminary drafts from the formation of an enforceable bargained-for exchange. Some lawyers and students refer to agreement-law issues as the law of offer and acceptance. But we will see that the reach of agreement law is much longer, including, among other things, the formation of huge deals between large corporations based on multiple drafts without a sequence of offer and acceptance at all.[107]

1.   The objective test of assent. We have already mentioned the example of Alice trying to "trap" you into making a contract, when your clearly manifested intent was only to negotiate.[108] Recall that Alice's attempt to bind you legally would fail. However, if you outwardly expressed an intention to be bound, for example, "I promise you this piano for $400, and will deliver it promptly upon your acceptance," Alice could form a contract by accepting your offer, even though you were really joking. In short, under the objective test of assent, contract law generally enforces the apparent, not necessarily real intention of the promisor.[109]

Nowhere is this point made more dramatically than in the classic case of *Lucy v. Zehmer*.[110] Lucy and Zehmer were enjoying cocktails at a restaurant and chatting. Lucy offered Zehmer $50,000 for Zehmer's farm, which Zehmer had refused to sell to Lucy in the past. Zehmer claimed that he thought Lucy made the offer in jest.

---

104. Id. § 86(2)(b).

105. Id. § 86, cmt. i ("[A] promise is not enforceable under [Section 86] beyond the amount of the benefit.").

106. For a definition of agreement, see Restatement (Second) of Contracts § 3 ("An agreement is a manifestation of mutual assent on the part of two or more persons.").

107. See infra note 241, and accompanying text.

108. See the introduction to this chapter.

109. E. Allan Farnsworth, Contracts 117 (3d ed. 1999) (indicating that under the objective approach, what controls are "the external or objective appearance of the parties' intentions as manifested by their actions.").

110. 84 S.E.2d 516 (Va. 1954).

Zehmer also asserted that he decided to play along and therefore wrote on the back of a guest check, "We hereby agree to sell to W.O. Lucy the Ferguson Farm complete for $50,000.00, title satisfactory to buyer."[111] Both Zehmer and his wife then signed the writing. Zehmer also claimed that he was "high as a Georgia pine" at the time of these events and that they were "just a bunch of two doggoned drunks bluffing to see who could talk the biggest and say the most."[112]

Lucy and his wife sought to enforce the writing through a court order called specific performance. (We cover this remedy in Chapter 5, section A(8).) First, the court discounted Zehmer's claim that he was drunk, primarily because he was able to testify about what had occurred.[113] Next, the court found "persuasive" evidence that the parties' agreement was a "serious business transaction rather than a casual, jesting matter."[114] For example, the parties negotiated for forty minutes, they wrote two drafts, and they had Mrs. Zehmer sign the contract. In addition, the court noted the "the completeness of the instrument," which suggested a serious business deal.[115]

You may be asking yourself about now whether this court is for real. Obviously, lots of evidence suggested that Zehmer was joking, such as the setting of the "negotiations," the drinking, and Zehmer's previous reluctance to sell the farm. In addition, with respect to the "completeness of the agreement," compare the handwritten agreement scribbled on the back of a guest check with the more usual three or four page printed form contract to purchase real estate, which includes, among other things, long descriptions of the property, title provisions, mortgage commitments, and provisions on the closing. Whether the court made accurate fact findings, however, is less important than understanding the law the court applied to the facts it did find.

The court ruled that it " 'must look to the outward expression of a person as manifesting his intention rather than to his secret and unexpressed intention.' "[116] According to the court, Zehmer's actual intentions therefore were irrelevant. What was important was Lucy's reasonable belief based on Zehmer's behavior. The court held that the parties entered an enforceable contract even if Zehmer was not serious because Lucy reasonably believed Zehmer was serious.[117]

---

111. Id. at 518.

112. Id. at 520.

113. Id.

114. Id. at 521.

115. Id.

116. Id. (quoting First Nat'l. Exch. Bank of Roanoke v. Roanoke Oil Co., 192 S.E. 764, 770 (Va. 1937)).

117. Id. at 521–22.

Although contract law does not care about Zehmer's (the promisor's) subjective beliefs, Lucy's belief about Zehmer's intentions must be both reasonable *and* honest, according to most courts.[118] Contract law seeks to protect promisees who rely on their contracts and to encourage such reliance, something that would be impossible if a promisor could avoid liability simply by claiming that he was joking.[119] Nevertheless, it is hard to find a reason for enforcing a promise that appears serious when the promisee actually knows that the promisor was joking. Such a promisee has no moral claim for enforcement, nor would any expectations about or reliance on the "promise" be reasonable. Therefore, if Lucy actually knew that Zehmer was joking, contract law should not enforce their agreement.

Lucy v. Zehmer teaches us not to be fooled by the barrage of language in judicial decisions about enforcing the parties' intentions.[120] In reality, the objective test of assent trumps actual intentions. Judge Learned Hand (what a great name for a judge) saw this in an often-quoted passage:

> A contract has, strictly speaking nothing to do with the personal, or individual, intent of the parties. * * * If * * * it were proved by twenty bishops that either party, when he used the words, intended something else than the usual meaning which the law imposes upon them, he would still be held, unless there were some mutual mistake, or something else of the sort.[121]

In fact, contract law may have always applied an objective approach to contract formation,[122] despite the propensity of courts, especially in the nineteenth century, to fill their opinions with language about the "will theory" of contract (promises are enforced according to the subjective wills of the parties).[123]

118. See, e.g., Embry v. Hargadine, McKittrick Dry Goods Co., 105 S.W. 777, 780 (Mo. Ct. App. 1907) ("It was only necessary that [the promisee], as a reasonable man, had a right to and did so understand [that the promisor intended to contract].").

119. See Lon L. Fuller & William R. Perdue, Jr., The Reliance Interest in Contract Damages, 46 Yale L.J. 52, 61 (1936) ("[T]here is ... a policy in favor of promoting and facilitating reliance on ... agreements.").

120. See, e.g., Haber v. St. Paul Guardian Ins. Co., 137 F.3d 691, 702 (2d Cir. 1998) ("[I]t is the intent of the parties which controls the interpretation of contracts."); Octagon Gas Sys., Inc. v. Rimmer, 995 F.2d 948, 953 (10th Cir.

1993) ("In construing the meaning of a written contract, the intent of the parties controls."); Holbrook v. United States, 194 F.Supp. 252, 255 (D. Or. 1961) ("[T]he intention of the parties ... controls the contract's interpretation and when that is ascertained, it is conclusive.").

121. Hotchkiss v. National City Bank of New York, 200 F. 287, 293 (S.D.N.Y. 1911), aff'd, 201 F. 664 (2d Cir. 1912), aff'd, 231 U.S. 50 (1913).

122. Joseph M. Perillo, The Origins of the Objective Theory of Contract Formation and Interpretation, 69 Fordham L. Rev. 427, 427–29 (2000).

123. Id. at 429–30.

From this discussion, you should understand that contract law evaluates a promisor's intent to contract objectively, meaning that contract law enforces an agreement when a reasonable person would believe the promisor intended to be bound (and the promisee actually believes it). Contract law determines what a reasonable person would believe by examining the circumstances, including the language of the alleged agreement, the length of negotiations, the subject matter of the contract, the setting of negotiations, the previous conduct of the parties, and anything else that may be relevant. Moreover, the objective test applies whether the promisor claims that he was joking, as in *Lucy v. Zehmer,* mistaken,[124] or misunderstood.[125] Finally, we are about to see that courts apply the objective test of assent to the many issues of contract formation discussed below.

2. Offer and acceptance. Probably most prospective contracting parties form their agreements after some back and forth. For example, a retail store might place an advertisement in a newspaper but leave out most of the details, thereby inviting buyers to come to the store to consider purchasing the goods. Several communications and meetings may preface a business deal, including huge ones between corporate titans and more modest ones between small entrepreneurs. You and Alice may engage in several discussions about the sale of your piano. In each of these settings, a dispute may arise about whether the parties ever committed themselves to a deal. Contract law must resolve these disputes clearly and consistently in order to give contracting parties the guidance they need and desire.

Contract law's general approach is to look for a particular communication that constitutes an offer and another communication that constitutes an acceptance. An offer and acceptance form an agreement that is legally enforceable (a contract). We will see later that some transactions do not lend themselves particularly well to this analysis because of their complexity and the absence, realistically, of any particular time when contract law can confidently find that the parties have reached an agreement. However, we should first understand the traditional approach to offer and acceptance before immersing ourselves in the complexities.

124. Cargill Commission Co. v. Mowery, 161 P. 634 (Kan. 1916), opinion modified 162 P. 313 (Kan.1917) (seller intended to sell 3,500 bushels, but was obligated to sell 35,000 because he mistakenly used a term that meant 35,000).

125. Embry v. Hargadine, McKittrick Dry Goods Co., 105 S.W. 777, 780 (Mo. Ct. App. 1907) (employee reasonably understood as assent employer's statement, "[g]o ahead, you're all right ... don't let that worry you").

a. Offer. According to one of the leading treatise writers of the twentieth century (in any legal field), Arthur Corbin, "[a]n offer is an expression by one party of assent to certain definite terms, provided that the other party involved in the bargaining transaction will likewise express assent to the same terms."[126] Note first that an offer is "an expression * * * of assent," not necessarily *actual* assent. This is consistent with the objective test of assent we have just investigated.[127] According to Corbin's definition, contract law must determine whether a reasonable person, acquainted with all of the circumstances, would believe that the author of the communication alleged to be an offer intended to be bound upon assent (acceptance) by the other party.

Suppose, for example, that a department store advertises "1 Black Lapin Stole, Beautiful, worth $139.50 * * * $1.00. First come First Served."[128] If you trotted down to the store, showed up first, and requested to purchase the stole, would the store be bound to sell it to you for $1? This depends on whether the store's communication was an offer or merely an invitation for you to come to the store to negotiate about the stole. The issue boils down to whether a reasonable person would believe the store intended to be bound upon your acceptance. Just as in *Lucy v. Zehmer*,[129] the court looking at this issue should examine the totality of circumstances in making its decision. In *Lefkowitz v. Great Minneapolis Surplus Store, Inc.*,[130] the department store case, the court held that the advertisement did constitute an offer. A reasonable person would believe the store intended to be bound upon an acceptance because the advertisement was "clear, definite, and explicit, and [left] nothing open for negotiation."[131]

Often the circumstances suggest that an advertisement is *not* an offer. In fact, for many analysts, the very fact that a communication appears in a newspaper is strong evidence that the advertiser did not intend to be bound to any particular reader.[132] Courts prone to view advertisements only as invitations to negotiate, however, usually seize upon additional evidence that reenforces their view

---

126. 1 Arthur L. Corbin, Corbin on Contracts 28 (2d ed.1993).

127. See supra notes 109–125, and accompanying text; see also Restatement (Second) of Contracts § 24 ("An offer is the manifestation of willingness to enter into a bargain, so made as to justify another person in understanding that is assent to that bargain is invited and will conclude it.").

128. Lefkowitz v. Great Minneapolis Surplus Store, Inc., 86 N.W.2d 689, 690 (Minn. 1957).

129. See supra notes 110–125, and accompanying text.

130. 86 N.W.2d 689, 690 (Minn. 1957).

131. Id. at 691.

132. Restatement (Second) of Contracts § 26, cmt. b; Williston, supra note 5, at 285–88. But see Melvin Aron Eisenberg, Expression Rules in Contract Law and Problems of Offer and Acceptance, 82 Calif. L. Rev. 1127, 1167 (1994) ("The black-letter advertising rule ... has the matter precisely upside down.").

that the advertiser lacked an intention to be bound. For example, in *Lefkowitz*, the court failed to enforce as an offer another advertisement for fur coats that did not set forth their value because the value was "speculative."[133] In *Ford Motor Credit Co. v. Russell*,[134] a car dealer advertised a Ford Escort for $7826. The advertisement set forth monthly payments of "159.29, based on a 60–month loan at 11% A.P.R."[135] The court held that the advertisement was not an offer for financing at 11% because a reasonable person would understand that "not everyone qualifies for financing."[136] An additional reason offered by the court, that reasonable people know that the dealer did "not have an unlimited number of Ford Escorts to sell,"[137] seems less persuasive. After all, a reasonable person reading the advertisement would understand that the offer (if there was one) stayed open only until the dealer ran out of Escorts.

Newspaper advertisements are not the only type of communication that call for offer analysis. Suppose two merchants write a series of letters back and forth (hard copy or electronic) and then one claims that the parties have made an enforceable agreement. As with advertisements, a court must determine whether one of the communications constitutes an offer (and another an acceptance—but we will study acceptance law shortly[138]). For example, a court declined to find an offer based on a communication from a seller that it "want[ed]" a certain amount for goods, [139]and that it has "about 1800 bushels or thereabouts" of seed.[140] Neither communication exhibits the degree of definiteness required to satisfy a reasonable person that the seller intended to be bound upon an acceptance. On the other hand, suppose that a prospective purchaser sends a letter to the seller asking for the lowest price at which the seller is willing to sell certain jars. The seller responds with price quotations and with the admonition: "for immediate acceptance." A court faced with these facts had no trouble finding that the seller's communication was an offer even though the purchaser could decide, among other things, the quantity of each size jar and the precise delivery dates.[141]

These decisions illustrate the importance of evaluating all of the surrounding circumstances (a student of mine once pointed out that "surrounding circumstances" is redundant, but lots of courts use the phrase), and that no one factor controls whether a party

---

133. 86 N.W.2d at 690.

134. 519 N.W.2d 460 (Minn. Ct. App. 1994).

135. Id. at 462.

136. Id. at 463.

137. Id. at 463.

138. See infra notes 145–155, and accompanying text.

139. Nebraska Seed Co. v. Harsh, 152 N.W. 310, 311 (Neb. 1915).

140. Id. at 310.

141. Fairmount Glass Works v. Crunden–Martin Woodenware Co., 51 S.W. 196 (Ky. 1899).

has made an offer. Still, some elements may be more equal than others. For example, a request for a firm offer by one party followed by "quotations" by the other, is powerful evidence that the latter is making an offer and a reasonable person would usually so believe.

Another factor of great importance is whether the supposed offer is too good to believe. For example, the opinion in *Lucy v. Zehmer* does not clearly reveal the fair market value of the farm Zehmer supposedly offered to Lucy. Recall that the purchase price was $50,000. Suppose the fair market value of the farm was $250,000. I trust the court would have found that a reasonable person would believe, and that Lucy actually believed, that the "agreement" was a joke. But, you say, what about the lapin stole in *Lefkowitz* that was "offered" for $1. The court didn't treat this offer as a joke. Compare the two contexts. In *Lucy*, there was plenty of other evidence to suggest that Zehmer was joking. An offer that was too good to believe probably would have compelled the court to come out in favor of Zehmer. However, department stores often make offers of "loss leaders," items they sell at a loss in order to attract people into their store. So an offer of a limited number of items for nominal consideration would not seem so unreasonable.

Outlandish propositions that recipients attempt to turn into offers are frequent news items in newspapers. For example, during the good old days of President Clinton and Monica Lewinsky, Geraldo Rivera promised $10,000 if anyone could find a criminal prosecution of an individual for lying about a sexual matter. A criminal defense lawyer turned up several such cases and insisted that Geraldo had made an offer. NBC paid his claim.[142] For another example, in a television commercial, PepsiCo. promised to award a Harrier fighter jet worth $23 million to anyone who collected seven million "Pepsi Stuff" points off its packaging or through direct purchase.[143] The latter is a good example of an "offer" that is too good (or too outrageous) to believe.[144]

b. Acceptance. According to the Restatement (Second) of Contracts, "[a]cceptance of an offer is a manifestation of assent to the terms thereof made by the offeree in a manner invited or required by the offer."[145] The key word here again is "manifestation." Consistent with the objective test of assent, contract law asks whether a reasonable person would believe the offeree intends to accept the offeror's terms and form a contract, not whether the

---

142. See Nat'l L.J., Feb. 22, 1999, at A28.

143. See Leonard v. Pepsico, 88 F.Supp.2d 116 (S.D.N.Y. 1999).

144. See generally Keith A. Rowley, You Asked for It, You Got It ... Toy Yoda: Practical Jokes, Prizes, and Contract Law, 3 Nev. L. J. 526 (2003).

145. Restatement (Second) of Contracts § 50(1).

offeree actually intended to do so.[146]

Acceptance issues often present themselves when an offeree authors a "wishy-washy" response to an offer and then one of the parties has second thoughts about contracting. Was the offeree's communication an acceptance that formed a contract, so that neither party can renege? For example, suppose that you offer Alice your piano for $400. You tell her that you will deliver the piano "during the weekend," and that the deal is "as is," meaning without any warranties as to the quality of the piano. Let us assume your offer is "clear, definite, and explicit,"[147] and a reasonable person would believe you intended to be bound upon an acceptance by Alice. Suppose Alice responds with the following. "I will purchase the piano. I am concerned about the quality of the piano. Can you assure me it is first rate?"

The issue is whether a reasonable person would believe Alice "definitely" and "unequivocally" intended to be bound by the offer. The answer is likely no. Alice does not say she "accepts." Further, the use of the phrase "I will purchase," although indicative of a commitment to follow, appears to mean that she has not yet accepted. Further, she wants assurances about quality before she commits.

Real cases abound with similar issues. In one, for example, the offeree of real estate signed a purchase agreement for certain real estate, but his lawyer included a letter with the contract stating in part:

> "My clients are concerned that the following items remain with the real estate: a) dining room set and tapestry wall covering in dining room; b) fireplace fixtures throughout; c) the sun parlor furniture. I would appreciate your confirming that these items are a part of the transaction, as they would be difficult to replace."[148]

The court held that despite the signed purchase agreement, the letter rendered the offeree's entire communication a "qualified acceptance," which, as a legal matter, is no acceptance at all.[149] The court found that "[t]he letter does not unequivocally state that even without the enumerated items [the offeree] is willing to complete the contract."[150] The seller-offerors were therefore allowed to walk away from the deal.

---

146. Ardente v. Horan, 366 A.2d 162, 165 (R.I. 1976) ("We must be concerned only with the language actually used, not the language [the offeree] thought he was using or intended to use."); see also Thacker v. Massman Constr. Co., 247 S.W.2d 623, 629–30 (Mo. 1952) ("An uncommunicated inten-

tion to accept an offer is not an acceptance.").

147. Lefkowitz v. Great Minneapolis Surplus Store, Inc., 86 N.W.2d 689, 691 (Minn. 1957).

148. Ardente, 366 A.2d at 163.

149. Id. at 166.

150. Id.

Silence as an acceptance You send a written offer to sell your piano to Alice. Alice does not respond. Has she accepted? Contract law treats silence like any other response to an offer. In short, it applies the objective reasonable person test to determine whether a party has accepted.[151] Would a reasonable person believe Alice intended to accept your offer? Sorry, ordinarily silence suggests that a party *doesn't* want to contract. Decisions often recite the principle that silence does not constitute an acceptance,[152] but in reality such language means that, in the usual case, a reasonable person would not believe the silent offeree intends to be bound.

You may be wondering at this point what are examples of situations where silence *would* constitute an acceptance. The Restatement (Second) of Contracts enumerates a few. For example, suppose one early spring day, you watch from a window as employees of Bob's Lawn Mowing Service unload their lawnmowers from a truck and mow your lawn. Although you hadn't responded to Bob's formal offer to mow your lawn this year, you had used Bob's for several years without formally accepting any arrangement. Your silence constitutes an acceptance because you had reason to know Bob's expected payment and you took the benefit of the service with a reasonable opportunity to stop Bob's.[153]

Suppose Alice had purchased many items of furniture from you in the past and had mentioned that she wanted your piano if you ever decided to sell it. She bumps into you again and reiterates her desire to buy your piano. She may have created a reasonable expectation that she would take the piano when you offer it for a fair price, especially if you do so soon after her statement. Alice therefore may have the duty to notify you if she does not want the piano.[154]

Restatement (Second) section 69(2) states that an offeree is bound to an offer when she "does any act inconsistent with the offeror's ownership of offered property." This rule could present problems when a merchant sends unsolicited goods in the mail. You might receive a DVD of the movie "Zombie Island Massacre," even though you didn't order it or want it.

Nevertheless, curiosity causes you to open and play the movie. Have you accepted the DVD and do you have to pay for it? Federal law now declares the mailing of unordered goods to be "an unfair trade practice," and allows you to keep the DVD as a gift.[155] (Some gift!)

151. See supra notes 108–125, and accompanying text.

152. Ducommun v. Johnson, 110 N.W.2d 271, 274 (Iowa 1961).

153. Restatement (Second) of Contracts § 69(1)(a).

154. Id. § 69(1)(c).

155. 39 U.S.C. § 3009 (1994).

3. The offeror has the power to prescribe the terms of the offer. An offeror does not have to make an offer. But if an offeror decides to make one, she can set forth any terms she likes, which the offeree must accept to form a contract.[156] For example, you don't have to offer to sell your piano, you can keep it! (But if you play like me, you might want to sell.) If you do decide to make an offer to sell your piano, however, you are free to set any terms that you desire. You can set any price you want for the piano, and choose your delivery and warranty terms. If the price is outrageously high, of course, Alice doesn't have to accept your offer and form a contract. She can make a counteroffer instead: "Your price for the piano of $1000 is too high. However, I offer to buy the piano for $400."[157] Contract law treats a counter-offer the same as any offer by inquiring whether a reasonable person would believe Alice intends to contract upon your acceptance of the $400 selling price.[158] Of course, if you don't want to sell for $400 you can refuse to accept the counteroffer. If Alice wants to be sure of getting the piano, she must comply with your terms.[159]

An offeror can also prescribe terms concerning the manner in which an offeree must accept an offer.[160] Courts have wrestled with the problem of determining the difference between *prescriptions* in offers, terms that the offeree must follow in order to form a contract, and *suggestions*, terms in the offer that the offeree does not have to comply with in order to accept.[161] For example, in an e-mail message, you offer to sell your piano to an acquaintance, Alec, in another town. You would like to hear from Alec by September 12, but you are willing to wait longer. You might write, "I would like to hear from you by September 12." This date is a suggestion and Alec can form a contract by sending you a message on September 13.[162] (But we will see later that your offer does not stay open forever.)[163]

On the other hand, if hearing by September 12 is very important to you, for example, because you have other prospective

---

156. Restatement (Second) of Contracts § 58.

157. Id. § 59 ("A reply to an offer which purports to accept it but is conditional on the offeror's assent to terms additional to or different from those offered is not an acceptance but is a counter-offer.").

158. See supra notes 126–127, and accompanying text.

159. Restatement (Second) of Contracts § 58 ("An acceptance must comply with the requirements of the offer as to the promise to be made or the performance to be rendered.").

160. Restatement (Second) of Contracts § 60.

161. See Allied Steel & Conveyors, Inc. v. Ford Motor Co., 277 F.2d 907, 910–11 (6th Cir. 1960) (distinguishing a prescribed and a suggested method of acceptance).

162. See id. at 909, 911 (offer stating that "[a]cceptance should be executed on acknowledgment copy which should be returned to the buyer" was only a suggestion).

163. See infra notes 186–190, and accompanying text.

purchasers of the piano, you could write, "I must hear from you by receiving a return e-mail by 6 p.m., September 12." If Alec tried to accept on September 13, it would be too late.

How does contract law sort out the difference between prescriptions and suggestions when the language of the offeror is ambiguous? Are you shocked to learn that the test is an objective one? Would a reasonable person believe the offeror *required* the offeree to follow a method of acceptance or only *suggested* that method.[164] Resolving this issue requires examining all of the circumstances. In sale-of-goods cases, the UCC creates a presumption that any "reasonable" manner or medium of acceptance is satisfactory unless the offeror "unambiguously" indicates otherwise by the "language or circumstances."[165] This rule places on the offeror the burden of proving that a reasonable person would believe that the offer contains a prescription as to the manner or medium of acceptance. Your requirement of receiving an e-mail by 6:00 p.m. on September 12, should satisfy the "unambiguously indicated" standard, so if Alice does not comply, you and she haven't formed a contract.

4.   Offers for unilateral and bilateral contracts. Now you know that offerors can prescribe the manner required for acceptance of an offer. It follows, therefore, that they can require either a return promise as an acceptance or a return performance as an acceptance. (Recall too that a return promise or a performance can constitute consideration.[166]) For example, if you offer to sell your piano to Alice for $400 if Alice *promises* to purchase it for $400, and Alice makes the promise, she has accepted your offer for what is called a bilateral (two-promise) contract. On the other hand, if you promise to sell your piano for $400 if Alice *pays* you $400, you have made an offer for a unilateral (one-promise, namely your promise) contract and the contract is formed when she pays you the money. When you make an offer for a unilateral contract, you have prescribed that the *only* way for Alice to accept is for her to pay you the money. Her promise to pay you would not be an acceptance and form a contract.

The language of unilateral and bilateral contract has fallen out of favor in the Restatement (Second) of Contracts, but the concepts remain the same: Offerors can require offerees "to accept by rendering a performance" or by a promise.[167] Despite the Restatement drafters' conclusion that the terminology "unilateral and

164. See supra notes 109–125, and accompanying text.

165. UCC § 2–206(1)(a).

166. See supra note 17, and accompanying text.

167. Restatement (Second) of Contracts § 45(1).

bilateral" contract was obsolete,[168] the terms are still helpful in encapsulating the concepts and you should not hesitate to use them. (If anybody criticizes you, please tell them to call me.)

One challenge with offers for unilateral and bilateral contracts (see, I'm using the terminology) is to determine which kind of offer an offeror has made. If the language of an offer is ambiguous so that a reasonable person cannot determine whether the offeror wants a promise or a performance as an acceptance, a court may presume that the offer was for a bilateral contract.[169] The Restatement (Second) of Contracts provides that an offeree can accept an ambiguous offer *either* by promising or performing.[170] An example of an ambiguous offer is where an uncle in a letter offers to leave his house to his niece "if she comes and takes care of him until his death." In the same letter, however, the uncle writes, "please let me hear from you by the end of the month." The first part of the uncle's letter suggests the uncle sought a performance as acceptance, but the second suggests he wants her to promise to come and render care.[171] In the absence of ambiguity, however, contract law is clear: The offeree can accept only by following the offeror's prescription. For example, if a reasonable person would believe the offeror required a return promise as an acceptance, the promisee can accept only by promising.

But now a slight catch: The offeree can still accept an offer for a bilateral contract by beginning performance if a reasonable person would believe that the offeree's conduct in performing *constitutes* a promise to perform. For example, in one case a property owner wrote a builder that "[u]pon an agreement * * * you can commence at once" to improve the property owner's offices.[172] What kind of an offer is this? C'mon, you know—it is an offer for a bilateral contract because the property owner wants "an agreement" (thereby requiring a promise) before the builder starts. In the actual case, the builder began work by purchasing and working on lumber, but none of the work was earmarked for the particular job, nor was it performed at the site. The court held that this act was not an acceptance because it was "no indication to the other party of an acceptance."[173] The implication of the court's reasoning, however, is that if the work did indicate an acceptance (suppose the

---

168. The Restatement once included language recognizing the distinction between unilateral and bilateral contracts. See Restatement (First) of Contracts § 45.

169. See, e.g., National Dairymen Ass'n v. Dean Milk Co., 183 F.2d 349, 352–53 (7th Cir. 1950), cert denied, 340 U.S. 876 (1950); Davis v. Jacoby, 34 P.2d 1026, 1030 (Cal. 1934); Knight v. Hamilton, 233 S.W.2d 969, 972 (Ky. 1950).

170. Restatement (Second) of Contracts § 32.

171. For similar facts, see Davis, 34 P.2d 1026.

172. White v. Corlies, 46 N.Y. 467, 467 (1871).

173. Id. at 470.

builder started work at the property owner's premises), the result would have been different.[174]

5. Duration of offers. The Restatement (Second) of Contracts sets forth several "offer-terminators."[175] When an offer terminates, the offeree can no longer accept the offer because it no longer exists. Important offer terminators include a "rejection or counter-offer by the offeree," a "lapse of time," the offeror's revocation, and the failure of the offeree to comply with any condition of acceptance.[176] We have already encountered the latter offer-terminator. We said that an offeror can prescribe the manner of acceptance.[177] If the offeree does not satisfy all of the conditions of acceptance, no contract is formed. Further, the offer is "off the table" (meaning that there is no offer that the offeree can accept) and the offeree cannot now comply with its terms.[178] Now let's look at additional offer terminators.

a. Rejection or counter-offer. When a reasonable person would believe the offeree does not accept an offer, contract law treats the offeree's decision as a rejection of the offer.[179] You offer to sell your piano to Alice for $400. She replies, "Pianos, we don't need no stinking pianos." We can say pretty confidently that a reasonable person would believe that Alice has rejected the piano.

A rejection terminates the offer. Alice cannot come back to you, even minutes later, and say that she accepts your offer. Her rejection terminates the offer.[180] This rule allows you to rely on her rejection and to look for opportunities to sell elsewhere.[181] In a well-known case, two employees orally offered their resignations at a meeting with their employer, but their employer did not accept the

174. See Allied Steel & Conveyors, Inc. v. Ford Motor Co., 277 F.2d 907, 911 (6th Cir. 1960) ("It is well settled that acceptance of an offer by part performance in accordance with the terms of the offer is sufficient to complete the contract.").

175. Restatement (Second) of Contracts § 36.

176. Id. § 36(1)(a)-(c), (2).

177. See supra notes 156–165, and accompanying text.

178. See, e.g., Lewis v. Adams, 979 S.W.2d 831, 834 (Tx. App. 1998) ("[A]n acceptance must not change or qualify the terms of an offer; if it does ... the modification ... becomes a counteroffer."); Restatement (Second) of Contracts § 59, cmt. a ("A qualified or conditional acceptance ... is a counter-offer and ordinarily terminates the power of

acceptance of the original offeree."); see also Restatement (Second) of Contracts § 39(2).

179. Akers v. J. B. Sedberry, Inc., 286 S.W.2d 617, 622 (Tenn. Ct. App. 1955) (quoting Williston, supra note 5, at 145) (" 'An offer is rejected when the offeror is justified in inferring from the words or conduct of the offeree that the offeree intends not to accept the offer . . . .' ").

180. See, e.g., Energy Mktg. Servs., Inc. v. Homer Laughlin China Co., 186 F.R.D. 369, 374 (S.D. Ohio 1999) ("When an offer is rejected, it ceases to exist, and a subsequent attempted acceptance is inoperative to bind the offeror."); Akers v. J. B. Sedberry, Inc., 286 S.W.2d 617, 621 (Tenn. Ct. App. 1955).

181. See Farnsworth, supra note 109, at 165–66.

resignations. A few days later, in what must have been a big surprise to the two employees, the employer sent a telegram to them stating that "we accept your kind offer of resignation effective immediately."[182] The court held that the offers to resign were no longer open when the employer sent the telegram, so there was nothing to accept.[183]

We have already seen examples of counter-offers.[184] You offer to sell your piano for $400. Alice replies, "that is too high, I'll take the piano for $350 and no more." Would a reasonable person believe Alice rejected your offer of $400? Most likely. (She could argue that she was trying to negotiate without rejecting the offer,[185] but, judged objectively, her language is too strong, especially the use of the language "and no more.") Would a reasonable person believe Alice intended to be bound to purchase for $350 upon your acceptance? Again the answer is yes. The legal ramification of the counter-offer is that your offer of $400 is off the table. If you do not accept $350, she cannot come back and accept your offer of $400. (She can make a new offer of her own for $400, which you can accept or reject.)

b. Lapse of time. Offerors can prescribe the length of time their offers will stay open. If an offeror fails to specify an amount of time the offer will stay open, and the offeror claims that an acceptance came too late, contract law must fill the gap. Contract law's general approach is to hold that an offer remains open for a "reasonable time"[186] In effect, this means determining how long a reasonable person would believe the offer would stay open,[187] which in turn depends on an analysis of all the circumstances.

Contract law holds, for example, that when the parties are engaged in a personal conversation, offers made during the conversation terminate at the end of it.[188] If you offer Alice your piano for $400 during a conversation and she does not reply, she cannot call you up later and accept. You could have specified a time after which

182. Akers, 286 S.W.2d at 620.

183. Id. at 622.

184. See supra notes 157–159, and accompanying text.

185. See Restatement (Second) of Contracts § 38(2) ("A manifestation of intention not to accept an offer is a rejection unless the offeree manifests an intention to take it under further advisement."); see also Eisenberg, supra note 132, at 1159 ("In the ordinary case ... the proposition that a counter-offer implies a rejection and takes the offer off the table seems incorrect....").

186. See, e.g., Akers, 286 S.W.2d at 621; Restatement (Second) of Contracts § 41(1).

187. Restatement (Second) of Contracts § 41, cmt. b.

188. Akers, 286 S.W.2d at 621; see also Restatement (Second) of Contracts § 41, cmt. d ("Where the parties bargain face to face or over the telephone, the time for acceptance does not ordinarily extend beyond the end of the conversation unless a contrary intention is indicated.").

your offer would expire, but you did not. Contract law therefore fills the gap. A reasonable person would believe the offer made during your conversation would terminate at the end of the conversation, so Alice is out of luck. It is worth emphasizing that the conversation rule does not apply when other evidence suggests a different amount of time for your offer to stay open. Remember contract law's quest here is to determine how long a reasonable person in the shoes of the offeree would think the offer will stay open. Suppose, for example, that you and Alice had bought and sold many items over the years, each of you making offers during conversations, and neither of you ever claiming that the offer expired at the end of a conversation. In fact, each of you had accepted many offers later over the telephone without incident. A reasonable person understanding this course of dealing probably would believe that your offer would stay open for at least a few days beyond the opening conversation.

The issue of duration of offers obviously comes up in a variety of contexts. For example, suppose Alice is injured in an automobile accident and the other driver's insurance company offers to pay her $25,000 for her injuries. The insurance company makes the offer exactly one month before the statute of limitations (the time in which Alice can sue) would expire. Alice tries to accept the offer about five weeks later, over a week after the statute of limitations has run out. The insurance company refuses to pay anything, claiming that a reasonable time for accepting its offer expired when Alice could not longer sue its insured.[189] At first blush the insurance company's argument seems quite compelling. After all, why would a reasonable person believe the insurance company intended to hold its offer open after Alice could no longer sue its insured for the accident? However, a court that considered similar facts held that the running of the statute of limitations was "relevant," but not conclusive in determining a reasonable time for acceptance.[190] A principal reason for the holding also presents a good lesson for aspiring lawyers. The court noted that the insurance company could have prescribed in its offer that the time for acceptance terminated when the statute of limitations expired, but the company failed to do so. The implication was that the failure of the insurance company to so specify meant that a reasonable person would believe that the offer would stay open beyond the running of the statute of limitations. The lesson for the lawyer: Advise your client to specify in its offer how long the offer will stay open!

---

189. These are essentially the facts of Vaskie v. West American Ins. Co., 556 A.2d 436 (Pa. Super. Ct. 1989).

190. Id. at 440.

c. Revocation. A revocation occurs when a reasonable person would believe the offeror has withdrawn the offer.[191] A revocation becomes effective when the offeree receives the information that the offer is no longer open.[192] One exception to this rule involves offers for unilateral contracts, such as a reward offer for capturing a criminal or finding a lost pet. Revocations are effective in such reward-offer cases when the offeror gives the revocation the same notoriety as the offer. For example, if the offeror makes an offer of a reward by publishing the offer in a newspaper, a revocation becomes effective as soon as the offeror publishes it in the same paper.[193] So, all you bounty hunters out there, be sure to check for revocations in the same medium that you saw the reward offer.

A revocation can come directly from the offeror in a conversation or a written or electronic notice. For example, you tell Alice that you revoke your offer to sell your piano or you send a message to her to that effect. This withdraws the offer. A revocation can also consist of information the offeree receives that makes it clear to a reasonable person that the offeror cannot intend for the offer to remain open.[194] For example, suppose Alice finds out you have sold your piano to someone else. Such information constitutes an effective revocation of your offer to sell your piano to her. Once a court determines that there has been an effective revocation, and so long as the offeree receives the revocation before the offeree has accepted the offer, the revocation takes the offer off the table. We discuss the time when an acceptance of an offer becomes effective shortly.[195]

d. Bars to revocation—option contracts. Suppose on January 17 you say to Alice, "I offer to sell you my piano for $400 and I promise to keep the offer open until January 31." On January 20, you tell Alice that you have changed your mind and that you are going to keep the piano. Or you tell her that you have sold the piano to someone else. Either notification constitutes an effective revocation under the principles discussed earlier.[196] (A reasonable person would believe you have withdrawn the offer.) But, what about your promise to keep the offer open? Recall the distinction

---

191. See Restatement (Second) of Contracts § 42 ("An offeree's power of acceptance is terminated when the offeree receives from the offeror a manifestation of an intention not to enter into the proposed contract.").

192. Id.

193. Shuey v. United States, 92 U.S. 73 (1875).

194. See, e.g., Hoover Motor Exp. Co. v. Clements Paper Co., 241 S.W.2d 851, 853 (Tenn. 1951) ("It is sufficient to constitute a withdrawal [of an offer] that knowledge of acts by the offer[or] inconsistent with the continuance of the offer is brought home to the offeree."); Dickinson v. Dodds, 2 Ch. D. 463 (1876).

195. See infra notes 231–239, and accompanying text.

196. See supra notes 191–195, and accompanying text.

between gift promises and bargained-for exchanges.[197] Your promise to keep the offer open was not supported by consideration—you didn't extract something as the price of your promise. So your promise to keep the offer open is a gift promise and unenforceable.[198]

Of course, we have seen (and will continue to see) instances in which technical contract law produces unhappy results, which, in turn, have inspired courts and lawmakers to develop counter-principles and exceptions. (Think, for example, of contract law's treatment of the preexisting duty rule.[199]) The rule allowing revocation of offers after assurances that they will stay open for a period of time is no exception. A series of exceptions mitigates the harshness of the rule by creating bars to revocation. First, consider the option contract exception. Suppose you promised to leave your offer open until January 31 in exchange for Alice paying you $10. You and Alice have entered a bargained-for exchange, called an option contract, and your promise to leave the offer open until January 31 is enforceable.[200] This should not be controversial because the option contract is like any other enforceable contract. Note, of course, that the option contract is secondary to the principal proposed exchange, namely the sale of your piano. By paying the $10, Alice has purchased the right until January 31 to contemplate whether to purchase the piano.

How silly of me to say that option contracts are not controversial. You have studied enough law or read enough books about law or political science to know that *all* rules are controversial in some way. What if you asked for twenty-five cents instead of $10 to keep your offer open? Could you later claim that this was a "sham" (fake) consideration, mentioned only to get around the bargain requirement, and could you revoke your offer before January 31? Option contracts often arise in real estate transactions and courts have often considered the issue of "sham" consideration in this context. Generally, courts have not been receptive to your sham consideration argument, arguing that a fair price for an option is too difficult to ascertain and that courts are supposed to leave the

---

197. See supra notes 1–12, and accompanying text.

198. Dickinson, 2 Ch. D. 463 (1876); see also Restatement (Second) of Contracts § 42, cmt. a ("the ordinary offer is revocable even though it expressly states the contrary, because of the

doctrine that an informal agreement is binding as a bargain only if supported by consideration.").

199. See supra notes 72–83, and accompanying text.

200. See, e.g., Marsh v. Lott, 97 P. 163 (Cal. Dist. Ct. App. 1908).

adequacy of consideration to the parties anyway.[201] One suspects that the real reason courts enforce these suspect option contracts is because they believe the option mechanism supports real estate transactions (parties frequently utilize them)[202] and because courts don't enjoy allowing an offeror to wiggle out of a promise to leave an offer open.

The Restatement (Second) of Contracts substantiates the position that option contracts do not require real consideration. Offers that are in writing and signed by the offeror are enforceable as option contracts if they propose a fair exchange "within a reasonable time" and "recite[] a *purported* consideration."[203] A purported consideration is fake consideration, such as twenty-five cents, which the offeror did not really bargain for. By requiring a writing and the reciting of fake consideration such as twenty-five cents, the Restatement approach theoretically satisfies the formal reasons for enforcing promises (evidentiary, cautionary, and channeling functions), discussed earlier.[204] In light of the apparent importance of option contracts to business people, we have both formal and substantive reasons for enforcing them.

The Restatement (Second) also provides that option contracts are enforceable if "made irrevocable by statute."[205] An important statute governing option contracts for the sale of goods is section 2–205 of the UCC. Section 2–205 enforces promises to leave offers open when made by a merchant (somebody who "deals in goods" that are the subject matter of the contract[206]), in writing, and signed by the offeror. Note that, unlike the Restatement approach, such offers do not have to recite any fake consideration. But the section limits the duration of a promise to leave an offer open to the time stated or three months (whichever is less) or, if the offer does not mention any time, for a reasonable time, not to exceed three months. So, a promise by a merchant in a signed writing to leave an offer open for two months is enforceable without consideration for two months. A promise by the merchant to leave an offer open for six months is enforceable without consideration for three months. A promise to leave an offer open forever would be enforceable for a reasonable time, up to three months.

---

201. Id. at 165.

202. Restatement (Second) of Contracts § 87, cmt. a (the option contract "serves a useful purpose even though no preliminary bargain is made: it is often a necessary step in the making of the main bargain proposed, and it partakes of the natural formalities inherent in business transactions.").

203. Restatement (Second) of Contracts § 87(1)(a) (emphasis added).

204. See supra notes 34–40, and accompanying text.

205. Restatement (Second) of Contracts § 87(1)(b).

206. UCC § 2–104(1) defines the term "merchant."

e. Bars to revocation—beginning performance of unilateral contracts. Contracts professors (at least ancient ones) love to play with this issue. So read with care. Suppose Alice offers to pay you $400 if you sell and deliver your piano to her. Notice that Alice has made an offer for a unilateral contract—she wants your sale and delivery of the piano, not a promise to sell it.[207] Suppose you prepare the piano for delivery and, because she lives down a hill from you and the piano is on wheels, you push it out of your house and hop on while the piano rolls down the hill. (I once delivered a piano this way. Honest.) Suppose, however, that Alice yells out to you as you coast down the hill, "I revoke my offer." She then claims that her revocation is effective because you had not accepted her offer, which required the actual delivery of the piano before you received her revocation.

O.k., this is an unusual example, but it raises an important, fairly common issue. How should contract law treat a revocation of an offer after an offeree has begun, but not finished, performance of a unilateral contract? This issue arises in important settings. For example, an employer may create an employee benefits package in the form of an offer for a unilateral contract: "If you work for us for twenty years, you will earn a pension."[208] Does contract law protect the employee if the employer "revokes" the pension after 15 years? For another example, an offeror may promise compensation to a family member if the latter cares for the offeror during the offeror's "golden" years and until death.[209] What are the family member's rights if the offeror revokes after the offeree has tendered years of care?[210] (Remember, at the time of the revocation, the family member hasn't accepted by caring for the offeror until his death.)

Although one analyst writing in the Yale Law Journal originally thought (he later reneged) that the offeror of a unilateral contract had the right to revoke without any liability even after the offeree has begun performance,[211] the modern view protects the offeree who is trying to perform. (See, don't believe everything you read in the Yale Law Journal.) The first Restatement of Contracts achieved this purpose by binding the offeror on condition that the offeree complete or at least tender full performance.[212] (A tender is an " 'offer of performance * * * accompanied with manifested

---

207. See supra notes 166–174, and accompanying text.

208. See Mark Pettit, Modern Unilateral Contracts, 63 B. U. L. Rev. 551, 564–67 (1983).

209. See, e.g., Brackenbury v. Hodgkin, 102 A. 106 (Me. 1917).

210. See id.

211. I. Maurice Wormser, The True Conception of Unilateral Contracts, 26 Yale L. J. 136, 136–38 (1916). His retraction appears in I. Maurice Wormser, Book Review, 3 J. of Legal Educ. 145, 146 (1950).

212. Restatement (First) of Contracts § 45.

present ability to make it good.' "[213]) The second Restatement utilizes the option contract conception—once you begin to deliver the piano or tender it, you have created an option contract that binds Alice to allow you to complete performance.[214] (Although a legal fiction, think of your beginning performance as consideration to support Alice's promise to keep the offer open, like the $10 consideration discussed earlier that supported your promise to leave your offer open until January 31.[215]) As with the first Restatement, the second Restatement then creates a condition precedent to Alice's liability, namely your "completion or tender of the invited performance."[216] It should also not be surprising to learn that an offeree who has begun performance of a unilateral contract must "exercise[] reasonable diligence" to notify the offeror if the offeror otherwise reasonably would not learn of the performance.[217] More on this in a moment. In cases involving the sale of goods, without exception, the offeree must notify the offeror of beginning performance "within a reasonable time."[218]

The policy behind creating fictitious option contracts when an offeree begins or tenders performance should not be hard to see. Contract law protects an offeree who relies on an offer when the only way to accept requires the offeree to begin performance. In fact, perhaps the option contract approach is not so fictitious after all. Isn't Alice implying that if you rely on her offer and begin the shipment of the piano, she will give you a chance to finish? So as not to end a section with a rhetorical question, I'll answer myself: "Yes!"

In addition, so as not to end a section with the implication that everything here is clear and straightforward, I'll mention two additional issues. First, parties sometimes dispute whether an offeree has begun performance, and the answer is not always so clear. For example, suppose you offer to sell your piano to Alice if she pays you $400 first. Has Alice begun performance (so that you cannot revoke your offer) by taking the cash out of the bank, traveling to your house, and stating that she was there to pay for the piano? One leading case suggests that the answer is no.[219] But a strong dissent, which I would argue is more persuasive, thought

---

213. Farnsworth, supra note 109, at 559 (quoting Restatement (Second) of Contracts § 263, cmt. b).

214. Restatement (Second) of Contracts § 45(1) ("Where an offer invites an offeree to accept by rendering a performance and does not invite a promissory acceptance, an option contract is created when the offeree tenders or begins the invited performance or tenders a beginning of it.").

215. See supra note 200, and accompanying text.

216. Restatement (Second) of Contracts § 45(2).

217. Id. § 54(2)(a).

218. UCC § 2–206(2).

219. Petterson v. Pattberg, 161 N.E. 428 (1928).

that similar actions did constitute performance of the offer for a unilateral contract.[220]

Second, when must an offeree who begins performance notify the offeror? According to the second Restatement, the offeree does not have to notify the offeror at all unless the offeror asks for notification or the offeree "has reason to know" that the offeror will not otherwise learn of the performance "with reasonable promptness and certainty."[221] In the latter case, the offeree must exercise "reasonable diligence" to notify the offeror unless the offeror actually learns of the offeree's performance in a reasonable time or the offer stated that the offeree did not have to notify the offeror.[222]

f. Bars to revocation—offers for bilateral contracts. Suppose Alice offers to purchase your piano for $400 if you *promise* to deliver it. Quickly, what kind of offer did she make? Right, her offer is for a bilateral contract.[223] You might think that an offer for a bilateral contract does not involve revocation issues pertaining to the reliance of the offeree, such as we have just seen with offers for unilateral contracts.[224] After all, the offeree who receives an offer for a bilateral contract merely has to promise to perform. But if you think there are no revocation issues, you would be wrong.

Consider the great case of *Drennan v. Star Paving Co.*[225] Drennan was a general contractor who made a bid to construct a school. In formulating his bid, Drennan relied on subcontractors' bids for various portions of the job. Star Paving, one of the subcontractors, made a bid over the telephone to perform the paving work for Drennan for $7,131.60. Drennan asked Star Paving to repeat the bid, which it did. Star Paving's bid was the lowest bid for the paving and Drennan incorporated it into his bid for the general contract. Drennan was awarded the general contract. The next morning, Drennan visited Star Paving's office and introduced himself. Before Drennan could say anything else, Star Paving's construction engineer told Drennan that Star Paving had made a mistake and could not perform the work for the amount it bid. Drennan then found another paving subcontractor who agreed to do the work for $10,948.60, and sought damages from Star Paving.

Was Star Paving's bid enforceable? Remember, the bid basically constitutes an offer for a bilateral contract: "We promise to do

---

220. Id.

221. Restatement (Second) of Contracts § 54.

222. Id.

223. See supra notes 166–167, and accompanying text.

224. See supra notes 207–218, and accompanying text.

225. 333 P.2d 757 (Cal. 1958).

the paving work, if you promise to pay us $7,131.60." Although Drennan had used Star Paving's bid in compiling its own bid for the general contract, Drennan had not yet accepted by promising to pay at the time Star Paving revoked its offer because of its claimed mistake.[226] It looks like Drennan is in trouble!

The first few conclusions of the court seemed to substantiate that Drennan was in a fix. First, the court found that Star Paving had not promised to keep its bid open in exchange for Drennan's use of the bid. In other words, the parties had not entered an option contract (with Drennan's use of the bid as consideration for Star Paving's promise to leave the bid offer open) because the evidence did not support the existence of such an intention on the part of the parties. Next, the court held that Drennan's use of Star Paving's bid was not an acceptance of Star Paving's offer for a bilateral contract. A reasonable person would not believe that Drennan's use of Star Paving's bid showed that Drennan intended to be bound to Star Paving's offer. (Apparently, the custom in the construction industry allowed a general contractor to replace a subcontractor after receiving the general contract, although the general contractor could not delay doing so too long.[227]) To accept Star Paving's offer for a bilateral contract, Drennan would have had to promise to use Star Paving, which it did not do before Star Paving revoked during that fateful morning meeting between the parties.

Notwithstanding these findings, the court still held in favor of Drennan. The court focused on Drennan's reliance on Star Paving's bid. Calling the problem of revocation of offers for unilateral contracts an "analogous problem," the court held that "it is only fair" to allow Drennan an opportunity to accept Star Paving's bid when Star Paving had reason to understand that Drennan would rely on the bid and Drennan did rely on it.[228] The court also invoked Restatement (Second) of Contracts, section 90, which enforces promises when the promisor should reasonably expect the promisee

---

226. See Klose v. Sequoia Union High Sch. Dist., 258 P.2d 515, 517 (Cal. Dist. Ct. App. 1953) ("A subcontractor bidder merely makes an offer that is converted into a contract by a regularly communicated acceptance conveyed to him by the general contractor.").

227. Drennan, 333 P.2d at 415 ("[A] general contractor is not free to delay acceptance after he has been awarded the general contract in the

hope of getting a better price."); see also Holman Erection Co. v. Orville E. Madsen & Sons, Inc., 330 N.W.2d 693, 698 (Minn. 1983) ("Binding general contractors to subcontractors because a particular bid was listed in the general bid or was utilized in making the bid would remove a considerable degree of needed flexibility.").

228. Drennan, 333 P.2d at 759–60.

to rely on the promise. (We study section 90 in almost nauseating detail in Chapter 3.) *Drennan* and other decisions that follow its reasoning have thus created a new revocation bar, namely reasonable reliance on an offer for a bilateral contract.

The decision in *Drennan* causes me some concern. First, one can question the analogy to offers for unilateral contracts where, we have said, the only way to accept is by relying on the offeror to keep the offer open and by beginning performance. An offeree of a bilateral contract, on the other hand, can bind her offeror by promising to perform *before* relying on the contract. One can therefore argue that any reliance by Drennan before he accepts is at his own risk. Further, section 90 of the second Restatement applies only when a promisor should reasonably expect the promisee to rely. Why should an offeror of a bilateral contract reasonably expect an offeree to rely on the offer before acceptance?[229] Suppose you offer to sell your piano to Alice for $400 and, before replying, Alice purchases expensive accessories for the piano. I doubt that you would reasonably have expected her to do this. After all, you and she had not formed a contract to sell the piano. (What are piano accessories anyway?)

In support of the court's decision in *Drennan*, apparently general contractors customarily relied on subcontractors' bids before accepting them, just as Drennan had done. Taking custom into account, Star Paving reasonably should have expected such reliance. I know of no such custom with piano accessories, however.

Finally, with respect to the *Drennan* case, I have always been suspicious of Drennan's trip to Star Paving the day after Drennan was awarded the general contract. Why did he stop off there and not at some other subcontractor's office or just go to his own place of work? Perhaps Drennan was himself suspicious that Star Paving had made a mistake. (The court stated, however, that Drennan "had no reason to know that defendant had made a mistake in submitting its bid since there was usually a variance of 160 per cent between the highest and lowest bids for paving in the desert * * *."[230]) We will see in Chapter 9 that such a suspicion (if he had it) would probably be sufficient to allow Star Paving relief from its bid.

---

229. See James Baird Co. v. Gimbel Bros., Inc., 64 F.2d 344 (2d Cir. 1933). But see G. Richard Shell, Opportunism and Trust in the Negotiation of Commercial Contracts: Toward a New Cause of Action, 44 Vand. L. Rev. 221, 248 (1991) ("Gimbel's approach toward the subcontractor-contractor relationship has been rejected by most modern courts.").

230. Drennan, 333 P.2d at 761.

6. Bargaining at a distance. This subsection takes up an issue that soon may be of historical interest only. The issue concerns contract formation when the parties are separated by some distance and use the mail (or telegram) as their medium of communication. (Most students seem addicted to e-mail and the internet, so you should be able to guess why this issue may soon be obsolete.) Despite innovative ways of communicating and forming contracts, at least a brief look at the old stuff is still in order. This is because a major question facing lawmakers today is whether the traditional rules of contract formation ought to apply to the new technology. In order to understand this set of issues, we need to look at the traditional rules and then test them out in the new electronic environment.

a. Communication via the mail or telegram (the old stuff). The main problem when parties communicate via the mail is that both parties cannot know at the same time whether they have formed a contract. The offeror doesn't know when and if the offeree put a letter of acceptance in the mail until the offeror receives the letter. The offeree doesn't know when and if the offeror received the acceptance until the offeror sends a confirmation. As an early case said, "[a]nd so it might go on ad infinitum."[231] Who should contract law favor, the offeror or the offeree?

Of course, an offeror can prescribe in the offer that the offeror must *receive* an acceptance before a contract is formed, thereby assuring that the offeror is first to know when a contract is formed. Suppose, for example, on July 1 you send a letter to Alice in which you offer her your piano for $400. You specify that you must receive an acceptance by mail (and by no other medium) by July 20. We have learned that contract law will honor your prescriptions as to the time and manner of acceptance.[232] Alice's letter of acceptance that is posted on July 19 and arrives on July 21 is no good. (We have also seen that you can revoke your offer even before July 20 unless one of the bars to revocation apply.[233] Gee, we've covered a lot already.)

Now suppose you fail to include any language in your July 1 offer with respect to the time or manner of acceptance. Contract law must determine who gains the advantage with respect to knowing when a contract is formed. For example, suppose on July 8, Alice posts a letter of acceptance to you, which you receive on July 11. Is the contract formed on July 8 or July 11? The date of

231. Adams v. Lindsell, 106 Eng. Rep. 250, 251 (K.B. 1818).

232. See Lewis v. Browning, 130 Mass. 173, 175–76 (1880) ("[T]he person making the offer may always, if he chooses, make the formation of the contract which he proposes dependent upon the actual communication to himself of the acceptance."); see also supra notes 156–165, and accompanying text.

233. See supra notes 196–206, and accompanying text.

formation is not important if both parties perform the deal without incident. But suppose you sent a letter to Alice on July 6 revoking your offer, which Alice received on July 9. Recall that revocations are not effective until the offeree receives them, here July 9.[234] So, if Alice's letter of acceptance forms a contract when posted on July 8, your revocation is no good. But if Alice's letter of acceptance forms a contract when you receive it on July 11, the revocation Alice received on July 9 is effective and you are not bound.

After some debate in the courts, contract law has settled on the "acceptance-is-good-when-posted" rule, so Alice's letter posted on July 8 forms the contract and your revocation is ineffective.[235] You should have prescribed when the acceptance becomes effective, namely when you receive it. In fact, a fairly persuasive argument in favor of the acceptance-is-good-when-posted rule is that offerors can protect themselves from the uncertainty concerning when a contract has been made and offerees cannot. If an offeror fails to avail itself of that protection by prescribing a time of acceptance in the offer, then the law should favor the offeree.[236]

Courts have also offered other reasons for the acceptance-is-good-when-posted rule. One is that the offeror, by choosing to use the mail, has made the post office her agent. As soon as an offeree posts an acceptance, constructively it is in the hands of the offeror.[237] Another explanation, at least for adhering to the rule, is that contract law requires certainty as to when contracts are formed and most courts have already settled on the acceptance-is-good-when-posted rule. Courts should not change this settled rule now.[238]

Regardless of the reasons for the acceptance-is-good-when-posted rule, its ramifications are clear. In the absence of a prescription in an offer otherwise, a posted acceptance forms a contract and neither party can change her mind. If Alice posts an acceptance before she receives a revocation of the offer, a contract is formed. If she posts her acceptance, but the postal service loses it, a contract

---

234. Restatement (Second) of Contracts § 42 ("An offeree's power of acceptance is terminated when the offeree receives from the offeror a manifestation of an intention not to enter into the proposed contract."); see supra note 192, and accompanying text.

235. See, e.g., Lewis, 130 Mass. at 175 ("[T]he contract has been deemed to be completed as soon as the letter of acceptance has been put into the post-office duly addressed.").

236. Morrison v. Thoelke, 155 So.2d 889, 904 (Fla. Dist. Ct. App. 1963) ("[T]he offeror can always expressly

condition the contract on his receipt of an acceptance and, should he fail to do so, the law should not afford him this advantage.").

237. Farnsworth, supra note 109, at 176.

238. Morrison, 155 So.2d at 904–05 ("Outmoded precedents may, on occasion be discarded and the function of justice should not be the perpetuation of error, but, by the same token, traditional rules and concepts should not be abandoned save a compelling ground.").

is still formed. If she posts her acceptance but retrieves it from the post office (modern rules allow this), a contract is still formed.[239]

b.   Electronic offer and acceptance. Electronic contracting raises lots of issues, but the most basic is whether the contract rules of agreement (the material of Part B of this chapter) should apply to this new medium in total, with some refinement, or not at all. Obviously, if the latter, electronic contracting would require a whole new set of rules. Although we are still fairly early in the development of electronic commerce, I am not aware of anyone asserting persuasively the position that contract law must begin anew in the field of electronic contracting. Basic principles, such as that contract law should enforce agreements supported by consideration, that contract law should use an objective "reasonable person" test to determine whether the parties have made an agreement, and that contract law should enforce the prescriptions in offers, seem to apply with equal strength to the electronic contracting medium. But *some* changes in contract law may be necessary to suit this new manner of contracting. For example, in Chapter 6, we will investigate some problems of consumer standard-form contracting that the new medium exacerbates.[240] (We will see, for example, that internet sellers may take advantage of our impatience and our tendency to be "click happy" by including unfair terms in our standard-form agreements.) However, here we focus on whether the rules of bargaining at a distance heretofore applied to the mail and telegram should also apply to electronic contracting. More specifically, should the "acceptance is good when posted" idea apply to internet and to e-mail so that an internet form or e-mail acceptance becomes effective when sent?

Only a brief discussion seems necessary. Although the problem of delay in communication is largely eliminated with electronic contracting, there will be occasional glitches. For example, a party may accept by sending an e-mail or by clicking on an "I accept" button on an internet page, but the transmission may fail to go through. Is a contract formed at the time the offeree sends the message?

Note that, just as in a paper world, an offeror can protect herself by requiring the receipt of an electronic message before a contract is formed. By failing to do so, the equities lie with the offeree. The acceptance should therefore be effective when sent. In

---

239. Id. at 905 ("[A]n unqualified offer was accepted and the acceptance made manifest. Later, the offerees sought to repudiate their initial assent ... adopting the view that the acceptance was effective when the letter of acceptance was deposited in the mails [sic], the repudiation was equally invalid....").

240. See Chapter 6 at notes 254–276, and accompanying text.

short, the same reasoning applies to both electronic and paper communication.

7. Limitations of agreement law. I do not mean to alarm you when I report that some lawyers and contracts writers claim that most of what we have reviewed in Part B of this chapter is archaic and irrelevant. They do not base their claim so much on the inroads of electronic technology, but on their view that the actual processes of contracting are very different from the neat offer and acceptance scenarios often described in cases and textbooks (and here). For example, businesses often make preliminary agreements of many different kinds:

> Especially when large deals are concluded among corporations and individuals of substance, the usual sequence of events is not that of offer and acceptance; on the contrary the businessmen who originally conduct the negotiations, often will consciously refrain from ever making a binding offer, realizing as they do that a large deal tends to be complex and that its terms have to be formulated by lawyers before it can be permitted to become a legally enforceable transaction. Thus the original negotiators will merely attempt to ascertain whether they see eye to eye concerning those aspects of the deal which seem to be most important from a business point of view. * * * When the lawyers take over, again there is no sequence of offer and acceptance, but rather a sequence of successive drafts. * * * After a number of drafts have been exchanged and discussed the lawyers may finally come up with a draft which meets the approval of all of them, and of their clients. It is only then that the parties will proceed to the actual formation of the contract, and often this will be done by way of a formal "closing" * * * [241]

If deals between "corporations and individuals of substance" (I guess that excludes you and me) do not have an identifiable sequence of offer and acceptance, the traditional approach to agreement formation, namely looking for "the offer" and "the acceptance," obviously will not be very helpful in this context. In such situations, contract law requires a different *modus operandi*.

Similarly, in sales of goods between businesses, the parties often utilize purchase orders and acknowledgment forms, but often fail to read the fine print on the forms. Sometimes the two forms do

---

241. Rudolph B. Schlesinger, Manifestation of Assent Without Identifiable Sequence in Offer and Acceptance, II Formation of Contracts 1583, 1584 (Rudolph B. Schlesinger ed., 1968); see also William Whitford, Ian Macneil's Contribution to Contracts Scholarship, 1985 Wis. L. Rev. 545, 547 ("If relational contracts lacking a grand meeting of the minds are to be enforced, there is no way to explain the results reached within the structure of classical contract law. . . .").

not match. For example, suppose a buyer's purchase order includes a term requiring arbitration of disputes, but the seller's acknowledgment form specifically calls for adjudication in a court. If a dispute develops and the seller sues the buyer for breach of contract in a court, the court must determine whether the parties made an enforceable contract (after all the acknowledgment form does not match the purchase order) and whether it should hear the dispute or require arbitration.

A third instance of contract formation where traditional rules of offer and acceptance are problematic involves what some people call "rolling contracts," often between a business and a consumer. Suppose a consumer orders a computer over the telephone and pays by giving her credit card information. The seller sends the computer in a package that also contains all of the terms of the deal. Is a contract formed? What are its terms?

Before turning to contract law's approach to these problems, I owe you a brief defense of traditional offer-and-acceptance analysis. After all, we just spent lots of time reviewing it. The law of offer and acceptance remains important because critics underestimate the number of contracts made via this traditional route. In addition, courts still employ offer-acceptance analysis even when this framework does not fit very well. In order to understand the analysis, we must be conversant with offer and acceptance law. Restatements, statutes, and international conventions also continue to pay lots of attention to offer and acceptance law. Finally, we will see that contract law's response to instances where the exchange lacks a clear offer and acceptance still resembles the traditional approach.

a. The legal significance of business draft agreements. Now let's get to the substance of the problem. How should contract law determine when the parties become bound when the parties produce lots of drafts, turn things over to lawyers, and then sign papers at a closing? You might think that this is not a hard question: Contract formation must occur at the closing when the parties sign the final documents. However, sometimes the parties sign earlier drafts, denominated "agreement to agree," "preliminary agreement," "memorandum of intent," or the like, and sometimes they intend these earlier drafts to have a legal effect. What result when the parties fail to reach a final agreement, but one party claims that a signed draft constitutes a legally enforceable contract?

For example, suppose that Ajax Piano Co. and Neighborhood Music Co. intend to combine forces and create one large music company. One of the many documents they sign is a "memorandum of intent," that contains most of the details of the merger. The memorandum also states that the parties' lawyers "will proceed as promptly as possible to prepare an agreement acceptable to Ajax and Neighborhood for the proposed combination of businesses." Further, under the heading "conditions," the memorandum states that the obligations of the parties shall be subject to the "preparation of the definitive agreement for the proposed combination in form and content satisfactory to both parties and their respective counsel." The parties also issue a press release stating that they had "agreed to cooperate in an enterprise that will serve the music industry." Soon after publication of the press release, Neighborhood decides not to proceed with the merger. Does Ajax have any legal rights?[242]

Ajax's rights depend on how contract law treats the memorandum of intent. There are at least three possibilities. First, contract law could find that the memorandum is not legally enforceable at all.[243] The parties simply meant to memorialize their tentative oral understandings in a writing so that they can refer to them later. At the other extreme, contract law could find that the memorandum is a legally enforceable contract.[244] The parties sought to bind themselves while they complete the remaining terms and refine the agreement. In the middle, contract law could find that the memorandum constitutes a legal obligation to make a reasonable effort to conclude the deal.[245] The parties have come far enough to expect that their counterpart will not simply change its mind without a good business reason related to the particular deal.

You should not be surprised to learn that contract law sorts out these alternatives by determining which category the parties intended. Also not surprising, contract law determines the parties' intentions objectively under the reasonable person test.[246] Would a reasonable person believe that Ajax and Neighborhood intended not to be bound by their memorandum of intent, intended to be bound

---

242. See Arnold Palmer Golf Co. v. Fuqua Indus., Inc., 541 F.2d 584, 587 (6th Cir. 1976).

243. Restatement (Second) of Contracts § 27, cmt. b ("[I]f either party knows or has reason to know that the other party regards the agreement as incomplete and intends that no obligation shall exist until other terms are assented to or until the whole has been reduced to another written form, the preliminary negotiations and agreements do not constitute a contract.").

244. Id. § 27, cmt. a ("Parties who ... before the final writing is made, agree upon all the terms which they plan to incorporate therein ... orally or by exchange of several writings. It is

possible thus to make a contract the terms of which include an obligation to execute subsequently a final writing which shall contain certain provisions....").

245. Arcadian Phosphates, Inc. v. Arcadian Corp., 884 F.2d 69, 72 (2d Cir. 1989) ("[T]he parties can bind themselves to a concededly incomplete agreement ... in the sense that they accept a mutual commitment to negotiate together in good faith in an effort to reach final agreement....") (quoting Teachers Insurance & Annuity Ass'n. v. Tribune Co., 670 F.Supp. 491, 498 (S.D.N.Y. 1987)).

246. See supra notes 108–125, and accompanying text.

to an enforceable contract, or intended to be bound to use best efforts to complete the final deal?

Contract law determines what a reasonable person would believe no differently here than in other contexts. For example, recall the court's approach in *Lucy v. Zehmer*.[247] The court examined all of the circumstances to determine whether a reasonable person would believe Zehmer intended to contract. As with that inquiry, in cases such as the Ajax—Neighborhood merger, courts investigate, the language of the writing, the degree of detail, the importance of the subject matter, statements and conduct of the parties both inside and outside the formal negotiations, and any other relevant contextual matters.[248]

What does this portend for Ajax and Neighborhood? Their memorandum of intent uses language of commitment: The lawyers *"will* proceed as promptly as possible to prepare an agreement * * *."* Further, the memorandum already includes most of the terms. The parties also issued a press release stating that they had "agreed to cooperate." On the other hand, the parties clearly contemplated that they would enter a later, final agreement and would "condition" enforcement of the final agreement on their satisfaction with it. In such situations, courts often decide that the parties intended to bind themselves to make a reasonable or good faith effort to conclude their deal.[249] A reasonable effort requires more than simply changing one's mind about entering the contract for reasons independent of the terms of the final draft.[250]

---

247. 84 S.E.2d 516, 522 (Va. 1954) ("[T]he law imputes to a person an intention corresponding to the reasonable meaning of his words and acts. If his words and acts, judged by a reasonable standard, manifest an intention to agree, it is immaterial what may be the real but unexpressed state of his mind."); see supra notes 110–125, and accompanying text.

248. Arnold Palmer Golf Co., 541 F.2d at 589 ("[T]he entire document and relevant circumstances surrounding its adoption must be considered in making a determination of the parties' intention."); Restatement (Second) of Contracts § 27, cmt. c (factors for determining the formation of a contract include "the extent to which express agreement has been reached on all the terms to be included, whether the contract is the type usually put in writing, whether it needs a formal writing for its full expression, whether it has few or many details, whether the amount involved is large or small, . . . and whether either

party takes any action in preparation for performance during the negotiations.").

249. Liberty Envtl. Sys., Inc. v. County of Westchester, 2000 WL 1752927, at 3 (S.D.N.Y.2000) ("each party [must] act in good faith towards the other party and . . . refrain from engaging in conduct designed to defeat or obstruct the other party's ability to perform or fulfill the requirements of the [memorandum of understanding]."); Teachers Insurance & Annuity Association v. Tribune Co., 670 F.Supp. 491, 498 (S.D.N.Y. 1987); ("[P]arties can bind themselves to concededly incomplete agreement in the sense that they accept a mutual commitment to negotiate together in good faith in an effort to reach final agreement within the scope that has been settled in the preliminary agreement.").

250. Teachers Insurance & Annuity Ass'n, 670 F.Supp. at 498 ("The obligation . . . bar[s] a party from renouncing the deal, abandoning the negotiations, or insisting on conditions that do

b. The requirement of certainty in business agreements. A party such as Neighborhood, that is contesting the enforcement of a draft agreement, has another defense. Even if the parties intended their preliminary draft to have legal effect, the draft may not be enforceable if the draft omits too many important terms.[251] Courts in such situations decline to enforce the contract on the grounds of uncertainty. Even if the parties intended to contract, a court may reason that it would not know what to enforce.[252] Although the doctrine of uncertainty applies to all kinds of contracts, it is especially prevalent with regard to business agreements.

Suppose, for example, that a renewal clause in a lease states that "the Tenant may renew this lease for an additional period of five years at annual rentals to be agreed upon." A court may decline to enforce this agreement-to-agree on the ground that the contract fails to inform the court of any basis for determining the renewal rate.[253] On the other hand, if the contract called for a renewal rate at market value or some percentage above the existing rent, a court would not hesitate to enforce the lease.[254]

Despite some decisions to the contrary,[255] courts should make every effort to fill gaps and enforce agreements when the parties intended to contract. Recall that in *Wood v. Lucy, Lady Duff–Gordon*,[256] Judge Cardozo found that, although Wood had not expressly promised to market Lucy's designs, the evidence showed that he had agreed to make reasonable efforts to do so. We can apply this lesson to the lease-renewal problem. If the parties were serious about granting the tenant an option to renew, the court should enforce the obligation. The court could find that the parties impliedly agreed to a reasonable renewal rate based, for example,

not conform to the preliminary agreement.").

251. Joseph Martin Jr., Delicatessen, Inc. v. Schumacher, 436 N.Y.S.2d 247, 249 (Ct. App. 1981) ("[I]t is rightfully well settled ... that a mere agreement to agree, in which a material term is left for future negotiations, is unenforceable").

252. Nebo Constr. Co. v. Southeastern Elec. Constr. Co., 200 F.Supp. 582, 587 (W.D.La.1961) ("The sheer indefiniteness of this purported contract renders it unenforceable."); see also Joseph Martin, Jr., Delicatessen, Inc., 417 N.E.2d at 543 ("[B]efore the power of law can be invoked to enforce a promise, it must be sufficiently certain and specific so that what was promised can be ascertained.").

253. Id. at 544 ("[renewal clause's] simple words leave no room for legal construction or resolution of ambiguity. Neither tenant nor landlord is bound to any formula. There is not so much as a hint at a commitment to be bound by the 'fair market rental value' ... or the 'reasonable rent'....").

254. Id. at 544 ("This is not to say that the requirement for definiteness ... could only have been met by explicit expression.... if a methodology for determining the rent was to be found within the four corners of the lease....").

255. Joseph Martin, Jr., Delicatessen, Inc., 436 N.Y.S.2d 247.

256. 118 N.E. 214 (N.Y. 1917); see supra notes 59–64, and accompanying text.

on the market value of the leasehold. Some decisions reflect this line of reasoning.[257] In addition, Article 2 of the UCC relaxes the uncertainty test. Section 2–204(3) states that "[e]ven though one or more terms are left open a contract for sale does not fail for indefiniteness if the parties have intended to make a contract and there is a reasonably certain basis for giving an appropriate remedy."[258]

c. Form contracts between sellers and buyers of goods.

Let's investigate further the example above involving a buyer's purchase order of goods and a seller's acknowledgment form that contradict each other and let's fill out the facts. Although there are lots of variations, here is a typical (although simplified) case: The buyer, Ajax Piano Co., wants to purchase certain lumber for manufacturing pianos from Seaman's Lumber Co. Ajax's manager telephones Seaman's selling agent and orders the lumber. The parties do not discuss the details (beyond price and delivery date) because they contemplate the exchange of a purchase order and acknowledgment form. Ajax then fills out and mails one of its purchase order forms, prepared by its lawyers and loaded with terms favorable to Ajax. The purchase order includes a term requiring arbitration of disputes. Before Seaman's receives the purchase order, it sends its acknowledgment form (prepared by *its* lawyers and full of provisions favorable to Seaman's) to Ajax, so the two forms cross in the mail. Seaman's form calls for adjudication of disputes in a court. After each party receives the other's form, Seaman's delivers and Ajax pays the first installment of the purchase price of the lumber. Ajax is not satisfied with the lumber and, after some unsatisfactory discussions with Seaman's, Ajax refuses to pay the next installment. Seaman's sues Ajax in a court. The court must determine whether the parties formed a contract, and if so, whether the contract requires arbitration.

Obviously this is a tough case for anyone trying to resolve it by using basic offer and acceptance rules. The parties likely did not form a contract during their telephone conversation because they contemplated an exchange of forms and because business people understand that a writing is required to close a contract for the sale of goods of $500 or more.[259] If the parties are not bound by the

---

257. Mutual Paper Co. v. Hoague–Sprague Corp., 8 N.E.2d 802, 807 (Mass. 1937) ("In . . . the case at bar there is set forth an elaborate method of determining the rent to be paid during the extended period. It cannot be supposed it was the intent of the parties that, at the end of the original tenancy, both parties would then be free to bargain with reference to a new lease.").

258. UCC § 2–204(3).

259. UCC § 2–201(1). See Chapter 4 at note 6, and accompanying text.

telephone call, Ajax's purchase order probably constitutes an offer under the "reasonable person" test of offer-acceptance law.[260] If so, Seaman's acknowledgment form must be a counteroffer, since it is not a "mirror image" of the offer but, instead, includes provisions that contradict the offer, such as the requirement that the parties adjudicate disputes in court. Ajax's acceptance of the lumber, then, must constitute an acceptance of Seaman's counteroffer. A contract is thus formed on Seaman's terms and the arbitration provision in Ajax's purchase order drops out.

The problem with this analysis, of course, is that the parties have not read their forms at all, so to speak of an agreement between the parties to decide disputes in court, not through arbitration, is pure fiction. In addition, the offer and acceptance analysis arbitrarily favors the party who sends its form last. In defense of this approach, one can argue that each party *should* read their forms so that Ajax should be on notice of Seaman's terms and Ajax should not accept the lumber unless it is willing to accept Seaman's terms. Most courts and analysts, however, assume that business parties simply do not read the forms regardless of the legal incentives.[261] If true, perhaps it is unwise arbitrarily to favor the party who has the "last shot" at denominating the terms.

The drafters of UCC section 2–207 saw the problems with traditional offer and acceptance analysis of the "battle of the forms" and sought to draft a solution. Unfortunately, the UCC approach has not been successful. It is itself complex, controversial, and the subject of lots of litigation. It may soon be amended by the state legislatures (we will briefly look at the proposed amendment below[262]). Fortunately, we need only cover the basics of section 2–207 here because the section is an important subject in most upperclass commercial law courses. (But if your school covers the section exclusively in contracts and you find what follows too basic, an excellent source of additional reading is James J. White & Robert S. Summers, The Uniform Commercial Code, 29–48 (5th ed. 2000)).

Section 2–207 is important enough to quote in full:

260. See supra notes 108–125, and accompanying text.

261. See, e.g., American Parts Co. v. American Arbitration Ass'n, 154 N.W.2d 5, 16 (Mich. Ct. App.1967) ("[B]usinessmen use forms that do not always fit their circumstances and which frequently contain significant modifications of the simple oral agreement of the parties in the form of boiler plate which generally is not read by the other contracting party and perhaps is not expected to be read."); James J. White & Robert S. Summers, Uniform Commercial Code 30 (5th ed. 2000) ("[S]ometimes the parties will fall into dispute even before occasion for performance.... In all these cases the parties will haul out their forms and read them—perhaps for the first time...").

262. See infra notes 276–278, and accompanying text.

Additional Terms in Acceptance or Confirmation

(1) A definite and seasonable expression of acceptance or a written confirmation which is sent within a reasonable time operates as an acceptance even though it states terms additional to or different from those offered or agreed upon, unless acceptance is expressly made conditional on assent to the additional or different terms.

(2) The additional terms are to be construed as proposals for addition to the contract. Between merchants such terms become part of the contract unless:

(a) the offer expressly limits acceptance to the terms of the offer;

(b) they materially alter it; or

(c) notification of objection to them has already been given or is given within a reasonable time after notice of them is received.

(3) Conduct by both parties which recognizes the existence of a contract is sufficient to establish a contract for sale although the writings of the parties do not otherwise establish a contract. In such case the terms of the particular contract consist of those terms on which the writings of the parties agree, together with any supplementary terms incorporated under any other provisions of this Act.[263]

First, note that the section applies both to situations where a writing constitutes a confirmation of a deal already made, and to situations such as ours, where the purchase order constitutes an offer and the acknowledgment form constitutes a "definite and seasonable expression of acceptance."[264] Professors White and Summers point out that section 2–207 contemplates three contract-forming avenues in offer-acceptance situations such as the Ajax–Seaman's contract.[265] We will now analyze each of these routes.

Route 1 Route 1 consists of subsection 1 up to the comma, which language abrogates the common-law mirror-image rule ("operates as an acceptance even though it states terms additional to or different"). Route 1 also consists of subsection 2 of section 2–207, which explains what happens to the "additional terms" in the acceptance.

Here is one important source of confusion in section 2–207: Note that subsection 2 speaks only of "additional terms" and says

---

263. UCC § 2–207.

264. UCC § 2–207(1) ("A definite and seasonable expression of acceptance or a written confirmation....").

265. White & Summers, supra note 261, at 31–36.

nothing about what happens to "different terms." Most interpreters of section 2–207 understand the difference between "additional" and "different" terms in the following way: Because Ajax's form called for arbitration and Seaman's form provided for court adjudication, Seaman's form contains a "different" term. On the other hand, if Ajax's form did not address the forum for resolving disputes and Seaman's called for arbitration, Seaman's term would be "additional."[266]

At any rate, what is the significance of subsection 2's reference to "additional" terms and not "different" terms? Among the possibilities, the drafters could have meant "additional" in subsection 2 to refer to both "additional or different" terms in subsection 1.[267] Alternatively, perhaps they intended subsection 2 to apply only to "additional" terms. If the latter, section 2–207 gives no guidance on what happens to "different" terms. Some commentators and courts believe that "different" terms knock each other out of the contract, with the court to fill the gap.[268] Applied to the Ajax–Seaman's problem, this approach would mean that the arbitration provision and court-adjudication term knock each other out of the contract. Court adjudication would then be the mode of dispute settlement, not because Seaman's form called for it, but because court adjudication is the form of dispute resolution that applies when the contracting parties have left a gap with respect to the issue. Contracts lawyers use the name "default rules" to refer to sources of law that apply when the parties have not drafted a rule for themselves. The default rule with respect to the forum for resolving contracts disputes is the courts.

If subsection 2 applies to both "additional or different" terms, the following analysis applies: The first sentence of subsection 2 says that Seaman's court-adjudication term is a "proposal[] for addition to the contract." The next sentence, containing provisions (a) through (c), applies only if the parties are "merchants."[269] Merchants, under Article 2 of the UCC, include people "who deal in goods of the kind * * *."[270] Here, Ajax and Seaman's "deal" in

---

266. See, e.g., id. at 32–33 ("[I]t would be more than a little difficult to view a different term in an acceptance as a proposal for addition to the contract where the offer already includes a contrary term.").

267. UCC § 2–207, cmt. 3 ("additional or different terms" come under subsection 2).

268. See, e.g., Lea Tai Textile Co., Ltd. v. Manning Fabrics, Inc. 411 F.Supp. 1404, 1407 (S.D.N.Y. 1975) ("Since the arbitration clauses are in hopeless conflict, I find that no contract

to arbitrate was made."); see also White & Summers, supra note 261, at 34 ([T]he two terms cancel one another. On this view the seller's form was only an acceptance of terms in the offer which did not conflict with any terms in the acceptance. The ultimate deal would not include the arbitration clause.).

269. UCC § 2–207(2) ("Between merchants such terms become part of the contract....").

270. UCC § 2–104(1).

lumber because Seaman's sells it and Ajax builds pianos with it, so they are merchants and the second sentence of subsection 2, with provisions (a) through (c), applies. Before applying it, let's see what would happen if the parties were not merchants. In that case, only the first sentence of subsection 2 would apply and we would have to determine what happens to "proposals for addition to the contract" when the parties go through with their deal.[271] Again, section 2–207 leaves us hanging. One can argue that if Seaman's court-adjudication term is only a proposal (and not a counteroffer), it would drop out if not expressly accepted by Ajax. The parties would have to arbitrate their dispute.

Because the parties are merchants, subsections (2)(a) through (c) apply. Subsection (2)(a) provides that Seaman's court-adjudication term becomes part of the contract unless Ajax's offer "expressly limits acceptance" to Ajax's terms. Assume that no such language appeared in Ajax's form. Subsection (2)(b) states that Seaman's court-adjudication term becomes part of the contract unless it "materially alter[s]" the offer. Presumably, a term that changes the manner in which disputes will be settled *is* a material alteration. Seaman's term therefore drops out of the contract. The term would also have dropped out under subsection (2)(c) if Ajax had notified Seaman's or notified it within a reasonable time that Ajax objected to the court-adjudication term. Apparently, the drafters did not contemplate that Ajax's arbitration term in its purchase order would constitute notification to Seaman's that Ajax objects to court adjudication. Ajax must state this intention explicitly.

Note that the result of the Ajax-Seaman's dispute under section 2–207, route 1, is the exact opposite of the result under common-law offer and acceptance rules: Ajax gets arbitration. The party that sent its form first prevails. As with common law, however, there is no particularly compelling explanation for why the law should favor the first party when neither party reads their forms.

Route 2 Contract formation under route 2 consists of subsection 1 after the comma: "unless acceptance is expressly made conditional on assent to the additional or different terms." With this language, the drafters embraced the idea that a party such as Seaman's has the power to make a counteroffer. But it is not enough for a party to simply include an "additional or different" term (as here) for the communication to constitute a counteroffer. According to case law, Seaman's form would have to track the

---

271. UCC § 2–207(2) ("The additional terms are to be construed as proposals for addition to the contract."); see also UCC § 2–207, cmt. 2 ("'[A]ny addi- tional matter contained in the confirmation or in the acceptance falls within subsection (2) and must be regarded as a proposal for an added term. . . .'").

language of the statute, including something like "acceptance expressly conditional on Ajax agreeing to judicial resolution of disputes."[272]

If route 2 applies to Ajax and Seaman's, Ajax's acceptance of the goods and payment would constitute an acceptance of Seaman's counteroffer and Seaman's court-adjudication term would prevail. This, of course, is the common-law outcome.[273]

Route 3 Section 2–207(3) provides the third route of contract formation. Most commentators conclude that the section applies when the parties' forms hopelessly conflict and obviously do not establish an intention to be bound, yet the parties act as if they have a contract, such as by delivering and paying for the goods.[274] One challenge, of course, is determining precisely when the writings conflict so much that route 3 applies. For example, one can argue that section 2–207(3) should govern the Ajax–Seaman's transaction, not section 2–207(1) and (2). Recall that each party's form heavily favors its drafter and several additional conflicts therefore likely exist. Further, the forms crossed in the mail so one can take issue with the conclusion that Seaman's acknowledgment form constituted "a definite and seasonable expression of acceptance" under route 1. Of course, the lack of clarity even as to which route to follow does not add to the general luster of section 2–207.

If subsection (3) does apply, it specifies the governing terms. Specifically, the contract consists of the matching terms in the two forms and, to fill remaining gaps, terms supplied by other provisions of Article 2. (Article 2 contains gap-filler provisions, for example, with respect to the price of goods, the place of delivery, and the time for delivery.[275]) Ajax would not be entitled to arbitration because the parties did not agree to arbitrate and Article 2 does not supply a term that requires arbitration of disputes.

Amended section 2–207 You are not alone if you read through the previous explanation of section 2–207 and exclaimed, "what a mess" (not my explanation, section 2–207 itself). As you know, for the past decade, the ALI and NCCUSL have been busy amending Article 2 for possible adoption by the state legislatures.[276] These

---

272. See White & Summers, supra note 261, at 37, 39 (citing cases).

273. Restatement (Second) of Contracts § 59 ("A reply to an offer which purports to accept it but is conditional on the offeror's assent to terms additional to or different from those offered is not an acceptance but is a counter-offer.").

274. UCC § 2–207, cmt. 7 ("In many cases, as where goods are shipped,

accepted and paid for before any dispute arises, there is no question whether a contract has been made.... [T]he only question is what terms are included in the contract, and subsection (3) furnishes the governing rule.").

275. See UCC §§ 2–305, 2–308, 2–309.

276. See Chapter 1 at text accompanying notes 5–6.

bodies have spent considerable time trying to resolve some of the ambiguities of section 2–207.

The draft of the section recently approved by the two organizations largely follows route 3 (subsection 3) of existing section 2–207:

> * * * If (i) conduct by both parties recognizes the existence of a contract although their records do not otherwise establish a contract, (ii) a contract is formed by an offer and acceptance, or (iii) a contract formed in any manner is confirmed by a record that contains terms additional to or different from those in the contract being confirmed, the terms of the contract, subject to Section 2–202, are:
>
> (a) terms that appear in the records of both parties;
>
> (b) terms, whether in a record or not, to which both parties agree; and
>
> (c) terms supplied or incorporated under any provision of this Act.

A "record" under the Article 2 amendments includes both written and electronic agreements.[277] Section 2–202 refers to the parol evidence rule, which we take up in Chapter 7 (and can ignore for now).[278]

Under amended section 2–207, the Ajax–Seaman's exchange would constitute either a contract recognized by the parties, but not by their records under (i), or a contract formed by offer and acceptance under (ii). (This parallels contract formation under routes 3 and 1 respectively under existing section 2–207.) Either way, subsections (a) through (c) establish the terms. Ajax's arbitration provision was not in each record under (a), and the parties did not agree to arbitrate outside of their records under (b). Subsection (c) therefore applies and Article 2 would supply the gap filler on dispute resolution. As with existing section 2–207, Ajax would not be entitled to arbitration because the parties did not agree to it and Article 2 does not supply a term that requires arbitration of disputes.

Amended section 2–207 may improve analysis of the "battle of the forms" because it is simpler. Still, courts will have to wrestle with new ambiguities, such as how to prove whether parties "agree" to terms outside of their records. Suppose, for example, that Ajax's form was silent on dispute resolution and Seaman's included an arbitration provision. Did Ajax agree to arbitration by taking and paying for the goods?

277. Amended UCC § 2–103(1)(m) (proposed final draft April 18, 2003).

278. See Chapter 7 at notes 4–56, and accompanying text.

d. Rolling contracts. The final example of a situation in which offer-acceptance analysis is problematic involves "rolling contracts." In rolling contracts, consumers order and pay for goods before having an opportunity to read most of the terms, which are contained on or in the goods' packaging. The terms of "rolling contracts" thus just keep rolling along as the deal progresses.

Consider the leading case of *Hill v. Gateway 2000.*[279] The Hills ordered a computer from Gateway over the telephone and gave their credit card information to the salesperson. Soon thereafter, Gateway delivered the computer in a box that contained a set of terms, including a declaration that the terms would govern the transaction unless the Hills returned the computer in 30 days.[280] After using the computer for more than 30 days, the Hills became dissatisfied with its performance, and sued Gateway in federal court. One of the terms in Gateway's box required arbitration of disputes.

The court found that Gateway's shipment of the computer with the terms, including the 30–day-return right, constituted an offer. The Hills accepted the offer, according to the court, by keeping the computer for more than 30 days. The contract, which was formed at the end of the 30 day period, therefore included the arbitration provision and Gateway's other terms.[281]

So far this looks like an ordinary offer and acceptance case, at least according to the court. However, the Hills maintained that the contract was formed when they paid for the computer and Gateway shipped it. Further, because nothing in UCC section 2–207(2) limits it applicability to merchants or to "battle of the forms" situations, the "additional" terms that followed contract formation, including the arbitration provision, drop out as proposals that the Hills did not accept.[282]

The court did not accept the Hills' argument in part because it found that Gateway conditioned contract formation on the Hills' examination of the goods and the terms, something they could not do until long after the telephone order and payment. The court neglected to apply section 2–206(1)(b) of the UCC, which provides:

> Unless otherwise unambiguously indicated by the language or the circumstances . . . an order or other offer to buy goods for

279. 105 F.3d 1147 (7th Cir. 1997).

280. Id. at 1148 ("[A] box arrives, containing the computer and a list of terms, said to govern unless the customer returns the computer within 30 days.").

281. Id. at 1150 ("By keeping the computer beyond 30 days, the Hills accepted Gateway's offer, including the arbitration clause."); see also Brower v. Gateway 2000, 676 N.Y.S.2d 569, 572 (App. Div. 1998) ("no contract was formed here . . . until the merchandise was retained beyond the 30–day period.").

282. UCC § 2–207(2) ("The additional terms are to be construed as proposals for addition to the contract.").

prompt or current shipment shall be construed as inviting acceptance either by a prompt promise to ship or by the prompt or current shipment of conforming or non-conforming goods * * * .[283]

According to section 2–206(1)(b), the Hills version of offer and acceptance was correct unless the language of the contract or the circumstances showed "unambiguously" that contract formation was postponed until 30 days after delivery of the computer to the Hills. But the truth is that the parties likely gave little thought to the legal question of when their contract was formed. Rather, the parties were concerned with the procedure for ordering, delivering, and returning the computer, and when the Hills would receive the terms. Thus, section 2–206(1)(b) appears to favor the Hills' version of the facts.

Perhaps a better approach to "rolling contracts," would be to focus less on offer and acceptance, which does not appear to produce very definitive results on when a contract is formed, and more on the fairness of the terms that come in the box. Courts should strike unconscionable terms, a category of terms that we will discuss fully in Chapter 6 (where we again take up *Hill v. Gateway*).[284] For now, understand that the crux of the matter is whether the manner of revealing the terms or what they say is fundamentally unfair. Because "terms in the box" are common, cost efficient, and similar to travel tickets, insurance agreements, and countless other terms-after-payment transactions, courts have not found this method of doing business unfair. In *Brower v. Gateway* 2000,[285] however, the court found Gateway's arbitration provision unconscionable, not because of Gateway's method of supplying the terms, but because it required the purchaser to incur "excessive costs" to arbitrate its dispute.[286]

---

283. For a discussion of UCC § 2–206(1)(b)'s applicability, see Shuba Ghosh, Where's the Sense in Hill v. Gateway 2000?: Reflections on the Visible Hand of Norm Creation, 16 Touro L. Rev. 1125, 1132–33 (2000).

284. See Chapter 6 at notes 141–184; 221–247, and accompanying text.

285. Brower, 676 N.Y.S.2d 569 (App. Div. 1998).

286. Id. at 575 ("Thus, we modify the order on appeal to the extent of finding that portion of the arbitration provision requiring arbitration before the ICC to be unconscionable. . . .").

Chapter Three
ADDITIONAL THEORIES FOR ENFORCING PROMISES

In Chapter 2, we studied the principal theory for enforcing promises, namely the bargain theory of consideration. This chapter covers three additional theories for enforcing promises, promissory estoppel, unjust enrichment, and warranties. Each of these theories allows the court to enforce promises or obligations that contract law would not necessarily enforce under a bargained-for exchange theory. These statements are not very meaningful in the abstract (but I had to write an introduction), so let's get to the material. After reading this chapter, you will have a more complete picture of the legal enforcement of promises and obligations. Part A deals with promissory estoppel, Part B takes up unjust enrichment, and Part C treats warranties.

A. Promissory Estoppel

1. Development of the doctrine. You have learned that a promise is legally enforceable if the promisee supplies consideration in return for the promise. A gift promise, on the other hand, is not enforceable. But very early on, courts began to squirm over cases where a gift promise had induced a promisee to rely. Shouldn't the law protect these promisees if their reliance was reasonable and provable? In an early case, *Kirksey v. Kirksey*, for example, a brother-in-law invited his sister-in-law to move to his land after his brother died.[1] The brother-in-law promised to give his widowed sister-in-law "a place to raise her family."[2] At some expense, she left the land she was planning to purchase, and moved to her brother-in-law's land. After two years, the brother-in-law asked her to leave. The sister-in-law sought to have her brother-in-law's promise enforced. The court held that the brother-in-law's promise was "a mere gratuity" and refused to enforce the promise.[3] But the judge who wrote the opinion volunteered in *dicta* that the law *should* enforce the promise because the promise induced the sister-in-law to rely, resulting in "loss and inconvenience" to her. In fact, the judge went so far as to urge that this detriment was "a sufficient consideration to support the promise * * *."[4]

Obviously, the judge's language went too far by suggesting that the sister-in-law's reliance constituted consideration. Nothing in

1. Kirksey v. Kirksey, 8 Ala. 131 (Ala. 1845).

2. Id. at 131.

3. Id.

4. Id.

the facts suggested that the brother-in-law had any other motive than to make a gift, with the sister-in-law's travel to the land a necessary condition to receive the gift.[5] By calling the move consideration, the judge was manipulating doctrine (using it when it doesn't really apply) and trying to achieve a just result. The cost of such a strategy, of course, is to introduce confusion into the law. Does promise enforcement require real consideration or doesn't it?

As time passed, courts became more willing to hold in favor of relying promisees, but often in a manner that did bend and stretch the doctrine of consideration. So, for example, courts began to enforce promises made to charities, often focusing on the charity's reliance on the promise, and insisting that the reliance proved the promise to be "abundantly supported" by consideration.[6] In addition, courts of equity applied equitable exceptions to the requirement of consideration. For example, equity holds that a promise of a gift of land is enforceable if the promise induces the promisee to improve the land.[7] Although such non-bargain situations demonstrated courts' focus on the promisee's detrimental reliance, still courts could not completely divorce themselves from the language of consideration. For example, the same court that declared a gift promise of land enforceable because the promisee relied and made improvements also claimed that the promisee's reliance "constitute[d] in equity, a consideration for the promise * * *."[8]

In 1932, the ALI encapsulated a new theory for enforcing promises in section 90 of its Restatement of Contacts. The section

5. See, e.g., Affiliated Enters. v. Waller, 5 A.2d 257, 260 (Del. Super. Ct. 1939) (" 'If a benevolent man says to a tramp,—'if you go around the corner to the clothing shop there, you may purchase an overcoat on my credit', no reasonable person would understand that the short walk was requested as the consideration for the promise, but that in the event of the tramp going to the shop the promisor would make him a gift.' ") (citing 1 Samuel Williston & George J. Thompson, A Treatise on the Law of Contracts § 112 (Rev. Ed. 1936)); Dorman v. Publix–Saenger–Sparks Theatres, Inc., 184 So. 886, 889 (Fla. 1938); Chapter 2 at notes 3–5, and accompanying text.

6. Ryerss v. Presbyterian Congregation of Blossburg, 33 Pa. 114, 117 (Pa. 1859) ("Where a party encourages a congregation, in the manner and to the extent [defendant] did, to go on and build a church in a specified locality, promising a subscription or gift of $100, and recognising and repeating that promise under such circumstances as are detailed in the evidence—and they go on, within a reasonable time, and build a church in substantial conformity with the understanding and intention of the promissor, it is in vain for him afterwards to deny the contract, its consideration, or its obligatory force.").

7. Seavey v. Drake, 62 N.H. 393, 394 (N.H. 1882) ("[E]quity protects a parol gift of land equally with a parol agreement to sell it, if accompanied by possession, and the donee has made valuable improvements upon the property induced by the promise to give it.").

8. Id.

was based on the growing number of reliance cases in the courts. Samuel Williston, the chief reporter, found the "binding thread" in these cases to be "justifiable reliance of the promisee."[9] The formulation of a distinct theory of obligation clarified the law while, at the same time, expanded promissory liability. The section reads in full:

Promise Reasonably Inducing Definite and Substantial Action

A promise which the promisor should reasonably expect to induce action or forebearance of a definite and substantial character on the part of the promisee and which does induce such action or forebearance is binding if injustice can be avoided only by enforcement of the promise.

2. Section 90 in the second Restatement. Section 90(1) of the second Restatement, adopted by the ALI in 1981, contains a few changes:

A promise which the promisor should reasonably expect to induce action or forbearance on the part of the promisee or a third person and which does induce such action or forbearance is binding if injustice can be avoided only by enforcement of the promise. The remedy granted for breach may be limited as justice requires.

You can see that the Restatement (Second) drops the requirement that reliance be "of a definite and substantial character." However, it retains the "injustice" requirement, and we shall see that there is little injustice in refusing to enforce a promise if the reliance was not definite and substantial.[10] The second Restatement's version of section 90 also provides that the "remedy granted for breach may be limited as justice requires." You will see in Chapter 5 that courts have interpreted this language to allow damages based on either the extent of a promisee's detrimental reliance or the value of the promise.[11] Section 90(2) drops the requirement of reliance for the enforcement of promises to charities or promises that are part of a marriage settlement.[12]

Section 90 of both Restatements, usually referred to by those in the know as "promissory estoppel" (the promisor is literally

---

9. Explanatory Notes in Restatement (First) of Contracts, 245–50 (limited ed. 1928) (comments of Williston).

10. See infra note 51, and accompanying text.

11. See Chapter 5 at notes 327–339, and accompanying text.

12. Restatement (Second) of Contracts § 90(2) (1981) ("A charitable subscription or a marriage settlement is binding ... without proof that the promise induced action or forbearance.").

"stopped" from claiming the absence of consideration[13]), contains several important elements. Let's refine your understanding of these elements with a discussion of each.

   a. Promise. First, there must be a promise. One court (in another setting) aptly defined a promise as follows: "[A] promise is an assurance, in whatever form of expression given, that a thing will or will not be done."[14] Many courts declare that the promise must be "clear and definite."[15] Issues pertaining to this standard often arise in the employment setting. A statement that employment is "permanent" usually does not satisfy this standard.[16] Courts have more difficulty when a terminated employee claims that her employer's practice was to dismiss employees only for good cause and that this practice constitutes a "clear and definite" promise to her.[17]

   In some cases, courts may have been too willing to assume the absence of factual issues on whether an employer made a promise and to grant summary judgment in favor of the employer. For example, in *Corradi v. Soclof*,[18] an employee claimed that the president of the company told her that he had "big plans" for her.[19] Later, after reading a newspaper advertisement seeking someone for her position (not a good day for the employee), the employee confronted her supervisor by asking whether she should look for a new job. The supervisor said that she should not look for a new job. In fact, he "advised her that her job was secure and that there was no need for her to look for other employment."[20]

13. See, e.g., Wheeler v. White, 398 S.W.2d 93, 96 (Tex. 1965) ("The function of the doctrine of promissory estoppel is, under our view, defensive in that it estops a promisor from denying the enforceability of the promise."); see also Comeau v. Mt. Carmel Med. Center, Inc., 869 F.Supp. 858, 863 (D. Kan. 1994) ("Promissory estoppel is a doctrine by which courts view performance in reasonable reliance on a promise as sufficient to create a legally binding contract where a contract otherwise lacks consideration.").

14. Baehr v. Penn–O–Tex Oil Corp., 104 N.W.2d 661, 664–65 (Minn. 1960); see also Restatement (Second) of Contracts § 2.

15. See Cohen v. Cowles Media Co., 479 N.W.2d 387, 391 (Minn. 1992) (en banc), remanded on reh'g 481 N.W.2d 840 (Minn.1992); E. A. Farnsworth, Contracts 95 (3d ed. 1999) (citing cases).

16. See, e.g., Fox v. T–H Cont'l Ltd. P'ship, 78 F.3d 409, 414 (8th Cir. 1996)

("[Employer] characterized the director of sales position as 'permanent.' This statement does not constitute a clear and definite promise of continued employment terminable only for cause.").

17. Compare Burns v. Brinkley, 933 F.Supp. 528, 533 (E.D.N.C. 1996) ("Nor would a custom or practice of terminating employees only for good cause somehow alter the at-will nature of an employment relationship.") with Eisenberg v. Alameda Newspapers, Inc. 88 Cal. Rptr.2d 802, 824 (Cal.App.1999) ("In determining the existence of such a promise of termination only for cause, we look to the entire relationship of the parties, including . . . the personnel policies and practices of the employer. . . .").

18. 1995 WL 322311 (Ohio Ct. App. 1995).

19. Id. at *1.

20. Id.

Notwithstanding these allegations, the court affirmed the trial court's grant of summary judgment in favor of the employer. The court held that the "big plans" statement was not a "specific promise of continued employment."[21] Further, the court thought that the supervisor's representation that the employee's job was "secure" was "conclusory" and did not promise employment for a "specific period of time."[22] But the combined statements of the president and supervisor probably should have been enough for the court to deny summary judgment. Arguably, a factual issue remained over whether a reasonable person would have believed that the statements constituted a definite promise of continued employment for a reasonable time.[23]

Dickens v. Equifax Services, Inc.[24] is another case that tests the patience of those who support a liberal interpretation of the "promise" requirement of promissory estoppel. Dickens, an employee of Equifax in Phoenix, alleged that his supervisor made the following promises about his prospective employment with Equifax in Denver:

> (1) he would continue to have a career with Equifax until age sixty-five, (2) he would be promoted if he moved to Denver, (3) he would receive annual pay increases and annual bonuses, (4) the amount of his bonus would compensate for his loss of his wife's income, (5) he would be a manager in Denver, (6) he would be taken care of by the company, and (7) he would remain employed by the company.[25]

Dickens claimed that in reliance on these promises, he moved to Denver. Alas, Equifax terminated Dickens on January 5, 1993, his fifty-fifth birthday, after offering him an inferior position, which he refused. (Before you start to seethe at Equifax's cruelty, you should also know that his pension vested on his birthday under Equifax's retirement plan.)

Despite Dicken's allegations, the Tenth Circuit affirmed a summary judgment in favor of Equifax. The court stated that the supervisor's statements "were not sufficiently definite to be legally enforceable promises for purposes of establishing promissory estop-

---

21. Id. at *5–6.

22. Id. at *6.

23. Fed. R. Civ. P. 56(c) sets forth the summary judgment rule:

The judgment sought shall be rendered forthwith if the pleadings, depositions, answers to interrogatories, and admissions on file, together with the affidavits, if any, show that there is no genuine issue as to any material fact and

that the moving party is entitled to judgment as a matter of law. . . .

See Miguel v. City of Laredo, 1996 WL 269466 at *1 (Tex. Ct. App.1996) (in applying summary judgment courts should afford the party fighting the motion "[e]very reasonable inference" and resolve any doubts in that party's favor).

24. 83 F.3d 431 (10th Cir. 1996).

25. Id. at *5.

pel.''[26] Further, the statements were "vague assurances or unsupported predictions, and as such, were not statements upon which Mr. Dickens could reasonably rely.''[27]

Yikes! The statements alleged by Dickens seem pretty definite to me.[28] At any rate, not all courts have been so parsimonious about what constitutes a promise for promissory estoppel purposes. For example, some courts relax the "clear and definite promise" requirement when persuaded that a party has reasonably relied on a less than clear assurance.[29]

Courts must distinguish a promise from a mere present intention, such as "I intend to keep the business open.''[30] If the business fails, the party who stated this intention should not be liable on the basis of promissory estoppel because the party never promised that the business would stay open. In addition, a party who makes a conditional promise should not be liable if the condition is not satisfied. For example, if an employer promises its employees to continue running its business *if it is profitable*, the promisor can abandon the business if it is not profitable, without sustaining liability based on promissory estoppel.[31]

b. Promisor's reasonable expectations. The second element of promissory estoppel is that the promisor must "reasonably expect [the promise] to induce action or forbearance.''[32] Although the rule focuses on what a promisor reasonably should expect, many courts translate the requirement into an inquiry about the

---

26. Id. at *6.

27. Id.

28. Compare Silcott v. Rio Linda Chem. Co., No. 95APE11–1512, 1996 WL 303679, *2 (Ohio Ct. App. 1996) ("In the absence of an employer's assent to a definite term of employment, statements manifesting praise for an employee's performance which lead to a 'personal but objectively unfounded sense of job security' are insufficient to alter the nature of the employment relationship.") (quoting Weiper v. W.A. Hill & Assocs., 661 N.E.2d 796, 799 (Ohio Ct. App. 1995)).

29. Neiss v. Ehlers, 899 P.2d 700, 707 (Or. Ct. App. 1995) ("The fact that a promise is indefinite, incomplete or even incapable of enforcement according to its own terms, does not mean that no redress should be possible for the damage that directly flows from the promisee's reliance on the promise."); Hellbaum v. Burwell, 463 P.2d 225, 229 (Wash. Ct. App. 1969) ("The doctrine of promissory estoppel has been applied to render enforceable a gratuitous or some-

what indefinite promise to obtain insurance.").

30. See Baehr v. Penn–O–Tex Oil Corp., 104 N.W.2d 661 (Minn. 1960) (oil company's agent's expressed intention to pay lesee's rent did not constitute a promise to pay the rent).

31. Local 1330, United Steel Workers v. United States Steel Corp., 631 F.2d 1264, 1277 (6th Cir. 1980) (" 'The condition precedent of the alleged contract and promise—profitability of the Youngstown facilities—was never fulfilled, and the actions in contract and for detrimental reliance cannot be found for plaintiffs.' ") (quoting 492 F.Supp. 1 (N.D. Ohio 1980)); see also Watson v. City of Salem, 934 F.Supp. 643, 661 (D.N.J. 1995) ("the promise made to Plaintiff was clearly conditional and contingent, as opposed to clear and definite . . . .").

32. Restatement (Second) of Contracts § 90.

reasonableness of the promisee's reliance.[33] This makes sense, in most cases, because a promisor ordinarily should not expect unreasonable actions on the part of the promisee. If an employer promises an employee six months employment, the employer should not reasonably expect the employee to do something rash, such as sign a ten-year lease on her apartment.

c. Inducement of action or forbearance. Further, the promise must actually "induce" action or forbearance.[34] In other words, the promisee must act because of the promise. Suppose Nephew learns that if he continues to smoke cigarettes he will damage his heart. Nephew therefore quits smoking. Later, unaware of Nephew's new resolve, Uncle promises Nephew $1000 if he quits smoking. Uncle's promise did not induce nephew's action and is not enforceable under promissory estoppel.[35]

Despite promissory estoppel's origins as a theory to compensate a party for detrimental reliance, some theorists report that promissory estoppel cases actually do not require reliance. For example, one study reported that courts enforce any promise made "in furtherance of an economic activity" regardless of whether a party relied on the promise.[36] Another study posited that courts enforce "serious" promises regardless of whether the promisee relied on them.[37] These articles caused a stir in the secondary literature on promissory estoppel.[38] However, my recent study of promissory

33. See, e.g., McKenny v. John V. Carr & Son, Inc., 922 F.Supp. 967, 980 (D. Vt. 1996) ("Plaintiff must show that his reliance on the promise was reasonable."); McDonald's Corp. v. Miller, 1994 WL 507822, *10 (D.N.J.1994) ("[Plaintiff] could not, as a matter of law, reasonably rely on these conditional 'promises' of a franchise award.").

34. Restatement (Second) of Contracts § 90; see also B & W Glass, Inc. v. Weather Shield Mfg., Inc., 968 F.2d 19 (10th Cir.1992) ("[Defendant's agent] gave the [plaintiffs] a quote of $101,725 for this project without including any exceptions, or modifications, in the quote. Given these facts, it was reasonable for the [plaintiffs] to rely on the quote. Any assumptions which the [plaintiff] made were induced by the actions which [defendant's agent] took.").

35. See McKenny, 922 F.Supp. at 980 (employee failed to offer evidence that a promise of "just cause employment" induced him to sell his stock to his employer); Alden v. Presley, 637 S.W.2d 862 (Tenn. 1982) (Elvis Presley's estate not liable to the plaintiff who claimed that she relied on "the King's"

promise to pay off the plaintiff's mortgage when plaintiff knew at the time she relied that the King's estate would not pay off the mortgage).

36. Daniel A. Farber and John H. Matheson, Beyond Promissory Estoppel: Contract Law and the "Invisible Handshake," 52 U. Chi. L. Rev. 903, 905 (1985).

37. Edward Yorio and Steve Thel, The Promissory Basis of Section 90, 101 Yale L.J. 111, 111 ("Judges actually enforce promises rather than protect reliance in Section 90 cases.").

38. See, e.g., James Gordley, Enforcing Promises, 83 Cal. L. Rev. 547, 569 (1995) ("Farber and Matheson suggested, and Yorio and Thel have recently confirmed, that most often the promisee recovers under the doctrine [of promissory estoppel] without proving he changed his position in reliance on the promise. Indeed, sometimes he recovers when it is fairly clear his position did not change."); Randy E. Barnett, The Death of Reliance, 46 J. Legal. Educ. 518, 522 (1996).

estoppel cases decided in the mid 1990s reports the continued importance of reliance in judicial decisions.[39] The following language in opinions is typical in its emphasis on the importance of reliance, although it goes too far in dispensing with the need for a real promise:

> The evil to be rectified through promissory estoppel is not the breach of the promise, but the harm that results from the promisor's inducement and the promisee's actions in reliance. The fact that a promise is indefinite, incomplete or even incapable of enforcement according to its terms, does not mean that no redress should be possible for the damage that directly flows from the promisee's reliance on the promise.[40]

d. Injustice. Section 90 states that a promise is binding "if injustice can be avoided only by enforcement of the promise."[41] Obviously, courts enjoy lots of discretion under an "injustice" standard. Some courts characterize the issue as a "policy decision."[42] For example, one court enforced a newspaper's promise to preserve a source's anonymity because of the "importance of honoring promises of confidentiality" and the "resultant harm" to the source that resulted from the broken promise.[43] In another case, the court declined to enforce a promise of long-term employment because enforcement might undermine "the employer's discretion and independent judgment in employment decisions."[44] The Restatement (Second) of Contracts supports such results by noting that the "injustice" inquiry should include relevant "policies."[45]

Another policy issue that often arises in promissory estoppel cases is whether a promisee who quits her current job in reliance on the promise of a prospective employer offering "at will" employment can recover for breach of that promise. At will employment constitutes a job without a guaranteed duration, meaning that the employer can terminate the employee at any time. Employers can argue that there is no injustice in refusing to enforce a promise of at will employment, even if it induces an employee to leave a job, because the employee is taking the risk that the new job won't

---

39. See Robert A. Hillman, Questioning the "New Consensus" on Promissory Estoppel: An Empirical and Theoretical Study, 98 Colum. L. Rev. 580 (1998).

40. Neiss v. Ehlers, 899 P.2d 700, 707 (Or. Ct. App. 1995).

41. Restatement (Second) of Contracts § 90.

42. Cohen v. Cowles Media Co., 479 N.W.2d 387, 391 (Minn. 1992) (en banc) ("[T]his is a legal question for the court,

as it involves a policy decision."), remanded on reh'g 481 N.W.2d 840 (Minn. 1992).

43. Cohen, 479 N.W.2d at 392; see also Ruzicka v. Conde Nast Publications, Inc., 999 F.2d 1319, 1323 (8th Cir. 1993) (promise involved "matters of utmost privacy").

44. Spanier v. TCF Bank Sav., 495 N.W.2d 18, 20 (Minn. Ct. App. 1993).

45. Restatement (Second) of Contracts § 90, cmt. b.

last.[46] This argument has not been very successful. One court stated, for example, that the employee "had a right to assume he would be given a good faith opportunity to perform his duties to the satisfaction of [the employer] once he was on the job."[47]

Some courts raise the "injustice" prong of promissory estoppel to substantiate a decision against applying promissory estoppel made on other grounds. Suppose, for example, an employer tells an employee that her employment probably will be renewed when her term ends. Subsequently, the employer changes the job description so that the employee no longer is qualified for the job and the employer does not renew her. It is hard to say that there is an injustice done to the employee by refusing to apply promissory estoppel because the employer did not make a promise. On comparable facts, courts have used all of their ammunition and found that there was no promise *and* no injustice.[48] This approach also follows the Restatement (Second), which notes the role of both the reasonableness of reliance and the formality of the promise in adjudicating the injustice element.[49]

We have already mentioned that the Restatement (Second) dropped the requirement that reliance must be "definite and substantial."[50] The "injustice" requirement captures this element too because it is hard to think of a case where there would be injustice in refusing to enforce a promise that induced indefinite and insubstantial reliance.[51] If you promise to mow Alice's lawn on Saturday morning, which induces her to go shopping at that time (to avoid

---

46. Cf. Grouse v. Group Health Plan, Inc., 306 N.W.2d 114, 116 (Minn. 1981) (en banc) ("The parties focus their arguments on whether an employment contract which is terminable at will can give rise to an action for damages if anticipatorily repudiated. [Employer] contends that recognition of a cause of action on these facts would result in the anomalous rule that an employee who is told not to report to work the day before he is scheduled to begin has a remedy while an employee who is discharged after the first day does not.")

47. Grouse, Inc. 306 N.W.2d at 116; see also Goff–Hamel v. Obstetricians & Gynecologists, P.C., 588 N.W.2d 798, 801 (Neb. 1999) (applying promissory estoppel in overturning trial court's conclusion "that since Goff–Hamel was to be employed at will, her employment could be terminated at any time, including before she began working."); cf. Sharon v. Yellow Freight System, Inc.,

872 F.Supp. 839, 848 (D. Kan. 1994) aff'd 107 F.3d 21 (10th Cir. 1997).

48. See, e.g., Faimon v. Winona State University, 540 N.W.2d 879, 884 (Minn. Ct. App. 1995) ("[P]romise to appellant was one that a benefit would probably be given and that it would probably be given to appellant. We can find no precedent for application of the doctrine of promissory estoppel to enforce a promise with benefits as uncertain as these, and we conclude that this is not the kind of commitment calling for special judicial action in the name of avoiding injustice."); see also Silberman v. Roethe, 218 N.W.2d 723, 730 (Wis. 1974) (no injustice in failing to enforce an informal implied promise).

49. Restatement (Second) of Contracts § 90, cmt. b.

50. See supra note 10, and accompanying text.

51. See supra note 42, and accompanying text.

the noise of the mower), I doubt that any court would entertain Alice's promissory estoppel claim if you don't show up.

3. Expansion of promissory estoppel. Although most, if not all, of the cases that inspired Williston to draft section 90 involved gift promises, courts soon expanded the theory by applying it in cases where a bargain was unenforceable because of some defense available to the promisor. For example, in *Wheeler v. White*,[52] the court enforced White's promise to procure or make a loan so that Wheeler could develop his property, after Wheeler relied by tearing down an existing building and preparing the property for new construction. The elaborate contract between the parties was unenforceable because they failed to agree on key terms, including the interest rate of the loan (they only agreed on a ceiling rate). Nevertheless the court enforced White's promise on the ground of promissory estoppel. Another court enforced Aretha Franklin's promise to appear in a broadway musical even though she and the producer had contemplated, but had not yet signed, a final agreement.[53] The court failed to give Franklin's defense of no signed contract any r-e-s-p-e-c-t and applied promissory estoppel because she had informed the producer she would perform and showed enthusiasm for the project. In addition, Franklin should have known that the producer would commit to major expenditures before she would be available to sign the contract.

In perhaps the leading case on the expansion of promissory estoppel into the realm of bargained-for transactions, a grocery store chain called Red Owl Stores represented to Joseph Hoffman and his wife that it would grant them a Red Owl franchise for $18,000.[54] During prolonged negotiations, Red Owl kept "upping the ante" by asking for more money and additional commitments from Hoffman and his family. Red Owl's representations induced the Hoffmans to sell the fixtures and inventory of their grocery store, buy and then sell a bakery building, and commit to a new building lot, all in preparation for becoming a Red Owl franchisee. The parties never completed the deal because Red Owl kept changing the terms, and the Hoffmans did not get their franchise. After the deal fell apart, the Hoffmans sued Red Owl for damages suffered in relying on Red Owl's representations. The trial court prepared a special verdict form for the jury based on the theory of promissory estoppel and the jury awarded Hoffman money damages. On appeal, the court affirmed, holding that Red Owl's "promissory representations" induced the Hoffmans to rely to their detriment. The case therefore established promissory estoppel as a

52. 398 S.W.2d 93 (Tex.1965).

53. Elvin Associates v. Franklin, 735 F.Supp. 1177 (S.D.N.Y. 1990).

54. Hoffman v. Red Owl Stores, 133 N.W.2d 267 (Wis. 1965).

very powerful doctrine. Under promissory estoppel, a party can be liable for representations made during negotiations prior to the culmination of a contract.

Writers began to emphasize the importance of promissory estoppel after witnessing its expansion in cases such as *Hoffman*.[55] One scholar claimed that "the principle of section 90 * * * has become perhaps the most radical and expansive development of this century in the law of promissory liability."[56] Further, theorists predicted that promissory estoppel would "swallow up" the bargain theory of contract and become the dominant theory for enforcing promises.[57] The theory has not been very successful in the courts, however, with many claims brought but few plaintiffs successful.[58] What went wrong? Perhaps claimants on the whole bring weak claims because promissory estoppel is not usually a plaintiff's primary theory of recovery. Perhaps most claimants simply "tack on" a promissory estoppel claim in a lawsuit brought on a breach of contract or other theory.[59]

Another explanation for the lack of success of promissory estoppel is that courts may be reluctant to apply the theory in exchange settings because it subverts important doctrines of contract law that bar enforcement. For example, the court in *Wheeler v. White* applied promissory estoppel after finding that the contract requiring White to make Wheeler a loan was too indefinite to enforce.[60] But if the contract is unenforceable because the parties left too many gaps, why should a court subvert the policy behind this decision by enforcing White's promise on promissory estoppel grounds? One response is that the *Wheeler* court held that Wheeler's recovery would be limited to "reliance damages measured by the detriment sustained."[61] Thus, because of the contract's indefiniteness, Wheeler could not recover expectancy damages for breach of contract, a measure likely to be greater than reliance damages. (We introduced the difference between these measures of damages

---

55. Charles L. Knapp, Reliance in the Revised Restatement: The Proliferation of Promissory Estoppel, 81 Colum. L. Rev. 52, 53 (1981).

56. Id. See also Stanley D. Henderson, Promissory Estoppel and Traditional Contract Doctrine, 78 Yale L. J. 343 (1969) (tracing the proliferation of promissory estoppel).

57. See Grant Gilmore, The Death of Contract 72 (1974).

58. See generally Hillman, supra note 39.

59. Id. at 596.

60. Wheeler, 398 S.W.2d at 95 n.2 (accepting plaintiff's argument that "if for any reason said contract is not sufficiently specific and definite, then nevertheless defendant is estopped to so claim and to set up any insufficiency because of the defendant's act in entering into said contract and exhorting plaintiff to clear the premises to make ready for the construction. . . ."); see also Kolkman v. Roth, 2002 WL 1429524, at *3 (Iowa Ct. App.), aff'd 656 N.W.2d 148 (Iowa 2003) ("We agree with plaintiff that there is a fact question as to whether promissory estoppel renders the evidence of the alleged oral contract admissible.").

61. Id. at 97.

in Chapter 1, and we will take them up in full in Chapter 5.[62]) The problem with this justification for promissory estoppel is that some courts have awarded expectancy damages to successful promissory estoppel claimants.[63]

Promissory estoppel is usually not available when an *enforceable* contract governs a relationship. In such a context, promissory estoppel "becomes * * * gratuitous duplication or, worse, circumvention of carefully designed rules of contract law."[64]

B. Unjust Enrichment

The theory of unjust enrichment has many alternative names, such as quantum meruit, restitution, quasi-contract, and contract implied in law. There are technical and historical differences among these principles, but at bottom they all refer largely to the following: When a party confers a benefit on another party and it would be unjust for the recipient to retain the benefit without paying for it, the law imposes an obligation on the recipient to pay or return the benefit.[65] As one court has said, an action for recovery based upon unjust enrichment "is based upon the universally recognized moral principle that one who has received a benefit has a duty to make restitution when to retain such benefit would be unjust."[66] The obligation arises in several settings related to exchange transactions, but as you can see from the above quotation, the theory is not based on an agreement between the parties, but on the justice of requiring one party to disgorge a benefit received from the other party.[67]

62. See Chapter 5 at notes 8–29; 322–339, and accompanying text.

63. See Hillman, supra note 39, at 601–02.

64. All-Tech Telecom, Inc. v. Amway Corp., 174 F.3d 862, 869 (7th Cir. 1999); see also id. ("When there is an express contract governing the relationship out of which the promise emerged, and no issue of consideration, there is no gap in the remedial system for promissory estoppel to fill."); LaSalle Nat'l Bank v. Metropolitan Life Ins. Co., 18 F.3d 1371, 1376 (7th Cir. 1994) ("[T]he doctrine of promissory estoppel ... 'has never been considered available when the parties have entered into a contract which is binding under contract law....'") (quoting Wagner Excello Foods, Inc. v. Fearn Int'l, Inc., 601 N.E.2d 956, 964 (Ill. App. Ct. 1992)).

65. See, e.g., Bloomgarden v. Coyer, 479 F.2d 201, 211 (D.C. Cir. 1973) ("Generally, in order to recover on a quasi-contractual claim, the plaintiff must show that the defendant was unjustly enriched at the plaintiff's expense, and that the circumstances were such that in good conscience the defendant should make restitution."); In re DeCecco, 234 B.R. 543, 545 (Bankr. M.D. Fla. 1999) ("[O]ne who benefits another should be rewarded, even absent of a contract, because the recipient of the benefit should not be unjustly enriched."); see also Andrew Kull, Restitution as a Remedy for Breach of Contract, 67 S. Cal. L. Rev. 1465, 1478 (1994) (" 'restitution' refers to ... those instances of liability imposed by law to prevent the unjust enrichment of one person at the expense of another.").

66. Arjay Inv. Co. v. Kohlmetz, 101 N.W.2d 700, 702 (Wis. 1960) (citing Frederic Campbell Woodward, The Law of Quasi Contracts 8 (1913)).

67. See Continental Forest Prods., Inc. v. Chandler Supply Co., 518 P.2d 1201, 1205 (Idaho 1974) ("As the es-

1. Unenforceable agreements. Unjust enrichment applies when one party to an agreement confers a benefit, but the agreement is unenforceable for some reason, including because it is incomplete or was not written down. Chapter 1 offers the following example: You and your neighbor, Alice, agree that you will care for her lawn in return for compensation, but you fail to specify how often you will work, the amount of compensation, or the duration of the arrangement. Courts cannot enforce this agreement because it is too uncertain—you left too many gaps for your arrangement to constitute an enforceable contract.[68] However, suppose you have already worked for Alice for three days. You have conferred a benefit on Alice that would be unjust for her to keep without compensation. Courts apply the theory of unjust enrichment in this context and allow you to recover the fair market value of your services.[69]

Several defenses bar unjust enrichment claims for unenforceable agreements (some of these defenses apply to other unjust enrichment contexts as well). We now turn to these.

a. Keeping the benefit is not unjust. One defense to an unjust enrichment claim is that the party claiming relief conferred the benefit as a gift.[70] In such situations, of course, it would be hard to claim that retaining the benefit is unjust. For example, if you offered to mow Alice's lawn as a favor while she is on vacation, she is enriched by your services, but not unjustly.

Generally, courts assume that family members or people in other close relationships intend to confer benefits on each other

---

sence of a contract implied in law lies in the fact that the defendant has received a benefit which it would be inequitable for him to retain...."); Farmers Nat'l Bank of Bloomsburg v. Albertson, 199 A.2d 486, 489 (Pa. Super Ct. 1964) ("Where one party has been unjustly enriched at the expense of another, he is required to make restitution. In order to recover, there must be both an enrichment and an injustice resulting if the recovery for the enrichment is denied.").

68. See, e.g., Joseph Martin, Jr., Delicatessen, Inc. v. Schumacher, 417 N.E.2d 541 (N.Y. 1981).

69. Cf. Gay v. Mooney, 50 A. 596, 597 (N.J. Sup. Ct. 1901) aff'd per curiam, 52 A. 1131 (N.J. 1902) ("[T]he service was not a gift, but a sale, and out of that determination the law deduces a right in him who sold the service to be

paid its value by him who bought it."); Kona Technology Corp. v. Southern Pacific Transp. Co., 225 F.3d 595, 606 (5th Cir. 2000) ("Recovery in quantum meruit will be had when non payment for the services rendered would 'result in an unjust enrichment to the party benefitted [sic] by the work.'") (quoting City of Ingleside v. Stewart, 554 S.W.2d 939, 942 (Tex. Civ. App. 1977)).

70. Brown v. Brown, 524 A.2d 1184, 1187 (D.C. Cir. 1987) ("When ... there is an applicable presumption that the services were rendered gratuitously—as occurs, for example, in the context of a parent-child relationship—a promise to pay obviously cannot be implied by the mere rendition and acceptance of valuable services."); see generally Dan B. Dobbs, Handbook on the Law of Remedies § 4.9 (1973).

gratuitously.[71] However, evidence that a family member or a person in a close relationship conferred a benefit pursuant to an unenforceable agreement rebuts the assumption.[72] For example, you could rebut the argument that you mowed Alice's lawn as a gift by proving that you had made an agreement with her that she would pay you (assume again that the agreement is unenforceable for lack of certainty). Of course, this approach is somewhat inconsistent with the idea that the agreement is too uncertain to enforce.[73] On the other hand, the agreement is unenforceable because of its uncertainty, not because anyone suspects that the parties never made such an agreement. The agreement is therefore reliable evidence that you did not mow Alice's lawn as a gift.

Suppose, however, that an agreement is unenforceable for lack of a writing. For example, you agree to mow Alice's lawn each week for two years for $50 per week. (We will see in Chapter 4 that certain agreements, including those for a duration of more than one year, must be in writing to be enforceable.[74]) You mow the lawn once and Alice does not pay you. Assume you can't sue for breach of contract. Can you bring an unjust enrichment action and offer evidence of your oral two-year agreement to show that you did not mow the lawn as a gift?[75] The purpose of the legal requirement of a writing is to bar false claims of an oral contract. Sure, in my hypo you did make the oral agreement. But what about all those deadbeats out there who make false claims of oral agreements? Allowing you to testify that you made an oral agreement thwarts the general purpose of the writing requirement.[76] Nevertheless, courts can justify allowing the testimony because the remedies for breach of contract and unjust enrichment are generally different. This remedial difference arguably preserves a role for the writing requirement: It serves to deny an expectancy recovery to a party who confers a benefit under an unenforceable oral agreement. Such a party can only recover the value of his services.

71. Brown, 524 A.2d at 1187; Offord v. Jenner's Estate, 189 S.W.2d 173, 176 (Mo. Ct. App. 1945) ("Where the close and intimate family relationship exists, there arises the presumption that the services were intended to be gratuitous, and in such a case there can be no recovery....").

72. See, e.g., Gay, 50 A. at 597 ("In order to rebut a presumption that the service was rendered and received as a gratuity, the plaintiff put in evidence tending to show an understanding between himself and the deceased that the latter would devise a certain dwelling house to the plaintiff's children in return for what he should receive as a member of the family.").

73. See Joseph M. Perillo, Restitution in a Contractual Context, 73 Colum. L. Rev 1208, 1215–16 (1973).

74. See Chapter 4 at notes 23–26, and accompanying text.

75. Perillo, supra note 73, at 1215–16.

76. See Chapter 4 at notes 7–17, and accompanying text.

b. No benefit. Needless to say, another issue in unjust enrichment cases is what constitutes a benefit.[77] The issue often arises in cases where a party requests services, but then doesn't use them. You ask an architect to draw plans for an addition on your house, but then you don't build the addition. You orally agree to purchase a house after the seller makes several requested alterations. Then you do not purchase the house.[78] You hire an oil exploration company to look for oil on your land, but the company doesn't find oil.[79] Suppose in each of these examples that the agreement is unenforceable because it is too uncertain.[80] Are you nevertheless liable to these service providers on the basis of unjust enrichment?

Unsurprisingly, courts have answered this question in the affirmative on the theory that, in each case, you requested the services.[81] Therefore, even if you chose not to accept the benefit, or the services prove fruitless, you have benefitted to the extent of the fair market value of the services rendered. Some writers believe that you didn't really receive a benefit in these cases, and that the true ground for recovery is justifiable reliance.[82] Some courts appear to agree.[83]

2. Breach of an enforceable contract. Unjust enrichment issues also arise after a breach of an enforceable contract. The injured (non-breaching) party may seek a recovery under the theory of unjust enrichment instead of breach of contract. If a breaching

---

77. See Anderco, Inc. v. Buildex Design, Inc., 538 F.Supp. 1139 (D.D.C. 1982).

78. Kearns v. Andree, 139 A. 695 (Conn. 1928).

79. Willis v. International Oil and Gas Corp. 541 So.2d 332, 334 (La. Ct. App. 1989).

80. See Chapter 7 at note 117, and accompanying text.

81. Kearns, 139 A. at 698 ("[I]f the work done on the property to adapt it to the desires of the defendant was done under the terms of an oral agreement for the sale of the premises, in good faith, and in the honest belief that the agreement was sufficiently definite to be enforced, the plaintiff is entitled to recover reasonable compensation there-

for."); see also Zirnhelt v. Ransom County, 137 N.W.2d 785, 789 (N.D. 1965) ("A contract is implied where a person performs services, furnishes property, or expends money for another, at such other's request, and there is no express agreement as to compensation.").

82. See, e.g., John P. Dawson, Restitution Without Enrichment, 61 B.U. L. Rev. 563, 582–83 (1981).

83. See, e.g., Kearns, 139 A. at 697 ("[A] plaintiff, who cannot bring an action upon a special contract for some reason other than his own fault, is permitted a recovery for the reasonable value of the services which he has performed, without regard to the extent of the benefit conferred upon the other party to the contract.").

party has conferred a benefit on the injured party that exceeds the injured party's damages, the breaching party may make an unjust enrichment claim. In each of these situations, the unjust enrichment theory is often called "restitution," because the party who has received the benefit must return it or its money equivalent to the other party.

a. Injured parties may recover under unjust enrichment. After a breach of contract, the injured party can sue either for breach of contract or for unjust enrichment.[84] Obviously, the injured party will proceed on whichever theory affords a greater recovery. Therefore, when the fair value of an injured party's performance is greater than the contract price of that performance, the injured party will use unjust enrichment. For example, suppose an employee agrees to perform services for one year for $4000 per month. After the first month, the employer wrongfully fires the employee before paying him. The fair market value of the services rendered by the employee for that month was $8000. Assuming that the employee can obtain another comparable job for the rest of the year, the employee will have contract damages only for the first month of $4000. But the employee can instead elect to recover on the ground of unjust enrichment—the employee has conferred a benefit on the employer of $8000 that would be unjust for the employer to keep.[85]

Courts justify using unjust enrichment to allow an injured party to recover more than the contract rate by arguing that the law should not allow the party who repudiated the contract to then use the contract as a shield to insulate her from liability for the actual benefit she received.[86] But not every court or writer agrees

---

84. Hunter v. Vicario, 130 N.Y.S. 625, 628 (N.Y. App. Div. 1911) ("[P]laintiff may at his option either sue for the breach and recover damages, or abandon the contract altogether, repudiate it because of defendant's repudiation, and recover under quantum meruit."); Posner v. Seder, 68 N.E. 335, 335 (Mass. 1903) ("[T]he innocent party may either sue on the contract for damages for the breach, or, if he so elects, he may regard the action of the defendants as indicating a purpose on their part to repudiate the contract, may accept the repudiation, and recover upon a quantum meruit the value of his services . . . .").

85. Battaglia v. Clinical Perfusionists, Inc., 658 A.2d 680, 683 (Md. 1995) ("[B]ack wages may be recovered either by claiming the value of the work performed (*quantum meruit*), or by including the back wages as part of a claim for breach of the express contract."); Posner, 68 N.E. at 335.

86. Constantino v. American S/T Achilles, 580 F.2d 121, 125 (4th Cir. 1978) (Winter, J. concurring and dissenting) (" 'The defendant cannot refuse to abide by the contract and at the same time claim its protection when the other party is not in default.' ") (quoting 12 Samuel Williston & Richard A. Lord, A

with this policy. Some who champion freedom of contract believe that the parties' own contractual measurements of value should limit recovery regardless of breach: "[T]he parties' own allocation of the market or other risks should be upset, if at all, by substantive doctrine and not by whether one chooses the label 'quantum meruit' or 'common count' on the one hand, or 'reliance damages' on the other."[87] These commentators suspect that a desire to punish the nasty contract breaker may be the real motivation when courts allow the injured party to recover greater damages under unjust enrichment.[88] Some courts have agreed with the commentators and hold that the contract price is a ceiling on recovery for unjust enrichment.[89]

Some of the courts barring recovery over the contract rate have created specific exceptions to the injured party's right to claim unjust enrichment after a breach of contract. Perhaps the most prominent exception is that "[t]he remedy of restitution in money is not available to one who has fully performed his part of a contract, if the only part of the agreed exchange for such performance that has not been rendered by the defendant is a [certain] sum of money * * *."[90] For example, if you agree to landscape Alice's yard for $500 and you complete the work, you cannot elect unjust enrichment if Alice does not pay, even if the fair value of your work is greater than $500. You have "fully performed" and all that is left is for Alice to pay you a certain amount, namely $500.

b. Breaching parties may recover under unjust enrichment. Not only may an injured party pursue a recovery based on unjust enrichment, a breaching party may as well, although this

Treatise on the Law of Contracts § 1485 at 312 (3d ed. 1970)).

87. Robert Childres & Jack Garamella, The Law of Restitution and the Reliance Interest in Contract, 64 Nw. U. L. Rev. 433, 439–40 (1969).

88. Andrew Kull, Restitution as a Remedy for Breach of Contract, 67 S. Cal. L. Rev. 1465, 1482–83 (1994) ("[C]ourts in some circumstances favor a punitive remedy for breach of contract, and that stripping a defendant of the benefits secured by a contract he has failed to perform has seemed to judges, in some circumstances, to be no more than poetic justice.").

89. Plaza Shoe Store, Inc. v. Hermel, Inc., 636 S.W.2d 53, 59–60 (Mo.

1982) (en banc) ("The better rule, undoubtedly, would be to use the contract price as an upper limit or ceiling on the amount the discharged attorney could recover."); Johnson v. Bovee, 574 P.2d 513, 514 (Colo. Ct. App. 1978) ("We believe using the contract price as a ceiling on restitution is the better-reasoned resolution of this question.... It is illogical to allow [plaintiff] to recover the full cost of his services when, if he completed the house, he would be limited to the contract price plus the agreed upon extras.").

90. Oliver v. Campbell, 273 P.2d 15, 20 (Cal. 1954) (citing Restatement (First) of Contracts § 350).

avenue for breaching parties is even more controversial. Why should a party who breached a contract be able to sue for unjust enrichment?

In the leading case of *Britton v. Turner*,[91] the court sought to answer this question. An employer hired an employee to work for one year for the bountiful sum of $120, but the employee quit without good cause after nine-and-one-half months (this case had nothing to do with that awful Kim Basinger movie called "9½ Weeks"). The employee sought to recover for the work he had performed. The trial court charged the jury that the breaching employee could recover the reasonable value of his labor and the jury awarded the employee $95.

On appeal, the employer contested the judge's charge to the jury, but the Supreme Court of New Hampshire affirmed. It set forth several reasons for allowing the employee to recover under unjust enrichment. First, the court pointed out that barring a recovery would penalize an employee who tried, but failed, to complete his contract, because the longer he worked before breaching the greater his harm.[92] Second, because the employment contract was "day to day," the court presumed that the employer had accepted and should pay for each day of the employee's work, notwithstanding the employee's failure to complete the whole contract: "[T]he party for whom the labor is done in truth stipulates to receive it from day to day, as it is performed, and although the other may not eventually do all he has contracted to do, there has been, necessarily, an acceptance of what has been done in pursuance of the contract * * *."[93] Third, the court asserted that the "general understanding of the community" is that an employer should compensate an employee for work performed even if the employee does not complete the contract term.[94] Fourth, the court pointed out that the parties did not expressly agree to deny the employee compensation unless he completed the term, even though they easily could have done so.[95] (Modern state labor laws generally

---

91. 6 N.H. 481 (N.H. 1834).

92. Id. at 485 ("the party who attempts performance may be placed in a much worse situation than he who wholly disregards his contract, and the other party may receive much more, by the breach of the contract, than the injury which he has sustained by such breach, and more than he could be entitled to were he seeking to recover damages by an action.").

93. Id. at 498.

94. Id. at 489.

95. Id. at 490 ("It is easy, if parties so choose, to provide by an express agreement that nothing shall be earned, if the laborer leaves his employer without having performed the whole service contemplated....").

forbid such a strategy, however.[96]) Fifth, the court worried that denying a recovery would create an incentive for employers to create unfavorable conditions near the end of an employee's term, with the hope that the conditions will persuade the employee to quit and lose all compensation.[97]

Some of the *Britton* court's arguments for granting a recovery to the breaching employee are better than others. For example, the final argument, concerning employers' incentives, ignores the likelihood that an employer who created unfavorable conditions would, by doing so, materially breach the contract first and owe the employee damages. Further, it is not always the case that an employer receives a benefit in each day's work of a long-term employment contract. For example, suppose during the first six to nine months the employer provided extensive training to the employee that would pay off only at the end of the term. Despite these qualms, contract law generally has accepted the *Britton* approach.[98] Among its more persuasive arguments is the "general understanding of the community" that employees should be paid for their efforts even if they cannot complete their term.

Unlike when an injured party recovers based on unjust enrichment, the contract price is a ceiling on a breaching party's recovery.[99] The employee in Britton cannot recover more than the contract rate of $10 per month, even if the market value of the work were a greater sum. Obviously, any other approach would create an incentive for parties to breach their contract when the other party was paying them less than fair market value for their goods or services. In addition, the breaching party is liable for any damages caused by breaching the contract. If the employer in Britton had to pay a substitute employee an extra $50 to do the remaining work, for example, the employee could only recover $45 ($95 minus $50). If the damages are greater than the benefit conferred on the employer, the employee cannot recover on the

---

96. See, e.g., N.Y. Labor Law § 191 (McKinney 2002).

97. Britton, 6 N.H. at 490 ("This rule, by binding the employer to pay the value of the service he actually receives, and the laborer to answer in damages where he does not complete the entire contract, will leave no temptation to the former to drive the laborer from his service, near the close of his term, by ill treatment, in order to escape from payment....").

98. Lancellotti v. Thomas, 491 A.2d 117, 119 (Pa. Super. Ct. 1985) ("The party who breaches after almost completely performing should not be more

severely penalized than the party who breaches by not acting at all or after only beginning to act."); Restatement (Second) of Contracts § 374.

99. Britton, 6 N.H. at 1176 ("The amount ... for which the employer ought to be charged, where the laborer abandons his contract, is only the reasonable worth, or the amount of advantage he receives upon the whole transaction, and, in estimating the value of the labor, the contract price for the service cannot be exceeded."); United States for Use of Palmer Constr., Inc. v. Cal State Elec., Inc., 940 F.2d 1260, 1265 (9th Cir. 1991) ("[T]he contract price represents a ceiling on the amount the non-breach-

basis of unjust enrichment and the employee will be liable for damages for breach of contract.[100]

3. Conferral of a benefit in the absence of a contract.

A party who confers a benefit without a contract may also recover under unjust enrichment. The theory applies, however, only when the party conferring the benefit did not intend to make a gift,[101] the benefit was not forced on the recipient,[102] and justice requires the party receiving the benefit to pay for it.[103] The last requirement, of course, grants courts lots of discretion. One way in which the "justice" issue arises concerns whether the party receiving the benefit reasonably should understand that the party conferring the benefit expects to be paid.[104] There would be no injustice in denying an unjust enrichment claim if the party receiving a benefit reasonably thought he received a gift. Courts resolve this question by focusing on the nature of the parties' relationship—whether it is a business or personal relationship—and the type of benefit conferred. Let's look more closely at these issues.

a. Business relationships.

Suppose a business person performs a service that is profitable for another party, but the parties did not discuss compensation. For example, Elmer Electrician, introduces a friend, Irwin Investor, to Dom Developer, another friend (cute names, heh?). Elmer knows that Dom is seeking investment capital for a real estate project. Elmer helps Irwin and Dom's negotiations move along by arranging meetings and serving as a go-between. Irwin and Dom ask Elmer what he expects for his efforts and Elmer tells them that he hopes to do the electrical work on the project. Irwin and Dom ultimately put together a lucrative business deal, but Elmer retires from his job as an electrician before construction begins. Irwin and Dom hire another electrician for the electrical work. Is Elmer nonetheless entitled to a finders'

---

ing party may be required to pay—*in toto.*").

100. Matter of Hallmark Builders, Inc., 64 B.R. 301, 305 (Bankr. M.D. Fla. 1986) ("[Creditors] are entitled to recover $565.00 in damages resulting from breach of contract which represents the amount of damages after computing an offset of the Debtor's quantum meruit recovery.").

101. Liautaud v. Liautaud, 221 F.3d 981, 988 (7th Cir. 2000) ("[A] a party may not recover damages for unjust enrichment pursuant to a gift relationship.").

102. Johnson Group, Inc. v. Beecham, Inc., 952 F.2d 1005, 1007 (8th Cir. 1991) ("To recover under quantum meruit under Missouri law, a plaintiff must

prove it provided services to the defendant at the request or with the acquiescence of the defendant. . . .").

103. Chadirjian v. Kanian, 123 A.D.2d 596, 598 (N.Y. App. Div. 1986) ("An agreement may be implied under the doctrine of unjust enrichment in order to prevent one person who has obtained a benefit from another without ever entering into a contract with that person from unjustly enriching himself at the other party's expense.").

104. Bloomgarden v. Coyer, 479 F.2d 201, 208–209 (D.C. Cir. 1973) ("[T]he party seeking payment must show (1) that the services were carried out under such circumstances as to give the recipient reason to understand (a) that they were performed for him and

fee for bringing Irwin and Dom together?[105] Let's try a variation. Suppose Elmer, in retirement, manages a piece of Dom's property (including collecting rents and maintaining and improving the property), without discussing any compensation. Is Elmer entitled to compensation for *this* service?[106]

Unjust enrichment law provides answers to both hypotheticals, taking into account whether Elmer conferred a benefit on Dom, whether he intended it as a gift, whether the benefit was foisted on Dom, and whether a reasonable person receiving such a benefit would expect to pay for it.[107] For example, although Elmer was friends with Dom and Irwin, Elmer's services were in a business context and Elmer expected a return on his services in the form of an electrical contract. And Dom and Irwin happily accepted Elmer's services. So far so good for Elmer. His services were not a gift, nor were they foisted on Dom and Irwin. However, Elmer did not request a finders' fee and told Irwin and Dom he expected only electrical work. Irwin and Dom therefore did not reasonably expect to pay Elmer a finder's fee and therefore Elmer cannot recover under the theory of unjust enrichment.[108] (Elmer can argue that Irwin and Dom should have realized that if, for some reason, Elmer did not get the electrical work, he would expect to be paid in another way for his efforts. But at least one court faced with similar facts did not accept this argument.[109]) In the second fact pattern, Elmer has a good unjust enrichment claim against Dom for the value of his managerial services, even though the two are friends. This benefit was not the kind that is usually a gift. Even good friends don't usually manage each other's businesses for free, so Dom reasonably should expect to pay.[110]

---

not for some other person, and (b) that they were not rendered gratuitously, but with the expectation of compensation from the recipient; and (2) that the services were beneficial to the recipient."); see also Midcoast Aviation, Inc. v. General Elec. Credit Corp., 907 F.2d 732, 740 (7th Cir. 1990) ("Parties who perform services altruistically or gratuitously, with some end other than payment in mind, cannot recover *quantum meruit;* with no expectation of payment for services rendered, a party can hardly claim that another has been *unjustly* enriched.").

105. See Bloomgarden, 479 F.2d 201.

106. See Sparks v. Gustafson, 750 P.2d 338 (Alaska 1988).

107. Bloomgarden, 479 F.2d 201.

108. See id., 479 F.2d at 212, n.66 ("No unfairness results from a denial of compensation to the claimant who had

no expectation of personal remuneration at the time of performance."); see also Lirtzman v. Fuqua Indus., Inc., 677 F.2d 548, 553 (7th Cir. 1982) ("[P]laintiff's services were ... rendered gratuitously with the expectation of developing future good will with [company].").

109. Bloomgarden, 479 F.2d at 211 ("Nor is compensation mandated where the services were rendered simply in order to gain a business advantage."). But see Midcoast Aviation, 907 F.2d at 740 ("But the facts belie [the] contention that [plaintiff] was working for free, that it did not expect payment.... The facts show that [plaintiff] expected payment: through extra work if a long-term contract was secured, otherwise, through immediate billing.").

110. Sparks, 750 P.2d at 343 ("[S]ervices that [plaintiff] performed for [his friend's] estate were not the sort which one would ordinarily expect to

Before we leave Elmer's travails, we should note that Elmer has another theory to pursue in both scenarios sketched above. When it is applied to disputes such as Elmer's, the unjust enrichment theory is also called "contract implied-in-law" or "quasi-contract." This is because Dom's obligation does not arise because of a real contract between the parties.[111] It is grounded in the idea that Elmer conferred a benefit that would be unjust for Dom to keep without paying for it.[112] But Elmer can also claim that Dom and Irwin broke a "contract implied-in-fact," which, as the name denotes, *is* a real contract.[113] The parties form this type of contract not by expressly agreeing to perform, either orally or in writing, but by manifesting their intentions to enter a contract through their conduct. As a "real" contract, an implied-in-fact contract must satisfy all of the contract requisites that we are learning in this book (so keep reading!).

Did Elmer enter an implied-in-fact contract with Dom or Irwin with respect to either of the services Elmer performed? Elmer told Dom he expected to gain by doing the electrical work, not by earning a finder's fee. Therefore the evidence does not support an implied-in-fact contract claim for a finders' fee.[114] On the other hand, Elmer's work for Dom was not the kind ordinarily done

receive from a friend as a mere gratuity."); see also Burton v. McLaughlin, 217 P.2d 566, 570 (Utah 1950) ("If these services were as extensive as we have indicated the evidence shows, then they were not the kind of services that strangers usually give without expecting compensation.").

111. Bloomgarden, 479 F.2d at 208 ("A quasi-contract, on the other hand, is not a contract at all, but a duty thrust under certain conditions upon one party to requite another in order to avoid the former's unjust enrichment.").

112. See Opelika Production Credit Ass'n., Inc. v. Lamb, 361 So.2d 95, 99 (Ala. 1978) ("The remedy of quasi-contract is founded upon the familiar principle of avoiding unjust enrichment. Where the plaintiff has suffered a detriment, and the defendant has received a benefit as a result, it is said that justice demands the repayment by the defendant of the plaintiff's loss.").

113. Bloomgarden, 479 F.2d at 208 ("An implied-in-fact contract is a true contract, containing all necessary elements of a binding agreement; it differs from other contracts only in that it has

not been committed to writing or stated orally in express terms, but rather is inferred from the conduct of the parties in the milieu in which they dealt."); see also Roebling v. Anderson, 257 F.2d 615, 619 (D.C. Cir. 1958) (" 'Contracts are express when their terms are stated by the parties and are often said to be implied when their terms are not so stated. The distinction is not based on legal effect but on the way in which mutual assent is manifested.' ") (quoting 1 Samuel Williston & Walter H. E. Jaeger, A Treatise on the Law of Contracts 8–11 (3d ed. 1957)).

114. Bloomgarden, 479 F.2d at 112 ("[Plaintiff] had no enforceable claim for recompense because it appeared without dispute that at the time he introduced the parties he did not expect to be personally compensated for so doing."); see also Brown v. Brown, 524 A.2d 1184, 1189 (D.C.App.1987) ("[A claimant] should have the burden to demonstrate, by a preponderance of the evidence, the existence of either an express or implied agreement that he or she expected to be paid and that the decedent intended to make payment.").

gratuitously by a friend. Accordingly, Elmer has a strong claim based on an implied-in-fact contract.[115]

Although unjust enrichment and implied-in-fact contract yield the same results as to liability in the Elmer problems above, this will not always be the case. For example, if Elmer mistakenly paid Dom some money that he meant to pay Irwin, Elmer could recover the money on unjust enrichment grounds, but he could not recover on the basis of implied-in-fact contract. In this hypo, the circumstances do not support an implication that Elmer paid the money to Dom as part of a real contract.[116] However, Elmer did confer a benefit on Dom and justice requires Dom to return it. (But if Dom reasonably believed he was entitled to Elmer's money and detrimentally relied by spending it, Elmer could not recover from Dom.[117])

Before we leave unjust enrichment in business settings, I want to mention the problem of the over-exuberant entrepreneur. Suppose Alice is in the swimming pool construction business. Alice knows you are on a trip to _____ (fill in the blank here and daydream about the fabulous place you select, but not for more than two minutes). Alice, eager for her business to be successful, proceeds to construct a pool in your yard while you are away. She sends you a bill upon your return. The pool increases the market value of your house and is aesthetically pleasing. Still, the law of unjust enrichment does not require you to pay Alice because she forced the benefit on you without your consent.[118] Needless to say, the law should not and does not encourage this kind of entrepreneurship.

115. Sparks, 750 P.2d 338; see also Alliant Food Serv., Inc. v. Powers, 2003 WL 21434786 at *4 (Ohio Ct. App.2003) ("In implied-in-fact contracts, the parties' meeting of the minds is shown by the surrounding circumstances including the parties' conduct and declarations, making it reasonably inferable that the parties intended to create binding and certain obligations.").

116. Gary–Wheaton Bank v. Burt, 433 N.E.2d 315, 323 (Ill. App. Ct. 1982) ("A contract implied in fact arises not by express agreement but by a promissory expression which may be inferred from the facts and circumstances which show an intent to be bound.").

117. See, e.g., Ferguson v. Cotler, 382 So.2d 1315, 1316 (Fla. App. 1980) (relief granted to party conferring a benefit by mistake if the other party "has not relied upon the mistake to his detriment.").

118. Bank of Nova Scotia v. Bloch, 533 F.Supp. 1356, 1362 (D.C. V.I.) aff'd, 707 F.2d 1388 (3d Cir. 1982) and aff'd Appeal of Bloch, 707 F.2d 1388 (3d Cir. 1982) ("Except in certain circumstances, a person who confers a benefit on another, such as by increasing the net value of property, should not be permitted to require the other to pay therefor, unless the one conferring the benefit had a valid reason for so doing."); Western Coach Corp. v. Roscoe, 650 P.2d 449, 456 (Ariz. 1982) ("It is well established that a person who has been unjustly enriched at the expense of another is required to make restitution to the other. The principle is applicable, however, only if the person conferring the benefit is not an 'officious intermeddler.' "); see also Dan B. Dobbs, Handbook on the Law of Remedies § 4.9 (1973).

b. Personal relationships. Unjust enrichment claims also arise in the context of personal relationships, such as between unmarried people who live together. After a breakup, one party may seek compensation on unjust enrichment grounds in order to share in the wealth accumulated during the relationship.[119] For example, one party may have taken care of children, performed housekeeping services, helped out in a business, and cooked meals, giving the other party more time to make money. Courts have recognized unjust enrichment claims in such contexts, especially when the parties have behaved as if they were married.[120] Courts reason that if the parties had been married, the claimant would have been entitled to share in the marital estate.[121] When both act as if they are married, the party receiving the benefit reasonably should understand that the other party expects to share in the wealth of the relationship.[122]

C. Warranties

Contract law enforces warranties made by sellers, lessors, and others concerning the quality of performance. When you purchase or rent a residence, the seller or lessor may make a warranty of habitability. When you purchase an air conditioner from Sears, it may make an express warranty with respect to the quality of the air conditioner, may warrant that the appliance is fit for its

119. See, e.g., Lawlis v. Thompson, 405 N.W.2d 317 (Wis. 1987); Watts v. Watts, 405 N.W.2d 303, 307 (Wis.1987) ("The plaintiff alleges that during the parties' relationship, and because of her domestic and business contributions, the business and personal wealth of the couple increased. Furthermore, the plaintiff alleges that she never received any compensation for these contributions to the relationship and that the defendant indicated to the plaintiff both orally and through his conduct that he considered her to be his wife and that she would share equally in the increased wealth.").

120. Watts, 405 N.W.2d at 313 ("According to the plaintiff's complaint, the parties cohabited for more than twelve years, held joint bank accounts, made joint purchases, filed joint income tax returns, and were listed as husband and wife on other legal documents. Courts have held that such a relationship and 'joint acts of a financial nature can give rise to an inference that the parties intended to share equally.' ") (citing Beal v. Beal, 577 P.2d 507, 510 (Or. 1978)); see also Bright v. Kuehl, 650 N.E.2d 311, 315 (Ind. Ct. App. 1995)

("[U]nmarried couples may raise equitable claims such an implied contract and unjust enrichment following the termination of their relationships where one of the parties attempts to retain an unreasonable amount of the property acquired through the efforts of both.").

121. Watts, 405 N.W.2d at 307 ("[P]laintiff alleges that she never received any compensation for these contributions to the relationship and that the defendant indicated to the plaintiff both orally and through his conduct that he considered her to be his wife and that she would share equally in the increased wealth.").

122. Watts, 405 N.W.2d at 313 ("[Plaintiff] alleges that the defendant accepted and retained the benefit of services she provided knowing that she expected to share equally in the wealth accumulated during their relationship."); see also Carr v. Carr, 576 A.2d 872, 880 (N.J. 1990) ("[U]nmarried cohabitants ... may acquire rights as a result of enduring, intimate personal relationships founded on mutual trust, dependence, and raised expectations.").

ordinary purpose, and may warrant that it is fit for a particular purpose.

Warranty law is a huge, complex, and largely statutory subject. Most contracts courses leave much of the material for other courses. So I will simply give you a brief introduction to the UCC sale-of-goods provisions that create warranties with respect to the quality of goods. Our discussion will include three sections of the UCC. UCC section 2–313 governs express warranties, which arise from statements or conduct of the seller. UCC section 2–314 deals with the implied warranty of merchantability, and section 2–315 involves the implied warranty of fitness for a particular purpose. Implied warranties arise "by operation of law," meaning that these warranties do not depend on anything the seller says or does. The implied warranties are therefore similar to unjust enrichment in the sense that they are not consensual in nature.

Before you get too happy about all this potential warranty protection for that faulty computer you just purchased, you should know that the UCC allows sellers to disclaim (contract out of) most warranties. We'll consider this topic too.

1. Express warranty. UCC section 2–313 provides:

Express Warranties by Affirmation, Promise, Description, Sample.

(1) Express warranties by the seller are created as follows:

(a) Any affirmation of fact or promise made by the seller to the buyer which relates to the goods and becomes part of the basis of the bargain creates an express warranty that the goods shall conform to the affirmation or promise.

(b) Any description of the goods which is made part of the basis of the bargain creates an express warranty that the goods shall conform to the description.

(c) Any sample or model which is made part of the basis of the bargain creates an express warranty that the whole of the goods shall conform to the sample or model.

(2) It is not necessary to the creation of an express warranty that the seller use formal words such as 'warrant' or 'guarantee' or that he have a specific intention to make a warranty, but an affirmation merely of the value of the goods or a statement purporting to be merely the seller's opinion or commendation of the goods does not create a warranty.

A few issues dominate judicial treatment of the creation of express warranties. The first issue involves understanding how sections 2–313(1)(a) and 2–313(2) work together. How do we decide whether a statement by the seller is an "affirmation of fact or promise" or "merely the seller's opinion or commendation of the goods?"[123] Courts sometimes refer to a seller's opinion as "puffing" or "sales talk,"[124] and this description sheds light on the distinction the section is trying to make. Section 2–313 enforces real commitments by the seller, but attempts to exclude the kind of sales chatter that would not induce reliance among reasonable people, who would realize that a sales pitch cannot form the basis of a lawsuit. Are you getting "deja vu all over again?"[125] Yes, the task for courts here is similar to the general test for determining the legal significance of communications between parties: What would a reasonable person believe about what the seller said or did?[126]

Several factors can help us decide what a reasonable buyer would believe about whether a statement constitutes a warranty or a sales pitch. For example, is the statement specific or vague?[127] "This is a great used car" is so general and vague that a reasonable person would understand that the seller is just trying to sell the old clunker. Another factor is whether a statement is verifiable.[128] A reasonable person would believe that the assurance, "this car gets 32 miles per gallon on the open road" is more than sales jabber because it relates to a particular fact that can be checked. A third factor is whether a statement is definitive, meaning that it makes a commitment.[129] For example, a reasonable person would hardly

123. Keith v. Buchanan, 220 Cal. Rptr. 392, 395 (Cal. Dist. Ct. App. 1985) ("In deciding whether a statement made by a seller constitutes an express warranty under this provision, the court ... must determine whether the seller's statement constitutes an 'affirmation of fact or promise' ... or whether it is rather 'merely the seller's opinion or commendation of the goods' under section 2313, subdivision (2).").

124. Sessa v. Riegle, 427 F.Supp. 760, 765 (E.D. Pa. 1977) aff'd, 568 F.2d 770 (3d Cir. 1978) ("[W]ords to the effect that 'The horse is sound' spoken during the telephone conversation between [seller] and [buyer] constitute an opinion or commendation rather than express warranty."); Cf. Platsis v. E.F. Hutton & Co. Inc., 642 F.Supp. 1277, 1293 (W.D. Mich. 1986) aff'd 829 F.2d 13 (6th Cir. 1987) ("A statement of opinion or belief such as occurs in 'puffing' generally cannot constitute a misrepresentation.").

125. This quote is attributed to Yankee great, Yogi Berra.

126. See Chapter 2 at notes 108–125, and accompanying text.

127. James J. White & Robert S. Summers, Uniform Commercial Code

347 (5th ed. 2000); see also Keith, 220 Cal.Rptr. at 395 ("Commentators have noted several factors which tend to indicate an opinion statement. These [include] a lack of specificity in the statement made ..."); Snow's Laundry & Dry Cleaning Co. v. Georgia Power Co., 6 S.E.2d 159, 162 (Ga. Ct. App. 1939) ("For a representation to be construed as a warranty the statement made must be affirmed as a fact; it must be understood by the parties as having that character; it must be positive and unequivocal and not merely a vague, ambiguous and indefinite statement of the seller regarding the property.").

128. Boud v. SDNCO, Inc., 54 P.3d 1131, 1135 (Utah 2002) ("To qualify as an affirmation of fact, a statement must be objective in nature, i.e., verifiable or capable of being proven true or false.").

129. White & Summers, supra note 127, at 348–349; see also Whitehorse Marine, Inc. v. Great Lakes Dredge & Dock Co., 751 F.Supp. 106, 108 (E.D. Va. 1990) ("Express warranties are not presumed and will not be inferred from ambiguous, inconclusive, or general discussions. The language employed must indicate a clear intention to enter into a contract of warranty when it is viewed

think that a seller intends to make a commitment when he says, "I think you'll love this car."[130] A fourth factor is whether a statement is oral or in writing.[131] Writings command more attention and, therefore, a reasonable person may take more stock in a writing.[132]

The second express-warranty issue involves the nature of descriptions that become warranties under section 2–313(1)(b). Suppose you purchase an air conditioner at Sears. You open the carton at home only to find an electric fan and instructions to aim the fan at a large block of ice. Suppose further that none of the documentation refers to any warranties, but the salesperson told you an air conditioner was in the carton. "Air conditioner" is a generic title that courts should treat as a description express warranty. In light of the salesperson's representation, a reasonable person would believe that he was buying a machine with a condenser and freon, and all that other good stuff.[133]

The third issue involves the "basis of the bargain" requirement of section 2–313(1)(a), (b) and (c). For example, even if the seller makes a statement that constitutes an affirmation, promise, or description, the statement is an express warranty only if it is a "basis of the bargain." So, what does this strange term mean? Comment 3 to section 2–313 suggests that every seller statement that meets the other conditions for creating an express warranty *is* presumed to be a basis of the bargain unless the seller proves otherwise.[134] The comment adds that "no particular reliance on such statements need be shown in order to weave them into the fabric of the agreement."[135] So how does a seller show that a statement is not a "basis of the bargain?" In fact, because of the lack of clear direction from comment 3 and the inherent ambiguity of the term "basis of the bargain," courts have not been consistent

in light of all the facts and circumstances surrounding the transaction.").

130. Cf. Bologna v. Allstate Ins. Co., 138 F.Supp.2d 310, 323 (E.D.N.Y. 2001) ("Here, Allstate's assertion, 'You're in good hands with Allstate,' is general, subjective, and cannot be proven true or false.... [Defendant's] allegation that Allstate's slogan created an express warranty which Allstate thereafter breached ... must fall....").

131. White & Summers, supra note 127, at 347.

132. See Chapter 2 at notes 33–40, and accompanying text, dealing with the role of formalities in the law.

133. See White & Summers, supra note 127, at 349.

134. UCC § 2–313, cmt. 3 ("In actual practice affirmations of fact made by the seller about the goods during a bargain are regarded as part of the description of those goods....").

135. Id.; see also Keith, 220 Cal. Rptr. at 397–98 ("It is clear from the new language of this code section that the concept of reliance has been purposefully abandoned."); Winston Indus., Inc. v. Stuyvesant Ins. Co., Inc., 317 So.2d 493, 497 (Ala. Civ. App. 1975) ("As this court perceives it, the determining factor in this case under the newly enacted Uniform Commercial Code is not reliance by the purchaser on the seller's warranty, but whether it is part of the 'basis of the bargain.' ").

in deciding whether the seller must show that the buyer has not relied on the statement.[136]

Perhaps the most helpful approach to "basis of the bargain" would be to follow the "mixed motives" idea of bargained-for-exchange theory and the interpretation strategy of agreement law.[137] Recall that, for a court to find consideration to support a promise, only one of the promisor's motives must be to extract something from the other party.[138] Similarly, the promisee may have many motives for performing or returning a promise, only one of which must be induced by the promisor.[139] Perhaps a statement is a basis of the bargain so long as the seller's utterance is at least "one of the inducements for the purchase of the product."[140] Further, the test should be whether, as a result of the statement, a reasonable buyer would be induced and whether the buyer actually was induced.[141]

The fourth issue involving express warranties deals with samples and models that create express warranties under section 2–313(1)(c). According to comment 6, a sample is "actually drawn from the bulk of goods which is the subject matter of the sale * * *." A model is not drawn from the goods, but is something the seller offers for inspection.[142] A sample creates a stronger presumption that it is a "basis of the bargain" than a model.[143] A seller should be able to avoid creating an express warranty under this subsection by clearly telling the buyer that she is showing him an item for illustrative purposes only, and that the goods sold may be different.[144]

---

136. Keith, 220 Cal.Rptr. at 397 ("Some [commentators] have indicated that [the 'basis of the bargain' test shifts the burden of proving non-reliance to the seller, and others have indicated that the code eliminates the concept of reliance altogether."]; Hobco, Inc. v. Tallahassee Assocs., 807 F.2d 1529, 1533 (11th Cir. 1987) ("Under Florida law, an express warranty may arise only where justifiable reliance upon assertions or affirmations is part of the basis of the bargain.").

137. See Chapter 2 at notes 14–15; 108–125, and accompanying text.

138. See Chapter 2 at notes 14–15, and accompanying text.

139. Restatement (Second) of Contracts § 81(2).

140. Keith, 220 Cal.Rptr. at 397; see also Allied Fidelity Ins. Co. v. Pico, 656 P.2d 849, 850 (Nev. 1983) ("If, however, the resulting bargain does not rest at all on the representations of the seller, those representations cannot be considered as becoming any part of the 'ba-

sis of the bargain' within the meaning of [the code].").

141. Austin v. Mitsubishi Elecs. America, Inc., 966 F.Supp. 506, 516 (E.D. Mich. 1997) ("An express warranty may . . . arise if the statements would lead a reasonable buyer to believe that such statements had been made to induce the bargain."); Chapter 2 at notes 118–119, and accompanying text.

142. UCC § 2–313, cmt. 6; White & Summers, supra note 127, at 356–360.

143. UCC § 2–313, cmt. 6.

144. Logan Equipment Corp. v. Simon Aerials, Inc., 736 F.Supp. 1188, 1198 (D. Mass. 1990)("While plaintiff may well have taken the [demonstration of the] Ontario Hydro boomlift as an example of [defendant] SAI's skill and expertise in the equipment design field, the 42–foot unit cannot have created an express warranty which survived the generation of a new set of agreed-upon specifications for [defendant's] proposed 80–foot machine.").

2. The implied warranty of merchantability. UCC section 2–314 states in part:

> (1) Unless excluded or modified, * * * a warranty that the goods shall be merchantable is implied in a contract for their sale if the seller is a merchant with respect to goods of that kind. * * *

> (2) Goods to be merchantable must be at least such as * * *

> (c) are fit for the ordinary purposes for which such goods are used * * *.

Several additional factors in section 2–314(2) help define merchantability,[145] but courts have focused on whether the goods are fit for their ordinary purpose. Before turning to the meaning of fitness, notice that the merchantability warranty arises only if the seller is a merchant. A merchant is "a person who deals in good of the kind or otherwise by his occupation holds himself out as having knowledge or skill peculiar to the practices or goods involved in the transaction * * *."[146] If you are a thriving Wall Street lawyer (be careful, the job isn't for everyone) and you sell your old piano to Alice, she has no merchantability warranty protection because you don't "deal" in pianos. People who "deal" in goods, for example, sell their inventory to consumers and other buyers.[147] People who have "knowledge or skill peculiar" to the goods include craftspeople such as "electricians, plumbers, carpenters, [and] boat builders * * *."[148]

What does it take for goods to be fit for their ordinary purpose? To some extent, the answer is obvious. An air conditioner has to cool air. A piano has to make music (at least if the right person plays it). Many of the disputes between buyers and sellers involve goods that injure a buyer, either in person or in the pocketbook, even though the goods *are* quite ordinary. For example, fish chowder ordinarily contains bones, so a person who chokes on a bone would not have a cause of action for breach of the merchantability

---

145. UCC § 2–314(2) states in full:

(2) Goods to be merchantable must be at least such as

(a) pass without objection in the trade under the contract description; and

(b) in the case of fungible goods, are of fair average quality within the description; and

(c) are fit for the ordinary purposes for which such goods are used; and

(d) run, within the variations permitted by the agreement, of even kind, quality and quantity within each unit and among all units involved; and

(e) are adequately contained, packaged, and labeled as the agreement may require; and

(f) conform to the promises or affirmations of fact made on the container or label if any.

146. UCC § 2–104(1).

147. White & Summers, supra note 127, at 362.

148. Id.

warranty.[149] Fish chowder that contains a lizard's head, on the other hand, would not be merchantable.

3. The implied warranty of fitness for a particular purpose. UCC section 2–315 states:

> Where the seller at the time of contracting has reason to know any particular purpose for which the goods are required and that the buyer is relying on the seller's skill or judgment to select or furnish suitable goods, there is unless excluded or modified * * * an implied warranty that the goods shall be fit for such purpose.

This implied warranty focuses on the time of contracting. A fitness warranty arises if, at that time, the seller has reason to know that the buyer wanted the goods for a particular purpose and the buyer relied on the seller's expertise to "select or furnish" the goods.[150] Suppose you go to a bicycle store and tell the salesperson that you are about to embark on a cross-country bike trip for six weeks. You ask him to recommend a suitable bike for the trip. The salesperson, who never rode a bike in his life, picks out a heavy mountain bike with only three gears, which is not very practical for long-distance road riding. If you rely on the seller's selection of the bike and your reliance is reasonable, you have rights under section 2–315.

But was your reliance reasonable? Perhaps a reasonable person who was going to ride cross country would be aware that a heavy mountain bike would be inappropriate for the trip. Perhaps a reasonable person would know that the salesperson is a novice. If either is true, you did not reasonably rely on the seller.[151] At any

---

149. Webster v. Blue Ship Tea Room, Inc., 198 N.E.2d 309, 312 (Mass. 1964) ("[W]e consider that the joys of life in New England include the ready availability of fresh fish chowder. We should be prepared to cope with the hazards of fish bones, the occasional presence of which in chowders is, it seems to us, to be anticipated, and which, in the light of a hallowed tradition, do not impair their fitness or merchantability.").

150. Metowski v. Traid Corp., 104 Cal.Rptr. 599, 604 (Cal. Ct. App. 1972) (implied warranty of fitness "arises only where the purchaser at the time of contracting intends to use the goods for a particular purpose; the seller at the time of contracting has reason to know of this particular purpose; the buyer relies on the seller's skill or judgment to select or furnish goods suitable for the particular

purpose; and the seller at the time of contracting has reason to know that the buyer is relying on such skill or judgment."); see also Wallman v. Kelley, 976 P.2d 330, 334 (Colo. Ct. App. 1998) ("Here, the trial court [correctly] found that plaintiff could not have relied on [defendant's] skill or judgment to select [herbal remedy] JBH because, in her deposition, she unambiguously stated that she had decided to buy [herbal remedy] JBH before she entered [defendant's] store, and she did not otherwise testify about any representations made by [defendant] that influenced her decision.").

151. Cf. Gumbs v. International Harvester, Inc., 718 F.2d 88, 93, n.6 (3d Cir. 1983) ("The relative state of the knowledge of the two parties about the product is highly relevant, and in the unusual case in which the buyer is more

rate, you can see that, unlike section 2–314's implied warranty of merchantability, reliance *is* the key here.[152] Another difference between the two implied warranties is that goods can be merchantable (fit for their *ordinary* purpose), but not fit for a *particular* purpose. The heavy mountain bike may be just dandy for riding up mountains, and therefore merchantable, but unfit for your cross-country road trip.

4. Disclaimers. UCC section 2–316 deals with "exclusion or modification of warranties." (Remember, I told you there was going to be some bad news.) The section provides in full:

(1) Words or conduct relevant to the creation of an express warranty and words or conduct tending to negate or limit warranty shall be construed wherever reasonable as consistent with each other; but subject to the provisions of this Article on parol or extrinsic evidence (Section 2–202) negation or limitation is inoperative to the extent that such construction is unreasonable.

(2) Subject to subsection (3), to exclude or modify the implied warranty of merchantability or any part of it the language must mention merchantability and in case of a writing must be conspicuous, and to exclude or modify any implied warranty of fitness the exclusion must be by a writing and conspicuous. Language to exclude all implied warranties of fitness is sufficient if it states, for example, that "There are no warranties which extend beyond the description on the face hereof."

(3) Notwithstanding subsection (2)

(a) unless the circumstances indicate otherwise, all implied warranties are excluded by expressions like "as is", "with all faults" or other language which in common understanding calls the buyer's attention to the exclusion of warranties and makes plain that there is no implied warranty; and

(b) when the buyer before entering into the contract has examined the goods or the sample or model as fully as he desired or has refused to examine the goods there is no implied

---

knowledgeable than the seller, the seller may win on the grounds the buyer did not rely.") (citing James J. White & Robert S. Summers, Handbook of the Law Under the Uniform Commercial Code 360 (2d ed. 1980)).

152. Keith v. Buchanan, 220 Cal. Rptr. 392, 399 (Cal. Ct. App. 1985)

("The major question in determining the existence of an implied warranty of fitness for a particular purpose is the reliance by the buyer upon the skill and judgment of the seller to select an article suitable for his needs.").

warranty with regard to defects which an examination ought in the circumstances to have revealed to him; and

(c) an implied warranty can also be excluded or modified by course of dealing or course of performance or usage of trade.

a. Disclaiming express warranties. Section 2–316(1) governs the exclusion or modification of express warranties. The section constitutes a small victory for buyers. Although it directs courts to try to construe language creating and nullifying express warranties consistently, the section codifies the idea that the seller is responsible for any inconsistencies between statements that cannot be resolved. If the contract states that a used car will get 36 miles per gallon, but also disclaims all warranties, section 2–316(1) directs courts to construe the ambiguity created by the contradiction against the seller. The express warranty of 36 miles per gallon should survive.[153]

Notice that section 2–316(1) includes a reference to section 2–202, the parol evidence rule. This reference creates an exception to the rule that inconsistencies go against the seller. We consider the parol evidence rule in awesome detail in Chapter 7 of this book.[154] For now understand that the rule is supposed to protect parties who rely on their written contracts from false allegations of prior promises or agreements that contradict the writing. In the context of warranty disclaimers, the problem arises when a buyer alleges that the seller made an oral express warranty ("this car will get 36 miles per gallon on the open road"), but the written contract either disclaims all warranties or specifically warrants lower gas mileage. If the parol evidence rule of section 2–202 did not supplement section 2–316(1), the buyer would be able to offer evidence of the 36 mile-per-hour statement and, if the trier of fact believed the evidence, it would create an express warranty that contradicts the writing. However, section 2–202 bars admission of the evidence. Under the UCC, the buyer cannot even prove that the seller made the statement.

If the last paragraph doesn't make much sense to you now, please read the materials on the parol evidence rule and then reread the paragraph. If you read the parol evidence material and still don't understand the above, at least you will know how to spell parol.

---

153. Hartman v. Jensen's, Inc., 289 S.E.2d 648, 649 (S.C. 1982) ("The trial court found the disclaimer in this case confusing in that the heading, which read 'TERMS OF WARRANTY' in bold print, suggested a grant of warranty rather than a disclaimer.... [P]lacing alleged disclaimer under the bold heading of 'Terms of Warranty' created an ambiguity and was likely to fail to alert the consumer that an exclusion of the warranty was intended.").

154. See Chapter 7 at notes 4–56, and accompanying text.

b.   Disclaiming implied warranties. Getting rid of implied warranties is easy for sellers. To disclaim the implied warranty of merchantability, the seller must mention the term merchantability by name, and, if in writing, the disclaimer must be conspicuous (stand out).[155] The seller can disclaim an implied warranty of fitness for a particular purpose in a conspicuous writing, but in this case the seller does not have to use the magic words "fitness for a particular purpose."[156]

You are an attentive reader, and you just thought you learned how sellers can disclaim implied warranties. Well, you did, sort of. Read section 2–316(3), however. The preamble to section 2–316(3) says "[n]otwithstanding subsection (2)," which means that subsection 3 is about to reveal some exceptions to subsection (2). Generally, under section 2–316(3)(a), a seller can disclaim all implied warranties by including language such as "as is," "with all faults," or the like. The seller doesn't have to mention merchantability or disclaim conspicuously after all.

Sections 2–316(3)(b) and (3)(c) constitute additional disclaimers based on the buyer's inspection (or refusal to inspect) the goods, and based on "course of dealing, or course of performance, or usage of trade" respectively. Courts often use the latter sources of evidence to reveal the meaning of a contract, and we study them further in Chapter 7.[157] For now you need only grasp the general idea: If, for example, the seller and buyer had made several contracts over the years with the understanding that the seller was selling "as is," their next deal will be "as is" too unless the parties expressly negate this previous "course of dealing."

5.   Article 2 amendments. The recent Article 2 amendments[158] change some of the above-described warranty scheme. Here are the highlights: First, unlike existing section 2–313, the amended section makes clear that express warranties extend to the immediate buyer only. An immediate buyer buys directly from the

---

155. UCC § 2–316(2); see also Myrtle Beach Pipeline Corp. v. Emerson Elec. Co., 843 F.Supp. 1027, 1038 (D. S.C. 1993) ("The court concludes that the various factors to be considered by a court in determining whether a document is conspicuous for purposes of disclaiming an implied warranty pursuant to subsection ... 2–316(2) include the following: (1) the color of print in which the purported disclaimer appears; (2) the style of print in which the disclaimer is written; (3) the size of the disclaiming language, particularly in relation to other print in the document; (4) the location of the disclaimer in the contract; (5) the appearance of the term 'merchantability' with respect to color, style, size, and type of print in the disclaimer clause; and (6) the status of the parties contesting the validity of the disclaimer, namely whether they be consumers or commercially sophisticated entities.").

156. UCC § 2–316(2).

157. See Chapter 7 at notes 73–99, and accompanying text.

158. See Chapter 1 at notes 5–6, and accompanying text.

seller.[159] In other words, if you buy a Compaq computer at Best Buy, any rights you have under section 2–313 are against Best Buy, not against Compaq. In Chapter 10, we will study two new sections that are part of amended Article 2 that deal with a manufacturer's liability (such as Compaq) to parties who are not "immediate buyers" (such as you).[160]

The second important amendment to Article 2 warranties includes a new subsection, 2–313(4), that introduces the concept of a "remedial promise." If a seller makes promises to remedy defects, the promise "creates an obligation."[161] Preliminary official comment 11 to the amended section explains the reason for the introduction of the "remedial promise" concept. Basically, a remedial promise does not have to satisfy the "basis of the bargain" test. In addition, amended Article 2 treats a remedial promise differently for statute of limitations purposes (the statute of limitations sets forth how much time a buyer has to sue).

Third, amended section 2–316(2) creates special rules for disclaimers of implied warranties in cases involving consumer purchasers. In order to disclaim the implied warranty of merchantability, the disclaimer must conspicuously state that "[t]he seller undertakes no responsibility for the quality of the goods except as otherwise provided in this contract * * *."[162] Further, the language must be in a "record." A record includes a writing, but also includes information that is stored in a computer.[163] To disclaim the fitness for a particular purpose warranty, the language must conspicuously state that "[t]he seller assumes no responsibility that the goods will be fit for any particular purpose for which you may be buying these goods, except as otherwise provided in the contract* * *."[164] Sellers may have mixed feelings about the language they must use in order to disclaim. On the one hand, they provide a "safe harbor," meaning that sellers can be sure that courts will enforce their disclaimers if they use the language. On the other hand, the language sellers must employ may create the misleading impression that they do not intend to stand behind the quality of their products at all.

Amended section 2–316 continues the policy of allowing sellers to disclaim using "as is" and "with all faults" language.[165] Consumers enjoy new protection under this section, however, because the language must be conspicuous. Are you jumping for joy about your new protection?

---

159. Amended UCC § 2–313(1) (proposed final draft April 18, 2003).

160. See Chapter 10 at notes 52–62, and accompanying text. The two new sections are 2–313A and 2–313B.

161. Amended UCC § 2–313(4).

162. Amended UCC § 2–316(2).

163. Amended UCC § 2–103(1)(m).

164. UCC § 2–316(2).

165. Amended UCC § 2–316(3).

6. Caveat. Please understand that proving the existence of a warranty and the absence of an effective disclaimer does not mean that the buyer is ever going to see any compensation. The buyer must also prove that the goods did not comply with the warranty, that the buyer was injured because of the defect, that the buyer suffered provable damages, and that no other affirmative defenses (such as the statute of limitations or the lack of notice) apply.[166] You can pursue all of these issues in an upper class commercial law course.

---

166. See generally White & Summers, supra note 127, at 342–343.

*

Chapter Four

THE STATUTE OF FRAUDS

Under the statute of frauds, certain agreements must be in writing to be enforceable. For example, if you and your neighbor, Alice, orally agree that you will sell her your car for $6000, the agreement will not be enforceable under the UCC sale-of-goods statute of frauds.[1] As the first sentence implies, however, not all contracts must be in writing. This chapter discusses the kinds of agreements that must be in writing to be enforceable. In addition, we discuss what a writing must entail to satisfy the statute of frauds. Further, we examine certain exceptions to the writing requirement in cases that ordinarily would require a writing.

Well, I have only written one paragraph in this chapter and already I must issue a caveat. Contract law is trying to keep up with dramatic technological advances in communication. In the computer age, we are all making contracts over the internet and even via e-mail. "Writings" may soon be largely a thing of the past. So, a proposed amendment to the statute of frauds for the sale of goods (which may soon be adopted by the states) requires only the "authentication or adoption" of certain contracts in a "record."[2] A record includes a writing, but also information stored in a computer.[3] Technology has also driven changes in laws affecting the statute of frauds for other kinds of agreements. Laws in flux can be challenging to describe. My strategy in this chapter will be to discuss the traditional statute of frauds, but to supplement the discussion by highlighting the proposed or adopted changes.

As you read this chapter, please also bear in mind another point that often confuses students. Up to this point in this book, we have focused on the requirements for an enforceable agreement, promise, or obligation. This chapter discusses an additional requirement for some agreements, namely a writing (or record). But (and here comes the confusing part), ordinarily, a writing does not make an otherwise unenforceable agreement enforceable. For example, a writing does not make an agreement enforceable if it lacks consideration or is too indefinite, and so on.

---

1. UCC § 2–201 (1996); see infra note 6, and accompanying text.

2. See infra notes 45–48, and accompanying text.

3. See id.

A. Background

The statute of frauds was first adopted in England in 1677,[4] and each of our state legislatures has enacted a statute of frauds much like the English version.

The Hawaii statute of frauds (a representative example we shall employ throughout this chapter), provides a list of contracts that must be in writing to be enforceable:

Certain contracts, when actionable. No action shall be brought and maintained in any of the following cases:

(1) To charge a personal representative, upon any special promise to answer for damages out of the personal representative's own estate;

(2) To charge any person upon any special promise to answer for the debt, default, or misdoings of another;

(3) To charge any person, upon an agreement made in consideration of marriage;

(4) Upon any contract for the sale of lands, tenements, or hereditaments, or of any interest in or concerning them;

(5) Upon any agreement that is not to be performed within one year from the making thereof;

(6) To charge any person upon any agreement authorizing or employing an agent or broker to purchase or sell real estate for compensation or commission;

(7) To charge the estate of any deceased person upon any agreement which by its terms is not to be performed during the lifetime of the promisor * * *

unless the promise, contract, or agreement upon which the action is brought, or some memorandum or note thereof, is in writing, and is signed by the party to be charged therewith, or by some person thereunto by the party in writing lawfully authorized.[5]

---

4. An Act for prevention of Frauds and Perjuryes (Statute of Frauds) 1677, 29 Car. 2, c. 3 § 4 (Eng.), reprinted in 4 Chitty's Statutes 1140 (W. H. Aggs ed., 6th ed. 1911).

[N]o action shall be brought (1) whereby to charge any executor or administrator upon any special promise, to answer damages out of his own estate; (2) or whereby to charge the defendant upon any special promise to answer for the debt, default or miscarriages of another person; (3) or to charge any person upon any agreement made upon consideration of marriage; (4) or upon any contract or sale of lands, tenements or hereditaments, or any interest in or concerning them; (5) or upon any agreement that is not to be performed within the space of one year from the making thereof; (6) unless the agreement upon which such action shall be brought, or some memorandum or note thereof, shall be in writing, and signed by the party to be charged therewith, or some other person thereunto by him lawfully authorized.

5. Haw. Rev. Stat. § 656–1 (2002).

In addition to the traditional categories enumerated above, we will study one other category of agreement that requires a writing, namely sales of goods (of $500 or more).[6] UCC section 2–201(1) provides: "[A] contract for the sale of goods for the price of $500 or more is not enforceable by way of action or defense unless there is some writing sufficient to indicate that a contract for sale has been made between the parties and signed by the party against whom enforcement is sought * * *."

England abolished most provisions of its statute of frauds in 1954, but our states have preserved it. To understand why the statute of frauds is controversial, we must think about the reasons for the writing requirement in the first place. England enacted the statute of frauds to combat fraud by people who might falsely claim they had an oral contract.[7] For example, the statute of frauds protects you from Alice's false claims that you agreed to sell her your car (assuming you did not). The notion of a statute of frauds made a lot of sense when it was enacted in 1677 because, at that time, the party claiming the existence of a contract could not testify at trial or be cross-examined.[8] In addition, judges of the time had much less control over jury decisions that were against the weight of the evidence.[9]

As procedural reforms made fact finding by juries much more reliable, reformers feared that the statute of frauds now caused as

---

6. See infra notes 19, 28, 38, 50–53, 60–70, 74–77, and accompanying text.

7. McIntosh v. Murphy, 469 P.2d 177, 179 (Haw. 1970) ("The first English Statute was enacted almost 300 years ago to prevent 'many fraudulent practices, which are commonly endeavored to be upheld by perjury and subornation of perjury.' ") (citing Statute of Frauds, 29 Car. 2, c. 3 (1677)); see also Estate of Stephens, 49 P.3d 1093, 1101 (Cal. 2002) (Kennard, J., dissenting) ("By requiring that the specified transactions be in writing and signed by the parties, the statute of frauds avoids the likelihood that permitting oral proof of such transactions would encourage fraudulent claims by swindlers gambling that they can glibly persuade a jury to enforce a nonexistent oral agreement.").

8. Lionel Morgan Summers, The Doctrine of Estoppel Applied to the Statute of Frauds, 79 U. Pa. L. Rev. 440, 441 (1931) ("Trial by jury was even more imperfect than now; there were no rules of evidence to speak of, and parties to the suit were not allowed to testify in

their own behalf. It can readily be seen that, under such circumstances, it was of paramount importance to have written evidence of contracts, else a plaintiff could come into court and have a friend testify to a feigned contract, which a defendant would be powerless to disprove by his own testimony.").

9. Thomson Printing Mach. Co. v. B.F. Goodrich Co., 714 F.2d 744, 746 (7th Cir. 1983) ("[C]ourts then could not throw out jury verdicts manifestly contrary to the evidence."); see also James J. O'Connell, Jr., Comment, Boats Against the Current: The Courts and the Statute of Frauds, 47 Emory L.J. 253, 257 (1998) ("In 1677 ... [j]uries were no longer composed of knowledgeable locals who were familiar with the parties to the litigation and the nature of the dispute, but they were not yet 'panels of disinterested strangers composing a tabula rasa on which the law of evidence would permit only certain facts to be inscribed.' ") (quoting Friedrich Kessler et al., Contracts: Cases and Materials 418, 754 (3d. ed. 1986)).

much or more fraud than it prevented.[10] English lawmakers were concerned that people who had actually made oral agreements could use the absence of a writing as a shield to avoid their commitments.[11] Suppose you actually had agreed to sell Alice your car, and now you were hiding behind the statute of frauds (shame on you). Notwithstanding this concern, our lawmakers see reasons to retain the statute of frauds.[12] For example, a writing helps satisfy the cautionary and evidentiary functions, a subject we took up in Chapter 2, when we investigated the purposes of the requirement of consideration.[13] You don't remember and are too tired to look up the footnote cite? Well, the theory is that you understand the seriousness of what you are doing when you put your contract to sell your car in writing. And, of course, the writing serves as a memorial of the agreement you made.

Notwithstanding the statute of fraud's continuing role in this country, judges resist employing it when they are convinced the parties actually made an oral agreement. As a result, judicial decisions have gradually reduced the impact of the rule by interpreting the categories of contracts that require a writing narrowly. For example, as one court has stated:

> [A] promise to pay the debt of another has been construed to encompass only promises made to a creditor which do not benefit the promisor (Restatement of Contracts § 184 (1932));

10. 43 L. Q. Rev. 1 (1927) ("Perhaps it is not inopportune to suggest that a dinner [in honor of the Statute's 250th anniversary] be given in one of the Inns of Court. A suitable number of litigants, who have been cheated of their rights by means of this interesting and aged Statute, might be invited to give relish to the affair. If some of the defendants who have sheltered themselves behind its useful provisions are also asked, care will have to be taken that none of the silver disappears."); H. C. & J. G. Ouston v. G. Scammell & Nephew Ltd., 1 All E.R. 59, 66 (Eng. C.A. 1940) ("[T]hat statute ... has enabled more frauds to be committed than it has ever prevented....").

11. Vernon v. Findlay, 4 All E.R. 311, 317 (K.B. 1938) ("I feel bound to say that this is a contract upon which no action can be brought. I say it with regret, because I think that undoubtedly [plaintiff] did work for these defendants.... I am bound to administer the law as I believe it to be...."); Wakeham v. MacKenzie, 2 All E.R. 783, 785 (Ch. 1968) ("Nothing could have been more fraudulent to the way of thinking of the old equity lawyers than that [the promisor] ..., having induced performance of the contract and enjoyed the benefits of that performance, should have repudiated his obligations in reliance on the statute.").

12. Summerlot v. Summerlot, 408 N.E.2d 820, 828 (Ind Ct. App.1980) ("The reason for the statute of frauds is quite simply to preclude fraudulent claims which would probably arise when one person's word is pitted against another's and which would open wide those ubiquitous 'flood-gates of litigation.'"); Lawless v. Temple, 150 N.E. 176, 176 (Mass. 1926) ("The reason for the adoption of the rule requiring acceptance in writing, like the underlying reason for the statute of frauds and similar statutes, 'is that sound policy requires some substantial evidence of the contract, and more reliable in its nature than the statement or recollection of witnesses.'") (quoting Selma Sav. Bank v. Webster County Bank, 206 S.W. 870, 872 (Ky. 1918)).

13. See Chapter 2 at notes 33–40, and accompanying text.

3 Williston, Contracts § 452 (Jaeger ed. 1960); a promise in consideration of marriage has been interpreted to exclude mutual promises to marry (Restatement, *supra* § 192; 3 Williston, *supra* § 485); a promise not to be performed within one year means a promise not performable within one year (Restatement, *supra* § 198; 3 Williston, *supra* § 495); a promise not to be performed within one year may be removed from the Statute of Frauds if one party has fully performed (Restatement, *supra* § 198; 3 Williston, *supra* § 504); and the Statute will not be applied where all promises involved are fully performed (Restatement, *supra* § 219; 3 Williston, *supra* § 528).[14]

We'll look further at some of these judicial contractions of the statute of frauds shortly.[15]

Not only have courts whittled down the categories presented in the original statute of frauds, they have created exceptions. For example, part performance usually is enough to avoid the writing requirement.[16] In addition, courts use other theories to enforce a promise that the statute of frauds would normally bar. For example, a court may enforce an oral promise based on the theory of promissory estoppel or unjust enrichment.[17]

We now proceed to consider more systematically the major issues that arise under the statute of frauds. First, does the statute of frauds apply? Second, does a writing satisfy the statute? Third, does an exception to the writing requirement apply? Finally, is a promise that is unenforceable for lack of a writing still enforceable under another theory, such as promissory estoppel or unjust enrichment?

B.   Does the Statute of Frauds Apply?

Look again at the Hawaii statute of frauds set forth above.[18] Add UCC section 2–201, which requires a writing for the sale of goods of greater than $500,[19] and the list of transactions that require a writing is quite complete. (Of course, various states have enacted additional writing requirements, but don't sweat these unless your teacher has assigned them for study.)

Many contracts courses focus on three categories of contracts that must be in writing to be enforceable. These are contracts for the sale of land or any interest in land (subsection 4 of the Hawaii statute), contracts that cannot be performed within one year from

---

14. McIntosh, 469 P.2d at 180 n.3.

15. See infra notes 18–27, and accompanying text.

16. See infra notes 50–59, and accompanying text.

17. See infra notes 71–81, and accompanying text.

18. See supra note 5, and accompanying text.

19. See supra note 6, and accompanying text.

the time of contract formation (subsection 5 of the Hawaii statute), and contracts for the sale of goods (UCC section 2–201). Let's discuss each of these briefly.

Contracts for the sale of land must be in writing.[20] That is easy enough. But don't forget that contracts for "any interest in or concerning" land also must be in writing to be enforceable.[21] A lease of your apartment, therefore, requires a writing. An oral promise of a leasehold won't do.[22]

Law professors have lots of fun with contracts that are "not to be performed within one year from the making thereof."[23] Recall that courts have whittled down this category to require a writing only when the promise *cannot* be performed in a year.[24] So, if you hire a young man to work for you for his life, the statute of frauds does not require a writing. The contract can be performed within one year, if (God forbid) the young man dies in a week.[25] He worked for you for his life. But if you hire a 98–year-old man to work for you for 366 days, even though he was diagnosed with a terminal case of the plague when he was 80 and given one year to live (he's a walking miracle), the statute of frauds requires a writing. The contract to employ the 98–year-old man cannot be performed in a year, even though he might die before 366 days pass. The old guy's death would end the contract, but the contract would not have been performed, it would only be excused.[26]

The revisers of Article 2 are spoilsports and have taken all the fun out of sale-of-goods contracts that fall under the longer-than-one-year statute of fraud's category. They added a new subsection that states: "A contract that is enforceable under this section is not

20. Haw. Rev. Stat. § 656–1(4).

21. Id.; see also

Purcell v. Miner, 71 U.S. 513, 517 (1866) ("Every day's experience more fully demonstrates that this statute was founded in wisdom, and absolutely necessary to preserve the title to real property from the chances, the uncertainty, and the fraud attending the admission of parol testimony.").

22. Kent v. Humphries, 275 S.E.2d 176, 180 (N.C. Ct. App. 1981) (" Plaintiff may not rely on the oral lease, however, because it is barred by the statute of frauds....").

23. Haw. Rev. Stat. § 656–1(5).

24. See supra note 14, and accompanying text.

25. Doherty v. Doherty Ins. Agency, Inc., 878 F.2d 546, 551–52 (1st Cir. 1989) ("A contract for lifetime employment is not subject to the statute of frauds, because the contract may be per-

formed within one year if the employee happens to die within the year."); see also Price v. Mercury Supply Co., 682 S.W.2d 924, 933 (Tenn. Ct. App. 1984).

26. Restatement (Second) of Contracts § 130, cmt. b (1981); see also Ferrera v. Carpionato Corp., 895 F.2d 818, 820 (1st Cir. 1990) ("It is true that [plaintiff] could have died within one year from the agreement's inception. His death, however, would not have amounted to 'performance' of the contract. Rather, death would simply have excused him from performing the contract."); Deaton v. Tennessee Coal & R. Co., 59 Tenn. 650, 652 (Tenn. 1874) ("The performance of the contract might be defeated by the death of all the parties for whose benefit it was made, within the year; but that would not operate as a performance of the contract.").

unenforceable merely because it is not capable of being performed within one year or any other period after its making."[27] Contracts for more than one year do not have to be in writing under amended Article 2.

As I already mentioned several times, section 2–201 of the UCC requires a writing when the sale of goods is "for the price of $500 or more." But at the time of this writing, the ALI and NCCUSL also have approved an amendment to section 2–201 that shows the effect of inflation. Under the amendment, contracts for the sale of goods of a price of $5000 or more require a writing.[28] This provision will not be law in any given state until its legislature enacts the change.

C. Does a Writing Satisfy the Statute of Frauds?

1. The nature of the writing. If the statute of frauds requires a writing, what kind of writing will suffice? The Hawaii statute of frauds' answer is typical: A party seeking to enforce a "promise, contract, or agreement" must show a writing or "some memorandum or note thereof * * * signed by the party to be charged therewith, or by some person thereunto by the party in writing lawfully authorized."[29] Let's translate this from legalese into English.

The actual "promise, contract, or agreement" that the promisee is trying to enforce must be in writing, or at least be referenced in "some memorandum or note" in writing that proves the existence of the "promise, contract, or agreement."[30] The point is that the statute of frauds does not require a formal written contract, just something in writing that proves the contract's existence. In order to satisfy such a proof requirement, the writing must "reasonably identif[y] the subject matter of the contract"[31] (for example,

---

27. Amended UCC § 2–201(4) (proposed final draft April 18, 2003).

28. Amended UCC § 2–201(1).

29. Haw. Rev. Stat. § 656–1; see also Spiegel v. Lowenstein, 147 N.Y.S. 655 (App. Div. 1914) ("Anything under the hand of the party sought to be charged admitting that he had entered into the agreement will be sufficient to satisfy the statute, which was only intended to protect parties from having parol agreements, dependent upon human recollection and veracity, imposed upon them.").

30. Bank of Am., N.A. v. Bradley, 54 Va. Cir. 351, 355 (Va. Cir. Ct. 2000) ("[T]he court finds that there was an oral contract.... The court further finds that [promissor's] ... July 15 letters, read together, are sufficient written memoranda of the oral contract to satisfy the statute of frauds, thereby making the oral contract valid and enforceable."); Brewer v. Horst–Lachmund Co., 60 P. 418, 419 (Cal. 1900).

31. Restatement (Second) of Contracts § 131(a); see also Taylor v. Lester, 12 S.W.2d 1097, 1098 (Tex. Civ. App. 1928) ("The several writings signed by the parties by reference clearly identify the subject-matter of the contract and fully meet the requirements of the Statute of Frauds.").

"sale of house at 313 Windsor Drive"), and include "with reasonable certainty the essential terms of the unperformed promises in the contract" (for example, identify the price).[32] Several writings as a group may satisfy these statute of frauds requirements, so long as at least one of them is signed by the promisee.[33] When there are several writings, the signed writing must establish "a contractual relationship between the parties,"[34] the unsigned documents must refer expressly to the same agreement,[35] and evidence must prove the relationship of the unsigned and signed documents.[36]

A writing may satisfy the statute of frauds even if the parties did not intend to contract or to create evidence of a contract.[37] For

32. Restatement (Second) of Contracts § 131(c); see also Janus v. Sproul, 458 S.E.2d 300, 301 (Va. 1995) ("To satisfy the Statute of Frauds, a writing must contain the essential terms of the agreement it memorializes."); Cage Realty, Inc. v. Hanna, 881 S.W.2d 254, 255 (Mo. Ct. App. 1994) ("A writing is sufficient to satisfy the Statute of Frauds if it sets forth the essential terms of the agreement including the parties, the subject matter, the consideration, the price, and the promises upon both sides.").

33. Schremp v. Dubrowin, 263 A.2d 827, 833 (Md. 1970) ("This Court has fully accepted the rule that the memorandum required by the Statute of Frauds may consist of two writings if each indicates it relates to the same transaction and, though only one be signed by the party to be charged...."); Papaioannou v. Britz, 285 A.D. 596, 599–600 (N.Y. App. Div. 1955) ("[T]he several writings may arise from an exchange of correspondence, only part of which is signed by the promisor, where the signed portion connects or unites the unsigned portion by internal identification or reference.").

34. See Crabtree v. Elizabeth Arden Sales Corp., 110 N.E.2d 551, 554 (N.Y. 1953) ("[A]t least one writing, the one establishing a contractual relationship between the parties, must bear the signature of the party to be charged....").

35. Horn & Hardart Co. v. Pillsbury Co., 888 F.2d 8, 11 (2d Cir. 1989) ("The signed writing must identify the transaction sufficiently to permit connection between the signed and unsigned writings."); Crabtree, 110 N.E.2d

at 554 ("[S]igned and unsigned writings [may] be read together, provided that they clearly refer to the same subject matter or transaction.").

36. Restatement (Second) of Contracts § 132; Hunt Oil Co. v. FERC, 853 F.2d 1226, 1241 (5th Cir. 1988) ("A 'writing' for purposes of the statute of frauds may consist of separate writings, connected together by express reference to each other or internal evidence of their unity, relation, or connection...."); Marks v. Cowdin, 123 N.E. 139, 145 (N.Y. 1919) ("The memorandum exacted by the statute does not have to be in one document. It may be pieced together out of separate writings, connected with one another either expressly or by the internal evidence of subject matter and occasion.").

37. Restatement (Second) of Contracts § 133; Crabtree, 110 N.E.2d at 553 ("Each of the two payroll cards—the one initialed by defendant's general manager, the other signed by its comptroller—unquestionably constitutes a memorandum under the statute. That they were not prepared or signed with the intention of evidencing the contract, or that they came into existence subsequent to its execution, is of no consequence; it is enough, to meet the statute's demands, that they were signed with intent to authenticate the information contained therein and that such information does evidence the terms of the contract."); see also Heffernan v. Keith, 127 So.2d 903, 904 (Fla. Dist. Ct. App. 1961) ("In the instant case, the plaintiff has met the requirements of the statute by presenting a telegram which by its terms refers to a certain proposed contract ....").

example, suppose you and Alice contemplate the sale to her of your residence at 313 Windsor Drive. You write a letter to her referring to the sale of 313 Windsor Drive, even before reaching a final agreement. The letter may satisfy the statute of frauds against you. Remember, however, that this does not mean that you are liable to Alice if you decide not to sell the property. You can still prove that you never completed a contract to sell the property. All that we are saying here is that you cannot use the defense of a lack of writing under the statute of frauds.

UCC section 2–201 also provides that an informal writing satisfies the statute of frauds. The language of section 2–201(1) requires only "some writing sufficient to indicate that a contract for sale has been made between the parties * * *."[38] So, under the UCC, you can write a memorandum for the sale of your car on the back of a claim check in a restaurant where you and Alice have ironed out the deal, and, if you both sign it, neither of you will have a statute of frauds problem.

The last sentence of section 2–201(1) provides that "[a] writing is not insufficient because it omits or incorrectly states a term agreed upon * * *." However, a contract based on a flawed writing is not enforceable "beyond the quantity of goods shown in such writing." Under this provision, the parties don't have to get everything straight in their writing. Parties can prove that the terms are different from the writing. However, a party cannot prove a contract beyond the quantity of goods stated in the writing. If the writing says two giraffes, the seller can't prove three giraffes.

Notwithstanding the informality of the writing requirement, I beg of you, I plead with you, bear in mind the admonition at the beginning of this chapter: Even if a promisee produces a formal or informal writing that satisfies the statute of frauds, she has not won the war. She has satisfied the statute of frauds, but she still must contend with all of the issues of contract enforceability we are learning about in this book, such as whether she supplied consideration to support the promise, whether a reasonable person would believe the parties intended to contract (of course, the writing is *evidence* of intention), whether the contract is sufficiently certain, and so on and so on.

---

38. Wells, Waters & Gases, Inc. v. Air Prods. & Chems., Inc., 19 F.3d 157, 161 (4th Cir. 1994) ("Section 2–201(1), by its terms, does not bar the enforcement of the contract against [plaintiff] provided that the writing 'indicates that a contract for sale has been made between the parties. . . .' "); Migerobe, Inc. v. Certina USA, Inc., 924 F.2d 1330, 1333 (5th Cir. 1991) ("In the case before us, the integration of two signed documents and one unsigned document tends to show that the parties had made a contract for sale.").

2. Who must sign. The definition of "signed" is very broad and largely uncontroversial. The UCC approach is typical: " 'Signed' includes using any symbol executed or adopted with present intention to adopt or accept a writing."[39] You can sign a writing with an "X," if you executed that symbol intending to accept the writing.[40] The harder statute of frauds question is: Who must sign?

Under the Hawaii statute of frauds, the writing must be signed "by the party to be charged therewith," meaning the party who breaks a promise.[41] So, stifle that false impression that most people have about signing contracts that require a writing, namely that both parties must sign. UCC section 2–201(1) makes this even more explicit for sale-of-goods cases: The writing must be "signed by the party against whom enforcement is sought * * *."[42] The net result is that if you and Alice draft a written contract for the sale of your car for $6000, signed only by you, Alice can sue you if you don't deliver the car, but you cannot sue Alice if she repudiates the contract before delivery. Life is sometimes unfair. (If you deliver the car, however, you can sue for breach of contract under the part-performance exception or you can sue for unjust enrichment, but we are getting ahead of ourselves.[43])

Both the Hawaii and UCC statute of frauds also provide that an authorized person may sign the writing on behalf of a contracting party.[44] The law of agency governs the meaning of "authorization," a subject beyond the scope of most first-year contracts courses.

3. Electronic contracts. More and more, people are purchasing goods and services over the internet and through e-mail. (You didn't need me to tell you this.) A largely paperless society may be in our future.[45] Perhaps you have wondered whether the purchase you made over the internet was enforceable, since you didn't sign a writing.

---

39. UCC § 1–201(37).

40. See Monetti, S.P.A. v. Anchor Hocking Corp., 931 F.2d 1178, 1185 (7th Cir. 1991) ("It was a writing on [defendant's] letterhead, so it satisfied the writing and signature requirements of the UCC statute of frauds."); see also Barber & Ross Co. v. Lifetime Doors, Inc., 810 F.2d 1276, 1280 (4th Cir. 1987) ("The written sales brochures given by [defendant] to [plaintiff] met the requirements of the statute of frauds. The writings met the signature requirement because the [defendant's] trademark appeared on the documents and that was sufficient to authenticate the documents.").

41. Haw. Rev. Stat. § 656–1.

42. UCC § 2–201(1).

43. See infra notes 49–59; 71–81, and accompanying text.

44. Haw. Rev. Stat. § 656–1; UCC § 2–201(1).

45. See Patricia Fry, X Marks the Spot: New Technologies Compel New Concepts for Commercial Law, 26 Loy.

Amended UCC Article 2, which, I have indicated, is in the works,[46] will take care of this issue. Amended section 2–201 provides in part:

> A contract for the sale of goods for the price of $5000 or more is not enforceable by way of action or defense unless there is some record sufficient to indicate that a contract for sale has been made between the parties and signed by the party against which enforcement is sought or by the party's authorized agent or broker.

Section 2–103(1)(p) sets forth the definition of "sign": " 'Sign' means, with present intent to authenticate or adopt a record: (i) to execute or adopt a tangible symbol; or (ii) to attach to or logically associate with the record an electronic sound, symbol, or process." Finally, under section 2–103(1)(m), a " 'record' " means information that is inscribed on a tangible medium or that is stored in an electronic or other medium and is retrievable in perceivable form."

First notice that most of your internet sales transactions will not come under the statute of frauds because amended section 2–201 requires a "record" only for sales contracts of $5000 or more. Even for large purchases of over $5000, your internet contract (or e-mail contract, for that matter) satisfies the statute of frauds under amended Article 2. When you click "I agree" on your internet sales contract, you have "signed" a "record" that "indicate[s] that a contract for sale has been made * * *."

In 2000, new federal legislation was passed allowing parties to execute binding online contracts using electronic signatures.[47] The law governs, among other things, banking, insurance and brokerage contracts.[48]

L. A. L. Rev. 607 (1993); see also Roger Edwards v. Fiddes & Son, Ltd., 245 F.Supp.2d 251, 261 (D. Me. 2003) (accepting plaintiff's argument that email's "clearly constitute a writing, and the fact that the party to be charged with enforcement ... authored emails with his salutation [sic] is sufficient to constitute a signature.").

46. See Chapter 1 at notes 5–6, and accompanying text.

47. Electronic Signatures in Global and National Commerce Act, 15 USC § 7001 (2000) (Section 7001(a)(1) provides that a contract cannot be thrown out "solely because it is in electronic form").

48. For a discussion, see, e.g., Holly K. Towle, E–Signatures-Basics of the U.S. Structure, 38 Hous. L. Rev. 921 (2001); see also Specht v. Netscape Communications Corp., 306 F.3d 17, 27, n. 11 (2d Cir. 2002) ("The parties do not dispute, nor could they, that the software license agreement at issue ... is a 'written provision' despite being provided to users in a downloadable electronic form. The latter point has been settled by the Electronic Signatures in Global and National Commerce Act...."); Roger Edwards v. Fiddes & Son, 245 F.Supp.2d 251, 261 (D. Me. 2003) ("[E]-mails are sufficient under Maine law to meet the requirements of [the Statute of Frauds].... This conclusion is consistent with [the Electronic Signatures in Global and National Commerce Act]....").

D. Does an Exception to the Writing Requirement Apply?

Even if the statute of frauds applies to an oral transaction, an exception may "take the case out of the statute" (legalese meaning that contract law does not require a writing when an exception applies). The most prominent example is part performance.[49] But what exactly constitutes part performance and when does the exception apply?

Let's start with section 2–201(3)(c) of the UCC, which codifies the part performance rule for sales of goods: A contract that does not satisfy the statute of frauds is enforceable "with respect to goods for which payment has been made and accepted or which have been received and accepted * * *."[50] Note that under the section, the contract is enforceable only to the extent of the part performance. You orally agree to sell Alice three pianos (don't ask for realism in all my hypos) for $6000. You deliver one of the pianos, which she accepts, but she does not pay. The statute of frauds is no impediment to your claim for payment for the piano you delivered, but it would bar full enforcement of the contract for the sale of three pianos. Likewise, if you had failed to deliver any pianos after Alice paid for one of them, she could enforce the contract for only one piano.[51]

Suppose you orally agreed to sell one piano to Alice for $2000, and she paid you a portion of the purchase price, say $500. She is not limited to enforcing a contract for only one quarter of the piano. Most courts allow her to enforce the entire contract, free

---

49. See, e.g., McNamee Schmetterer Euro RSCG Inc. v. Aegis Group PLC, 711 N.E.2d 953, 956 (N.Y. 1999) ("[T]he doctrine of part performance is based on principles of equity, and, specifically, recognition of the fact that it would be a fraud to allow one party to a real estate transaction to escape performance after permitting the other party to perform in reliance on the agreement. Part performance alone, of course, is not sufficient. The performance must be unequivocally referable to the agreement."); Richardson v. Taylor Land & Livestock Co., 171 P.2d 703, 709 (Wash. 1946) ("[T]he doctrine of part performance was established for the same purpose for which the statute of frauds itself was enacted, namely, for the prevention of fraud, and arose from the necessity of preventing the statute from becoming an agent of fraud, for it could not have been the intention of the statute to enable any party to commit a fraud with impunity.") (quoting 49 Am. Jur. 725, Statute of Frauds, § 421); Brown v. Sutton, 129 U.S. 238, 242

(1889) ("[T]here can be little doubt that the delivery of possession to sufficient part performance to take the case out of the statute of frauds.").

50. UCC § 2–201(3)(c); see also Casazza v. Kiser, 313 F.3d 414, 418 (8th Cir. 2002) ("Under the part-performance exception to the statute of frauds, a writing is not required 'with respect to goods for which payment has been made and accepted or which have been received and accepted.'") (quoting Minn. Stat. § 336.2–201(3)(c) (2000)).

51. In re Augustin Bros. Co., 460 F.2d 376, 380 (8th Cir. 1972) ("[P]art performance of an oral contract for the sale of goods that is capable of apportionment is enforceable only as to that portion that has been either fully or partially performed.... [E]nforcement of an oral contract for goods in which an advance payment has been made by the buyer is limited to that quantity of goods which the advance payment would buy at the market price.").

from a statute of frauds defense.[52] Remember, however, all she has shown by proving the $500 payment is that the statute of frauds doesn't apply; in order to recover, she still must prove the other prerequisites for contract enforcement, including agreement and consideration.[53] (I hope you don't mind that I keep making this crucial point.)

Restatement (Second) of Contracts, section 129, sets forth an approach for contracts involving land that is both narrower and broader than Article 2's part performance doctrine (don't worry, I'll explain this):

> A contract for the transfer of an interest in land may be specifically enforced notwithstanding failure to comply with the Statute of Frauds if it is established that the party seeking enforcement, in reasonable reliance on the contract and on the continuing assent of the party against whom enforcement is sought, has so changed his position that injustice can be avoided only by specific enforcement.[54]

In cases involving money damages for the breach of an oral land-sale contract, courts have been reluctant to apply the part performance exception to the statute of frauds (meaning that the statute bars money damages even if the injured party has partially performed).[55] So, the treatment of the part-performance exception in land sale contracts is narrower than for sales of goods. On the other hand, the Restatement rule creates a broader exception when the action is for specific performance. The express language of Restatement (Second) section 129 authorizes specific performance of an oral land sale when the injured party has "change[d] * * * position" in reliance on the oral contract. A change of position is

---

52. See, e.g., Sedmak v. Charlie's Chevrolet, Inc., 622 S.W.2d 694, 699 (Mo. Ct. App. 1981) ("The present contract could not have contemplated less than one car. If the part payment is believed, it must have been intended to buy the entire car not a portion of the car. Thus, denying the contract because part payment cannot be apportioned encourages fraud rather than discouraging it.").

53. See Chapter 2.

54. See Hayward v. Morrison, 241 P.2d 888, 894 (Or. 1952) (Plaintiff performed "acts of part performance which were performed in strict accordance with the oral agreement and directly in reference thereto. In such circumstances it would result in gross injustice and be wholly inequitable and unconscionable to permit defendant ... to now take a

position completely at variance with her prior acts and conduct.").

55. Winternitz v. Summit Hills Joint Venture, 532 A.2d 1089, 1092 (Md. Ct. Spec. App. 1987), cert. denied, 538 A.2d 778 (Md. 1988) ("The law is clear and well established that 'part performance' is an equitable doctrine available only where the principal relief sought is specific performance of the oral agreement. It has no application in an action at law for money damages."); Trollope v. Koerner, 470 P.2d 91, 98 (Ariz. 1970) ("This court has squarely held that notwithstanding the procedural merger of law and equity, the equitable doctrine of part performance is inapplicable in a suit where only money damages are sought."); see also Restatement (Second) of Contracts § 129, cmt. c.

broader than part performance.[56] For example, part performance by a buyer would include paying all or part of the purchase price and taking possession of the land.[57] But a buyer also changes position, for example, when she makes improvements on the subject property with the seller's assent.[58] Obviously, the more of these acts the purchaser completes the better for avoiding the statute of frauds, because the real question is whether the purchaser's actions tend to show that the parties really made a contract.[59]

UCC section 2–201 sets forth several additional exceptions to the statute of frauds specific to the sale of goods. Section 2–201(2) applies to contracts between merchants. (To review, merchants "deal" in the kind of goods the contract concerns or represent to the public that they have "knowledge or skill peculiar to the practices or goods involved in the transaction* * *."[60]) Section 2–201(2) provides that when two merchants make an oral contract

56. Johnson Farms v. McEnroe, 568 N.W.2d 920, 923–24 (N.D. 1997), ("Only one of the typically recognized acts of part performance—payment of the contract price—is generally expressly mentioned as a requirement under a contract. The two other most common acts that qualify under the doctrine of part performance—taking possession of the property and making improvements—may occur because of the existence of the contract, but they are not acts that are literally required for performance of the contract.") (quoting 14 R. Powell and P. Rohan, Powell on Real Property, para.880[2][a] at 81–63); William Henry Brophy Coll. v. Tovar, 619 P.2d 19, 22 (Ariz. Ct. App. 1980) ("Whether this doctrine is labeled 'estoppel' or 'part performance' does not affect the ultimate result of its application, which is that a party may be precluded from asserting the Statute of Frauds as a defense when he has induced or permitted another to change his position to his detriment in reliance on an oral agreement which would be within the Statute.").

57. In re Madsen's Estate, 259 P.2d 595, 606 (Utah 1953) ("[Decedent] orally agreed to convey the property in dispute to the respondent corporation ... at which time the latter paid him the purchase price and went into possession. There being part performance of that oral contract, the executor of [decedent's] estate cannot plead the statute of frauds as a bar to the respondent's action.").

58. Seavey v. Drake, 62 N.H. 393, 394 (N.H. 1882) ("[E]quity protects a parol gift of land equally with a parol agreement to sell it, if accompanied by possession, and the donee has made valuable improvements upon the property induced by the promise to give it."); William Henry Brophy Coll., 619 P.2d at 23 ("[Lesees'] making of improvements of a value approaching that of five months' rent is inconsistent with a monthly tenancy and referable, as we see it, to a longer term. We therefore find as a matter of law that the uncontradicted evidence is sufficient to establish part performance of the alleged oral lease by appellees in reliance thereon, and that appellants are estopped from asserting its invalidity under the Statute of Frauds.").

59. Johnson Farms, 568 N.W.2d at 923 ("[T]hree major categories of acts by the purchaser that may make an oral contract enforceable: paying the contract price, taking possession of the property, and making improvements."); id. at 924 ("The most important question is whether the part 'performance' is consistent only with the existence of the alleged oral contract." (quoting Buettner v. Nostdahl, 204 N.W.2d 187, 195 (N.D. 1973); Breen v. Phelps, 439 A.2d 1066, 1074 (Conn. 1982) ("[T]he complaint before us ... states acts of part performance which a trier might reasonably conclude to be sufficient to remove the case from the operation of the statute of frauds.").

60. See UCC § 2–104(1); Chapter 3 at notes 146–147, and accompanying

and one of them sends a written confirmation that is sufficient to satisfy the statute of frauds against the sender, and the recipient "has reason" to know its contents, the writing is good against the recipient, even though she did not sign it. The recipient has an opportunity to reject the confirmation, if she acts quickly. If she notifies the sender in writing within ten days of receiving the confirmation that she objects to "its contents," then the statute of frauds still applies.[61] Under this "merchant" exception to the signature requirement, merchants cannot safely avoid contracts simply by refusing to sign anything. Merchants had better read their mail. In fact, a confirmation suffices under the section even if it contains no "explicit words of confirmation nor express references to the prior agreement * * *."[62]

Another exception to the writing requirement in cases involving sales of goods is the "specially manufactured goods exception."[63] Under UCC section 2–201(3)(a), a writing is not required when goods are to be "specially manufactured" so that they are suitable only for the buyer, and the seller has started producing the goods or has committed to obtain them in circumstances that "reasonably indicate that the goods are for the buyer."[64] Suppose I quit law teaching and become a full-time fiction writer (probably a bad idea). I pick up the telephone and order a $600 sign for my office that

text.

61. UCC § 2–201(2); see also Azevedo v. Minister, 471 P.2d 661, 665 (Nev. 1970) ("The custom arose among business people of confirming oral contracts by sending a letter of confirmation. This letter was binding as a memorandum on the sender, but not on the recipient, because he had not signed it. The abuse was that the recipient, not being bound, could perform or not, according to his whim and the market, whereas the seller had to perform. Obviously, under these circumstances, sending any confirming memorandum was a dangerous practice. Subsection (2) of section 2–201 of the Code cures the abuse by holding a recipient bound unless he communicates his objection within 10 days."); Howard Constr. Co. v. Jeff–Cole Quarries, Inc., 669 S.W.2d 221, 226 (Mo. Ct. App. 1983).

62. Azevedo, 471 P.2d 661, 665 ("'All that is required is that the writing afford a basis for believing that the offered oral evidence rests on a real transaction.'") (quoting Harry Rubin & Sons, Inc. v. Consolidated Pipe Co., 153 A.2d 472, 476 (Pa. 1959)); Howard Constr. Co., 669 S.W.2d at 227 ("[I]f it is more probable than not that the writing evidences a deal between the parties, then the writing should be found sufficient.").

63. UCC § 2–201(3)(a); see Webcor Packaging Corp. v. Autozone, Inc., 158 F.3d 354, 356 (6th Cir. 1998) ("[W]here a manufacturer produces special goods for a buyer, courts may permit evidence of the oral agreement at trial.").

64. Colorado Carpet Installation, Inc. v. Palermo, 668 P.2d 1384, 1389 (Colo. 1983) ("[F]our distinct criteria are necessary to satisfy the 'specially manufactured goods' exception to the statute of frauds: (1) the goods must be specially made for the buyer; (2) the goods must be unsuitable for sale to others in the ordinary course of the seller's business; (3) the seller must have substantially begun to have manufactured the goods or to have made a commitment for their procurement; and (4) the manufacture or commitment must have been commenced under circumstances reasonably indicating that the goods are for the buyer and prior to the seller's receipt of notification of contractual repudiation.").

says, "Bob Hillman's Writing Sanctuary." If the manufacturer has begun making the sign by carving my name on it, the statute of frauds will not bar the manufacturer's lawsuit against me if I repudiate the oral contract. All of the requisites of section 2–201(3) are satisfied. The goods are specially manufactured, are suitable only for me (remember the sign includes my name), and are already under production. The reason for section 2–201(3) should not be difficult to surmise: "The long-accepted justification for this statutory rule lies in the assurance that, by virtue of the unique nature of the goods, the manufacturer would not have produced such unique goods absent an agreement with the alleged buyer."[65]

Still another exception to the statute of frauds in sale-of-goods cases is section 2–201(3)(b). This section reverses the uncomfortable contradiction at common law that allowed a party to admit in a pleading or other court document or testimony in court that the parties made a contract, but still hide behind the statute of frauds. Now, if a party admits a contract in "his pleading, testimony or otherwise in court," the statute of frauds defense falls away.[66] (Amended section 2–201 substitutes "under oath" for "in court" to make it clear that depositions and the like taken outside of court constitute admissions under the section.)[67] What's more, the promisor doesn't have to break down on the stand and admit "I did it, I made the contract," such as in an old Perry Mason episode (hope you've seen a rerun). It is enough if the promisor admits facts sufficient to show that the parties made a contract.[68] (For example, "I said I'd deliver the piano because she said she would pay me

---

65. Webcor Packaging Corp., 158 F.3d at 356; see also Impossible Electronic Techniques, Inc. v. Wackenhut Protective Sys., Inc., 669 F.2d 1026, 1036–37 (5th Cir. 1982) ("The Statute exempts contracts involving 'specially manufactured' goods from the writing requirement because in these cases the very nature of the goods serves as a reliable indication that a contract was indeed formed.").

66. UCC § 2–201(3)(b); see also Powers v. Hastings, 582 P.2d 897, 901 (Wash. Ct. App. 1978) ("[W]e disagree with the trial court's conclusion that the statute of frauds would bar enforcement of the parties' agreement. Our decision is supported in the record, which reveals that defendants on *six* different occasions admitted the existence of the lease with option to purchase in *writing* or *in testifying in open court*."); Nebraska Builders Prods. Co. v. Industrial Erectors, Inc., 478 N.W.2d 257, 268 (Neb. 1992) ("The statutory requirement can be satisfied by way of pleadings, bills of particulars, depositions, affidavits, admissions pursuant to notices to admit, and oral testimony, including admissions made on cross-examination.").

67. Amended UCC § 2–201, preliminary cmt.7.

68. Nelson v. Brostoff, 689 P.2d 1056, 1060 (Or. Ct. App. 1984) ("[O]nce the party asserting the statute admits facts from which the existence of *a contract* can be inferred, the statute ceases to be a defense and proof can be offered to show that an agreement containing the statutory elements was reached."); see also Nebraska Builders Prods. Co., 478 N.W.2d at 268 ("We do not hereby hold that an admission is made whenever the defendant utters the magic words contract or agreement. We acknowledge the possibility that laypeople might misuse legal terminology.... [T]he court should look at the other evidence presented by the defendant.... [Defendants'] conduct indicates that an agreement between the parties existed.").

$2000.") In addition, some courts refuse to dismiss or grant summary judgment on statute of frauds grounds before a promisee has the opportunity to examine the promisor under oath.[69] One important limiting factor of section 2–201(3)(b) is that the admission exception applies only with respect to the "quantity of goods" admitted.[70] If you made an oral agreement to sell Alice two pianos for $800 each, and she admits that she agreed to buy one piano, you can enforce a contract for one piano.

What do all of these exceptions have in common? They all involve situations where, even though an agreement is oral, evidence shows that the parties in fact made a contract. After all, it is not likely that a party made improvements on land, or manufactured a sign stating "Bob Hillman's Writing Sanctuary," or admitted a contract in court, or partly performed, unless that party really made an agreement.

E.   Does Another Theory Apply?

In Chapter 3, we discussed theories for enforcing promises other than bargained-for exchange, including promissory estoppel and unjust enrichment. Suppose parties make an oral agreement, the subject matter comes under the statute of frauds, and no exception to the writing requirement applies. A party cannot recover for breach of this oral agreement, but can she recover under promissory estoppel or unjust enrichment? In short, the answer is yes. Courts have enforced oral promises under both theories.[71] For

---

69. M & W Farm Serv. Co. v. Callison, 285 N.W.2d 271, 275 (Iowa 1979) ("[T]he party resisting the Statute should be given the opportunity to prove the alleged contract in two statutorily recognized ways: by the opposing party's failure to deny the existence of the contract in its responsive pleading and by the opposing party's emitting oral evidence of the contract.").

70. UCC § 2–201(3)(b).

71. On promissory estoppel, see, e.g., Alaska Democratic Party v. Rice, 934 P.2d 1313, 1316 (Alaska 1997) ("[A] promise which the promisor should reasonably expect to induce action or forbearance on the part of the promisee or a third person and which does induce the action or forbearance is enforceable notwithstanding the Statute of Frauds if injustice can be avoided only by enforcement of the promise....") (citing Restatement (Second) of Contracts § 139); McIntosh v. Murphy, 469 P.2d 177, 180–81 (Haw. 1970) ("The doctrine of estoppel to assert the statute of frauds has

been consistently applied by the courts of this state to prevent fraud that would result from refusal to enforce oral contracts in certain circumstances. Such fraud may inhere in the unconscionable injury that would result from denying enforcement of the contract after one party has been induced by the other seriously to change his position in reliance on the contract....") (quoting Monarco v. Lo Greco, 220 P.2d 737, 739 (Cal. 1950)).

On unjust enrichment, see Tenzer v. Superscope, Inc., 702 P.2d 212, 217 (Cal. 1985) ("[Defendant] has received the benefit of [plaintiff's] performance but relies upon the statute of frauds to avoid paying the agreed-upon price. [T]hese allegations suggest a case of unjust enrichment.... In such cases, the doctrine of estoppel to assert the statute of frauds may be applied in the interests of fairness."); Gay v. Mooney, 50 A. 596, 597 (N.J. 1901), aff'd per curiam, 52 A. 1131 (N.J. 1902) ("The bargain thus exhibited is not one on which an

example, a prospective employee, Taylor Plantations, leaves his job in California and travels to Detroit, relying on Ford Motor Company's oral promise of a two-year job. A landowner, Alice Williams, orally promises to convey land to Marvin Green's daughter in exchange for room and board at Marvin's home, which Marvin supplies for ten years. These exchanges would be enforceable as contracts only if they were in writing or an exception applied.[72] Nevertheless, courts have enforced them on the basis of promissory estoppel and unjust enrichment respectively.[73] Courts also have also enforced oral promises for the sale of goods after a party relies, even though UCC section 2–201 lists a series of exceptions that does not include promissory estoppel.[74] (Current section 2–201 includes a preamble stating that "[e]xcept as otherwise provided in this section," a sales contract requires a writing, suggesting that exceptions not listed in the section, such as promissory estoppel, do not constitute exceptions.[75] But courts sometimes apply promissory estoppel notwithstanding the preamble,[76] and amended section 2–201 omits the preamble, thereby inviting a greater use of promissory estoppel.[77])

If we assume that the parties in the above examples really made the agreements described, enforcing the promises on the basis of alternative theories relieves the apparent injustice of the statute of frauds. Further, a promisee's reliance on an oral promise or conferral of a benefit tends to show that the promise was genuine. However, critics charge that the use of alternative theories to circumvent the writing requirement contradicts the policies behind the statute of frauds, which was designed to prevent fraud.[78] For

---

action at law could be maintained, because it related to land, and was not susceptible of such proof as the statute of frauds requires; but when, in pursuance of a bargain, for this reason unenforceable, services have been rendered, the legal remedy is by an action on the *quantum meruit* for the value of the services.").

72. See supra notes 20–26, and accompanying text.

73. See supra note 71.

74. Warder & Lee Elevator, Inc. v. Britten, 274 N.W.2d 339, 342 (Iowa 1979) ("We have long recognized promissory estoppel as a means of defeating the general statute of frauds.... We see nothing in [state law] which purports to require a different rule under the Uniform Commercial Code.").

75. UCC § 2–201(1).

76. Warder & Lee Elevator, 274 N.W.2d at 341 ("Under this statute an oral contract for the sale of goods for a price of $500 or more is unenforceable, with certain stated exceptions. [Plaintiff] does not contend any of those exceptions is applicable. Promissory estoppel is not among them.... However, other courts which have considered the question have held the doctrine is available.").

77. Amended UCC § 2–201.

78. See Philo Smith & Co. v. US-LIFE Corp., 554 F.2d 34, 36 (2d Cir. 1977) ("The strongly held public policy reflected in New York's Statute of Frauds would be severely undermined if a party could be estopped from asserting it every time a court found that some unfairness would otherwise result."); McIntosh v. Murphy, 469 P.2d 177, 182 (Haw. 1970) (Abe, J. dissenting) ("I cannot agree, as intimated by this court, that we should circumvent the Statute of Frauds by the exercise of the equity

example, suppose Taylor Plantations made up Ford's promise of employment after traveling to Detroit to look for work. In addition, critics point out that a party may have to prove the existence of an oral agreement (something the statute of frauds is supposed to bar) in order to sustain a claim of promissory estoppel or unjust enrichment.[79] For example, unless Marvin can show that he and Alice agreed to an exchange of room and board for the conveyance to Marvin's daughter, a court may find that the benefit Marvin conferred on Alice was a gift.

Those concerned about using unjust enrichment or promissory estoppel to enforce oral promises that are unenforceable under the statute of frauds should note that courts may limit the remedies under the latter theories. For example, the remedy for breach of Taylor's employment contract would be Taylor's expected salary minus what he reasonably could make in a substitute job.[80] Under promissory estoppel, however, Taylor might recover only the costs incurred in his travel to Detroit and lost wages on his old job.[81] You will learn much more about remedial differences between claims based on breach of contract and those based on other theories in the next chapter.

---

powers of courts.... Thus, if the Statute of Frauds is too harsh as intimated by this court, and it brings about undue hardship, it is for the legislature to amend or repeal the statute and not for this court to legislate.").

79. Joseph M. Perillo, Restitution in a Contractual Context, 73 Colum. L. Rev. 1208 (1973).

80. See Chapter 5 at notes 109–132, and accompanying text.

81. See Chapter 5 at notes 322–339, and accompanying text; see also Jarboe v. Landmark Cmty. Newspapers, 644 N.E.2d 118, 122 (Ind. 1994) ("The doctrine of promissory estoppel may be available to an at-will employee, but the remedy is limited to damages actually resulting from the detrimental reliance and will not include the benefit of altering the employment....").

*

Chapter Five

REMEDIES

Chapter Five covers the remedies available to a contracting party who is entitled to recover for breach of contract, promissory estoppel, or unjust enrichment. We "in the know" call the party entitled to recover the "injured" party. First, we discuss several possible remedies for the injured party for breach of contract. The most common remedy, called "expectancy damages," seeks to give the injured party the money equivalent of what she expected from the contract so that she is in as good a position as if her contracting partner had not breached.[1] Another remedy for breach of contract is "reliance damages," which seeks to put the injured party in the position she was in before making the contract.[2] This remedy is different from expectancy damages because the injured party does not recover the value of the broken promise. A third remedy for breach of contract is "liquidated damages," which is the measure of damages contractually agreed to by the parties in case of breach.[3] We also discuss contract law's treatment of emotional distress damages and punitive damages for breach of contract.

We follow up all of these measures of *damages* for breach of contract with a discussion of two additional remedies for breach of contract. First, we look at a remedy called "restitution," which gives the injured party an amount of money measured by the benefit the injured party conferred on the contract breaker.[4] Second, we study "specific performance," in which a court orders the breaching party to perform the contract.[5]

We then turn to remedies for an injured party based on the theories of promissory estoppel and unjust enrichment. Remedies for promissory estoppel include damages measured by the value of

---

1. Restatement (Second) of Contracts § 344 (1981) (" '[E]xpectation interest' [is the] interest in having the benefit of [the] bargain by being put in as good a position as [the plaintiff] would have been in had the contract been performed....").

2. Id. (" '[R]eliance interest' [is the] interest in being reimbursed for loss caused by reliance on the contract by being put in as good a position as [the plaintiff] would have been in had the contract not been made....").

3. Black's Law Dictionary 395 (7th ed. 1999) ("An amount contractually stipulated as a reasonable estimation of actual damages to be recovered by one party if the other party breaches.").

4. Restatement (Second) of Contracts § 344 (" '[R]estitution interest' [is the] interest in having restored to [the plaintiff] any benefit that he has conferred on the other party.").

5. See, e.g., Curtice Bros. Co. v. Catts, 66 A. 935 (N.J. Eq. 1907).

the injured party's detrimental reliance or damages measured by the value of the promise.[6] The remedial goal in unjust enrichment cases is the same as in cases where an injured party elects restitution for breach of contract, namely to give the claimant a money remedy based on the benefit the injured party conferred on the other party.[7]

This little roadmap will not mean very much until you read and study what follows. So what are you waiting for?

A. Remedies for Breach of Contract

1. Expectancy damages—Introduction. You will find many references in judicial decisions, treatises, and law reviews to the remedial goal in cases of breach of contract (in fact, you already have seen several references to this goal right here in this valuable book[8]): The purpose of awarding damages is to compensate the injured party so that she is in the position she would have been in if the breaching party had performed the contract.[9] In short the injured party gets the monetary equivalent of what she expected (hence "expectancy damages") under the contract. She doesn't get more than her expectancy. For example, she cannot recover punitive damages, because contract law's goal is to compensate the injured party, not to punish the breaching party.[10] Nor, in theory, does the injured party get any less than her expectancy (although we will see that there are lots of limitations on the expectancy recovery so that injured parties rarely, in fact, receive the full money equivalent of what they expected).[11]

---

6. Goldstick v. ICM Realty, 788 F.2d 456, 464 (7th Cir. 1986) ("[T]he value of the promise is the presumptive measure of damages for promissory estoppel...."); Jarboe v. Landmark Cmty. Newspapers of Indiana, Inc., 644 N.E.2d 118, 122 (Ind. 1994) ("[T]he remedy [for promissory estoppel] is limited to damages actually resulting from the detrimental reliance....").

7. Ramsey v. Ellis, 484 N.W.2d 331, 333 (Wis. 1992) ([D]amages in an unjust enrichment claim are measured by the benefit conferred upon the defendant....).

8. See, e.g., supra note 1, and accompanying text.

9. See, e.g., P.C. Data Ctrs. of Pa., Inc. v. Federal Express Corp., 113 F.Supp.2d 709, 715 (M.D. Pa. 2000) ("[T]he purpose of awarding damages in breach of contract actions is to compen-

sate for damages actually incurred by placing the plaintiff in the position he would have occupied had the contract been fulfilled in accordance with its terms...."); Guard v. P & R Enter., Inc., 631 P.2d 1068, 1071 (Alaska 1981) ("The purpose of awarding damages for a breach of contract is to put the injured party in as good a position as that party would have been had the contract been fully performed.").

10. Hirst v. St. Paul Fire & Marine Ins. Co., 683 P.2d 440, 447 (Idaho Ct. App. 1984) ("[T]he purpose of awarding damages for breach of contract is to fully recompense the non-breaching party for its losses sustained because of the breach, not to punish the breaching party."); See infra notes 278–287, and accompanying text.

11. Robert A. Hillman, Contract Lore, 27 J. Corp. L. 505 (2002).

An example should clarify the idea of expectancy damages. Suppose you make an enforceable contract to sell your piano to your neighbor, Alice, for $1200, when the market value of the piano is $1400. You break your contract before you deliver the piano and before Alice has paid you anything. Alice's expectancy damages are $200, the difference between the market value of the piano and the contract price. If you had performed your contract, Alice's net worth would have increased by $200—she would have parted with $1200 to acquire an asset worth $1400. She can use the $1200 she would have paid you, plus the $200 in damages, to purchase an equivalent piano on the market for $1400. Alice is in as good a position as if you had not breached the contract. Expectancy damages measured by the market price-contract price differential are often called *general damages*.[12] (This example is a sale of goods, so Article 2 of the UCC would apply. We will see that under the UCC the result would be the same.)[13]

You are probably already worrying about several complications. For example, you may be concerned about whether contract law compensates Alice for her time and effort in finding and purchasing another piano. And suppose Alice is a piano teacher and loses income during the time she has no piano due to your breach. Contract law must compensate Alice for all of this harm in order to put her in as good a position as if you had not breached. Recoveries of this nature are the *consequential damages* component of expectancy damages, and much more about them in due time.[14]

Why should injured parties in breach of contract situations receive expectancy damages? Most writers explain the expectancy goal as the best method for encouraging people to make and rely on their contracts, which benefits them and society.[15] For example, parties can rely on their contracts, assured that they will receive either performance or the equivalent in compensation for non-performance.[16] A damages measure any lower than lost expectancy would undermine people's confidence in their contracts, and a measure larger than expectancy would discourage them from making contracts because they would be wary of the extent of their liability for breach.[17]

---

12. Dan B. Dobbs, Law of Remedies 752 (2d ed. 1993) ("Expectancy damages are sometimes measured by 'general damages' or market measures. Such measures use the market value of the very thing promised, at the time of performance, as a basis for calculation.").

13. See infra notes 173–176, and accompanying text.

14. See infra notes 60–63, and accompanying text.

15. See Hillman, supra note 11, at 506.

16. See L.L. Fuller & William R. Perdue, Jr., The Reliance Interest in Contract Damages, 46 Yale L.J. 52, 62 (1936) (explaining that "[t]o encourage reliance we must ... dispense with its proof.").

17. E.I. DuPont de Nemours and Co. v. Pressman, 679 A.2d 436, 446 (Del. 1996) ("Punitive damages would increase the amount of damages in excess of the promisee's expectation interest and lead to inefficient results.") (citing 3 E. Allan Farnsworth, Farnsworth on Contracts 155–56 (1990)); see also E.

Lawyers interested in economics offer another rationale for awarding expectancy damages. (Please continue to read even if you hated economics in college.) According to the "theory of efficient breach," expectancy damages correctly *encourage* a party to breach when the breach is *efficient,* in that the breach makes some parties better off without making anyone worse off.[18] On the other hand, expectancy damages dissuade a party from breaching when a breach would cause more losses than gains.[19] Suppose, for example, you agree to sell your piano to Alice for $1200. As above, the piano is worth $1400. But, alas, you have more than one neighbor in this example. Another neighbor, Bob, offers to buy the piano from you for $1800. According to the lawyer-economists, expectancy damages allow, even encourage, you to break your contract with Alice, to pay her $200 (her expectancy damages measured by the market price-contract differential), and to deliver the piano to Bob, who outbid Alice for the piano. You gain enough from selling to Bob instead of Alice ($600) so that you can pay Alice her expectancy damages and still come out $400 ahead.[20] Bob, who bid the highest for the piano is also better off because he valued the piano more than the $1800 he paid (otherwise he would not have made the deal). Alice is no worse off because she recovers her $200 expectancy. Everybody is happy. What a wonderful world.

Lawyer-economists point out that awarding damages greater than an injured party's lost expectancy would be undesirable because it would discourage breach when breach would be efficient.[21] Suppose, for example, that Alice could recover $200 lost expectancy damages and $600 punitive damages. You would not breach because it would not be profitable for you, even though we have just demonstrated that, without the punitive damages liability, breaching would make you and Bob better off and no one worse off (hence

Allan Farnsworth, Contracts 763 (3d ed. 1999) (noting that the ban on punitive damages preserves efficient breaches).

18. Giampapa v. American Family Mut. Ins. Co., 64 P.3d 230, 251 (Colo. 2003) ("'The theory of 'efficient breach' posits that the purpose of contract law is not to discourage all breaches. To the contrary, certain breaches, such as those where the breaching party's gains exceed the injured party's losses, are thought to be desirable. When such a situation arises, the measure of damages under contract law—the expectancy interest—provides an incentive to encourage the breach.") (Bender, J. concurring).

19. Richard A. Posner, Economic Analysis of Law 120 (6th. ed. 2003) ("[I]n some cases a party would be tempted to break his contract simply because his profit from breach would exceed his profit from completion of the contract. If it would also exceed the expected profit to the other party from completion of the contract, and if damages are limited to the loss of that expected profit, there will be an incentive to commit a breach.").

20. See, e.g., Robert A. Hillman, The Richness of Contract Law 217–19 (1997).

21. But see William S. Dodge, The Case for Punitive Damages in Contracts, 48 Duke L.J. 629, 663 (1999) ("Allowing a party to breach a contract and pay damages is not as efficient as forcing that party, with the threat of punitive damages, to negotiate with the other party for a release from the contract.").

a breach would be efficient). Awarding damages any lower than expectancy also would be undesirable because you would have the incentive to breach even when your gain from doing so would be less than Alice's real loss.[22]

Please understand that this introduction to expectancy damages (and efficient breach) requires lots of elaboration (to come). For example, the efficient breach idea is controversial and we will introduce many counter arguments.[23] Further, lots of damages rules often limit the recovery of injured parties to well below lost expectancy. For example, contracting parties usually must pay their own lawyers and can rarely recover prejudgment interest.[24] These costs of litigation apply across most areas of the law.[25] Further, contract law denies injured parties damages that were not reasonably foreseeable or not proven with certainty, even though such damages may be real and large.[26] In addition, courts rarely award certain kinds of damages, such as emotional distress damages and sentimental losses.[27]

Such limitations on expectancy damages make sense. For example, we will see that contract law bars the recovery of unforeseeable consequential damages in part to encourage parties to disclose potential losses at the time of contracting.[28] (I can't resist giving you a brief explanation of this point right here. Before making the piano contract, Alice has the incentive to disclose to you that she is a piano teacher and will lose profits if you fail to deliver the piano because, if she doesn't disclose, she cannot recover the lost profits if you breach.) In addition, contract law awards only provable damages to encourage parties to enter contracts in the first place.[29]

---

22. Id. at 664 ("If the breaching party is not responsible for the non-breaching party's full losses, then there is an incentive to breach even when the breach would not be efficient.").

23. See infra notes 256–261, and accompanying text. For a discussion of various criticisms of the efficient breach theory, see Hillman, supra note 20, at 220–24.

24. See, e.g., Robert S. Summers & Robert A. Hillman, Contract and Related Obligation: Theory, Doctrine, and Practice 278–79 (4th ed. 2001).

25. See Deborah L. Rhode, Legal Scholarship, 115 Harv. L. Rev. 1327, 1350 (2002) ("Studies of medical malpractice, unsafe products, and auto and airline accidents consistently find that most victims do not recover the majority of their costs.").

26. See infra notes 89–97; 133–165, and accompanying text.

27. See infra notes 265–277, and accompanying text; see also John A. Sebert, Jr., Punitive and Nonpecuniary Damages in Actions Based Upon Contract: Toward Achieving the Objective of Full Compensation, 33 U.C.L.A. L. Rev. 1565, 1568 (1986) ("[C]ontract plaintiffs normally may recover for emotional distress only infrequently and in narrowly restricted circumstances.").

28. See Ian Ayres & Robert Gertner, Filling Gaps in Incomplete Contracts: An Economic Theory of Default Rules, 99 Yale L. J. 87, 101 (1989) (arguing that the unforeseeable damages rule promotes overall efficiency by inducing the more informed party to reveal pertinent information to the other party).

29. Joseph M. Perillo, Misreading Oliver Wendell Holmes on Efficient Breach and Tortious Interference, 68 Fordham L. Rev. 1085, 1096 (2000) ("[The Hadley v. Baxendale foreseeabil-

(Would you want to enter the contract to sell your piano to Alice if you thought your liability would not be limited to damages she could prove with sufficient certainty?) You can see that the study of expectancy damages involves understanding the policies in favor of these damages and the counter-policies that sometimes restrict recoveries to less than expectancy.

2. Methods of measuring expectancy damages. It is easy to say that the goal of contract damages is to put the injured party in as good a position as she would have been in had there been no breach. Actually achieving this goal is another story.

One fundamental question is whether a party's lost expectancy under a contract should be measured objectively, based on the market value of the promised performance "to some hypothetical reasonable person,"[30] or subjectively, based on the value of performance "to the injured party himself" in light of the party's "particular circumstances."[31] For example, you promise to sell a piece of your land to a developer. The developer promises to build a wall to divide your remaining land from the development. Although you realize that the wall will actually decrease the market value of your remaining land, you are peculiarly adverse to development and wish not to see it from your land. The developer breaks its promise to build the wall. The cost of getting someone else to build the wall is $3000, but the wall actually will diminish the value of your remaining land by $1000. In other words, you are better off on your balance sheet *without* the wall. Should you recover $3000, the value of performance to you in light of your circumstances and proclivities or should you get nothing and be thankful that you saved $1000 on your balance sheet?

So as to not keep you in suspense, some courts would award you the $3000.[32] Such decisions theorize that contract law should measure lost expectancy based on the injured party's subjective perspective.[33] Notice, however, that I said that "some" courts would do so. The issue is, in fact, controversial and a number of important cases have wrestled with it.

The opinion in *Groves v. John Wunder Co.*,[34] includes forceful majority and dissent discussions of how to measure lost expectancy. Wunder leased a piece of Groves' land in order to excavate gravel. Wunder promised in the lease to "leave the property 'at a uniform grade, substantially the same as the grade now existing at the

---

ity requirement] encourages contract-making").

30. Restatement (Second) of Contracts § 347, cmt. b.

31. Id.

32. E.g., Radford v. De Froberville, 1 All Eng. Rep. 33 (Ch. 1977).

33. Id. at 34.

34. 286 N.W. 235 (Minn. 1939).

roadway * * *.' "[35] At the end of the lease, Wunder returned the land without honoring the promise to restore it to a uniform grade. The cost of restoration would have been more than $60,000, but restoration would only have increased the value of land by a little more than $12,000.[36] The case presents the issue of whether Groves' expectancy damages should be measured by the actual cost of restoration or by how much restoration would increase the value of the land.

The majority opinion held that Groves was entitled to the cost of restoration ($60,000), provided that the contract actually required Wunder to remove gravel from the premises in order to restore the grade, which, apparently, constituted a large part of the expense.[37] The dissent, however, would have awarded $12,000 damages, on the theory that Groves suffered only a $12,000 loss in the value of the land as the result of the breach.[38] Who is right?

Both the majority and dissent agreed that Groves was entitled to expectancy damages and that two methods of measuring those damages existed. They strongly disagreed, however, on the correct measurement under the facts of the case. For example, the majority volunteered that Wunder's breach was "deliberate" and "wilful."[39] A court positing whether to award a larger or smaller measure of damages naturally would be inclined to require a "nasty" contract breaker to pay the larger amount. But the dissent observed that there was no "finding that the contractor 'wilfully and fraudulently' violated the terms of its contract."[40]

You have learned that the goal of contract remedies is to make the injured party whole, not to punish contract breakers,[41] so different perspectives concerning the motives of Wunder in breaking the contract cannot be all that separated the majority and dissent. In fact, more important was the majority's and dissent's different views of the probable intentions of Groves after Wunder returned the land. The majority appears to have opted for cost-of-restoration damages because they believed that Groves would keep the land and that its condition was important to Groves. The majority likened Groves' position to a property owner who contracted for a foolish monument on his property that will actually diminish the value of his land: " 'A man may do what he will with his own, * * * and if he chooses to erect a monument to his caprice or folly on his premises, and employs and pays another to do it, it

---

35. Id. at 235.

36. Id. at 236.

37. Id. at 238–39.

38. Id. at 241 (Olson, J., dissenting).

39. Id. at 236.

40. Id. at 239. (Olson, J., dissenting).

41. Highland Inns Corp. v. American Landmark Corp., 650 S.W.2d 667, 674 (Mo. Ct. App. 1983) ("The essential objective of a contract remedy is to compensate, not punish. . . .").

does not lie with a defendant who has been so employed and paid for building it, to say that his own performance would not be beneficial to the plaintiff.' "[42] The majority's position was that Groves may be objectively irrational to have contracted for restoration (a $60,000 investment for a $12,000 return), but a landowner ought to have the right to do what it wants with its land.

The dissent argued, however, that the parties contemplated "put[ting] the property in shape for general sale"[43] and that nothing supported the view that Groves wanted the property for a "unique or personal use."[44] Further, the property was not special because of its location or because of a future contemplated use.[45] In short, according to the dissent, restoration of the land was not important to Groves, and was only an incidental term of the contract. The dissent therefore concluded that, although Groves could have contracted for a foolish monument, and would then have been entitled to the cost of restoration, "that is not what [Groves] contracted for."[46] Implicit in the dissent's opinion is the concern that if Groves were awarded $60,000, Groves would pocket the money and receive a windfall instead of investing the money to restore the land.[47]

Whether the majority or dissent is correct about the appropriate measurement of Groves' lost expectancy thus depends on who is right on the facts. If Groves wanted the land restored so that it could enjoy its beauty, Groves should get $60,000. If Groves was simply going to sell the land, which would be worth only $12,000 once restored, Groves should recover only $12,000. The majority thought that Groves was more like the former than the latter, whereas the dissent thought the opposite.

One aspect of the case that went unexplored by both the majority and dissent that would have shed light on Groves' motives, is the nature of the parties' bargaining over the restoration clause at the time of contracting. Did Groves insist on the clause or was it part of a standard form that the parties ignored? If the former, did Groves reveal why it wanted the clause? Did Groves actually *pay* for the restoration clause, for example, by discounting the price of renting the land, so that Wunder would agree to restore it?

Let's illustrate the latter point. Wunder paid $105,000 for the lease.[48] Suppose the fair rental value of the land was $165,000, but that Groves discounted the price because Wunder promised to restore the land, which the parties calculated to cost $60,000.

---

42. Groves, 286 N.W. at 237 (quoting Chamberlain v. Parker, 45 N.Y. 569, 572 (N.Y. 1871)).

43. Id. at 241 (Olson, J., dissenting).

44. Id.

45. Id.

46. Id. at 244.

47. Id. at 244–45.

48. Groves, 286 N.W. at 235.

Under these facts, restoration must have been important to Groves (after all, he gave up $60,000 in rent for it). Groves' lost expectancy would therefore be $60,000. Neither the majority nor dissent discussed this issue, perhaps suggesting that the parties did not calculate the cost of restoration at the time of contracting.

In *Peevyhouse v. Garland Coal & Mining Co.*,[49] often a companion case to *Groves* in the casebooks, the Peevyhouses brought an action against Garland Coal for failing to restore the Peevyhouses' land after strip mining, as promised by Garland Coal. The cost of restoration was about $29,000, but restoration would increase the value of the land by only about $300. The majority focused on the huge discrepancy between these amounts and denied the Peevyhouses cost-of-restoration damages. The court reversed a jury verdict of $5000 and awarded $300.[50]

Based on our discussion above in *Groves,* however, the Peevyhouses may have been shafted (this is a great pun if strip mining creates shafts). The dissent pointed out that the Peevyhouses "insisted that the * * * [restorative and remedial] provision be included in the contract and that they would not agree to the coal mining lease unless the above provision were included."[51] So the Peevyhouses should have recovered $29,000 because the restoration provision was important to them. At minimum, the majority should have affirmed the jury's award of $5000 because this measure appeared to constitute a compromise between the cost of restoration and the diminution in value. Alternatively, perhaps the jury thought that the Peevyhouses gave Garland Coal a $5000 discount on the lease because the parties thought that was the cost of restoration. Unanticipated circumstances after the parties signed their contract may have driven up the cost of restoration.[52]

The *Peevyhouse* case, decided by the Oklahoma Supreme Court, was cast into doubt by *Rock Island Improvement Company v. Helmerich & Payne, Inc.*,[53] a federal court case applying Oklahoma law. In still another instance where the cost of land restoration was hugely disproportionate to the increase in land value by restoration, the court applied the cost-of-restoration measure.[54] The wrinkle was that by the time the court decided the case, the Oklahoma legislature had adopted a statute declaring that land conservation was the

---

49. 382 P.2d 109 (Okla. 1962).

50. Id. at 114.

51. Id. at 115; see also Judith L. Maute, Peevyhouse v. Garland Coal & Mining Co. Revised: the Ballad of Willie and Lucille, 89 Nw. U. L. Rev. 1341 (1995).

52. See Melvin Aron Eisenberg, The Responsive Model of Contract Law,

36 Stan. L. Rev. 1107, 1163–64 (1984) ("[I]n many cases the disparity between cost of completion and diminished market value results in large part from circumstances that were not anticipated when the contract was made.").

53. 698 F.2d 1075 (10th Cir. 1983).

54. Id. at 1061.

policy of the state and requiring the miner to restore the land regardless of the cost.[55] The *Rock Island* decision included this telling passage:

> When the parties negotiated the contract in question, they expressly included a reclamation clause and required the lessee to bear the cost of reclamation. Given the attention focused by Oklahoma on the importance of reclaiming stripmined lands, it is more logical to assume that the parties meant what they said, calculated their costs and benefits under the contract accordingly, and intended the provision to insure proper reclamation of the land, than it is to assume that they expected the reclamation clause to have no force.[56]

In Oklahoma, the state policy created a strong presumption that the contract right of landowners to reclamation was not merely incidental to the contract, but an important, bargained-for term. Although the cost of the restoration was grossly disproportionate to the increase in value of the land, the landowner was therefore entitled to the cost of restoration.[57]

3. Expectancy damages—general damages and consequential damages. An injured party's lost expectancy consists of two basic components. First, certain damages, sometimes called "general damages," arise "naturally" or "ordinarily"[58] from a breach, meaning that every injured party under the circumstances suffers these damages. When you contract to sell your piano, worth $800, to Alice for $1000, you will suffer $200 damages if she repudiates the contract before either party performs. You were going to sell an asset worth $800 for $1000, so your balance sheet would improve by $200 if Alice performed the contract. In fact, every seller who has a contract to sell an item worth $800 for $1000 would lose $200 by a breach.[59] Your $200 damages are therefore often denominated general damages.

"Special," also called "consequential" damages arise because of an injured party's particular circumstances.[60] Suppose you reasonably incur extra storage expenses after Alice refuses to take the piano. To make you whole, contract law must award you not only the contract price-market price differential, but also compensation for these expenses. But, of course, not all piano sellers would incur such costs, so they are called special or consequential damages.

---

55. Id. at 1078.

56. Id. at 1079.

57. Id. at 1080.

58. Hadley v. Baxendale, 156 Eng. Rep. 145, 151 (Ex. 1854).

59. UCC § 2–708(1) (1996).

60. Roanoke Hosp. Ass'n. v. Doyle & Russell, Inc., 214 S.E.2d 155, 160 (Va. 1975) ("Consequential damages are those which arise from the intervention of 'special circumstances' not ordinarily predictable.").

The distinction between general and consequential damages sometimes is blurred and confusing,[61] but, when clear, the distinction often helps clarify what the injured party must show in order to recover damages. For example, we will see that an injured party claiming consequential damages faces certain proof hurdles, such as showing that the damages were reasonably foreseeable to the breaching party at the time of contracting,[62] and not too speculative.[63] Contract law establishes these and other hurdles to the recovery of consequential damages because, by definition, not all injured parties suffer them. In the discussion that follows, we therefore will refer to general and consequential damages where appropriate.

4. Expectancy damages in various contexts. A helpful approach to the study of expectancy damages is to sample the expectancy damages awarded in various contexts. Here we consider construction contracts, employment and other service contracts, and sales of goods and land. Although the principles that emerge are not always unique to a particular context, after becoming familiar with how the principles operate in one context, you will be able to apply them to other types of contracts.

a. Construction contracts. First, let's consider construction cases. How much can a builder recover when the owner breaches a construction contract? How much can the owner recover when the builder breaches? Simple answer: Both can recover the money equivalent of their lost expectancies. Let's delve more deeply.

Injured builders: In order to put an injured builder in as good a position as if there had been no breach by the owner, contract law must give the builder the net profit it would have made on the contract and any amount already expended in furtherance of the project.[64] Suppose you repudiate a contract in which Ajax Construc-

---

61. Restatement (Second) of Contracts § 351, cmt. b ("These terms are often misleading, however, and it is not necessary to distinguish between 'general' and 'special' or 'consequential' damages for the purpose of the rule stated in this Section.").

62. Cancun Adventure Tours, Inc. v. Underwater Designer Co., 862 F.2d 1044, 1049 (4th Cir. 1988) ("To be recoverable, consequential damages must have been foreseen or reasonably foreseeable and the buyer must prove them with reasonable certainty.").

63. San Carlos Irrigation & Drainage Dist. v. United States, 111 F.3d 1557, 1563 (Fed. Cir. 1997) ("[C]ontract

law precludes recovery for speculative damages.").

64. Warner v. McLay, 103 A. 113, 113–14 (Conn. 1918) ("[T]he plaintiff ha[s] the right to recover such sum in damages as he would have realized in profits if the contract had been fully performed. To ascertain this, it [is] necessary to find the cost and expense of the work and materials necessary to complete the contract. This sum, deducted from the contract price, [gives] a balance which would have been the profit which would have accrued to the plaintiff out of the contract, if it had been fulfilled. This the plaintiff ha[s] a right to receive in addition to his expenditures for work

tion Company was going to build a house for you for $150,000 (sorry, these days that won't get you much). Ajax's total cost of building would have been $120,000, and you repudiated the contract before Ajax began performance. Ajax should recover $30,000—the amount of Ajax's net profit had it built the house. If you repudiated the contract after Ajax had already spent $50,000 of the cost of performance, Ajax should recover $30,000, the expected net profit, and $50,000, the amount Ajax expended before your repudiation. The $80,000 award takes Ajax from a minus $50,000 position after your repudiation to a plus $30,000 position, the position that Ajax would have been in had both parties performed the contract. Of course, if you had already made progress payments to Ajax, these would be subtracted from the recovery.[65]

The formula for an injured contractor can also be expressed in another way, namely contract price minus the cost of completion.[66] Ajax would have been paid $150,000 if there had been no breach. Now it can save $70,000 ($120,000 total cost minus $50,000 cost expended). So Ajax should recover the difference or $80,000 (again minus any progress payments you already made).

It is time to introduce an important limitation on lost expectancy recoveries that applies in all cases, variously called the mitigation principle, the duty to minimize damages, and the avoidable consequences principle.[67] This limitation is well-illustrated by injured builder situations. Suppose again that you repudiate after Ajax has already performed $50,000 of the work. Ajax ignores your repudiation and finishes the house, which costs an additional $70,000. Ajax then seeks $150,000, the contract price. Contract law doesn't reward Ajax's stubbornness, but will only award $80,000, as above.[68] The theory is that Ajax must act reasonably after a breach to minimize its loss. Ajax's unreasonableness, not your breach, caused the extra $70,000 loss to Ajax after your repudiation.[69] As

and labor supplied toward the completion of the contract.").

65. Williams v. Kerns, 265 S.E.2d 605, 609 (Ga. Ct. App. 1980) ("The basic component of damages recoverable by a contractor when a construction contract is wrongfully breached by the owner is the net profit to which the contractor would have been entitled had full performance of the contract been permitted.... [T]here must be deducted from the recovery those amounts received by the contractor from the owner as prepayment or progress payment.").

66. McGee Constr. Co. v. Neshobe Dev., Inc., 594 A.2d 415, 420 (Vt. 1991) ("[T]he proper measure of recovery is the contract price minus the cost of completion and other costs avoided.").

67. Davis v. First Interstate Bank, N.A., 765 P.2d 680, 681 (Idaho 1988) ("The duty to mitigate, also known as the doctrine of avoidable consequences, provides that a plaintiff who is injured by actionable conduct of the defendant, is ordinarily denied recovery for damages which could have been avoided by reasonable acts, including reasonable expenditures, after the actionable conduct has taken place.") (citing Dan B. Dobbs, Handbook on the Law of Remedies § 3.7, at 186 (1973)).

68. Rockingham County v. Luten Bridge Co., 35 F.2d 301 (4th Cir. 1929).

69. Clark v. Marsiglia, 1 Denio 317 (N.Y. Sup. Ct. 1845).

one early court put it: "the plaintiff had no right, by obstinately persisting in the work, to make the penalty upon the defendant greater than it would otherwise have been."[70] If Ajax finishes your job, it cannot collect damages for the portion completed after your repudiation.

In a great case illustrating the "mitigation" principle, Rockingham County hired Luten Bridge Company to build, you guessed it, a bridge.[71] However, the county decided not to build a road to and from the bridge and canceled the contract before Luten Bridge began construction. Luten Bridge built the bridge anyway "in the midst of the forest."[72] The court held that Luten Bridge "had no right * * * to pile up damages by proceeding with the erection of a useless bridge."[73] (Maybe this was the bridge that inspired Paul Simon to write "Bridge over Troubled Water.") The county was liable only for the damages Luten Bridge would have suffered had it stopped work at the time of the county's countermand.[74]

As we have said, the duty to mitigate damages requires an injured party to act reasonably after breach.[75] Occasions may arise where finishing work after a countermand *is* the most reasonable strategy for an injured party trying to minimize damages.[76] For example, a manufacturer of goods may act reasonably by completing the job after a repudiation if there is a rapidly rising market for the completed goods and the manufacturer can resell them for more than the contract price.[77] The same reasoning could apply to a developer who is selling lots and building upon them. However, it is difficult to see how an injured builder working on your land could avail itself of this principle.

The duty to mitigate damages also requires a builder who honors a repudiation to look for other work in order to minimize the loss.[78] If Ajax reasonably can make a net profit of $20,000 by constructing another building for a third party, a job Ajax can take

70. Id. at 318.

71. Rockingham County, 35 F.2d 301.

72. Id. at 307.

73. Id.

74. Id. at 308 ("The measure of plaintiff's damage, upon its appearing that notice was duly given not to build the bridge, is an amount sufficient to compensate plaintiff for labor and materials expended and expense incurred in the part performance of the contract, prior to its repudiation, plus the profit which would have been realized if it had been carried out in accordance with its terms.").

75. Schiavi Mobile Homes, Inc. v. Gironda, 463 A.2d 722, 724 (Me. 1983) ("[W]hen a contract is breached, the nonbreaching party has an affirmative duty to take reasonable steps to mitigate his damages.").

76. See Farnsworth, supra note 17, at 815–16.

77. See UCC § 2–704(2).

78. Complete Gen. Constr. Co. v. Ohio Dep't of Transp., 760 N.E.2d 364, 370 (Ohio 2002) ("[T]he contractor also has the duty to mitigate damages.... [I]f able, the contractor must take on other work to absorb the overhead allotted to the delayed project.").

only because your breach freed up time, contract law deducts the $20,000 from your damages liability. In the example above where you repudiated after Ajax had completed $50,000 of work, Ajax's recovery should be $60,000, consisting of $30,000 net profit, plus $50,000 costs expended, minus $20,000 made on the substitute job.

Now we introduce another damages principle nicely illustrated in the construction setting, which involves builders who "lose volume" as a result of a breach. Suppose Ajax is a large construction company that can satisfy all of the demand for construction in its area at any given time. (It can hire and lay off workers and rent machinery as needed.) Assume again that Ajax made a net profit of $20,000 on another job after your breach. Does this $20,000 decrease your $80,000 damages liability to Ajax, even when Ajax can do all of the construction jobs that people request? If Ajax has lost volume, because it could have done your job *and* the second job, the answer is a definitive no![79] The second job is not a *substitute* for your job and, if you had not breached, Ajax would have made a total of $50,000 net profit; $30,000 on your job and $20,000 on the second job. Contract law therefore ignores the $20,000 Ajax made on the second job to put it in as good a position as if you had not breached. Remember to apply this lost-volume idea only when an injured party can take on as many jobs as people request and, therefore, when any new jobs are not substitute jobs.[80]

A large construction company that can satisfy all of the demand for construction at any given time can still mitigate damages in the following situation. (This "wrinkle" drives people crazy, and not just law students, so pay attention.) Suppose you hired Ajax to build a house for you. Ajax retains a subcontractor, Acme Plumbing Company, to install all of the plumbing in the house. Acme is a large company that can perform all of the plumbing jobs it is hired to do at any given time. In short, Acme will lose volume if Ajax breaches. Ajax does breach; in fact, it stops all work on your house and thus breaches the contract with you too. You take over the general contracting yourself and hire Acme to do the same plumbing work it would have done as Ajax's subcontractor. Acme performs the work and you pay Acme the same amount Ajax would have paid it. Acme then sues Ajax for breach of contract and seeks lost profits as a lost-volume contractor. Can it recover?

---

79. Cf. R.E. Davis Chem. Corp. v. Diasonics, Inc., 826 F.2d 678, 683 n. 7 (7th Cir. 1987) ("[B]y definition, a lost volume seller cannot mitigate damages through resale. Resale does not reduce a lost volume seller's damages because the breach has still resulted in its losing one sale and a corresponding profit.").

80. See Restatement (Second) of Contracts § 350, cmt. d and § 347, cmt. f.

In a case with similar facts (only you weren't involved), *Olds v. Mapes–Reeves Construction, Co.*,[81] the court suggested that a subcontractor (Acme in the example) can recover lost profits from a general contractor (Ajax in the example) despite doing the same work for the landowner (you in the example).[82] The court reasoned in part that the subcontractor could have taken a completely different job, say doing plumbing work at the Watergate complex in D.C.[83] The profit made on that job would not have diminished the general contractor's damages liability because the subcontractor lost volume by virtue of the breach (the subcontractor could have done both jobs). So why should the subcontractor's work for the landowner be treated any differently?

This reasoning in *Olds* is faulty for at least two reasons. First, unlike the Watergate job, the subcontractor's job with the landowner is available only because of the general contractor's breach. The job for the landowner, in short, *is* a substitute job, whereas the Watergate job is not. As a substitute job, the subcontractor does not lose volume as the result of the breach (even though, in general, the subcontractor can do as many jobs as are available). The second reason the court's approach was inaccurate is that the subcontractor would never be in a position to take the Watergate job *instead* of the job with the owner precisely because the subcontractor is a lost-volume contractor. If Watergate offered the subcontractor a job and the landowner offered a job, the subcontractor reasonably should take both. In fact, if the subcontractor failed to take the landowner job, the subcontractor would not be acting reasonably to minimize its damages after the general contractor's breach.[84]

Injured landowners: Suppose Ajax breaches the contract to build your $150,000 home, instead of you. You hire another builder to do the same job for $160,000. This new contract is called a "cover" contract because it covers or substitutes for what Ajax was supposed to do. If Ajax had performed, you would have had the house for $150,000. Now you will get the same house for $160,000. You can recover $10,000. Of course, your substitute arrangement must be reasonable. You cannot hire a builder to build the same house for $160,000 if other builders reasonably were available who would have done the work for $150,000. Further, you cannot hire a builder to build a *better* house for $160,000 and still get the $10,000.[85] That would put you in a better position than if Ajax had performed. One exception to this last point: You might get the

---

81.   58 N.E. 478 (Mass. 1900).

82.   Id. at 479–80. Under the actual facts of *Olds*, the subcontractor performed the original and some extra work for the landowner. Id.

83.   Id. at 479.

84.   Schiavi Mobile Homes, Inc., 463 A.2d at 724 ("[W]hen a contract is breached, the nonbreaching party has an affirmative duty to take reasonable steps to mitigate his damages.").

85.   Thorne v. White, 103 A.2d 579 (D.C. Mun. Ct. App. 1954).

$10,000 if you contracted for the better house only because you reasonably could not find a builder willing to build the $150,000 house. In that case, you had no choice but to accept the more valuable house, which, contract law says, was "foisted" on you.[86]

Suppose, in the above example, Ajax had completed $10,000 of work before repudiating. You reasonably hire a substitute builder for $160,000. Do you still get the $10,000 difference between your cover and contract prices? Does this penalize the breaching builder who has done $10,000 of work? The answer is that you do get the $10,000 and the award does not penalize the builder. This is because the $160,000 price you paid to the substitute contractor takes into account the work Ajax did. Let's assume that Ajax's $10,000 of work reduced the cost of the substitute's construction by $10,000. Without Ajax's work, the substitute would have charged roughly $170,000. So Ajax's damages liability (cover minus contract price) would have been $20,000 without its work. With its work, Ajax owes you only $10,000. It therefore got full benefit for the work it did.[87]

The "hypos" keep coming. Suppose you hired Ajax to build a bed and breakfast for you. You tell Ajax about your plans. Ajax promises to complete the house by June 1, so that it will be ready during the busy summer months. Ajax delays completing the house until September 1 and you bring an action seeking lost profits for the summer months.

The lost profits you seek are a form of consequential damages, a topic introduced above.[88] As such, among other things, you must show both that the damages were reasonably foreseeable and that you can prove them with sufficient certainty.[89] The first of these hurdles is not a problem here because you told Ajax about your plans to open a bed and breakfast.[90] The second hurdle is more problematic. You are starting a new business and it will be very difficult for you to prove what your gross receipts and expenses would have been during the time you could not open your business

---

86. Cf. Handicapped Children's Educ. Bd. v. Lukaszewski, 332 N.W.2d 774 (Wis. 1983) (employment contract setting). For more on the "foisting" principle, see Chapter 3 at note 118, and accompanying text.

87. Morello v. J.H. Hogan, Inc., 468 A.2d 1248 (Conn. App. Ct. 1984).

88. See supra notes 58–63, and accompanying text.

89. Florafax Int'l, Inc. v. GTE Mkt. Res., Inc., 933 P.2d 282, 292 (Okla.

1997) ("[The] loss of future or anticipated profit—i.e. loss of expected monetary gain—is recoverable in a breach of contract action: 1) if the loss is within the contemplation of the parties at the time the contract was made, 2) if the loss flows directly or proximately from the breach . . . and 3) if the loss is capable of reasonably accurate measurement or estimate.").

90. See infra notes 133–165, and accompanying text for more difficult applications of the foreseeability hurdle.

because of Ajax's delay.[91] In short, your damages are very speculative and you probably cannot recover them.

Courts sometimes manipulate the "new business rule" (which bars a recovery of lost profits) and, for that matter, the general requirement of proving consequential damages with sufficient certainty. For example, a court that strongly believes that a breaching party actually caused a loss is more likely to relax the certainty requirement.[92] In addition, courts are more likely to award lost profits when a party willfully or negligently breaches than when the breach is innocent or common (such as a delay in a construction contract).[93] In fact, as a general matter, the certainty requirement seems on the wane. For example, an early case that denied lost profits required the injured party to prove damages with "reasonable certainty."[94] Later cases pronounce arguably more liberal standards, such as a "rational basis" for the computation.[95] Moreover, some courts largely reject the new business rule.[96]

All is not lost for you, incidentally, even if the new business rule bars your recovery of lost profits for your bed and breakfast. Most courts would still grant damages for the delay in construction measured by the lost rental value of your property (usually measuring the rental value of the improved property) on the theory that if the builder had not delayed, you could have rented the property as a bed and breakfast from the time the structure was due.[97]

Now suppose you hire Ajax to build an addition on your already existing bed and breakfast. Ajax breaches the contract and your

91. Evergreen Amusement Corp. v. Milstead, 112 A.2d 901 (Md. 1955).

92. Lakota Girl Scout Council, Inc. v. Havey Fund–Raising Mgmt., Inc., 519 F.2d 634, 643 (8th Cir. 1975) (" 'If the mind of the court is certain that profits would have been made if there had been no breach by the defendant, there will be a greater degree of liberality in allowing the jury to bring a verdict for the plaintiff, even though the amount of profits prevented is scarcely subject to proof at all.' ") (quoting 5 Arthur Linton Corbin, Corbin on Contracts, at 142–43 (1994)).

93. Compare Evergreen Amusement Corp., 112 A.2d 901 (delay by construction company) with Lakota Girl Scout Council, Inc., 519 F.2d 634 (fund raising company failed to reach expected goal).

94. Evergreen Amusement Corp., 112 A.2d at 904.

95. Lakota Girl Scout Council Inc., 519 F.2d at 640.

96. In re Merritt Logan, Inc., 901 F.2d 349, 357 (3d Cir. 1990) ("Recent cases have eroded the once generally accepted rule that lost profits damages for a new business were not recoverable.... The trend of the modern cases is plainly toward replacing the old rule of law with a rule of evidence—the unquestionable principle that damages for loss of profits must be proven with reasonable certainty and that the evidence must support that finding by the trier of fact."); Vickers v. Wichita State Univ., 518 P.2d 512 (Kan.1974).

97. Evergreen Amusement Corp., 112 A.2d at 904 ("[D]amages are recoverable for profits prevented by breach of contract 'only to the extent that the evidence affords a sufficient basis for estimating their amount in money with reasonable certainty', and that where the evidence does not afford a sufficient basis, 'damages may be measured by the rental value of the property.' ") (quoting Restatement (First) of Contracts § 331).

business loses good will. Good will is "the reputation that businesses have built over the course of time that is reflected by the return of customers to purchase goods and the attendant profits that accompanies such sales."[98] Claims for loss of good will or loss of reputation, for that matter, have not always been successful because of the difficulty of quantifying the loss.[99] Courts allow such a recovery only when there is "a reasonable basis from which to calculate damages."[100]

b. Employment and other services contracts. Now we take up an injured employer's expectancy damages after an employee breaks an employment contract and an injured employee's expectancy damages after a breach by the employer. In addition, we look at damages for breach of services contracts, which share many of the attributes of employment contracts.

Injured employers Recall that property owners typically hire a replacement builder after the original builder breaches a construction contract. Injured employers also usually hire a substitute. Not surprisingly, the employer's expectancy damages are the difference between the salary the employer must pay the new employee and the salary the employer would have paid the breaching employee.[101] The employer must hire a reasonable replacement, of course, meaning that the employer must "attempt to obtain equivalent services at the lowest possible cost."[102] If the only substitute employee available is more qualified than the breaching employee, contract law usually ignores any extra benefit the employer receives because the employer had no choice but to accept the benefit[103] (the "foisting" principle again[104]). For example, in *Handicapped Children's Education Bd. of Sheyboygan County v. Lukaszewski,*[105] after Lukaszewski broke her teaching contract with the Education Board, the court awarded the Education Board the full difference between the substitute teacher's salary and Lukaszewski's, even though the substitute teacher had more teaching experience than Lukaszewski. The court concluded that "[a]ny additional value the Board may have received from the replacement's greater experience was imposed upon it and thus cannot be characterized as a benefit."[106]

---

98. AM/PM Franchise Ass'n. v. Atlantic Richfield Co., 584 A.2d 915, 924 (Pa. 1990).

99. Stancil v. Mergenthaler Linotype Co., 589 F.Supp. 78, 84 (D. Haw. 1984); Quinn v. Straus Broadcasting Group, Inc., 309 F.Supp. 1208, 1209 (S.D.N.Y.1970).

100. AM/PM Franchise Ass'n., 584 A.2d at 926.

101. Handicapped Children's Educ. Bd., 332 N.W.2d 774.

102. Id. at 779.

103. Id.

104. See supra note 86, and accompanying text.

105. 332 N.W.2d 774 (Wis. 1983).

106. Id. at 779.

The reasoning of the court in *Handicapped Children's Education Bd.* should be familiar to any reader who has studied the material in Chapter 3 on the theory of unjust enrichment. Recall that a party who receives a benefit without the opportunity to reject it is not liable under the theory of unjust enrichment. (Remember the example where Alice is in the swimming pool construction business and she builds a pool in your yard while you are away. You don't have to pay for the pool.[107]) The crux of the problem is that the party receiving the benefit neither consented to nor wanted the benefit. Similarly, the Education Board received the benefit of the better teacher only because of Lukaszewski's breach and the unavailability of comparable teachers, not because the Education Board sought the benefit.[108] Hence, contract law ignores the benefit in determining Lukaszewski's damages liability.

Injured employees Suppose an employer wrongfully terminates an employee. The employee is entitled to any unpaid salary up to the time of the breach and her salary for the remaining term. But the employee must try to minimize her damages.[109] Contract law deducts from her recovery any salary she makes or could have made by accepting reasonable substitute employment.[110] If you have a contract to work for one year for Paul's Piano Tuners for $4000 per month and Paul's wrongfully terminates you after paying you for one month, you are entitled to $44,000 ($4000 per month for eleven months) minus what you make or could have made in a reasonable substitute job. The mitigation principle creates incentives for you to find substitute work instead of lying around and watching soap operas on TV.

What constitutes a reasonable substitute job? Obviously, the substitute job must be comparable or similar to the original job.[111] But what exactly is a comparable or similar job? The issue of a reasonable substitute arises not only when an injured employee has

---

107. See Chapter 3 at note 118, and accompanying text.

108. 332 N.W.2d at 779.

109. Boehm v. American Broadcasting Co., 929 F.2d 482, 485 (9th Cir. 1991) ("[A]n employee who has been wrongfully terminated has a duty to mitigate damages through reasonable efforts to achieve other employment.").

110. Id. at 485 ("The general rule is that the measure of recovery by a wrongfully discharged employee is the amount of salary agreed upon for the period of service, less the amount which the employer affirmatively proves the employee has earned or with reasonable effort might have earned from other employment.") (citing Parker v. Twentieth

Century–Fox Film Corp., 474 P.2d 689, 692 (Cal. 1970)).

111. Parker v. Twentieth Century–Fox Film Corp., 474 P.2d 689, 692 (Cal. 1970) ("[B]efore projected earnings from other employment opportunities not sought or accepted by the discharged employee can be applied in mitigation, the employer must show that the other employment was comparable, or substantially similar, to that of which the employee has been deprived; the employee's rejection of or failure to seek other available employment of a different or inferior kind may not be resorted to in order to mitigate damages.").

opportunities with third parties after a breach, but also when the breaching employer reconsiders and seeks to rehire the injured employee. In the latter case, courts especially have amplified the meaning of a "reasonable substitute."

Consider the decision in the wonderful case of *Parker v. Twentieth Century–Fox Film Corp.*[112] Fox hired Parker, also known as Shirley MacLaine, to act in a movie called "Bloomer Girl," a musical to be filmed in California. The contract gave Parker approval rights over the director and screenplay. Fox decided not to make "Bloomer Girl" and broke the contract with Parker. However, Fox offered Parker a part in another movie, "Big Country, Big Man," for the same salary.[113] This film was to be a western, shot in Australia. Parker also would lose her approval rights. Parker declined the job offer and sought full payment of her promised salary for "Bloomer Girl."

The Supreme Court of California affirmed a summary judgment in favor of Parker.[114] Applying the mitigation-of-damages principle, the court held that Fox's substitute offer was not "substantially similar" (therefore not a reasonable substitute) but, instead, was both "different" and "inferior."[115] Further, no factual issues challenged that conclusion.[116] (The court stated that Parker could ignore Fox's new offer if it was either "different *or* inferior," but the court believed that the facts supported both requirements in the case.)[117] Fox's substitute offer was "different" because "Big Country, Big Man" was a western to be filmed in Australia, not a musical to be shot in California.[118] Fox's offer was "inferior" because Parker lost her approval rights.[119] Parker was therefore reasonable in refusing to accept the substitute offer.[120]

A dissenting judge was chagrined by the majority's willingness to decide the case without a trial. The dissent thought that the question of whether the substitute offer was "different" should go to a jury because "[i]t has never been the law that the mere existence of *differences between two jobs in the same field* is sufficient, as a matter of law, to excuse an employee wrongfully discharged from one from accepting the other in order to mitigate damages."[121] According to the dissent, the jobs had to be "different in kind," a factual issue, before Parker could ignore the substitute offer. Further, whether loss of approval rights made "Big Country, Big Man" inferior was also a fact question.[122]

112. 474 P.2d 689 (Cal. 1970).

113. Id. at 691.

114. Id. at 694.

115. Id. at 693–94.

116. Id. at 693.

117. Id. at 693–94.

118. Id.

119. Id. at 694.

120. See id.

121. Id. at 696.

122. Id.

From *Parker* and similar cases,[123] we can glean some of the factors that are probative of whether a new offer of employment, whether from the breaching party or a third party, is a reasonable substitute. Is the offer for a job in the same field?[124] Parker certainly wouldn't have to take a job cleaning the animal cages used in "Big Country, Big Man." Does the employee have the same rights as in the original contract?[125] Recall that Parker lost her approval rights.[126] Does the employee have new duties or responsibilities?[127] Is the compensation different? How will the substitute job affect the injured party's career? Obviously, such factors will not always provide clear guidance to courts in any particular case.

A few policy concerns apply only to new offers made by the breaching party.[128] Although the court in *Parker* did not address the issue, courts should consider whether requiring an injured employee to accept a new offer from her breaching employer, even a reasonable one, impinges on freedom of contract. Parker contracted to perform in a musical in California, not a western in Australia. If the mitigation rule applied to Fox's offer, Parker would have to perform a different contract than she bargained for (or lose the amount she could have made by doing so). In addition, not only would Fox have the power to alter the contract unilaterally, but Parker would have to deal further with a party who had already demonstrated its lack of reliability and untrustworthiness. What would prevent Fox from coming up with still another substitute film offer, say for Parker to play a derelict in a horror film to be shot in Mongolia? Further, Parker may be so disgusted with Fox that she will create difficulties and decline to perform in "Big Country, Big Man" to the best of her abilities.

These policy concerns influence courts so that breaching employers have had an uphill battle arguing that an employee should have accepted a breaching party's new offer.[129] On the other hand, if the terms of the offer are similar enough (for example, if Fox simply sought to move the shooting date of "Bloomer Girl" forward by a few weeks), contract law requires the injured employee to take the offer in order to avoid the costs of breakdown.[130]

123. See, e.g., Boehm, 929 F.2d 482.

124. Parker, 474 P.2d at 695 ("Only work which is in the same field and which is of the same quality need be accepted.") (Sullivan, Acting C.J., dissenting).

125. Id. at 694.

126. Id.

127. Boehm, 929 F.2d 482.

128. See generally Robert A. Hillman, Keeping the Deal Together After Material Breach—Common Law Mitigation Rules, the UCC, and the Restatement (Second) of Contracts, 47 U. Colo. Law Rev. 553 (1976).

129. Farnsworth, supra note 17, at 807 ("The burden of showing that the injured party could have, but has not, taken appropriate steps generally rests upon the party in breach. . . .").

130. See Hillman, supra note 128, at 564–70.

Before we leave the issue of mitigation of damages in the employment context, one caveat: If an injured employee actually takes a clearly inferior job, the substitute salary made by the injured employee is still likely to reduce the damages liability of the original breaching employer.[131] Suppose again that Paul's Piano Tuners hires you for one year for $4000 per month and wrongfully terminates you after one month. You immediately take a job as a janitor at Elliot's Cleaners for $2000 per month, and remain with Elliot's for eleven months. You can recover $22,000 from Paul's ($44,000 expected from Paul's minus $22,000 made with freed-up time). Contract law does not account for your loss of prestige, but would award any consequential damages you suffer, such as the costs of a longer commute or other concrete inconveniences.[132]

Service contracts Hadley v. Baxendale[133] may be the most famous contracts case. Perhaps it is one of the most famous cases in any field of Anglo–American jurisprudence. Maybe it is the most important piece of writing in the English language. Well, I may be getting carried away, but please treat the case with appropriate veneration. The case involves what I am calling a "service contract," because a carrier promised a miller to deliver a broken crank shaft to a repair shop. The carrier was performing a service for the miller as an independent contractor, not as an employee. Nonetheless, as you will see, the *Hadley* rule applies to all kinds of contracts.

The carrier delayed delivering the crank shaft and the miller lost profits. The court would not award the lost profits to the miller, however, because the lost profits did not "aris[e] naturally" from the breach, nor were they "reasonably * * * in the contemplation of both parties, at the time they made the contract, as the probable result of the breach of it."[134] The lost profits did not "aris[e] naturally" because it was "obvious that, in the great multitude of cases of millers sending off broken shafts to third persons by a carrier under ordinary circumstances, such consequences would not, in all probability, have occurred."[135] The lost profits were not reasonably in the parties' contemplation because the special circumstances—the miller would lose profit without its crank shaft because it did not have a substitute shaft and the mill

---

131. Marshall School Dist. v. Hill, 939 S.W.2d 319 (Ark. Ct. App. 1997).

132. Smith v. American General Corp., 1987 WL 15144, at a 11 (Tenn. Ct. App. 1987) ("When calculating damages for wrongful discharge courts strictly apply the rules of foreseeability, mitigation, and certainty and rarely award consequential damages. Damages for injury to the employee's reputation, for example, are generally considered too remote and not in the parties' contemplation.").

133. 156 Eng. Rep. 145 (Ex.1854).

134. Id. at 151.

135. Id.

would have to shut down until the shaft was repaired and returned—were "never communicated" by the miller to the carrier.[136]

Hadley is famous for setting forth the "reasonably foreseeable" hurdle to the recovery of what are, in the typical case, consequential damages.[137] (The lost profits are consequential damages because not every miller would have lost profits because of the carrier's delay.[138] For example, some would have a substitute crank shaft to keep the mill running.) According to *Hadley*, the miller can recover lost profits only if the carrier, at the time of contracting, should have reasonably foreseen that its delay would cause such losses.[139] This objective test (because it depends on what a reasonable party would know) does not always require the injured party to explain the consequences of breach to the breaching party. For example, suppose the carrier previously had transported the miller's crank shaft and knew that the miller had to shut down the mill while the crank shaft was being repaired. Or suppose it was generally known that millers could legally own only one crank shaft. In either case, the miller could assert persuasively that the carrier reasonably should have known that the miller would lose profits if the carrier delayed delivering the crank shaft. Now suppose the carrier delivered crank shafts and nothing else. In this instance, a carrier reasonably should know more about the milling business and perhaps about the consequences to a customer of delay.[140]

In the actual case, the miller did not tell the carrier about the consequences of delay nor would a reasonable carrier have gleaned the ramifications from the circumstances. The lost profits were therefore not reasonably foreseeable and not recoverable.[141] By the way, don't be confused by the conflict between the rendition of the facts set forth at the beginning of the opinion, written by a court reporter ("the defendants' clerk * * * was told that the mill was stopped, that the shaft must be delivered immediately, and that a special entry, if necessary, must be made to hasten its delivery...."[142]), and the court's understanding of the facts in the middle of the opinion ("we find that the only circumstances here communicated by the plaintiffs to the defendants at the time the contract was made, were, that the article to be carried was the

---

136. Id.

137. Schroeder v. Barth, Inc., 969 F.2d 421, 425 (7th Cir. 1992) ("Ever since Hadley v. Baxendale, courts have allowed recovery in breach of contract actions for all damages that were reasonably foreseeable to the parties at the time of contract formation.").

138. See supra notes 58–63, and accompanying text for a discussion of general and consequential damages.

139. Hadley, 156 Eng. Rep. at 151.

140. Armstrong v. Bangor Mill Supply Corp., 145 A. 741 (Me. 1929) (crankshaft repair shop liable for lost profits after defective repairs).

141. Hadley, 156 Eng. Rep. at 151.

142. Id. at 145.

broken shaft of a mill, and that the plaintiffs were the millers of that mill."[143]). According to later courts, the *Hadley* court simply rejected the court reporter's version of the facts.[144]

Several policies support the *Hadley* rule, which awards only reasonably foreseeable damages.[145] The court notes the injustice of requiring the carrier to pay for losses it reasonably could not foresee. The court does not elaborate, but it must have thought that the carrier would have charged more, taken extra precautions, or insisted on a disclaimer of liability had it known of the miller's potential loss from delay.[146]

Another policy supporting the *Hadley* decision involves reducing the costs of contracting. The contract between the miller and carrier did not allocate the risk of the carrier's delay, meaning that the contract did not say whether the carrier was liable to the miller for its lost profits caused by delay. So the issue in the case boils down to how the court should fill the gap in the contract. Lawyer-economists argue that courts should fill the gap with the term the parties would have wanted had they dealt with the issue in their contract (assuming that their bargaining would be costless and each party had complete information).[147] This strategy serves economic efficiency because it reduces "transactions costs" (roughly, the cost in time and effort of reaching an agreement on the issue). Parties do not have to invest resources bargaining over terms, such as whether the carrier is liable for lost profits, because the court will fill the gap with the term the parties would have selected.[148]

How do courts find the term the parties would have selected? Lawyer-economists posit that the parties would have allocated the risk of lost profits to the "superior risk bearer," the party better able to bear the risk, such as by purchasing insurance, or to the "superior risk avoider," the party better able to prevent the loss from occurring in the first place.[149] In *Hadley*, for example, the superior risk bearer may be the miller, who can insure most cheaply against the risk of a broken crank shaft.

---

143. Id. at 151.

144. Spang Indust., Inc. v. Aetna Cas. & Surety Co., 512 F.2d 365, 371 n.8 (2d Cir. 1975) (relying on Victoria Laundry, Ltd. v. Newman Indus., Ltd., 2 K. B. 528, 537 (1949)).

145. Hadley, 156 Eng. Rep. at 151.

146. Id. at 151 ("[H]ad the special circumstances been known, the parties might have specially provided for the breach of contract by special terms as to the damages in that case; and of this advantage it would be very unjust to deprive them.").

147. See Posner, supra note 19, at 106.

148. See id.

149. Id.; see also In re Brame, 23 B.R. 196, 201 (Bankr. W.D. Ky. 1982) ("Economic analysis of loss-shifting suggests that losses should be borne by the 'superior risk-bearer'—a designation given, in the esoteric parlance of economics, to the party to a transaction who is in the best position to appraise the nature and extent of risks contractually assumed and the possibility of losses resulting from their occurrence.").

You may be a little concerned with this analysis. You may be thinking that the carrier is the superior risk avoider in *Hadley* because it can take precautions to ensure delivery of the crank shaft on time at a lower cost than the miller can insure against the risk of a broken shaft or can ensure that the mill does not stop after a crank shaft breaks.[150] You also may be thinking that this is all very speculative and that a court can easily manipulate the determination of who is the superior risk bearer or avoider. Although you are surely right, the superior risk bearer or avoider approach is a major theory of gap filling, which we pursue further in Chapters 7 and 9.[151]

Commentators also treat the *Hadley* rule as an example of a "penalty default," which penalizes a party for failing to reveal its superior information.[152] Specifically, *Hadley* penalizes the miller, who did not disclose its potential losses to the carrier at the time of contracting, by disallowing the miller's lost profits.[153] The decision therefore encourages future parties to reveal, at the time of contracting, any special losses they will incur if the other party breaches.[154] Further, were it not for the *Hadley* rule, the miller probably would not disclose these potential losses. Assuming most millers do not suffer lost profits due to a delay in the carriage of their crank shaft, the carrier will raise its price once the miller reveals its special circumstances (because the carrier is taking on a greater risk of liability than when it carries the average miller's crank shaft).[155] So, without the *Hadley* rule, the miller will not disclose because the result would only be that the miller would pay more for carriage of the crank shaft. With the rule, the miller will disclose so long as the benefit of a potential recovery of lost profits exceeds the higher price of carriage.[156]

The "penalty-default" explanation of *Hadley* is controversial. For one thing, the miller may not disclose its situation to the carrier under the *Hadley* rule because the costs of doing so may be even greater than an increase in the price of carriage.[157] A miller

150. See Ian Ayres & Robert Gertner, Filling Gaps in Incomplete Contracts: An Economic theory of Default Rules, 99 Yale L. J. 87, 101 (1989).

151. See Chapter 7 at notes 123–124, and accompanying text; Chapter 9 at notes 50–51, and accompanying text.

152. Ayres & Gertner, supra note 150, at 101 ("The holding in *Hadley* operates as a penalty default. The miller could have informed the carrier of the potential consequential damages and contracted for full damage insurance.").

153. Id.

154. Id. at 101–104.

155. See Jason Scott Johnston, Strategic Bargaining and the Economic Theory of Contract Default Rules 100 Yale L.J. 615, 622 (1990).

156. Ayres & Gertner, supra note 150, at 104.

157. Melvin Aron Eisenberg, The Principle of Hadley v. Baxendale, 80 Cal. L. Rev. 563, 595 (1992) ("In many cases the communication of information concerning consequential damages would involve a cost much more substantial than the cost of assembly and transmission. Information that is valuable to a

inclined to disclose will have to incur the costs of determining exactly what it will lose by a delay in carriage (which may not always be as obvious as in *Hadley*).[158] The miller also suffers the risk that the carrier will try to exploit the miller by charging more than a fair price for the carrier's extra liability.[159] The total costs of revealing information therefore often may outweigh the gains of potential carrier liability.[160] Moreover, even if the miller discloses, the carrier may not take the necessary precautions to avoid delivering late (which, after all, is the one of the main benefits of information disclosure).[161] If the carrier rarely delivers late and delivers oodles of crank shafts, it may be cheaper for the carrier to pay high damages very rarely than to try to process information from millers and make special arrangements as needed for each type of miller.[162]

Whatever the reasons for the rule of *Hadley v. Baxendale*, it has met with wide approval and adoption. For example, the drafters of the UCC codified the *Hadley* rule in section 2–715(2)(a): "Consequential damages resulting from the seller's breach include (a) any loss resulting from general or particular requirements and needs of which the seller at the time of contracting had reason to know and which could not reasonably be prevented by cover or otherwise * * *."[163] An official comment to the section expressly repudiates the "tacit agreement" test for the award of consequential damages.[164] Under that test, a breaching party might escape liability for foreseeable consequential damages. A breaching party would be liable only if she "tacitly consented" to be liable for the foreseeable damages.[165] In *Hadley*, for example, the carrier might not be liable for the miller's lost profits even if the miller told the carrier of the ramifications of delay. The carrier would be liable only if the circumstances showed that the carrier "tacitly agreed" to take on that potential liability. If you are having trouble thinking of how the miller could show the carrier's tacit agreement, you are not alone. That is why most courts and section 2–715 repudiated the rule.

party might lose much of that value when transmitted.").

158. Id. at 594–95.

159. Id. at 595–96.

160. Id. at 594–95.

161. Id. at 592–94.

162. Id. at 593.

163. UCC § 2–715(2)(a); see also Restatement (Second) of Contracts § 351.

164. UCC § 2–715, cmt. 2.

165. Lamkins v. International Harvester Co., 182 S.W.2d 203, 205 (Ark. 1944) ("[I]n order to render a seller liable to the buyer for special or consequential damages arising from delay in delivering the article of sale, it is necessary that at or before the time of the making of the contract of sale he knew of the special circumstances which would expose the buyer to special damages by reason of the delay in delivery, and that such seller at least tacitly consented to assume the particular risks arising from such delay.").

c.   **Sales of goods**. Part seven (the 700 sections) of Article 2 of the UCC governs remedies for breach of a sales contract. In addition, section 1–106(1) of the UCC sets forth the general expectancy measure as the cardinal remedial principle of the UCC (the rules of Article 1 apply to all of the UCC, including Article 2): "The remedies provided by this Act shall be liberally administered to the end that the aggrieved party may be put in as good a position as if the other party had fully performed * * *."[166] The remedial rules of Article 2, designed to achieve the goal of section 1–106, are a rich subject that is often taken up in upperclass commercial law courses. I will only provide a broad outline here.

Consequential and incidental damages We just encountered UCC section 2–715, dealing with consequential damages, and we saw that the section adopts the *Hadley* rule that consequential damages must be reasonably foreseeable.[167] If you break a contract to sell your piano to Alice, you will be liable for any reasonably foreseeable consequential damages.[168] If you have reason to know that Alice is a piano teacher, for example, you may be liable for her lost profits if she cannot give lessons. Further, section 2–715 provides that the lost profits must not be reasonably preventable.[169] If Alice reasonably could have obtained a substitute piano immediately after your breach and therefore could have avoided losing profits, you will not be liable for her lost profits.

Suppose Alice breaches the contract before you deliver the piano. Section 2–710 allows you, as a seller, to recover "incidental damages" consisting of any "charges, expenses or commissions incurred in stopping delivery," any expenses in transporting and caring for the goods after the breach, and any similar damages.[170] You can conceptualize incidental damages as a form of consequential damages for sellers, in that some, but not all, sellers will suffer such damages after breach.[171] Amended section 2–710 specifically allows sellers to recover consequential damages, although a comment suggests that sellers rarely will need to avail themselves of this right.[172]

General damages Obviously, buyers and sellers may incur greater damages than consequential or incidental damages. Article

---

166.   UCC § 1–106(1).

167.   See supra notes 163–165, and accompanying text.

168.   UCC § 2–715(2) ("Consequential damages resulting from the seller's breach include (a) any loss resulting from general or particular requirements and needs of which the seller at the time of contracting had reason to know and which could not reasonably be prevented by cover or otherwise . . .").

169.   Id.

170.   UCC § 2–710.

171.   See supra notes 58–63, and accompanying text, for a definition of consequential damages.

172.   Amended UCC § 2–710, cmt. 2 (proposed final draft April 18, 2003).

2 sets forth parallel provisions for buyers and sellers that allow them to recover their general damages as well.

Injured buyers Suppose you break your promise to sell Alice your piano for $1000 when the market price is $1200. Alice can recover $200 under the market price-contract price differential formula of section 2–713.[173] Under the section, courts must determine the market price "at the time when the buyer learned of the breach,"[174] because this is the time when a reasonable buyer could purchase a substitute piano. Amended section 2–713 substitutes the "time for tender" as the time for measuring the market price.[175] However, if the seller repudiates the contract before the time for tender, courts must determine the market price "at the expiration of a commercially reasonable time after the buyer learned of the repudiation," but no later than the time for tender.[176]

If Alice *actually* purchases a substitute, Alice can recover the cover price-contract price differential under section 2–712.[177] (The "cover" price is the price of the substitute purchase.) If the substitute purchase is "in good faith," is "without unreasonable delay," and is otherwise reasonable,[178] she can recover more under section 2–712 than she could under section 2–713. If Alice pays $1300 for the substitute piano, when the market price is $1200, she can recover $300 if her actions were reasonable. Alice's actions would be reasonable, for example, if she can get the $1300 piano soon enough to avoid losing profits in her piano teaching business. The theory for allowing Alice this remedy, of course, is that it better measures Alice's *actual* damages.

Article 2 is not very clear on what happens if Alice purchases a substitute piano for $1100 when the market value is $1200. Can she recover $200 under section 2–713? This seems inconsistent with the lost expectancy principle codified in section 1–106, because Alice lost only $100 in that she purchased a piano at less than the market price. However, section 2–712(1) says the buyer "may" cover, suggesting that the section is optional and that Alice can recover under section 2–713.[179] Further, Alice can claim that her

---

173. UCC § 2–713(1) ("[W]ith respect to proof of market price (Section 2–723), the measure of damages for nondelivery or repudiation by the seller is the difference between the market price at the time when the buyer learned of the breach and the contract price together with any incidental and consequential damages provided in this Article (Section 2–715), but less expenses saved in consequence of the seller's breach.").

174. Id.

175. Amended UCC § 2–713(1)(a).

176. Amended UCC § 2–713(1)(b).

177. UCC § 2–712(2) ("The buyer may recover from the seller as damages the difference between the cost of cover and the contract price together with any incidental or consequential damages as hereinafter defined (Section 2–715), but less expenses saved in consequence of the seller's breach.").

178. UCC § 2–712(1).

179. Id.

$1100 piano purchase was a separate investment and that she is going to sell that piano on the market for $1200. She will then have to pay $1200 for another piano and her damages are legitimately $200. The ambiguity in the UCC on Alice's recovery when she "covers" at less than the market price has never been satisfactorily resolved. Amended Article 2 includes a comment that the cover remedy "is not mandatory" and that "buyer is always free to choose between cover" and section 2–713.[180] But Amended Article 2 does not expunge the expectancy damages principle of section 1–106(1), so you can argue that giving Alice $200 puts her in a better position even under the revision.

Section 2–714 sets forth the remedy for a buyer who accepts and keeps defective goods. The remedy for breach of warranty is "the difference at the time and place of acceptance between the value of the goods accepted and the value they would have had if they had been as warranted * * *."[181] Suppose the market value of a piano like yours is $1100, and you contract to sell the piano to Alice for $1000. Neither you nor Alice know that the piano is defective and worth only $800. Alice keeps the piano. Under section 2–714(2), you owe her $300, the difference between the value of what she received ($800) and what you promised her ($1100).

*Injured seller*s We have already discussed sellers' incidental and consequential damages under the UCC.[182] We focus on sellers' general damages here. When a buyer breaches a contract, the injured seller can look to UCC sections 2–708(1) and 2–706 in much the same way as sections 2–713 and 2–712 work for injured buyers. For example, if Alice promises to purchase your piano for $1000 and it is only worth $900 "at the time and place for tender" (usually the time she breaches), you can recover the contract price-market price differential of $100 under section 2–708(1).[183] In the alternative, if you resell the piano for $850, and the resale is "in good faith and in a commercially reasonable manner," you can recover $150.[184] "Good faith" and commercial reasonableness roughly mean that the resale must be honest and comparable to other sales in the trade.[185] You can't sell at a discount in order to penalize Alice or to curry favor with a particular customer. As with the relationship between sections 2–713 and 2–712 on the buyer's side,[186] whether section 2–708(1) is available to a seller when the seller resells for more than the market price is unclear. If you resell

180. Amended UCC § 2–712, cmt. 6.

181. UCC § 2–714(2).

182. See supra notes 167–172, and accompanying text.

183. UCC § 2–708(1).

184. UCC § 2–706(1).

185. UCC § 1–201(19).

186. See supra notes 173–180, and accompanying text.

for $950 when the contract price is $1000 and the market value is $900, for example, can you claim the larger contract price-market price differential of $100, or are you stuck with a $50 damages award? Section 1–106, which sets forth the expectancy formula, would suggest the latter, but sections 2–708(1) and 2–706 are also written as if they were alternatives for the seller.[187]

Amended section 2–708(1)(b) provides that the time for measuring the market price when the buyer repudiates the contract before the time for tender is "at the expiration of a commercially reasonable time after the seller learned of the repudiation * * *." The explanation for the change is that "[t]his time approximates the market price at the time the seller would have resold the goods * * *."[188]

Lost volume sellers Suppose Alice contracts to purchase a piano from Peter's Retail Piano Store for $1000, instead of from you. She then breaches the contract, but Peter's sells the same piano to Leonard for $1000. (You may be thinking, "why is he going over this easy resale price-contract price example again?[189] I have enough to learn as it is.") If Peter's can obtain from the manufacturer-supplier as many pianos as Peter's requires to sell to the public, the resale price-contract price formula of section 2–706 will not put Peter's in as good a position as if Alice had performed. For that matter, neither will the contract price-market price differential of section 2–708(1). This is because, as the result of Alice's breach, Peter's has lost one sale and one profit ($1000 minus the price Peter's paid for the piano from the manufacturer). If Alice had not breached, Peter's would have sold two pianos. After the breach, Peter's sells only one. If Peter's was purchasing the pianos wholesale for $800 and selling retail for $1000, then Peter's lost $200 as a result of Alice's breach. A court explained this "lost volume" principle as follows (in an example dealing with cars):

> If the dealer has an inexhaustible supply of cars, the resale to replace the breaching buyer costs the dealer a sale, because, had the breaching buyer performed, the dealer would have made two sales instead of one. The buyer's breach, in such a case, depletes the dealer's sales to the extent of one, and the measure of damages should be the dealer's profit on one sale.[190]

---

187. UCC § 2–706(1) ("Under the conditions stated in Section 2–703 on seller's remedies, the seller *may* resell the goods concerned or the undelivered balance thereof.") (emphasis added).

188. Amended UCC § 2–708, cmt. 4.

189. See supra notes 184–185, and accompanying text.

190. Neri v. Retail Marine Corp., 285 N.E.2d 311, 314 (N.Y. 1972).

The drafters of UCC section 2–708(2) recognized the lost-volume predicament of the seller and provided that the seller can recover lost profits in lieu of another remedy.[191] The section has caused some confusion, however, because it also provides that the buyer should get "credit for payments or proceeds of resale."[192] In the example above, should Alice get credit for the proceeds of resale against what she owes Peter's? If so, this defeats the whole idea of allowing lost profits to a lost-volume seller. But don't worry. Courts and commentators interpret the "credit for resale" reference to apply only to a resale of a manufacturer's raw materials as scrap after a breach by the buyer.[193] The "credit for resale" clause should be ignored, in other words, in cases such as our example. Further, amended section 2–708(2) deletes the offending language, laying to rest the issue of what it means in retail sales cases.[194]

We have already seen that the "lost volume" idea applies not only to sales of goods, but in the construction contract arena as well.[195] In fact, it should apply in any context where the injured party loses volume as the result of a breach.

d. Sale of real property. Damages for breach of a real-property sales contract resemble damages for breach of a sale-of-goods contract, but with a few differences. Injured sellers can recover the difference between the contract price and market price of the land,[196] together with any consequential damages.[197] Under

---

191. UCC § 2–708(2) ("If the measure of damages provided in subsection (1) is inadequate to put the seller in as good a position as performance would have done then the measure of damages is the profit (including reasonable overhead) which the seller would have made from full performance by the buyer, together with any incidental damages provided in this Article (Section 2–710), due allowance for costs reasonably incurred and due credit for payments or proceeds of resale.").

192. Id.

193. Neri, 285 N.E.2d at 314 n.2 ("The concluding clause, 'due credit for payments or proceeds of resale,' is intended to refer to 'the privilege of the seller to realize junk value when it is manifestly useless to complete the operation of manufacture.' The commentators who have considered the language have uniformly concluded that 'the reference is to a resale as scrap under * * * Section 2–704.' Another writer, reaching the same conclusion, after detailing the history of the clause, says

that 'proceeds of resale' previously meant the resale value of the goods in finished form; now it means the resale value of the components on hand at the time plaintiff learns of breach.") (citations omitted).

194. Amended UCC § 2–708(2).

195. See supra notes 79–84, and accompanying text.

196. Gilmartin Bros. v. Kern, 916 S.W.2d 324, 332 (Mo. Ct. App. 1995) ("[W]here the seller of real estate brings suit for breach of contract against the buyer, the appropriate measure of damages is the difference between the contract price and the market value of the property on the date the sale should have been completed.").

197. Turner v. Benson, 672 S.W.2d 752, 754–55 (Tenn. 1984) ("[The injured party] may recover special damages, if any, that arise out of the breach of contract in order to compensate the [injured party] for any loss or injury actually sustained by reason of the [breaching party's] breach.").

one line of authority, injured purchasers of land also can recover the difference between the market price and contract price.[198] Another approach, however, limits the injured purchaser to restitution of the amount the purchaser has already paid, unless the seller's breach was willful or in bad faith.[199] In the absence of seller willfulness or bad faith, why should an injured purchaser be deprived of expectancy? The idea seems to be that sellers often breach inadvertently because of title problems, and such contract breakers should be treated more leniently.[200] More important to you, which "rule" should you apply on your exam or in practice? Know both of them for the exam, and indicate the result either way (that's how you should treat all "splits" in authority). When you are a lawyer, do research in your state to find out the rule applied there!

e. Summary of limitations on expectancy damages as illustrated by the various contexts. Although we have focused on contract expectancy damages in various contexts, general principles have emerged. The goal in each context is the same—to give the injured party the money equivalent of what she expected from performance. Moreover, we have set forth various formulae for achieving this goal. Each formula takes into account the position the injured party is in after the breach and the position the injured party would have been in had there been no breach. Contract law then awards money damages to move the injured party from the former to the latter position.

Of course, you also must be mindful of the limitations on expectancy recoveries that we have surveyed. For example, injured parties must mitigate their damages. Recall that an injured builder usually must quit work after a landowner's repudiation and an injured employee must accept a reasonable substitute offer.[201] In addition, injured parties must prove their damages with sufficient certainty. Courts may deny a new business owner lost profits, for example, because of the absence of persuasive proof of the amount the business lost.[202] Further, contracting parties also must prove that their damages were reasonably foreseeable. For example, courts may bar a miller unforeseeable lost profits when a carrier delays delivering the miller's broken crank shaft.[203]

---

198. See Charles L. Knapp, Nathan M. Crystal, Harry G. Prince, Problems in Contract Law 818–19 (5th ed. 2003) (citing cases).

199. Id.

200. Id.

201. See supra notes 67–78, 109–132, and accompanying text.

202. See supra notes 88–100, and accompanying text.

203. See supra notes 133–165, and accompanying text.

5. Reliance recoveries for breach of contract in lieu of expectancy damages. In limited situations in breach of contract cases, courts grant an injured party reliance damages instead of expectancy damages. You should not confuse the situations we are about to discuss in this section with those involving remedies after a finding of promissory estoppel.[204] In the cases to be discussed here, an injured party has proven that the other party has breached an enforceable contract. Still, the court awards reliance damages instead of expectancy damages. Later, we will look at the remedies after a party has succeeded in a promissory estoppel action.[205]

a. Reliance damages defined. First, what do we mean by reliance damages instead of expectancy damages? Suppose you are a concert promoter and you sign Lea Salonga (you know, from "Miss Saigon") to give a concert in Chicago on September 1. You project that the gross receipts from the concert will be $2,000,000 and the total costs of putting on the concert will be $1,400,000. You envision a nice profit of $600,000. Unfortunately, Lea breaks the contract so that she can perform elsewhere after you have already sunk $300,000 into the project. What can you recover?[206]

Recall that a serious impediment stands in the way of your recovering expectancy damages. You expected to make $600,000, and you now are out $300,000, so you would have to recover $900,000 to be in as good a position as if Lea had not breached. But you will have difficulty proving with sufficient certainty the amount of your expected profit. Has Lea performed before in comparable forums and under similar conditions so that you can prove your damages with sufficient certainty? Do you have other evidence that you would have grossed $2,000,000? Can you even prove that the concert would not have lost money? All of this seems very speculative,[207] so you can't count on recovering full expectancy damages.

What about your expenditures of $300,000 incurred before the breach and made in reliance on the contract? You should be able to prove this amount with sufficient certainty. (You kept records, didn't you?) So, your difficulty in proving lost profits should have no impact on your ability to collect your reliance losses.[208]

---

204. See Chapter 3 at notes 1–64, and accompanying text for a discussion of the theory of promissory estoppel.

205. See infra notes 322–339, and accompanying text.

206. This example is loosely based on Chicago Coliseum Club v. Dempsey, 265 Ill.App. 542 (Ill. App. Ct.1932).

207. See supra notes 89–97, and accompanying text.

208. Wartzman v. Hightower Prods., Ltd., 456 A.2d 82, 86 (Md. Ct. Spec. App. 1983) ("[P]rofits lost due to a breach of contract are recoverable. Where anticipated profits are too speculative to be determined, monies spent in part performance, in preparation for or in reliance on the contract are recoverable."); Chicago Coliseum Club, 265 Ill. App. at 554 ("The items recoverable are such items of expense as were incurred between the date of the signing of the

What if Lea claims that her concert would not have been a success, meaning that the costs of the concert would have been greater than the gross receipts? (Lea may not like the implications of this example concerning her "star" power, of course.) In fact, Lea claims that gross receipts would have been only $1,000,000, so that you would have lost $400,000 if Lea had not broken the contract. (Remember the costs of producing the concert would have been $1,400,000.) Contract law allows defendants in Lea's position to present this defense, but they must prove the amount of the loss with the same precision that you would have to prove the gain.[209] If Lea can prove gross receipts from the concert would have been $1,000,000, you should not recover any of your $300,000 reliance loss because you would have lost $400,000 if she had not breached. (But contract law does not reward Lea for breaching by allowing her to recover your $100,000 savings caused by her breach.) If neither party can prove with sufficient precision the amount of profits or losses on Lea's concert, which is the most likely outcome, courts give the benefit of the doubt to the injured party and therefore would award you the full $300,000 reliance loss,[210] provided you can jump other hurdles to the recovery of your reliance loss (to follow).

b. More hurdles to reliance recoveries. Do other hurdles stand in your way? In short, all of the limitations on expectancy recoveries discussed earlier also apply in the context of reliance recoveries for breach of contract.[211] This makes sense. After all, Lea should not be responsible for your expenditures if they were not reasonably foreseeable[212] or you could have avoided them after hearing about her breach.[213]

Further, suppose $100,000 of the $300,000 of your expenditures consisted of a payment to reserve a concert hall in Chicago for

agreement and the breach ... by the defendant and such as were incurred as a necessary expense in furtherance of the performance.").

209. L. Albert & Son v. Armstrong Rubber Co., 178 F.2d 182, 189 (2d Cir. 1949) ("[P]romisee may recover his outlay in preparation for the performance, subject to the privilege of the promisor to reduce it by as much as he can show that the promisee would have lost, if the contract had been performed."); Wartzman, 456 A.2d at 86; see Restatement (Second) of Contracts § 349 ("[T]he injured party has a right to damages based on his reliance interest, including expenditures made in preparation for performance or in performance, less any loss that the party in breach can prove with

reasonable certainty the injured party would have suffered had the contract been performed.").

210. L. Albert & Son, 178 F.2d at 188–89.

211. See supra notes 201–203, and accompanying text.

212. Landmark Land Co. v. FDIC, 256 F.3d 1365, 1378 (Fed. Cir 2001) ("In order to be recoverable as reliance damages, however, plaintiff's loss must have been foreseeable to the party in breach at the time of contract formation.").

213. Westfed Holdings, Inc. v. United States, 55 Fed. Cl. 544, 562 (Fed. Cl. 2003) ("A party may not recover for 'loss that the injured party could have avoided without undue risk, burden or

Lea's concert, but that you committed to the venue and paid the money *before* Lea had even signed your contract to perform. Can you recover this money as part of your reliance damages for breach of contract?

One argument against your recovery of the $100,000 is that you didn't make the expenditure in reasonable reliance on Lea performing for you because you knew that she might never sign the contract. You accepted that risk when you committed yourself.[214] On the other hand, when Lea did sign the performance contract, she reasonably should have understood that if she broke the contract you would lose any money you already had committed to the concert. In effect, by joining the project she impliedly agreed to indemnify you for any pre-contractual reliance.[215] Authority exists for adopting either of these propositions.[216]

   c. Fixed overhead. Recall that we are assuming that you are a promoter and that you arrange lots of concerts. One expense of your business is known as "fixed overhead," which, most basically, consists of the general cost of running your business. For example, you pay secretaries, for the heating and cooling of your office, rent, taxes, etc. to keep your business running.[217] Can you recover any of these expenses after Lea's breach?

At first blush, you may think not.[218] After all, you would have incurred these expenses even if Lea had never been born (which would have a been a real blow to musical theater). But consider the following. Suppose you had four projects for the accounting period at issue in our problem, including Lea's. You produced three other concerts that took place without a hitch (say the Indigo Girls, the Backstreet Boys, and Men at Work), each of which cost $150,000 to produce and grossed $230,000. You therefore made a total of $240,000 on the Girls, Boys, and Men ($230,000 minus $150,000 for each of three concerts). Suppose your total fixed overhead for this accounting period was $36,000. If Lea had not breached, your accountant would allocate $9,000 of the fixed overhead to each of

humiliation.'") (quoting Restatement (Second) of Contracts § 350(1)).

   214. Chicago Coliseum Club, 265 Ill.App. at 551 ("Any obligations assumed by the plaintiff prior to [signing of the agreement] are not chargeable to the defendant.").

   215. Anglia Television Ltd. v. Reed, 1 Q.B. 60, 64 (C.A. 1971) ("If the plaintiff claims the wasted expenditure, he is not limited to the expenditure incurred *after* the contract was concluded. He can claim also the expenditure incurred *before* the contract, provided that it was

such as would reasonably be in the contemplation of the parties as likely to be wasted if the contract was broken.").

   216. See, e.g., Chicago Coliseum Club, 265 Ill.App. 542 (precontractual reliance not recoverable); Anglia Television Ltd., 1 Q.B. 60 (precontractual reliance recoverable).

   217. Chicago Coliseum Club, 265 Ill.App. at 553.

   218. Id. (fixed overhead not recoverable).

the four events. If Lea breaches and you cannot recover $9,000 of the fixed overhead allocated to her concert, your accountant now has only three projects with which to allocate the fixed overhead. Your accountant therefore would allocate $12,000 of fixed overhead to each of the successful concerts. In effect, then, Lea's breach would reduce the net profit on each of the other projects by $3000 ($12,000 of overhead for each of the projects instead of $9000). You would not be in as good a position as if Lea had performed. So you should recover the $9000 fixed costs allocated to the Lea concert as reliance expenses. This should be the rule any time an injured party can prove that it could have "recouped its overhead expenses on other projects."[219]

d. More theories for awarding reliance damages. Up to this point in our discussion of reliance damages for breach of contract, we have been looking at situations in which full expectancy damages are too speculative. Another ground for awarding reliance damages in lieu of expectancy damages pertains to the strength of the contract claim itself. An example, based on an important case, helps illuminate this point.

In *Sullivan v. O'Connor*,[220] a doctor promised to improve a patient's nose in two operations. Instead, the doctor performed three operations, and the patient's nose actually became worse.[221] Among other things, the court discussed whether the patient should recover reliance or expectancy damages for the doctor's breach of a contract. Reliance damages would put the patient in the position she was in before the operation. She would recover damages for the pain and suffering of the three operations and for the worsening of her nose. She would also recover the fees she already paid to the doctor. These are all losses the patient suffered because she relied on the doctor's promise of a better nose.

Expectancy damages would put the patient in the position she would have been in had the doctor performed as promised. If the doctor had performed, she would have the value of an improved nose, and would have incurred the costs of getting that nose, namely two operations and the doctor's fees. Under an expectancy theory, she should recover the difference in value between that position and the woeful position she is in as a result of the doctor's breach (with a worse nose, three operations, and payment of her fees). You can see that, ordinarily, the patient would recover more under a lost expectancy theory than a reliance theory because the patient would recover the value of the promised nose (minus the

---

219. Autotrol Corp. v. Continental Water Sys. Corp., 918 F.2d 689, 693 (7th Cir. 1990).

220. 296 N.E.2d 183 (Mass. 1973).

221. Id. at 185.

costs of getting it) and not merely compensation to put her back in the position she was in before the operations.

The *Sullivan* court was wary of granting expectancy damages precisely because of the relative weakness of the contract theory of recovery. The court stated:

> It is not hard to see why the courts should be unenthusiastic or skeptical about the contract theory. Considering the uncertainties of medical science and the variations in the physical and psychological conditions of individual patients, doctors can seldom in good faith promise specific results. Therefore it is unlikely that physicians of even average integrity will in fact make such promises. Statement of opinion by the physician with some optimistic coloring are a different thing, and may indeed have therapeutic value. But patients may transform such statements into firm promises in their own minds, especially when they have been disappointed in the event, and testify in that sense to sympathetic juries.[222]

The court stopped short of declaring that all promises made by doctors should be unenforceable. The court feared that such a rule would create incentives for doctors to make promises that they could not keep in order to entice prospective patients. Instead, the court intimated that it supported a compromise position of enforcing doctors' promises, but awarding only reliance damages.[223] *Sullivan v. O'Connor* certainly illustrates the significant relationship between the theory for enforcing a promise and the remedy for breach of the promise.

The court reinforced its position in favor of reliance damages in this context by referring to two distinct remedial concerns. First, the court noted the difficulty of placing a firm monetary amount on the value of a good nose, something that the court could avoid by granting a reliance recovery.[224] Further, the court emphasized the large discrepancy between the doctor's fee and the doctor's potential liability for his patient's lost expectancy.[225]

---

222. Id. at 186.

223. Id. at 187–88 ("For breach of the patient-physician agreements under consideration, a recovery limited to restitution seems plainly too meager, if the agreements are to be enforced at all. On the other hand, an expectancy recovery may well be excessive. The factors, already mentioned, which have made the cause of action somewhat suspect, also suggest moderation as to the breadth of the recovery that should be permitted.... There is much to be said, then, for applying a reliance measure to the present facts....").

224. Id. at 188 ("To attempt, moreover, to put a value on the condition that would or might have resulted, had the treatment succeeded as promised, may sometimes put an exceptional strain on the imagination of the fact finder.").

225. Id. ("We should recall here that the fee paid by the patient to the doctor for the alleged promise would usually be quite disproportionate to the putative expectancy recovery.").

6. Liquidated damages. Within limits, contract law allows contracting parties to agree in their contract on their damages liability if they later breach.[226] Parties may want to include such a provision, called an "agreed" or "liquidated" damages provision for lots of reasons. In case of a breakdown, the parties can avoid the expense of calculating and proving damages.[227] Liquidated damages provisions also create an incentive for the parties to perform.[228] In addition, liquidated damages clauses ensure that an injured party can recover when damages would be too difficult to prove.[229]

Liquidated damages clauses are not always enforceable, however. Most courts apply some variation of two tests, both of which must be satisfied. First, the agreed damages must be a "reasonable forecast of just compensation for the harm that is caused by the breach."[230] Second, "the harm that is caused by the breach is one that is incapable or very difficult of accurate estimation."[231] Yes, you are correct—these requirements seem contradictory. How can the parties reasonably forecast damages if they are incapable of accurate estimation? Nevertheless, courts take the two-prong test seriously and appear willing to enforce agreed damages clauses only when prospective damages for breach are uncertain,[232] and the parties make a good faith effort to estimate them. Although these two requirements for enforcing agreed damages clauses focus on

226. Truck Rent–A–Center, Inc. v. Puritan Farms 2nd, Inc., 361 N.E.2d 1015, 1018 (N.Y. 1977) ("In effect, a liquidated damage provision is an estimate, made by the parties at the time they enter into their agreement, of the extent of the injury that would be sustained as a result of breach of the agreement. Parties to a contract have the right to agree to such clauses, provided that the clause is neither unconscionable nor contrary to public policy."); see also Scott M. Tyler, Note, No (Easy) Way Out: "Liquidating" Stipulated Damages for Builder Delay in Public Construction Contracts, 44 Duke L. J. 357, 357 (1994) ("Liquidated damages refers to an amount that contracting parties, at the time of contracting, agree shall be payable as compensation in the event of a breach.").

227. Leeber v. Deltona Corp., 546 A.2d 452, 455 (Me. 1988) ("[T]he traditional role of liquidated damages provisions [is to serve] as an economical alternative to the costly and lengthy litigation involved in a conventional breach of contract action."); Farnsworth, supra note 17, at 841 ("For both parties, stipulating a sum may fa-

cilitate the calculation of risks and reduce the cost of proof.").

228. Matthew T. Furton, Note, The Use of Penalty Clauses in Location Incentive Agreements, 70 Ind. L.J. 1009, 1018–1019 (1995).

229. Farnsworth, supra note 17, at 841, 845; see also Charles J. Goetz & Robert E. Scott, Liquidated Damages, Penalties and the Just Compensation Principle: Some Notes on an Enforcement Model and a Theory of Efficient Breach, 77 Colum. L. Rev. 554, 557 (1977) ("The expected cost of establishing true losses under conventional damage measures will ... induce parties who face uncertain or nonprovable anticipated losses to negotiate stipulated damage agreements.").

230. H.J. McGrath Co. v. Wisner, 55 A.2d 793, 785 (Md. 1947), quoting Restatement (First) of Contracts § 339 (1932).

231. Id.

232. See supra notes 89–97, and accompanying text for a discussion of the certainty requirement in another context.

the situation at the time of contracting,[233] some courts seem unable to resist looking at the situation at the time of the breakdown of the contract. These courts strike agreed damages clause when the actual damages at the time of the breach bear no relationship to the amount of agreed damages.[234]

When an injured party cannot satisfy either of the two tests for enforcement—the damages provision is either not a "reasonable forecast" of harm or the harm is not difficult to estimate[235]—a court will not enforce the agreed damages clause, calling it a "penalty."[236] Courts balk at penalty provisions even when the parties intend to include one to create incentives for performance:[237]

> A clause which provides for an amount plainly disproportionate to real damage is not intended to provide fair compensation but to secure performance by the compulsion of the very disproportion. A promisor would be compelled, out of fear of economic devastation, to continue performance and his promisee, in the event of default, would reap a windfall well above actual harm sustained.[238]

Suppose you contract to sell your piano, worth $1200, to Alice for $1000. Alice is not a piano teacher and would sustain no consequential damages if you breach. The contract provides that you will pay Alice $5,000 if you fail to deliver the piano. Courts will not enforce this term. Alice's damages of $200 (market price minus contract price) are easy to prove and the $5000 term looks like a vehicle to compel your performance, not a reasonable estimate of Alice's damages.

233. Truck Rent–A–Center, Inc., 361 N.E.2d at 1018 ("In effect, a liquidated damage provision is an estimate, made by the parties at the time they enter into their agreement, of the extent of the injury that would be sustained as a result of breach of the agreement.").

234. See, e.g., Massman Constr.Co. v. City Council of Greenville, 147 F.2d 925 (5th Cir. 1945) (no actual damages at the time of breach).

235. Melvin Aron Eisenberg, The Limits of Cognition and the Limits of Contract, 47 Stan. L. Rev. 211, 230–32 (1995); Farnsworth, supra note 17, at 844–847.

236. Atel Fin. Corp. v. Quaker Coal Co., 132 F.Supp.2d 1233, 1239 (N.D.Cal. 2001) ("A liquidated damages clause will generally be considered unreasonable, and hence unenforceable, if it bears no reasonable relationship to the range of actual damages that the parties could have anticipated would flow from a breach. An amount disproportionate to the anticipated actual damages is termed a 'penalty.' "). But see DJ Manufacturing Corp. v. United States, 86 F.3d 1130, 1134 (Fed. Cir. 1996) ("[F]ederal law 'does not look with disfavor upon 'liquidated damages' provisions in contracts.' ") (quoting Priebe & Sons v. United States, 332 U.S. 407, 411 (1947)).

237. See, e.g., Mason v. Fakhimi, 865 P.2d 333 (Nev. 1993) (" '[The] distinction between a penalty and liquidated damages is that a penalty is for the purpose of securing performance, while liquidated damages is the sum to be paid in the event of non-performance.' ") (quoting 22 Am. Jur. 2d Damages § 684 (1980)); Farnsworth, supra note 17, at 841.

238. Truck Rent–A–Center, 361 N.E.2d at 1018.

For reasons not self-evident, courts appear to be more willing to strike agreed damages clauses than most other provisions in contracts.[239] Courts and commentators offer several explanations. One is historical. A penal bond, the historical forerunner to modern penalty provisions, was a promise to pay a certain amount if the promisor broke a contract.[240] English courts of equity refused to enforce penal bonds,[241] focusing instead on awarding "just compensation,"[242] and modern courts have endorsed this response:[243] "[T]here is no sound reason why persons competent and free to contract may not agree upon [liquidated damages] as fully as upon any other, or why their agreement, when fairly and understandingly entered into with a view to *just compensation for the anticipated loss*, should not be enforced."[244] The focus on just compensation, both historically and today, presumably is meant to encourage people to enter contracts free from the fear of inordinate liability.[245] Of course, this does not explain why courts strike penalty provisions when the evidence demonstrates that both parties understood and sought the provision.

In fact, courts are also suspicious of the quality of the parties' bargaining over agreed damages provisions.[246] Some courts and analysts apparently believe that contracting parties do not pay attention to liquidated damages provisions[247] or understand their meaning. This is because parties may be too optimistic that nothing will go wrong[248] or may misunderstand the nature of their remedial

239. Farnsworth, supra note 17, at 841.

240. Id. at 842 ("A penal bond ... took the form of a promise to pay a stated sum, coupled with a provision that this obligation was 'null and void' if the promisor rendered the required performance under the contract.").

241. See A.W.B. Simpson, A History of the Common Law of Contract 119–125 (1975); see also Goetz & Scott, supra note 229, at 593 ("Since the roots of the penalty rule were nourished on fairness concerns, it is not surprising that generations of lawyers have clung to the view that penalties are 'bad.' "). For a brief discussion of courts of equity, see infra notes 290–296, and accompanying text.

242. Farnsworth, supra note 17, at 841 n. 3 (citing Jaquith v. Hudson, 5 Mich. 123 (1858)); see also Goetz & Scott, supra note 229, at 561.

243. Robert A. Hillman, The Limits on Behavioral Decision Theory in Legal Analysis: The Case of Liquidated Dam-

ages, 85 Cornell L. Rev. 717, 727 (2000) ("Modern courts apparently have greeted with open arms the equity court's response to penal bonds.").

244. Wise v. United States, 249 U.S. 361, 365 (1919) (emphasis added).

245. See supra note 17, and accompanying text.

246. See Hillman, supra note 243, at 727.

247. See Phillip R. Kaplan, Note, A Critique of the Penalty Limitation on Liquidated Damages, 50 S. Cal. L. Rev. 1055, 1072 (1977) (Courts do not believe that "parties have capitalized the risk of breach and included this value in the price.").

248. Jeffrey B. Coopersmith, Comment, Refocusing Liquidated Damages Law for Real Estate Contracts: Returning to the Historical Roots of the Penalty Doctrine, 39 Emory L. J. 267, 268 n.6 ("It is characteristic of men ... that they are likely to be beguiled by the 'illusions of hope,' and to feel so certain of their ability to carry out their engage-

rights.[249] The evidence in actual cases is not compelling to support these conclusions, however.[250]

Some lawyer-economists explain and support the judicial approach to liquidated damages on the basis of economic efficiency. The proof of the economic efficiency of the law here is complex and inconclusive and, for the most part, I am going to spare you.[251] One perspective from this school is worth mentioning, however. Recall our earlier discussion of efficient breach of contract.[252] Legal economists point out that if contract law enforced penalties, parties would be deterred from breaching even when the breaching party could pay off the injured party's expectancy damages and still come out ahead by dealing with a third party.[253] So, contract law strikes penalty provisions to encourage efficient breach of contract.

Recall in our earlier discussion of efficient breach, you agreed to sell your piano to Alice for $1200. The piano was worth $1400. Bob then offered to buy the piano from you for $1800. Recall that the efficient breach theory encourages you to breach your contract with Alice and to pay her $200 (her market price-contract price differential damages), and to deliver the piano to Bob, who outbid Alice for the piano.[254] (You and Bob are better off and Alice is no worse off.) But suppose your contract with Alice included an agreed damages clause that required you to pay her $700 if you did not perform. You will not breach the contract because you will lose $100 by doing so (you'll get $600 extra from Bob, but you will be liable to Alice for $700). The benefits of breaching described above (two people better off and no one hurt) will not be realized. Efficient breach adherents explain the lack of enforcement of the $700 agreed damages clause on the ground that contract law wants to encourage breach in this situation.[255]

ments in [the] future, that their confidence leads them to be willing to make extravagant promises and commitments as to what they are willing to suffer if they fail.") (quoting C. McCormick, Damages 601 (1935)).

249. Id.

250. Hillman, supra note 243, at 728.

251. See, e.g., 3 E. Allen Farnsworth, Farnsworth on Contracts 300 n.8 (2d ed. 1998) (citing the opposing views of Goetz & Scott and Clarkson, Miller & Muris).

252. See supra notes 18–27, and accompanying text.

253. See Posner, supra note 19 at 128 ("It might seem obvious that the law would not—and in fact does not—

enforce penalty clauses in contracts. A penalty would deter efficient as well as inefficient breaches, by making the cost of the breach to the contract breaker greater than the cost of the breach to the victim...."); David Brizzee, Liquidated Damages and the Penalty Rule: A Reassessment, 1991 B.Y.U. L. Rev. 1613, 1625 (1991); but see Lawyers Title Ins. Corp. v. Dearborn Title Corp., 118 F.3d 1157, 1161 (7th Cir. 1997) ("As for any concern that penalty clauses might discourage efficient breaches—breaches in which the profit from the breach exceeds the cost to the promisee—the promisee can always waive the penalty and will do so if compensated by the promisor.").

254. See supra notes 18–27, and accompanying text.

255. Posner, supra note 19, at 128.

I have now discussed the theory of efficient breach twice. It is time to discuss some of the important criticisms of the theory, lest you think that everyone agrees with it.[256] For example, we have already mentioned and seen in various contexts that, because of limitations on expectancy damages, injured parties are rarely put in as good a position as if the breaching party had performed.[257] But the efficient breach theory depends on the assumption that injured parties are made whole. (Remember, nobody is supposed to be worse off as a result of the breach.) In addition, breaching parties will rarely, if ever, know in advance the full amount of their liability for breach. For example, Alice may have reasonably foreseeable consequential damages that are very difficult to estimate at the time you contemplate breaching the contract, but that are provable with sufficient certainty at trial. Further, efficient breach theory does not adequately take into account the harm to your reputation by breaching the contract. Such harm may be too indistinct to include in your calculation of whether you should breach the contract, but it still may be very real. In addition, if you and Alice cannot agree on the precise amount of your damages liability, you may incur significant negotiation or litigation expenses. These costs may be much greater than the costs of an alternative strategy to breaching, namely negotiating a release from Alice of the obligation to deliver the piano.[258]

Perhaps the most worrisome aspect of efficient breach theory is that it ignores the potential harm caused by undermining people's faith in their contracting partner's promises. Although some have argued otherwise, people contract for performance, *not* the right to a monetary equivalent of performance.[259] If people thought that contract law actually encouraged parties to breach when it is profitable, people might be reticent to enter contracts in the first place. As Lon Fuller warned, the "regime of exchange would lose its anchorage and no one would occupy a sufficiently stable position to know what he had to offer or what he could count on receiving

---

256. See generally Daniel Friedmann, The Efficient Breach Fallacy, 18 J. Leg. Stud. 1 (1989).

257. See supra notes 201–203, and accompanying text.

258. Ian R. Macneil, Efficient Breach of Contract: Circles in the Sky, 68 Va. L. Rev. 947, 968–69 (1982) (" '[T]alking after a breach' may be one of the more expensive forms of conversation to be found, involving . . . engaging high-priced lawyers, and gambits like starting litigation, engaging in discovery, and even trying and appealing cases."); William S. Dodge, The Case for Punitive

Damages in Contracts, 48 Duke L. J. 629, 634 (1999) ("[B]ecause the transaction costs of negotiating a release are typically lower than the assessment costs of establishing damages at trial, contractual entitlements should be protected with property rules, including punitive damages.").

259. But see Oliver Wendell Holmes, The Path of the Law, 10 Harv. L. Rev. 457, 462 (1897) ("The duty to keep a contract at common law means a prediction that you must pay damages if you do not keep it, and nothing else.").

from another."[260] A related concern is the distaste that people would feel for a system that actually encourages what is arguably immoral behavior, namely breaking one's promise simply to get a better deal.[261]

Before we leave liquidated damages, we can sum up by focusing on what a lawyer drafting a contract should do to try to ensure the enforcement of an agreed damages clause. Most obviously, of course, the lawyer should make sure to satisfy the two tests of enforcement. Specifically, damages must be difficult to ascertain, but the estimate must be reasonable. To show that the agreed damages clause is a reasonable estimate, the lawyer should incorporate a sliding scale of damages based on the circumstances during performance. Obviously, courts will frown on a term providing for a fixed amount of damages no matter how serious the breach or when it occurs during the course of performance. So, in an equipment lease, for example, base the damages for a breach by the lessee on the amount of rent due at the time of breach, minus a reasonable estimate of what the lessor can save by the return of the equipment.[262]

Incidentally, don't be lulled into believing that if you draft an enforceable liquidated damages provision for your client, you are a brilliant lawyer and have saved your client from the prospect of breach by the other party. One of my favorite examples to make this point is *White v. Benkowski*.[263] The Benkowskis agreed to supply water to their neighbors, the Whites, through a well on the Benkowskis' property. The Whites claimed that the Benkowskis maliciously withheld water, and brought a lawsuit against them. The Whites prevailed on their substantive claim, but could not prove serious damages. What is important here, the judicial decision reports that the neighbors were initially friendly, but the relationship deteriorated to the point of hostility. Here's what actually happened, as revealed by a transcript of the trial:

> Gwynneth [White] testified that the relationship of the families was good until ... the Whites' daughter picked an apple in the Benkowskis' yard. Ruth Benkowski then called the daughter an "S.O.B." Gwynneth told Ruth that "she didn't like this." Later, Ruth called Gwynneth "a redheaded bitch." Virgil White

260. Lon L.Fuller, The Morality of Law 28 (rev. ed. 1969).

261. Patricia H. Marschall, Willfulness: A Crucial Factor in Choosing Remedies for Breach of Contract, 24 Ariz. L. Rev. 733, 734, 740 (1982) ("Even if the theory of efficient breach were realistic, the values that support it are of less importance to society than the principle of good faith and fair dealing in the performance and enforcement of contracts.... Courts ought to be putting more emphasis on the notion of sanctity of contract and the resulting moral obligation to honor one's promises.").

262. Truck Rent–A–Center, 361 N.E.2d at 1019.

263. 155 N.W.2d 74 (Wis.1967).

stated that Paul Benkowski lodged a complaint with Virgil's superior that Virgil had tried to run over Paul's child. The district attorney's investigation absolved Virgil. Paul Benkowski also complained to the police chief that Virgil ... had wild parties at home. Virgil was again absolved of any wrongdoing.[264]

The transcript reveals the deep animosity of the parties, leading to irrational behavior by the Benkowskis. I doubt that a liquidated damages clause in the agreement would have deterred the Benkowkis from turning off the water.

7. Emotional distress and punitive damages. Contract law is reluctant to grant emotional distress damages[265] and outright prohibits punitive damages.[266] Let's investigate the reasons.

a. Emotional distress damages. Suppose you hire Paul's Plumbing Co. to install a new hot tub in your master bath and, because of faulty installation, the hot tub floods your home and destroys your new home entertainment center, among other things. You must move out of your home for three weeks while workers repair the water damage. You can recover consequential damages for your inconvenience and property losses, but you may wonder whether you can recover for your emotional distress, of which you seem to have no shortage. After all, if contract damages are really supposed to put you in as good a position as if the contract had been performed, why shouldn't you recover for your suffering caused by the breach? Sorry, few courts would compensate you for your emotional distress.[267]

Contract law allows emotional distress damages only when a party suffers emotional distress because of the breach of a "personal agreement,"[268] as opposed to a "commercial" contract.[269] You have probably read enough of this book to understand that such

---

264. Summers & Hillman, supra note 24, at 17.

265. Chrum v. Charles Heating and Cooling, Inc., 327 N.W.2d 568, 570 (Mich. Ct. App. 1982)

266. E.I. DuPont de Nemours & Co. v. Pressman, 679 A.2d 436, 445 (Del. 1996) ("[P]unitive damages are not recoverable for breach of contract unless the conduct also amounts independently to a tort.").

267. See generally Restatement (Second) of Contracts § 353. But see B & M Homes v. Hogan, 376 So.2d 667 (Ala. 1979) (emotional distress damages recoverable for severe defects in home construction).

268. Stewart v. Rudner, 84 N.W.2d 816, 824 (Mich. 1957) ("When we have a contract concerned not with trade and commerce but with life and death, not with profit but with elements of personality, not with pecuniary aggrandizement but with matters of mental concern and solicitude, then a breach of duty with respect to such contracts will inevitably and necessarily result in mental anguish, pain and suffering.").

269. Chrum, 327 N.W.2d 568 at 570 ("Where an action is for a breach of a commercial contract, damages for mental distress are not recoverable.").

distinctions are not always very clear. Generally, "personal" contracts involve "deep, personal human relations"[270] or "personal rights of dignity."[271] For example, breaches of contract involving nursing home care of a family member, funeral home services, and medical treatment fit the bill, but not breaches involving the sale of goods or services, such as a sale of a furnace, construction of a home, or storage of personal goods.[272] In addition, breaches that cause damages to the person may qualify for emotional distress damages, but not breaches that cause only property damage.[273] What about breaches of employment contracts? These seem to involve personal relations, but few courts have awarded emotional distress damages to injured employees.[274]

Courts justify the distinction between personal and commercial contracts on the theory that emotional distress is not foreseeable in commercial or employment contracts.[275] Such reasoning may be true in the typical mundane commercial contract, but is less than persuasive in some commercial contexts and certainly is fallacious in many employment settings. Shouldn't the seller of your hot tub reasonably foresee that you would have emotional distress damages if the hot tub floods and causes water damage to your property? What could be more distressing (calm down, this is only a hypothetical)? Shouldn't an employer reasonably foresee that wrongfully terminating an employee from her livelihood would lead to emotional distress? A better explanation for the commercial-personal distinction may be courts' reluctance to allow juries to quantify emotional distress damages in commercial contract cases.[276] How can juries possibly establish an appropriate sum? Would juries be tempted to award a huge sum that would discourage commercial parties from offering their goods or services in the first place?[277] This may be a real concern.

270. Id.

271. Gaglidari v. Denny's Restaurants, Inc., 815 P.2d 1362, 1370 (Wash. 1991).

272. See Sullivan v. O'Connor, 296 N.E.2d 183 (Mass. 1973) (patient's condition worse after operations, emotional distress damages allowed); Avery v. Arnold Home, Inc., 169 N.W.2d 135 (Mich. Ct. App. 1969) (nursing home failed to notify plaintiff of mother's grave condition, emotional distress damages allowed); Chrum, 327 N.W.2d 568 (faulty furnace causes fire that destroys plaintiffs' home, emotional distress damages denied); Jankowski v. Mazzotta, 152 N.W.2d 49 (Mich. Ct. App. 1967) (faulty construction of home, emotional distress damages denied).

273. Chrum, 327 N.W.2d at 570 ("Where property loss is involved, the courts have generally not allowed recovery for mental distress in breach of contract actions.").

274. Gaglidari, 815 P.2d at 1370 ("'[T]ort damages for emotional distress caused by breach of an employment contract are not recoverable.'").

275. Sullivan, 296 N.E.2d at 188.

276. Id. ("To attempt ... to put a value on the condition that would or might have resulted, had the treatment succeeded as promised, may sometimes put an exceptional strain on the imagination of the fact finder.").

277. Gaglidari, 815 P.2d at 1374 ("The impact of allowing emotional distress damages for breach of contract would indeed be enormous.").

b. Punitive damages. The Restatement (Second) of Contracts restates (that's its job) the rule found in hosts of opinions and treatises: "Punitive damages are not recoverable for a breach of contract unless the conduct constituting the breach is also a tort for which punitive damages are recoverable."[278] We will discuss when torts arise in the exchange setting in Chapter 6.[279] For now, understand that in certain situations, often involving "professionals," including doctors, lawyers and engineers, courts have found that a duty exists, *independent of the contract*, to "exercise a reasonable degree of care, skill and ability, such as is ordinarily exercised under similar conditions * * *."[280] A tortious performance of contract, for example, requires unreasonable conduct, such as a doctor leaving a glove in her patient's intestines or a lawyer using a form lease when his client wanted to purchase a house. This section focuses on the rule barring punitive damages in situations not involving a tort. The section will be short, because, basically, you've just learned all there is to know. No punitive damages for breach of contract, even intentional breaches.[281] Courts award punitive damages only when a breach also constitutes an independent tort.[282]

What explains the aversion to punitive damages? To encourage contracting, contract damages are supposed to make people whole, not to punish the breaching party.[283] Many breaches are inadvertent and undeserving of punishment, and awarding punitive damages in such contexts would only discourage parties from making contracts in the first place. Further, as with agreed penalty clauses, punitive damages would discourage breach even when it would be efficient.[284] Suppose, as before, you agree to sell your piano to Alice for $1200. The piano is worth $1400. Bob then offers to buy the piano from you for $1800. Efficient breach theory encourages you to breach your contract with Alice and to pay her $200 (her market price-contract price differential damages), and to deliver the piano to Bob, who outbid Alice for the piano. You and Bob are better off

278. Restatement (Second) of Contracts § 355; See also 11 Samuel Williston and Walter H. E. Jaeger, Williston on Contracts 209–21 (3d ed. 1968); 11Arthur Linton Corbin, Corbin on Contracts 380–382 (Interim ed. 1993); Timothy J. Sullivan, Punitive Damages in the Law of Contract: The Reality and the Illusion of Legal Change, 61 Minn. L. Rev. 207, 207 (1977).

279. See Chapter 6 at notes 85–117, and accompanying text.

280. Mauldin v. Sheffer, 150 S.E.2d 150, 155 (Ga. Ct. App. 1966).

281. Thyssen, Inc. v. S.S. Fortune Star, 777 F.2d 57, 63 (2d Cir. 1985)

("[No punitive damages] although the breach is intentional or even when it has been effected with malicious intent.").

282. Federal Express Corp. v. Dutschmann, 846 S.W.2d 282, 284 (Tex. 1993) ("Recovery of punitive damages requires a finding of an independent tort with accompanying actual damages.").

283. Hillman, supra note 11, at 509 ("The goal is to make the injured party whole, not to punish contract breakers.").

284. See supra notes 253–255, and accompanying text.

and Alice is no worse off. But if you faced the prospect of punitive damages, you hardly will be enthusiastic about breaching.

Still another explanation for the lack of punitive damages in contracts cases involves the commercial contract-personal contract dichotomy, which we have just discussed with respect to emotional distress damages.[285] Contract law, the argument goes, "governs primarily commercial relationships, where the amount required to compensate for loss is easily fixed, in contrast to the law of torts, which compensates for injury to personal interests that are more difficult to value, thus justifying noncompensatory recoveries."[286]

O.k., you've already learned not to trust anyone who asserts absolute rules, such as "no punitive damages in contracts cases." And yes, there are a few exceptions, even beyond the tort exception. For example, courts have awarded punitive damages to an insured party when her insurance company refuses to settle a claim against her even though settlement would be in her best interest.[287] Suppose you cause a car crash and you are sued for $500,000. You have $25,000 of liability insurance and the plaintiff offers to settle for $20,000. The insurance company refuses to settle for $20,00 because, at most, it will lose only $5000 more, even though it is in your best interest to settle. The jury returns a judgment against you for $450,000. You may recover punitive damages against the insurance company.

8. Specific performance. Specific performance has been called an "extraordinary" contract-law remedy.[288] It is probably more accurate to say that the remedy is less common than money damages. Why is specific performance less favored than money damages? For that matter, what precisely is specific performance? These questions and more are the subject of this subsection.

First a little history.[289] In the middle ages in England, courts of equity and law existed side-by-side. These courts differed in procedure (for example, equity courts had no juries), substance, and remedy. Courts of law applied the common law, from which evolved some rather rigid legal rules, some of which you have already studied. For example, you saw that the donee of an oral gift of land who made improvements on the land in anticipation of receiving a

---

285. See supra notes 267–277, and accompanying text.

286. Thyssen, 777 F.2d at 63.

287. Id. at 57. For more detail, see Chapter 6 at notes 106–110, and accompanying text.

288. Barbers Local 552 v. Sealy, 118 N.W.2d 837, 839 (Mich. 1962) ("The remedy of specific performance is an ex-

traordinary one granted only in unusual cases to prevent irreparable harm. It is a matter of grace and not of right."); E. Allan Farnsworth, Legal Remedies for Breach of Contract, 70 Colum. L. Rev. 1145, 1154 (1970).

289. See generally Farnsworth, supra note 17, at 765–770.

deed could not recover anything in a law court if the donor broke the promise, because the donee supplied no consideration and the gift promise was not in writing.[290] Courts of equity arose in part because of the inflexibility of such legal rules, and the Chancellor and deputies, who administered the equity court, developed various equitable doctrines to alleviate harsh results in the law courts, including the outcome in the donee example. The donee's improvements barred the donor from asserting the statute of frauds and constituted "in equity" consideration for the donor's promise to convey the land.[291]

Courts of equity also developed remedial principles, including specific performance. The donee of land who made improvements could obtain a court order requiring the donor to convey the property.[292] This order was very different from the ordinary legal remedy consisting of a judgment that the donor owed the donee money damages, which judgment the donee could enforce by arranging for a sheriff to seize the donor's property to pay the judgment.[293] An order of specific performance was a direct order to the donor to convey, which the equity court enforced by exercising its contempt power.[294] A party, such as the donor of land, who ignored an order of specific performance could be held in contempt and could be thrown in jail, fined or both and the punishment could last until the party obeyed the court order.[295] In part because of the reluctance of equity courts to intrude on the law court's domain, equity courts granted specific performance only when the legal remedy of money damages was inadequate to make the injured party whole.[296]

---

290. See Chapter 3 at note 7, and accompanying text.

291. Seavey v. Drake, 62 N.H. 393, 394 (1882) ("[E]quity protects a parol gift of land equally with a parol agreement to sell it, if accompanied by possession, and the donee has made valuable improvements upon the property induced by the promise to give it.").

292. Akins v. Heiden, 177 Ark. 392, 403 (1928) ("[W]hen a donee enters into possession and makes valuable improvements on the land, the money thus expended on the faith of the gift is a consideration on which to ground a claim for specific performance.").

293. Farnsworth, supra note 288, at 1151–52 ("[I]f the sum was not paid, a writ of execution would issue empowering the sheriff to seize and sell so much of the defendant's property as was required to pay the plaintiff.").

294. Aaron S. Edlin & Alan Schwartz, Symposium: Private Law, Punishment, and Disgorgement: Optimal Penalties in Contracts, 78 Chi.-Kent. L. Rev. 33, 33 (2003) ("[A]n award of specific performance is enforced by the court's contempt power...."); Farnsworth, supra note 288, at 1152.

295. Farnsworth, supra note 288, at 1152–53.

296. Wolf v. Anderson, 334 N.W.2d 212, 215 (N.D. 1983) ("A complaint which requests the equitable remedy of specific performance must clearly show that the legal remedy of damages is inadequate."); Farnsworth, supra note 288, at 1154 ("Equity would stay its hand if the remedy at law was 'adequate.'").

The equity-law division of the English courts was carried over to the United States, but gradually both federal and most state courts eliminated the distinction and unified their courts into one court hearing all cases. Nevertheless, these courts retained many of the differences between substantive legal and equitable principles and between remedial legal and equitable principles. Of concern here, courts continued to grant specific performance only when money damages were inadequate.

Contract law presumes that land is unique, so courts grant specific performance when a seller of land breaks the contract.[297] The theory is that money damages are inadequate because the purchaser cannot use her damages award to purchase equivalent property.[298] If the breaching seller already has resold to a bona fide purchaser, obviously the injured purchaser cannot get specific performance. If you contract to sell your house and lot to Alice, but you convey the property to a bona fide purchaser instead (a bona fide purchaser is someone who doesn't know about your contract with Alice and pays a fair price for the property[299]), contract law obviously must deny Alice specific performance against you. Alice may recover damages, often including any amount you gained by breaching and selling to the bona fide purchaser. For example, if the market value of the property is $190,000, the contract price is $180,000, and you sell the property to Ms. BFP for $200,000, Alice can recover $20,000.[300]

Some courts grant specific performance of land sale contracts to sellers as well as buyers,[301] in part to create symmetry between the seller's and buyer's remedies. Obviously, the purchase price due a seller is not unique. Courts that grant specific performance to sellers typically condition their decree on the seller tendering a deed to the buyer.[302] Some courts don't buy the symmetry concern,

---

297. Farnsworth, supra note 288, at 1154.

298. Breitbach v. Christenson, 541 N.W.2d 840, 843 (Iowa 1995) ("[I]t is clear from our case law this court presumes real estate to possess a unique quality such that mere monetary damages may not always constitute adequate remedy for a breach of contract."); Kitchen v. Herring, 42 N.C. 190 (1851); see also Restatement (Second) of Contracts § 360, cmt. e ("Contracts for the sale of land have traditionally been accorded a special place in the law of specific performance. A specific tract of land has long been regarded as unique and impossible of duplication by the use of any amount of money.").

299. Black's Law Dictionary 1249 (7th ed. 1999) ("One who buys something for value without notice of another's claim to the item or of any defects in the seller's title; one who has in good faith paid valuable consideration for property without notice of prior adverse claims.").

300. Cf. Timko v. Useful Homes Corp., 168 A. 824 (N.J. Ch. 1933).

301. Jackson v. Schultz, 151 A.2d 284 (Del. Ch. 1959).

302. Summers & Hillman, supra note 24, at 338.

however, and deny specific performance to sellers.[303] These sellers can still get a money judgment.

Unlike contracts involving land, courts rarely grant specific performance to employers or employees.[304] First, let's review some Constitutional law (see how "rich" contract law is?). The Thirteenth Amendment prohibits involuntary servitude, remember?[305] Courts fail to grant employers specific performance because ordering an employee to work would be unconstitutional.[306] Courts have had less trouble barring an employee from working for someone else,[307] which often persuades the employee "voluntarily" to return to work for the injured employer. Courts also rarely grant specific performance to an employee, unless the employee's rights are based on a statute.[308]

UCC section 2–716 governs specific performance of contracts for the sale of goods. It provides in part: "Specific performance may be decreed where the goods are unique or in other proper circumstances."[309] Obviously, money damages cannot make an injured buyer whole when the goods are unique (one-of-a-kind), such as a Beatles record signed on the label by John Lennon. But the "other proper circumstances" language invites expansion of the remedy of specific performance. For example, a court may grant specific performance to a buyer even though substitute goods are available on the market, if the buyer reasonably cannot cover her losses because the seller's breach causes the buyer financial difficulties.[310]

303. Wolf, 334 N.W.2d at 215–16 ("We find nothing unique or special in these circumstances warranting the remedy of specific performance. In the instant case there is no indication that monetary damages will not adequately compensate the [seller]. Although [North Dakota law] supports a buyer's right to specific performance on the ground that monetary damages are presumed to be inadequate, no similar statutory presumption exists to support an action by the seller for specific performance.").

304. E.g., Pingley v. Brunson, 252 S.E.2d 560, 561 (S.C. 1979) ("Courts of equity will not ordinarily decree specific performance of a contract for personal services, particularly where the performance of the services contracted for would be continuous over a long period of time.").

305. American Broadcasting Co., Inc. v. Wolf, 420 N.E.2d 363, 366 (N.Y. 1981) ("It has been strongly suggested that judicial compulsion of services would violate the express command of [the Thirteenth] amendment.") (citing Arthur v. Oakes, 63 F. 310, 317 (7th Cir. 1894)).

306. Id. ("For practical, policy and constitutional reasons, therefore, courts continue to decline to affirmatively enforce employment contracts.").

307. Id. at 367 ("[W]here an employee refuses to render services to an employer in violation of an existing contract, and the services are unique or extraordinary, an injunction may issue to prevent the employee from furnishing those services to another person for the duration of the contract.").

308. Gargano v. Diocese of Rockville Centre, 888 F.Supp. 1274 (E.D.N.Y. 1995), aff'd, 80 F.3d 87 (2d Cir. 1996). I have refrained from textual footnotes throughout this book, but I can't resist mentioning that Rockville Centre is my home town. Go South Side High!

309. UCC § 2–716(1).

310. Stephan's Mach. & Tool, Inc. v. D & H Mach. Consultants, Inc., 417 N.E.2d 579 (Ohio Ct. App. 1979).

A court may also grant specific performance when a seller breaches a long-term supply contract and the buyer cannot procure a contract of similar length.[311]

Amended section 2–716 expands the right to specific performance still further. Section 2–716(1) adds that in contracts not involving consumers, "specific performance may be decreed if the parties have agreed to that remedy."[312] The remedy is not available, however, "if the breaching party's sole remaining contractual obligation is the payment of money."[313] If Fred's Used Car Lot agrees to purchase four cars from Ford Motor Company, the parties can provide for specific performance in the event of a breach. If Ford delivers the cars and all that is left is for Fred's to pay the purchase price, however, specific performance is not available. Ford can get a money judgment against Fred's, of course. Comment 3 to the section points out that courts can refuse to grant specific performance, even when the parties have agreed to it, in light of the court's "equitable discretion."[314]

The availability of specific performance becomes murkier when the subject matter of the contract is not land, employment, or sale of goods. Courts have ordered specific performance in favor of a lessee of a store in a shopping center because money damages could not compensate for "the almost incalculable future advantages that might accrue to it as a result of extending its operations into the suburbs."[315] On the other hand, courts often decline to specifically enforce construction contracts because of the need to continue supervising the project to make sure the builder doesn't mess up on purpose.[316]

As many of the above examples suggest, courts enjoy considerable discretion in determining whether to award specific performance.[317] Here are some additional "rules" that add to judicial discretion. Courts may refuse to grant specific performance when

---

311. Laclede Gas Co. v. Amoco Oil Co., 522 F.2d 33 (8th Cir. 1975) ("[Plaintiff] probably could not find another supplier of propane willing to enter into a long-term contract such as the [breached] agreement. . . .").

312. Amended UCC § 2–716(1).

313. Id.

314. Amended UCC § 2–716, cmt. 3.

315. City Stores v. Ammerman, 266 F.Supp. 766, 776 (D.D.C. 1967), aff'd, 394 F.2d 950 (D.C. Cir. 1968).

316. Id. (but specific performance awarded); Lester's Home Furnishers, Inc. v. Modern Furniture Co., 61 A.2d 743, 746 (N.J. Super. Ct. 1948) ("[T]he items of renovation and construction work are numerous, and noticeably diversified. Moreover by their nature they are such as to render their actual performance and accomplishment provocative of frequent disputes. 'The difficulty in supervision that would be necessary is obvious.' ") (quoting Fiedler, Inc. v. Coast Fin. Co., 18 A.2d 268 (N.J. 1941)).

317. Farnsworth, supra note 17, at 768–69; see also Anthony T. Kronman, Specific Performance, 45 U. Chi. L. Rev. 351, 369 (1978) ("There is . . . some basis for believing the uniqueness test [of specific performance] reflects the typical solution that contracting parties would arrange for themselves. . . .").

they believe that a plaintiff's conduct was unsavory.[318] Courts also may decline to award specific performance if the parties have omitted too many terms in their contract,[319] even if the contract is not too indefinite to enforce by granting money damages.[320] Courts also consider the hardship of a specific performance decree on the promisor.[321]

B. Remedies for Promissory Estoppel

1. Introduction. Under the theory of promissory estoppel, recall that a promisee can recover for a broken promise when the promisor reasonably should expect the promise to induce reliance, the promisee does rely, and justice requires enforcement of the promise.[322] At the time of the drafting of Restatement (First) of Contracts, section 90, which first encapsulated this principle, a controversy developed over the appropriate measure of damages. At an ALI meeting discussing the issue, the chief draft person, Samuel Williston, posited the following hypothetical: Johnny B. Goode (well, Williston just used Johnny) tells his uncle he wants to buy a Buick. His uncle promises Johnny $1000. Johnny buys the car because of the uncle's promise, but for $500. Is Johnny entitled to $1000 or $500?

Williston thought that Johnny should get $1000, the value of the promise. But a member of the Institute had this caustic reaction: "In other words, substantial justice would require that uncle should be penalized in the sum of $500."[323] The gist of the nervy guy's complaint was that Johnny's out of pocket loss was $500, which is precisely the harm that promissory estoppel addresses.[324] On the other hand, Williston thought that Johnny should get $1000 because "either the promise is binding or it is not."[325]

---

318. Wollums v. Horsley, 20 S.W. 781, 781 (Ky. 1892) ("Thus a hard or unconscionable bargain will not be specifically enforced, nor, if the decree will produce injustice or under all the circumstances be inequitable, will it be rendered.").

319. City Stores v. Ammerman, 266 F.Supp. 766 (D.D.C. 1967), aff'd, 394 F.2d 950 (D.C. Cir. 1968); Linderkamp v. Hoffman, 562 N.W.2d 734, 735 (N. D. 1997) (" 'specific performance of an agreement must be denied when its terms are not sufficiently certain to make the precise act which is to be done clearly ascertainable.' ") (quoting Beebe v. Hanson, 169 N.W. 31, 32 (N.D. 1918)).

320. See Summers & Hillman supra note 24, at 344.

321. Van Wagner Adver. Corp. v. S & M Enters., 492 N.E.2d 756, 761 (N.Y. 1986) ("It is well settled that the imposition of an equitable remedy must not itself work an inequity, and that specific performance should not be an undue hardship.").

322. See Chapter 3 at notes 1–64, and accompanying text.

323. Summers & Hillman, supra note 24, at 308.

324. See Chapter 3 at notes 1–64, and accompanying text.

325. Summers & Hillman, supra note 24, at 308.

Williston thought the promise *is* binding and therefore Johnny was entitled to expectancy damages.

The controversy over whether the Johnnys of the world (meaning people who detrimentally rely on promises) should get $500 (detrimental reliance damages) or $1000 (expectancy damages) still rages today. This is mainly so because the drafters of the Restatement (Second) did nothing to resolve the issue. In fact, they exacerbated the confusion by adding the following sentence to section 90: "The remedy granted for breach may be limited as justice requires." A comment confirms that the drafters' intent was to give courts plenty of discretion on this issue.[326] But how should courts decide which remedy is appropriate in a given case?

2. Judicial decisions. Some courts have considered the appropriate measure of damages in promissory estoppel cases, but the results reflect Section 90's fogginess. In short, some courts grant reliance damages, some grant what looks like lost expectancy.[327] Moreover, the decisions do not spend a lot of time explaining *why* they grant one measure of damages over the other.

Instead, they seem to assume that one or the other measure is the law. For example, in *Goodman v. Dicker*,[328] the court awarded reliance damages to the plaintiff, a prospective franchisee of Emerson radios, who incurred expenses preparing for the franchise after a distributor represented that the plaintiff would get the franchise and an initial delivery of radios. The court refused to grant the plaintiff lost profits, proclaiming that "[t]he true measure of damage is the loss sustained by expenditures made in reliance upon the assurance of a dealer franchise."[329]

In *Walters v. Marathon Oil Co.*,[330] on the other hand, the court awarded lost profits. Marathon Oil broke a promise to supply oil products to the Walters after they had improved a gas station in reliance on the promise.[331] Marathon Oil claimed that the Walters did not suffer reliance damages because the increase in the market value of the Walters' land more than made up for the cost of the improvements. Further, Marathon Oil insisted that the Walters could not recover lost profits in a promissory estoppel case.

---

326. Restatement (Second) of Contracts § 90, cmt., d.

327. See Robert A. Hillman, Questioning the "New Consensus" on Promissory Estoppel: An Empirical and Theoretical Study, 98 Colum. L. Rev. 580, 601–02 (1998) (exceptionally fine article analyzing the cases).

328. 169 F.2d 684 (D.C. Cir. 1948).

329. Id. at 685; see also Walser v. Toyota Motor Sales, U.S.A., Inc., 43 F.3d 396, 402 (8th Cir. 1994) ("[T]he district court [did not] abuse[] its discretion in limiting the award of damages on the promissory estoppel claim to out-of-pocket expenses.").

330. 642 F.2d 1098 (7th Cir. 1981).

331. Id. at 1099.

The court awarded the Walters lost profits on the theory that they forewent the opportunity to invest and make the profits elsewhere:

> [I]n reliance upon [Marathon Oil's] promise to supply gasoline supplies to them, [the Walters] purchased the station, and invested their funds and their time. It is unreasonable to assume that they did not anticipate a return of profits from this investment of time and funds, but, in reliance upon [Marathon Oil's] promise, they had foregone the opportunity to make the investment elsewhere.[332]

The court then discussed evidence of the number of gallons of gasoline previous owners of Walters' station had pumped, the amount of gasoline Marathon Oil had promised the Walters, and the amount of profit the Walters would have made on each gallon of gasoline they would have sold. Based on this evidence, the court concluded that the Walters proved lost profits with sufficient certainty.[333] The court therefore affirmed the trial court's computation of lost profits.[334]

In sum, the *Walters* court justified the recovery of lost profits on the theory that, but for the broken promise, the Walters would have made the profit elsewhere. Based on this reasoning, the Walters' lost profits were like a reliance recovery because Marathon Oil's promise induced the Walters to rely by foregoing other opportunities. To support this reasoning, the court had to make the leap that the Walters would have made a profit on another investment, in fact an identical profit to the one expected from the Marathon Oil project. This assumption is clouded by the court's additional conclusion that the Walters did not fail to mitigate damages by finding a substitute supplier because no other suppliers were reasonably available.[335] This conclusion is inconsistent with the position that the Walters would have made an equivalent profit on an alternative investment were it not for Marathon Oil's promise.

In one line of cases, courts appear comfortable with limiting the promissory estoppel recovery to reliance damages. These cases involve an employer's promise of a job that induces an employee to leave other employment and incur expenses relocating to the new employer's place of business. The employee usually cannot recover for breach of contract because the new employment is terminable at will.[336] Nevertheless, courts have found in favor of the employee on

---

332. Id. at 1100.

333. Id. at 1100–01 ("[Plaintiff] suffered a loss of profits as a direct result of their reliance upon the promise made by appellant, and the amount of

the lost profits was ascertained with reasonable certainty.").

334. Id. at 1101.

335. Id. at 1099.

336. Andrade v. Jamestown Hous. Auth., 82 F.3d 1179, 1186 (1st Cir. 1996)

the basis of promissory estoppel, although limiting the recovery to reliance damages: "The doctrine of promissory estoppel may be available to an at-will employee, but the remedy is limited to damages actually resulting from the detrimental reliance * * *."[337] This conclusion makes sense because the employer generally has the right to terminate the new employee before she has earned any salary, so her expectancy is very uncertain.

Notwithstanding the definitive turn to reliance damages in these employment cases, other questions persist. Can an employee recover lost salary from the job she quits in order to take the new job? Can she recover lost salary from other job offers that she declined in order to work for the defendant employer? Such recoveries would be consistent with the "opportunities forgone" rationale of reliance damages discussed above in the *Walters* case.[338] Some courts appear to agree with this analysis: "Since * * * the prospective employment might have been terminated at any time, the measure of damages is not so much what [the employee] would have earned from [the employer] as what [the employee] lost in quitting the job he held and in declining at least one other offer of employment elsewhere."[339]

C. Remedies for Unjust Enrichment

Recall that under the theory of unjust enrichment, a party who confers a benefit on another party can recover the benefit when it would be unjust for the party receiving the benefit to keep it without paying for it.[340] The remedial challenge when the remedy is the money equivalent of the benefit conferred and not specific restitution (return of specific property) is how to measure the benefit in dollars. The Restatement (Second) of Contracts, section 371, sets forth two possible measures:

> If a sum of money is awarded to protect a party's restitution interest, it may as justice requires be measured by either
>
>> (a) the reasonable value to the other party of what he received in terms of what it would have cost him to obtain it from a person in the claimant's position, or

("[I]t is well established that 'a promise to render personal services to another for an indefinite term is terminable at any time at the will of either party and therefore creates no executory obligations.'") (quoting School Comm. v. Board of Regents for Educ., 308 A.2d 788, 790 (R.I. 1973)).

337. Jarboe v. Landmark Comty. Newspapers, Inc., 644 N.E.2d 118, 122

(Ind. 1994); see also D & G Stout, Inc. v. Bacardi Imports, Inc., 923 F.2d 566, 568–70 (7th Cir. 1991).

338. See supra notes 330–335, and accompanying text.

339. Grouse v. Group Health Plan, Inc., 306 N.W.2d 114, 116 (Minn. 1981).

340. See Chapter 3 at notes 65–122, and accompanying text.

(b) the extent to which the other party's property has been increased in value or his other interests advanced.[341]

Suppose Alice hires you to level her backyard in preparation for the construction of a swimming pool. She agrees to pay you $1000. You complete the work, but she is not satisfied and refuses to pay you anything. The work cost you $1050, and it increases the market value of her land by $750. Alice could have hired someone else to do the work for $1200. (Why did you agree to do it for $1000? You didn't do your homework and thought the job was worth only $1000.)

If you sue Alice and prove that your work was perfectly acceptable and that she broke the contract, recall that you have an election to recover on the contract for expectancy damages or, in the alternative, to recover based on Alice's unjust enrichment.[342] With respect to the latter, she has a leveled yard and hasn't paid you anything. Contract law can measure this benefit in many ways. You bid too low for the work and should have gotten $1200, the fair market value of the work. Restatement (Second), section 371(a), authorizes an award of $1200. You increased the market value of her property by $750. Restatement (Second), section 371(b), allows a recovery based on this measure. A third possibility is to measure the benefit conferred by your cost of performing the services, here $1050.[343] A fourth measure of the benefit would be the contract price, not because you want the court to enforce the contract, but because the contract rate might be the best evidence of the true value of the benefit to Alice.[344]

Which measure is a court likely to adopt? Commentators have found a relation between the conduct of the breaching party and the likely measurement of restitution.[345] Alice has breached a contract, which does not put her in a favorable light right out of the starting block. To the extent the evidence shows willful or negligent reasons for her failure to pay, her stock with the court goes down even further. The worse Alice's conduct, the more likely the court will adopt the highest measure. The lesson from all this is that courts appear to enjoy considerable discretion in determining monetary remedies for unjust enrichment.

341. Restatement (Second) of Contracts § 371.

342. See Chapter 3 at notes 84–90, and accompanying text.

343. See City of Philadelphia v. Tripple, 79 A. 703 (Pa. 1911).

344. United States v. Zara Contracting Co., 146 F.2d 606, 611 (2d Cir. 1944) ("It is ... appropriate here, particularly in default of any challenging evidence, to base recovery on proper expenditures in performance or for extra work and to make use of the contract as fixing the basic price.").

345. Richard Craswell, Against Fuller and Perdue, 67 U. Chi. L. Rev. 99, 142 (2000) ("[T]here is some evidence that courts are influenced in their choice of measurement by how well or badly the breaching party behaved.").

Don't count on collecting your $1200 just yet, however, for two reasons. First, some courts have balked at allowing a recovery greater than the contract rate would permit (here $1000),[346] on the theory that contract law should not ignore the agreement you made with Alice even if she breaches the contract.[347] You agreed to do the work for $1000, why should you now get $1200?[348] However, probably a greater number of courts allow the $1200 recovery, reasoning that a nasty contract breaker should not be able to use the very contract that she breached as a shield against the additional liability.[349] Obviously, this reasoning has a punitive element to it, but the Restatement (Second) is quite explicit in allowing a recovery:

> The right of the injured party under a losing contract to a greater amount in restitution than he could have recovered in damages has engendered much controversy. The rules stated in this Section give him that right. He is entitled to such recovery even if the contract price is stated in terms of a rate per unit of work and the recovery exceeds that rate.[350]

Wait another minute before you celebrate your $1200 recovery. In cases such as yours, where you have completed all of the work prior to a breach by the other party, and all that is left to complete the contract is for the other party to pay you an agreed sum, courts

346. Johnson v. Bovee, 574 P.2d 513, 514 (Colo. Ct. App. 1978) ("We believe using the contract price as a ceiling on restitution is the better-reasoned resolution of this question. Had [plaintiff] fully performed, his recovery would be limited to the contract price, since he would be suing for specific performance of the liquidated debt obligation under the contract. It is illogical to allow him to recover the full cost of his services when, if he completed the house, he would be limited to the contract price plus the agreed upon extras.").

347. See, e.g., Robert Childres & Jack Garamella, The Law of Restitution and the Reliance Interest in Contract, 64 Nw. U. L. Rev. 433, 439–40 (1969) ("There is no justification for the position that the terms of the promise do not regulate the recovery of reliance damages in some cases which may be twisted into an 'action in *quantum meruit.*' ").

348. See Joseph M. Perillo, Restitution in a Contractual Context, 73 Colum. L. Rev. 1208, 1224 n.104 (1973) ("When restitution is awarded because of breach of contract, most courts have held that the contract rate does not set an upper limit. Such a result of course disturbs the allocation of risks made by the parties.").

349. Bausch & Lomb Inc. v. Bressler, 977 F.2d 720, 730 (2d Cir. 1992) ("The terms of the agreement do not control an award of restitution."); United States ex rel. Coastal Steel Erectors, Inc. v. Algernon Blair, Inc., 479 F.2d 638, 641 n.7 (4th Cir. 1973) ("[I]n suits for restitution there are many cases permitting the plaintiff to recover the value of benefits conferred on the defendant, even though this value exceeds that of the return performance promised by the defendant. In these cases it is no doubt felt that the defendant's breach should work a forfeiture of his right to retain the benefits of an advantageous bargain."); see also Andrew Kull, Restitution as a Remedy for Breach of Contract, 67 S. Cal L. Rev. 1465, 1482 (1994) ("[C]ourts in some circumstances favor a punitive remedy for breach of contract, and ... stripping a defendant of the benefits secured by a contract he has failed to perform has seemed to judges, in some circumstances, to be no more than poetic justice.").

350. Restatement (Second) of Contracts § 373, cmt. d.

may balk at giving you any more than the agreed sum: "The remedy of restitution in money is not available to one who has fully performed his part of a contract, if the only part of the agreed exchange for such performance that has not be rendered by the defendant is a sum of money constituting a liquidated debt."[351] (The parties don't dispute the amount of a "liquidated debt."[352]). Courts adopting this rule seem motivated by their unease over ignoring the contract rate of $1000. But if this is the reason for the rule, courts should explicitly say so. Creating an exception to the right to receive a recovery greater than the contract rate based on whether the plaintiff has completed performance only will confuse the law and lead to silly results. For example, under this rule, if you had completed 99% of the leveling job at the time of Alice's breach, you could collect more than the contract rate. But if you completed the last bit of work (say removing your tools), you would be limited to the contract rate.

351. Oliver v. Campbell, 273 P.2d 15, 20 (Cal. 1954) (quoting Restatement (First) of Contracts § 350).

352. Black's Law Dictionary 411 (7th ed. 1999) ("A debt whose amount has been determined by agreement of the parties or by operation of law.").

Chapter Six

POLICING CONTRACTS

If you have read this book from the beginning, you now understand the principal ground for enforcing a promise, namely the existence of an agreement supported by consideration (a bargained-for exchange).[1] In this chapter, we assume that the parties have made an agreement and that each promise is supported by consideration. What's left to talk about, you say? The agreement may be unenforceable even though it satisfies the requirements of a bargained-for exchange because the promisor may have defenses based on one or more of the following "policing" doctrines that we are about to study: duress, fraudulent misrepresentation, fraudulent concealment, innocent misrepresentation, tortious breach of contract, public policy, and unconscionability.[2] Further, we will see that misrepresentation, concealment, and other tort claims often entitle the injured party to affirmative recoveries. In this chapter, we also investigate the special problems of enforcement presented by standard-form contracts.

Policing doctrines generally deny enforcement of agreements when something is wrong with the process of forming the agreement or when the discrepancy between what each party receives is too large, or both.[3] For example, contract law declines to enforce an "agreement" between you and your neighbor, Alice, made while you are holding a gun to her head. In addition, contract law balks at enforcing an agreement in which you promise to pay $1 for Alice's $1000 watch, even if you didn't use your assault weapon to procure the contract. Of course, overturning the watch contract may be controversial because, motivated by the principle of freedom of contract, people are wary of the government impinging on private arrangements.[4] If your neighbor decided to sell her watch

---

1. See Chapter 2.

2. Additional rules sometimes lumped with policing doctrines involve the lack of capacity to contract. They include infancy and mental incapacity. See Restatement (Second) of Contracts § 12 (1981); E. Allen Farnsworth, Contracts 225–241 (3d ed. 1999).

3. Riesett v. W.B. Doner & Co., 293 F.3d 164, 172–173 (4th Cir. 2002) ("When the substantive terms of a contract are so one-sided that a court is led to conclude that some defect in bargain-

ing process (such as fraud, duress, or incompetence of a contracting party) led to the formation of the contract, then the unconscionability doctrine may be useful in helping courts ferret out such contracts, whose enforcement would neither promote the autonomy of the contracting parties nor enhance social welfare.").

4. See, e.g., Sanger v. Yellow Cab Co., Inc., 486 S.W.2d 477, 482 (Mo. 1972) ("[T]he general rule of freedom of

for $1 without being coerced, why shouldn't the contract be enforced?

One can see that contract law's challenge is drawing a coherent line between contracts that should not be enforced because they are procured unfairly or contain unfair terms and contracts that should be enforced on the basis of freedom of contract. This requires some thought about distinguishing "fair" bargaining and reasonable terms from overreaching and unconscionable ones. Moreover, we must draw these lines over a wide range of transactions, from important business deals, to standard-form contracts, to simple contracts between neighbors.

We will proceed systematically (would I do otherwise?) by looking at each of the policing doctrines. Does each doctrine draw the appropriate line between freedom of contract and wrongful overreaching?

A. Duress

Various courts and writers have tried to define duress, but with limited success. Consider the following definitions: "[T]here must be * * * some threatened exercise of power or authority over [a person's] person or property which can be avoided only by making the payment."[5] "[T]he plaintiff [must] show that the other party by wrongful acts or threats, intentionally caused [the plaintiff] to involuntarily enter into a particular transaction."[6] "[H]as the person complaining been constrained to do what he otherwise would not have done?"[7] Each of these definitions gropes towards a principle for defining when contract law should decline to enforce a promise because the promisor did not make the promise of her own free will,[8] but are the definitions successful in guiding courts in particular cases? For example, the last definition surely is too broad. You decided to attend law school, something you would not have done if you didn't need a job to put food on the table.[9] But

contract includes the freedom to make a bad bargain.").

5. Phelan v. City and County of San Francisco, 52 P. 38, 39 (Cal. 1898).

6. Totem Marine Tug & Barge, Inc. v. Alyeska Pipeline Serv. Co., 584 P.2d 15, 22 (Alaska 1978).

7. S. P. Dunham & Company v. Kudra, 131 A.2d 306, 309 (N.J. Super. Ct. 1957).

8. For more groping, see John D. Calamari & Joseph M. Perillo, The Law of Contracts 308–09 (4th ed. 1998) ("Today the general rule is that any wrongful act or threat which overcomes the free will of a party constitutes duress."); Kaplan v. Kaplan, 182 N.E.2d 706, 709 (Ill. 1962) ("Duress has been defined as a condition where one is induced by a wrongful act or threat of another to make a contract under circumstances which deprive him of the exercise of his free will...."); Shlensky v. Shlensky, 15 N.E.2d 694, 698 (Ill. 1938) ("Duress has been defined as a condition which exists where one is induced by an unlawful act of another to make a contract or perform or forego an act under circumstances which deprive him of the exercise of his free will.").

9. See generally Robert L. Hale, Coercion and Distribution in a Supposedly Non–Coercive State, 38 Pol. Sci. Q. 470, 471–73 (1923).

contract law hardly allows you to claim that you made your decision under duress.[10] So the real question is to determine what kinds of constraints on free will should bar enforcement of promises and what kinds should contract law ignore.[11]

First, an easy case. If someone beats you into signing a contract, or even threatens to pummel you if you don't sign, contract law treats your signing as void, meaning that you have no contract at all.[12] Such cases are not only easy, they are also rare.[13]

The best way to understand what courts are doing in harder cases, namely those involving economic duress, is to consider some examples. Suppose Standard Box, a company that manufactures (you guessed it) boxes, suddenly finds itself in the enviable position of supplying a commodity in very short supply.[14] The shortage is due to the famous earthquake that shook San Francisco in 1906. (I guess the ground opened up and swallowed all of San Francisco's boxes.) Mutual Biscuit Company needs boxes to package its products and will go out of business without them. Standard Box, aware of Mutual Biscuit's plight, offers to sell boxes at their market value and Mutual Biscuit purchases some boxes.[15] Later, Mutual Biscuit seeks a return of a portion of the purchase price on the theory that Standard Box charged more than it had under previous contracts with Mutual Biscuit and that Mutual Biscuit had paid under duress.[16] The court entertaining comparable facts made short shrift of Mutual Biscuit's argument (does anybody ever make long shrift of an argument?) because Standard Box simply charged market value for the boxes.[17]

Easy case, you say. But we can investigate the doctrine of economic duress further by posing some hypos based on these facts. Suppose Standard Box, aware of Mutual Biscuit's need, charges ten times the market value for the boxes. Mutual Biscuit, unable to secure an alternative source of supply in time, pays the inflated price, but then claims duress. In thinking about this example, consider one writer's more helpful (albeit somewhat tentative)

---

10. Michael J. Trebilcock, The Limits of Freedom of Contract 243 (Harvard University Press 1993); Gregory S. Alexander, Comparing the Two Legal Realisms—American and Scandinavian, 50 Am. J. Comp. L. 131, 145 (2002) ("All choices are constrained choices simply by virtue of the fact of being made in the context of society.").

11. Calamari & Perillo, supra note 8, at 310 ("[I]n determining whether a transaction may be avoided for duress, the main inquiry is to ascertain what acts or threats are branded as wrongful.").

12. Farnsworth, supra note 2, at 264; United States for the Use of Trane Company v. Lorna D. Bond, 586 A.2d 734, 738 (Md.1991).

13. Restatement (Second) of Contracts § 174, cmt. a.

14. Standard Box Co. v. Mutual Biscuit Co., 103 P. 938, 939 (Cal. Ct. App. 1909).

15. Id. at 939.

16. Id.

17. Id. at 944.

description of duress: "[I]t might be argued that deliberate exploitation by one party of another party's lack of choices to exact returns that exceed those normally realizable in a more competitive environment should be viewed as suspect."[18] In the example, Standard Box exploited Mutual Biscuit's lack of an alternative source of boxes by setting the price far above those "realizable" even under the exigent circumstances. Mutual Biscuit's claim of duress arguably should prevail.[19]

What if boxes became plentiful again before Mutual Biscuit purchased them for ten times their market value? No duress because Mutual Biscuit had other choices.[20] But what if Mutual Biscuit did not know about the market alternatives? This raises the question of whether Mutual Biscuit's lack of choice should be based on what a reasonable company would have known about the alternatives (an objective test) or on what Mutual Biscuit actually knew (a subjective test). Courts disagree on this issue,[21] but why should contract law protect Mutual Biscuit when it unreasonably did not avail itself of market alternatives?

What if Standard Box is not aware of Mutual Biscuit's situation when Standard Box decides to charge ten times the market price for the boxes? No duress because Standard Box's motive is not to take advantage of Mutual Biscuit's precarious position.[22]

Suppose boxes were plentiful (no earthquake), but Mutual Biscuit negligently failed to procure contracts from other suppliers and had to deal with Standard Box. Standard Box, aware of Mutual Biscuit's ineptitude, refuses to sell for less than ten times the

18. Trebilcock, supra note 10, at 243. See Totem Marine Tug & Barge, Inc. v. Alyeska Pipeline Service Co., 584 P.2d 15 (Alaska 1978).

19. See Charles Fried, Contract as Promise: A Theory of Contractual Obligation, 109–110 (Harvard University Press 1981). But see Joel Feinberg, Harm to Self, 246, 248 (Oxford University Press 1986) (B's consent valid when A exploits, but does not create B's lack of choice).

20. Pierce v. Atchison, Topeka & Santa Fe Ry. Co., 65 F.3d 562, 569 (7th Cir. 1995) ("[O]ne cannot successfully claim duress as a defense to a contract when he had an alternative to signing the agreement."); Merrill Lynch, Pierce, Fenner & Smith, Inc. v. Adcock, 176 F.R.D. 539, 545 (N.D. Ill. 1997) ("[Defendant's] choice negates any showing of duress.").

21. Zeilinger v. SOHIO Alaska Petroleum Co., 823 P.2d 653, 658 (Alaska

1992) ("In determining whether a reasonable alternative [is] available, we employ an objective test...."); Austin Instrument v. Loral Corp., 272 N.E.2d 533 (N.Y. 1971) (subjective test); S. P. Dunham & Co. v. Kudra, 131 A.2d 306, 309 (N.J. Super. A.D. 1957) ("[O]ur courts have finally rejected the objective test....");Wise v. Midtown Motors, 42 N.W.2d 404, 407 (Minn. 1950) ("The standards of resisting power of the victim are personal and subjective rather than objective...."); see generally Calamari & Perillo, supra note 8, at 309 ("[T]he overwhelming weight of modern authority uses a subjective test.... Still, an objective test governs in certain situations.").

22. Trebilcock, supra note 10, at 243. But see Grubel v. Union Mut. Life Ins. Co., 387 N.Y.S.2d 442, 443 (N.Y. App. Div. 1976) ("Actions, not motives, must cause economic duress.").

market value of the boxes. Mutual Biscuit purchases boxes at this price and then claims duress. This issue also causes courts consternation, but the better view is that courts should ignore how the party claiming duress got itself in its precarious position.[23] Contract law should not condone Standard Box's unsavory conduct of taking advantage of Mutual Biscuit's plight to achieve gains it could not otherwise have made, just because Mutual Biscuit negligently forewent other opportunities.[24] Likewise, if Ethan Entrepreneur charges $100 for a glass of water to a person dying of thirst (literally) in the desert, when Ethan charges one dollar to everyone else, the victim should be able to claim duress regardless of how she came to be in this precarious state.

Does the opportunity to go to court to adjudicate your contract rights negate a claim of lack of choice and hence duress? Most courts have abandoned the reasoning that access to a court is a reasonable alternative for a party under duress.[25] For example, if you agree to mow Alice's lawn for $50 per week and later, realizing that she cannot find another person to do the job, you refuse to mow unless she pays you $100, you cannot negate Alice's claim of duress because she has the right to sue you for breach of contract. Although we saw in Chapter 5 that contract law, in computing a party's lost expectancy damages, largely ignores the costs in time and resources of pursuing litigation,[26] contract law assesses these concerns (as it should) in the duress inquiry. Going to court simply may not be a viable alternative for Alice.

Putting all of this together, if you are investigating whether your client has a good economic duress claim, consider first the actions of the party accused of duress. Was her motive to take advantage of your client?[27] Second, did your client have other reasonable choices or was he stuck dealing with the party accused of duress? Third, did the accused party enjoy gains she otherwise wouldn't have made? If the answer to all of these questions is yes, your client has a good claim of duress and your law practice will gain a loyal client when you pursue the case.

23. John Dalzell, Duress by Economic Pressure I, 20 N.C. L. Rev. 237, 258 (1942) ("[T]he fact that [the debtor] did not create [the situation] should be treated as of little importance."); S. P. Dunham & Co. v. Kudra, 131 A.2d 306, 310 (N.J. Super Ct. App. Div. 1957) ("[Defendant's] argument . . . that plaintiff itself caused defendants to exert the duress. . . . is without the slightest substance.").

24. See Dalzell, supra note 23, at 257–258.

25. Totem Marine Tug & Barge, Inc. v. Alyeska Pipeline Serv. Co., 584 P.2d 15, 22 (Alaska 1978) ("An available alternative or remedy may not be adequate where the delay involved in pursuing that remedy would cause immediate and irreparable loss to one's economic or business interest."); S. P. Dunham & Co., 131 A.2d at 310 ("[A] public suit [does] not constitute adequate relief").

26. See Chapter 5 at notes 24–25, and accompanying text.

27. See Restatement (Second) of Contracts § 176(2)(c).

Before we leave duress, two additional points. First, what about duress induced by someone who is not a party to the contract? For example, suppose Alice wants to purchase a car on credit, but she needs someone to sign a contract with the dealer guaranteeing her performance. Alice threatens to fire an employee in Alice's music business if the employee doesn't agree to guarantee the car purchase. If Alice's threat constitutes duress (it looks like duress to me), the employee is not bound as a guarantor unless the car seller "gives value or relies materially" on the contract "in good faith and without reason to know of the duress."[28]

Second, I want to return to a subject discussed in Chapter 2, namely the preexisting duty doctrine.[29] Recall that if you agree to sell your piano to Alice for $400, then Alice agrees to pay $450, contract law originally declined to enforce the modification based on the preexisting duty rule.[30] You already promised to sell the piano for $400, so you had the "preexisting duty" to deliver at that price.[31] Alice's promise to pay $50 more therefore was not supported by consideration and was a mere gift promise.[32]

Recall that courts felt uncomfortable with this result when they believed that the parties freely and fairly entered their modification agreement.[33] Courts therefore devised methods of avoiding the preexisting duty rule, such as by finding a mutual rescission of the original contract, so that neither party had a preexisting duty to perform.[34] Of course, courts would not find a mutual rescission when they believed that one party was coerced into a modification, so the preexisting duty rule was highly manipulated by courts.[35]

---

28. Restatement (Second) of Contracts § 175(2).

29. See Chapter 2 at notes 72–83, and accompanying text.

30. See Chapter 2 at note 72, and accompanying text.

31. See id.

32. See, e.g., International Paper Co. v. Suwyn, 951 F.Supp. 445, 448 (S.D.N.Y. 1997) ("[A] promise to perform an existing legal or contractual obligation is, without more, insufficient consideration to support a new contract."); Schwartzreich v. Bauman–Basch, Inc., 131 N.E. 887, 889 (N.Y. 1921) ("Any change in an existing contract, such as a modification of the rate of compensation, or a supplemental agreement, must have a new consideration to support it.").

33. See Chapter 2 at note 73, and accompanying text.

34. Contempo Design, Inc. v. Chicago and N.E. Ill. Dist. Council of Carpen-

ters, 226 F.3d 535, 550 (7th Cir. 2000) ("[If the parties] agree to rescind the original contract, [they may] create a different contract on entirely new terms, without providing additional consideration."); Recker v. Gustafson, 279 N.W.2d 744, 755 (Iowa 1979) ("Rescission and entry into a new contract, in contrast to modification, does not require new consideration."); 1 Allan Farnsworth, Farnsworth on Contracts 501 (2d ed. 1998) ("In theory, this must leave both parties with at least an instant of freedom, during which they are no longer bound by the old contract and are under no duty to make a new one.").

35. McCallum Highlands, Ltd. v. Washington Capital Dus, Inc., 66 F.3d 89, 94 (5th Cir. 1995) ("[W]here an alleged rescission is coupled with a simultaneous re-entry into a new contract and the terms of that new contract are more favorable to only one of the parties, doubt is created as to the mutuality of

We said that if courts manipulate the preexisting duty rule to reach decisions based on whether the modification agreement appeared voluntary, contract law should move to a rule that focuses on that question.[36] And contract law has done just that, at least in cases involving the sale of goods. Article 2 of the UCC provides that "[a]n agreement modifying a contract within this Article needs no consideration to be binding."[37] An "official comment" to the section imposes a test of good faith on the party benefitting from the modification in order to deny enforcement of modifications achieved by "extortion."[38] Not surprisingly, in light of this language, courts have utilized a duress-like analysis in applying the good faith test.[39]

According to the UCC approach, Alice's promise to pay an additional $50 would be enforceable only if you negotiated this additional compensation in good faith. If you demanded an extra $50 after learning that Alice was a concert pianist who needed the piano to practice for a major concert and could not obtain another one in time, her promise to pay the $50 would not be enforceable under the UCC. You would be in bad faith. Notice that the elements of duress all would be satisfied. You deliberately exploited Alice's lack of alternatives to obtain $50 more than you would have realized in a "competitive environment."[40]

B. Fraudulent and Other Misrepresentation, Fraudulent Concealment, and Tortious Breach of Contract

Fraud and misrepresentation are torts.[41] So is (obviously) tortious breach of contract.[42] You might ask, "what are torts doing in a book about contracts principles?" You're right. Please purchase a book on "Principles of Tort Law" if you want to know all about tort law. However, this book does explore torts that arise in a contractual setting, that provide defenses to contractual obligations, and that lead to damages recoveries. So we need to think about some of the basics of tort law for this limited purpose.

A tort consists of one of many "miscellaneous civil wrongs,"[43] such as assault and battery, negligence, and trespass. Liability is based upon "socially unreasonable" conduct that interferes with

the agreement to rescind the original contract.").

36. See Chapter 2 at notes 79–83, and accompanying text.

37. UCC § 2–209(1) (1998).

38. UCC § 2–209, cmt. 2.

39. Robert A. Hillman, Policing Contract Modifications under the UCC: Good Faith and the Doctrine of Economic Duress, 64 Iowa L. Rev. 849, 860, 870–73 (1979).

40. Trebilcock, supra note 10, at 243; see also Austin Instrument v. Loral Corp., 272 N.E.2d 533 (N.Y. 1971).

41. William L. Prosser & W. Page Keeton, The Law of Torts § 1 (5th ed. 1984).

42. Id.

43. Id.

the rights of others.[44] The duty to act reasonably under tort law arises by operation of law,[45] meaning that lawmakers, either legislators or judges, create duties to act reasonably. Recall that the duty to pay for a benefit received under unjust enrichment law does not arise because of the parties' agreement, but because justice (as interpreted by lawmakers) demands it.[46] Similarly, lawmakers create the social duty to act reasonably and to avoid interfering with others' rights.[47] The duties we are about to discuss in this subsection arise, not because of the parties' agreement, but because society recognizes certain non-consensual duties in the contract setting.

1. Innocent, negligent and fraudulent misrepresentation

a. Innocent misrepresentation. Suppose Alice offers to sell her home to you for $250,000. She tells you that her property consists of 5.5 acres of land. She actually believes this based on a survey made at the time she purchased the house, but the survey was incorrect and the land consists of only 3.5 acres. Alice has misrepresented the size of her land,[48] albeit innocently. You rely on her misrepresentation and purchase the house. Do you have a remedy when you learn your new property's actual acreage? Assuming that Alice's misrepresentation is "material" (meaning, basically, that it is important to you in deciding to purchase the property),[49] Alice made the representation to induce you to purchase the land, and you reasonably relied on it, you do have a remedy.[50] You may rescind the purchase, convey the property back to Alice, and recover the purchase price, plus any damages neces-

---

44. Id.

45. Id. at 665 ("Tort obligations are in general obligations that are imposed by law ... to avoid injury to others."); St. Clair v. B & L Paving Co., 411 A.2d 525, 526 (Pa. Super. Ct. 1979) ("Those who undertake an activity pursuant to a contract have both a self-imposed contractual duty and a 'social' duty imposed by the law to act without negligence."); Busch v. Interborough Rapid Transit Co., 80 N.E. 197, 198 (N.Y. 1907) ("[A] tort ordinarily is a violation of a duty fixed by law, independent of contract or the will of the parties.").

46. See Chapter 3 at notes 65–67, and accompanying text.

47. Hargrave v. Oki Nursery, Inc., 636 F.2d 897, 898–899 (2d Cir. 1980) ("Tort liability is imposed on the basis of some social policy that disapproves

the infliction of a specific kind of harm irrespective of any agreement.").

48. Restatement (Second) of Contracts § 159 ("A misrepresentation is an assertion that is not in accord with the facts.").

49. Black's Law Dictionary 991 (7th ed. 1999) ("Of such a nature that knowledge of the item would affect a person's decision-making process").

50. Smith v. Richards, 38 U.S. 26, 36–37 (1839) (" 'If [one] takes upon himself to make a representation to another, upon the faith of which that other acts, no doubt he is bound; though his mistake was perfectly innocent'.... The misrepresentation must be of something material, constituting an inducement, or motive to the act, or omission of the other, and by which he is actually misled to his injury.") (quoting Ainslie v. Medli-

sary to restore you to your position prior to the contract.[51] In the alternative, you can keep the property and recover damages (the difference between the contract price and the actual value of what you got, plus any consequential damages).[52]

Innocent misrepresentation is closely related to the concept of express warranty, and, indeed, courts sometimes turn misrepresentation cases into warranty cases.[53] The primary ramification is that when the court characterizes the case as involving an express warranty, the injured party can recover expectancy damages.[54]

Consider, for example, *Johnson v. Healy*,[55] where a builder, Healy, sold a new home to Johnson, after Healy said that the "house was made of the best material * * * and that there was nothing wrong with it."[56] However, the house was defective because of improper fill placed on the land before Healy bought the house. Healy claimed that he should not be responsible for the defects because he did not know of the improper fill.[57] The court referred to sale-of-goods law, where statements about the quality of the goods constitute express warranties regardless of the seller's belief about the statements, and extended the concept to the sale of new homes.[58] Further, the court awarded expectancy damages, based on "the difference in value between the property had it been as represented and the property as it actually was."[59]

b. Negligent misrepresentation. Suppose Alice's misrepresentation as to the acreage was negligent in that she failed to

---

cot, 9 Vesey, 21); see also Stephens v. Guardian Life Ins. Co., 742 F.2d 1329, 1333 (11th Cir. 1984) ("The most innocent misrepresentation will afford a reason to rescind if the truth is ... material").

51. Calamari & Perillo, supra note 11, at 326 (4th ed. 1998); Pence v. Brown, 627 F.2d 872, 874 (8th Cir. 1980) ("When a contract has been procured by fraud or material misrepresentation, even though innocently and nonnegligently made, the injured party may rescind the contract."); Jennings v. Lee, 461 P.2d 161 (Ariz. 1969) (allowing both rescission and damages).

52. Restatement (Second) of Torts § 552C (1977); cf. Kinkade v. Markus, 589 P.2d 1142, 1144 (Or. Ct. App. 1979) ("The general rule is that one who is induced to enter a contract by fraud may, upon discovery of the fraud, elect his remedy—he may either rescind the contract and be returned to his former

position or he may affirm the contract and sue for damages suffered by reason of the fraud.").

53. Cooper Power Sys. v. Union Carbide Chems. & Plastics Co., 123 F.3d 675, 682 (7th Cir. 1997) ("Misrepresentations ... that ultimately concern the quality of the product sold, are properly remedied through claims for breach of warranty."); Johnson v. Healy, 405 A.2d 54, 57 (Conn. 1978) ("Extension of warranty liability for innocent misrepresentation to a builder-vendor who sells a new home is, as a matter of policy, consistent with the developing law of vendor and purchaser generally.").

54. Johnson, 405 A.2d at 59.

55. 405 A.2d 54 (Conn. 1978).

56. Id. at 55.

57. Id. at 56.

58. Id. at 57.

59. Id. at 59.

exercise reasonable care in ascertaining the size of her property. When a party such as Alice has a "pecuniary interest" in a transaction, "supplies false information for the guidance of others in their business transactions," and fails "to exercise reasonable care or competence in obtaining or communicating the information" that party has committed a negligent misrepresentation.[60] In order for you to recover for Alice's negligent misrepresentation, you must reasonably rely on it.[61] The remedy is the same as for innocent misrepresentation: You may rescind the purchase, convey the property back to Alice, and recover the purchase price, plus any damages necessary to restore you to your position prior to the contract;[62] or you can keep the property and recover the difference between the contract price and the actual value of what you received, plus any consequential damages.[63] Further, there is little reason why a court should not turn a negligent misrepresentation case into a warranty case, as it may do with innocent misrepresentation, and grant expectancy damages.[64] So, regardless of whether Alice was innocent or careless in reporting that she had 5.5 acres of land, the result should be the same.

    c. Fraudulent misrepresentation. Fraudulent misrepresentation constitutes a material, but false, factual representation that the maker either knows is false or asserts recklessly without knowing the truth.[65] The maker must intend for the other party to rely on the misrepresentation and the other party must reasonably rely and suffer damages.[66] To illustrate, Alice must be more despicable than in the above examples. She knows that she doesn't have 5.5 acres of land or has no idea of how many acres she has, but makes the assertion of 5.5 acres to induce you to make the purchase. As a consequence of Alice's misdeeds, you may have more remedial options than if your complaint was an innocent or negligent misrepresentation, at least if your purchase is a "business

---

60. Restatement (Second) of Torts § 552(1).

61. Kearney v. J.P. King Auction Co., 265 F.3d 27, 34 n.8 (1st Cir. 2001) ("Claims for ... negligent misrepresentation ... require that the defendant have made a false representation of present fact and that the plaintiff justifiably relied on the representation as true."); see also Jenkins v. KLT, Inc., 308 F.3d 850, 858 (8th Cir. 2002) ("A promisee can only recover damages for pecuniary loss incurred in reasonable reliance on a misrepresentation negligently made by the promisor.").

62. Calamari & Perillo, supra note 11, at 343.

63. Restatement (Second) of Torts § 552B(2).

64. Cf. Johnson v. Healy, 405 A.2d 54 (Conn. 1978).

65. Abt Assocs. v. JHPIEGO Corp., 104 F.Supp.2d 523, 536 (D. Md. 2000); Gibb v. Citicorp Mortgage, Inc., 518 N.W.2d 910, 916 (Neb. 1994).

66. Gibb, 518 N.W.2d at 916; Channel Master Corp. v. Aluminum Limited Sales, Inc., 151 N.E.2d 833, 835 (N.Y. 1958) ("'[O]ne 'who fraudulently makes

transaction."[67] In such a case, not only can you rescind and recover reliance and consequential damages, but you can also recover the benefit of the bargain (the difference between the value of what you received and what your neighbor promised).[68] Additionally, because fraudulent misrepresentation is a serious tort, we cannot rule out the possibility of punitive damages.[69]

Notice that all three versions of misrepresentation require the victim's reliance to be reasonable.[70] If you knew or should have known that Alice's assertion of 5.5 acres was false or unreliable, you cannot recover regardless of whether her misrepresentation was innocent, negligent, or fraudulent.[71] For example, suppose you hired your own surveyor who reported that Alice's land consisted of only 3.5 acres and you had no reason to doubt your surveyor. Alternatively, suppose you knew that Alice was intoxicated when she told you the size of her land. Finally, suppose you knew that Alice merely stated her opinion about the size of her land. You should have no claim against Alice in any of these scenarios, even if you relied on Alice's statement.[72] Your reliance was not reasonable. Harder cases involve the reasonableness of your conduct when you don't hire a surveyor but Alice claims you should have, or you don't know that Alice was drunk or merely gave her opinion, but Alice claims you should have known. Reasonableness in these instances is a question of fact and will depend on the circumstances.

a misrepresentation of . . . intention . . . for the purpose of inducing another to act or refrain from action in reliance thereon in a business transaction' is liable for the harm caused by the other's justifiable reliance upon the misrepresentation.") (quoting Restatement (Second) of Torts § 525); see also Restatement (Second) of Contracts § 162.

67. Restatement (Second) of Torts § 549(2) ("The recipient of a fraudulent misrepresentation in a business transaction is also entitled to recover additional damages sufficient to give him the benefit of his contract with the maker, if these damages are proved with reasonable certainty.").

68. Id.; Air Host Cedar Rapids, Inc. v. Cedar Rapids Airport Comm'n., 464 N.W.2d 450, 454 (Iowa 1990) ("The measure of damage in false representation claims is under the benefit of the bargain rule.").

69. Pesaplastic, C.A. v. Cincinnati Milacron Co., 750 F.2d 1516, 1527 (11th Cir. 1985) ("[I]n an action for fraudu-

lent misrepresentation, punitive damages may be awarded."); Hargrave v. Oki Nursery, Inc., 636 F.2d 897 (2d Cir. 1980).

70. Dexter Corp. v. Whittaker Corp., 926 F.2d 617, 620 (7th Cir. 1991) (The victim of fraud must prove not only that he relied to his detriment on the fraud but that he *reasonably* relied.; United States v. Perez–Torres, 15 F.3d 403, 407 (5th Cir. 1994)) ("[I]n cases . . . where estoppel is sought to be based on a misrepresentation [plaintiff must prove] a change in position in reasonable reliance on the misrepresentation.").

71. United States v. Perez–Torres, 15 F.3d at 407 ("Reliance is not reasonable if at the time of acting the party seeking to invoke estoppel could reasonably have known the truth of the matter."); Farnsworth, supra note 2, at 253.

72. See Farnsworth, supra note 2, at 253–260.

2. Fraudulent concealment. Insects, especially roaches and termites, have played a large role in the development of fraudulent concealment law. You can envision the scenario. Alice sells you her house, but she doesn't tell you that the house is infested with termites (or roaches). The gravamen of your complaint is not that Alice misrepresented anything, but that she did not disclose the true condition of her house.[73]

In one leading case involving termite infestation, the court decided that in a deal made "at arms length," the seller does not have to disclose, notwithstanding the "appeal to the moral sense" of a decision otherwise.[74] The court worried about the ramifications of a decision requiring disclosure: "If this defendant is liable * * * every seller is liable who fails to disclose any nonapparent defect known to him in the subject of the sale which materially reduces its value and which the buyer fails to discover."[75]

However, courts have narrowed the idea of *caveat emptor* (let the buyer beware).[76] Some courts now would find that Alice has fraudulently concealed her home's condition if she had knowledge of and purposefully concealed the condition, the infestation was "not within [your] reasonably diligent attention,"[77] and you were actually misled and damaged.[78] Perhaps the most difficult element of this test is whether a fact was within a party's "reasonably diligent attention." For example, should you have known about the infestation of Alice's house by inspecting the property? Of course, Alice will claim that you should have hired your own housing inspector to investigate the house's condition. Courts must determine in each case whether the party claiming a concealment acted

73. Weintraub v. Krobatsch, 317 A.2d 68, 71 (N. J. 1974) ("[R]elief may be granted to one contractual party where the other suppresses facts which he, 'under the circumstances, is bound in conscience and duty to disclose to the other party, and in respect to which he cannot, innocently, be silent.'") (quoting Keen v. James, 39 N.J.Eq. 527, 540–41 (1885)); Swinton v. Whitinsville Sav. Bank, 42 N.E.2d 808, 808 (Mass. 1942) ("The charge is concealment and nothing more; and it is concealment in the simple sense of mere failure to reveal, with nothing to show any peculiar duty to speak."); Gibb, 518 N.W.2d 910.

74. Swinton, 42 N.E.2d 808 at 808–809.

75. Id. at 808.

76. Holcomb v. Zinke, 365 N.W.2d 507, 511 (N.D. 1985) ("Historically, the rule of caveat emptor shielded the seller of real estate from any duty to disclose, the buyer assuming all risks.... While such a rule may have had some merit in the agrarian society in which it was applied, the same cannot be said for its continued application to the complexities of our society."); Wilhite v. Mays, 232 S.E.2d 141, 143 (Ga. Ct. App. 1976) ("[I]n cases of passive concealment by the seller of defective realty, we find there to be an exception to the rule of caveat emptor....").

77. Gibb, 518 N.W.2d at 916.

78. Id.; see also Wilhite, 232 S.E.2d at 143 (seller must disclose "in situations where he or she has special knowledge not apparent to the buyer and is aware that the buyer is acting under a misapprehension as to facts which would be important to the buyer and would probably affect its decision.").

reasonably in not learning the facts.[79] Of course, a person claiming fraudulent concealment has an easier time showing that she acted reasonably when the defects are latent (not readily observable)[80] or when the practice in the relevant community is not to hire inspectors.[81] In addition, some courts appear to have largely relaxed the "reasonably diligent attention" requirement.[82]

One thing is very clear in the cases. Partial disclosures that are themselves misleading may constitute fraud.[83] For example, if a seller advertises property as investment property, but the seller knows that the property violates building and zoning regulations, the seller's misrepresentation is fraudulent.[84]

3. Tortious breach of contract. Suppose, pursuant to a contract, Engineer furnishes plans to Architect for the heating, plumbing and electrical portions of improvements to several school buildings.[85] Architect incorporates Engineer's work into the plans he furnishes the school district. Unfortunately, Engineer is either lazy, incompetent, or reckless because (Dave Barry would say here, "I'm not making this up") Engineer reuses plans drawn for entirely different projects and, with regard to the school projects, the plans violate "the fundamental laws of physics."[86] Architect incurs

79. FDIC v. Deloitte & Touche, 834 F.Supp. 1129, 1154 (E.D. Ark. 1992) ("As soon as discovery has occurred or reasonably should occur, the doctrine of fraudulent concealment ceases to operate."); Fusco v. Johns–Manville Products Corp., 643 F.2d 1181, 1184 (5th Cir. 1981) ("There cannot be fraudulent concealment of facts which admittedly were or should have been known by [plaintiff]."); cf. Holcomb v. Hoffschneider, 297 N.W.2d 210 (Iowa 1980) ("[A] buyer cannot generally be held to be able to judge the contents of a parcel of land by the eye. Even though a buyer examines land before purchasing, he may normally rely upon the representations of the seller as to measurement.").

80. Weintraub, 317 A.2d at 74.

81. See generally Akins v. Couch, 518 S.E.2d 674, 676 (Ga. 1999) ("A jury ... is authorized to find that a purchaser exercised due diligence even without hiring an inspector.").

82. Kannavos v. Annino, 247 N.E.2d 708, 712–13 (Mass. 1969) ("[O]ur cases have not barred plaintiffs from recovery merely because they 'did

not use due diligence ... [when they] could readily have ascertained from ... records' what the true facts were.") (quoting Yorke v. Taylor, 124 N.E.2d 912, 916 (Mass. 1955)).

83. Kannavos, 247 N.E.2d at 711–12 ("Fragmentary information may be as misleading ... as active misrepresentation, and half-truths may be as actionable as whole lies....") (quoting Fowler V. Harper & Fleming James, Jr., The Law of Torts, § 7.14 (3d ed. 1996)).

84. See generally Crompton v. Beedle, 75 A. 331, 334–35 (Vt. 1910) ("Where one has full information and represents that he has, if he discloses a part of his information only, and by words or conduct leads the one with whom he contracts to believe that he has made a full disclosure, and does this with intent to deceive and overreach and to prevent investigation, he is guilty of fraud against which equity will relieve, if his words and conduct in consequence of reliance upon them bring about the result which he desires.").

85. Mauldin v. Sheffer, 150 S.E.2d 150, 151–52 (Ga. Ct. App. 1966).

86. Id.

large costs in redoing the plans and loses several other jobs as a result of Engineer's actions.

Needless to say, Architect sues, with one of his theories being that Engineer's conduct constitutes a tort. Engineer tests the sufficiency of the theory by moving to dismiss the complaint. Determining whether Architect can sue in tort is crucial because, if so, among other things,[87] Architect can recover punitive damages, which are not available in contract actions.[88]

In situations involving a "professional" such as a doctor, architect, lawyer, or engineer, courts have found that a duty exists, *apart from the contract,* to "exercise a reasonable degree of care, skill and ability, such as is ordinarily exercised under similar conditions."[89] The duty arises only when the professional actually performs her contract unreasonably, which courts call "misfeasance."[90] If Engineer had simply failed to furnish plans at all (nonfeasance), Architect could not have sued in tort.[91] Reckless or negligent performance of a contract by a professional, such as Engineer's performance in our example, would therefore give rise to a tort claim.

As we have said, the most significant effect of allowing a tort claim to arise out of a breach of contract is that the plaintiff can recover punitive damages.[92] Other remedial ramifications of recognizing a tort include the potential award of emotional distress damages and a relaxation of contract law's foreseeability-of-dam-

---

87. For a discussion of other differences between contract and tort, see Richard E. Speidel, The Borderland Of Contract, 10 N. Ky. L. Rev. 164 (1983).

88. See Chapter 5 at notes 278–287, and accompanying text.

89. Mauldin, 150 S.E.2d at 155; see also Housing Authority of City of Carrollton v. Ayers, 88 S.E.2d 368, 373 (Ga. 1955) ("The law imposes upon persons performing architectural, engineering, and other professional and skilled services the obligation to exercise a reasonable degree of care, skill, and ability, which generally is taken and considered to be such a degree of care and skill as, under similar conditions and like surrounding circumstances, is ordinarily employed by their respective professions.").

90. Mauldin, 150 S.E.2d at 154 ("[In cases of misfeasance] a cause of

action ex delicto may be had."); see also Courtright v. Design Irrigation, 534 N.W.2d 181, 182 (Mich. Ct. App. 1995) ("Misfeasance is negligence during performance of a contract. While performing a contract, a party owes a separate, general duty to perform with due care so as not to injure another. Breach of this duty may give rise to tort liability.").

91. Prosser & Keeton, supra note 41, at 657 ("There is no tort liability for nonfeasance, i.e., for failing to do what one has promised to do in the absence of a duty to act apart from the promise made."); Courtright, 534 N.W.2d at 182 ("[F]ailure to perform a contract altogether constitutes nonfeasance and gives rise only to a suit for breach of contract.").

92. See supra note 88, and accompanying text.

ages requirement,[93] the latter subject taken up in Chapter 5.[94] Although the award of punitive damages in a contract setting is a major development, courts seem more willing than ever to recognize torts arising in this context.[95] In fact, the requirement that the tort-feasor must be a "professional" seems to be disappearing: "The American courts have extended the tort liability for misfeasance to virtually every type of contract where defective performance may injure the promisee."[96]

Clearly, the conduct of the party accused of a tort in a contract setting must be egregious so that it is worthy of punishment through punitive damages.[97] Perhaps instead of analyzing the cases through the lens of contract and tort, courts should simply ask whether punitive damages are appropriate for a particular breach. Such an approach would consider the policies behind contract law's general rule against punitive damages in contracts cases and would consider whether exceptions should apply. Was a party's conduct sufficiently outrageous to warrant punishment, either to deter such conduct or for retributive purposes? Courts would also have to consider whether granting punitive damages in a particular case would discourage people from entering contracts because of the fear of potential punitive damages liability.[98]

Before leaving tortious breach, I want to mention a related topic, namely bad faith breach of contract. We will have occasion to study the concept of good faith performance in more detail in Chapter 7 of this book.[99] For now, recall that in Chapter 2, we discussed cases involving satisfaction clauses.[100] For example, you promise to purchase a water-color picture of your house "if you are satisfied with the picture." We saw that many courts interpret such

---

93. See Speidel, supra note 87, at 168–71; White v. Unigard Mut. Ins. Co., 730 P.2d 1014, 1017 (Idaho 1986) ("The measurement of recoverable damages in tort is not limited to those foreseeable at the time of the tortious act . . . ."); Crisci v. Security Ins. Co. of New Haven, Conn., 426 P.2d 173, 178 (Cal. 1967) ("The general rule of damages in tort is that the injured party may recover for all detriment caused whether it could have been anticipated or not.").

94. See Chapter 5 at notes 133–165, and accompanying text.

95. L.L. Cole & Son, Inc. v. Hickman, 665 S.W.2d 278, 281 (Ark. 1984) ("The courts . . . have tended to extend the tort liability for misfeasance whenever the misconduct involves a foreseeable, unreasonable risk of harm to the plaintiff's interests.").

96. Prosser & Keeton, supra note 41, at 660.

97. Cenex, Inc. v. Arrow Gas Service, 896 F.Supp. 1574, 1583 (D. Wyo.

1995) ("For punitive damages to be recoverable, there must be conduct on the part of the actor amounting to aggravation, outrage, malice or willful and wanton misconduct."); Bud Wolf Chevrolet, Inc. v. Robertson, 519 N.E.2d 135, 137–38 (Ind. 1988) ("[A jury may award punitive damages if there is clear and convincing evidence that the defendant] acted with malice, fraud, gross negligence or oppressiveness which was not the result of a mistake of fact or law, honest error or judgment, over-zealousness, mere negligence or other human failing, in the sum [that the jury believes] will serve to punish the defendant and to deter it and others from like conduct in the future.").

98. See Chapter 5 at notes 283–284, and accompanying text.

99. See Chapter 7 at notes 139–153, and accompanying text.

100. See Chapter 2 at notes 65–66, and accompanying text.

satisfaction clauses to require you to determine whether you are satisfied in good faith, meaning, in this context, that your decision must be honest.[101] Courts sometimes imply the good-faith obligation based on the parties' intentions as revealed by the circumstances (the circumstances show that you actually promised to decide whether you are satisfied based on the merits of the picture).[102] In other cases, courts establish the good-faith obligation based simply on the principle of fair dealing (fairness requires you to decide whether you are satisfied based on the picture's merits).[103] Regardless of why the court finds a good faith obligation, if you dishonestly reject the picture, say because you dislike the painter and not on the basis of the merits of the picture, you would commit a bad faith breach of contract.[104]

Your bad faith breach of contract ordinarily would trigger only contract remedies.[105] After all, your bad faith constituted a breach of contract. However, some bad-faith breaches are serious enough to merit even more severe treatment, including punitive damages.[106] A leading category of such bad faith cases arise when an insurance company breaches its contract with its insured by looking out for its own interests above the insured's.[107] Suppose you have an automobile insurance policy with a liability limit of $25,000. (Yikes, that's not enough these days. You should get more!) Suppose you are in an accident and you are sued for $2 million. The plaintiff is willing to settle for $10,000, well within your $25,000 limit. Your interests and the insurance company's may diverge because your potential liability is $2 million and its potential liability is only

101. See id.

102. See Chapter 7 at notes 139–153, and accompanying text.

103. See id.

104. San Bernardino Valley Water Development Co. v. San Bernardino Valley Municipal Water District, 45 Cal. Rptr. 793, 805 (Cal. Dist. Ct. App. 1965) ("[R]ejection of performance of a satisfaction contract [must] be made in good faith, with reasonable promptness, and with an explanation of the grounds of dissatisfaction so that defects in performance may be cured if possible."); Hood v. Meininger, 105 A.2d 126, 128 (Pa. 1954) ("[In contracts where] performance was conditioned on the satisfaction of the owner, the test of adequate performance was not whether the owner ought to have been satisfied but whether she was satisfied.... [T]he dissatisfaction must be genuine and not prompted by caprice or bad faith....").

105. See Chapter 5 at notes 278–287, and accompanying text.

106. Thomas v. Metropolitan Life Ins. Co., 40 F.3d 505, 510 (1st Cir. 1994) ("Under New York law, a plaintiff may recover punitive damages for 'bad faith' breach of contract where there is evidence of morally reprehensible conduct directed at the general public, or an extraordinary showing of a disingenuous or dishonest failure to carry out a contract.").

107. William M. Goodman & Thom Greenfield Seaton, Foreward: Ripe for Decision, Internal Workings and Current Concerns of the California Supreme Court, 62 Cal. L. Rev. 309, 346 (1974) ("The insurers' obligations are ... rooted in their status as purveyors of a vital service labeled quasi-public in nature. Suppliers of services affected with a public interest must take the public's interest seriously, where necessary placing it before their interest in maximizing gains and limiting disbursements.").

$25,000. It would be in your best interest to settle, for example, if the facts suggest you are liable and the plaintiff's damages are $50,000. If the insurance company refuses to settle because it is in its best interest not to settle, many courts would find the insurance company to be in bad faith.[108] These courts would find that an implied term of the insurance contract requires the company to conduct settlement negotiations based on your interests as well as its own.[109] Courts so finding may award insureds punitive damages and damages for mental distress on the theory that the bad-faith breach was a tort.[110]

Some employees have sought to extend the reasoning of the insurance cases to their situations. For example, in one case, an employee claimed he was fired because he had revealed negative information about a prospective supervisor.[111] The employee sought to recover damages from his employer based in part on "tortious breach of the implied covenant of good faith and fair dealing."[112] The court dismissed the action, finding important distinctions between insurance company and employer bad faith.[113] The court reasoned that, unlike employers, insurance companies supply services of a "quasi public nature," namely protecting people from harm.[114] Further, because of the availability of alternative employment, "a breach in the employment context does not place the employee in the same economic dilemma that an insured faces when an insurer in bad faith refuses to pay a claim to accept a

---

108. Pinto v. Allstate Ins. Co., 221 F.3d 394, 398 (2d Cir. 2000) ("Because an insurance company has exclusive control over a claim against its insured once it assumes defense of the suit, it has a duty under New York law to act in 'good faith' when deciding whether to settle such a claim, and it may be held liable for breach of that duty. The insurer acts in good faith when it gives equal consideration to its insured's interest in avoiding liability in excess of the policy limit as it does to its own interests when considering plaintiff's demand to settle a lawsuit."); Commercial Union Ins. Co. v. Liberty Mut. Ins. Co., 393 N.W.2d 161, 164 (Mich. 1986) ("If the insurer is motivated by selfish purpose or by a desire to protect its own interests at the expense of its insured's interest, bad faith exists, even though the insurer's actions were not actually dishonest or fraudulent."); Comunale v. Traders & General Ins. Co., 328 P.2d 198, 201 (Cal. 1958) ("The insurer, in deciding whether a claim should be compromised, must take into account the interest of the insured and give it at least as much consideration as it does to its own interest.").

109. Pinto v. Allstate Ins. Co., 221 F.3d 394, 396 (2d Cir. 2000) ("New York implies a duty of good faith in insurance policies requiring the company—when it decides whether to settle a claim—to give the same consideration to its insured's interests as it does its own."); Murphy v. Allstate Insurance Co., 553 P.2d 584, 586 (Cal. 1976) ("[T]he insurer must settle within policy limits when there is substantial likelihood of recovery in excess of those limits. The duty to settle is implied in law to protect the insured from exposure to liability in excess of coverage as a result of the insurer's gamble—on which only the insured might lose.").

110. Farnsworth, supra note 2, at 789; Crisci v. Security Ins. Co., 58 Cal. Rptr. 13 (1967) (mental distress).

111. Foley v. Interactive Data Corp., 765 P.2d 373 (Cal. 1988).

112. Id. at 374.

113. Id. at 394–96.

114. Id. at 390.

settlement offer within policy limits."[115] The court's conclusions about the availability of substitute employment and the greater importance of insurance are surely highly debatable, and for a time some courts extended the bad-faith tort to the employment arena.[116] However, most recent decisions have maintained the distinction between insurance and employment contracts and have refused to grant tort remedies for bad faith breach of the latter.[117]

C. Public Policy

There are lots of public policies. Freedom of contract is itself a public policy.[118] It calls for the enforcement of freely-made contracts in order to facilitate private exchange, which is good for the parties and society.[119] The task for a party seeking to avoid a contract or term based on public policy is to convince the court that the public policy the party urges is more important than freedom of contract.[120] Because of the importance of freedom of contract, this argument has been successful only in limited circumstances. We will now set forth some examples.

1. Exculpatory clauses. An exculpatory clause absolves a contracting party from liability to the other party for any number of acts or omissions or, for that matter, from any liability at all.[121] For example, a lease may include a clause stating that the landlord is not liable to anyone for injuries suffered on the premises. The

115. Id. at 396.

116. E.g., Seaman's Direct Buying Service, Inc. v. Standard Oil Co., 686 P.2d 1158 (Cal. 1984).

117. See, e.g., VanLente v. University of Wyoming Research Corp., 975 P.2d 594, 598 (Wyo. 1999) ("The situations are rare in which ... a special relationship exists when employment is at will."); Freeman & Mills, Inc. v. Belcher Oil Co., 900 P.2d 669, 675 (Cal. 1995) ("[Language in recent decisions] strongly suggests courts should limit tort recovery in contract breach situations to the insurance area, at least in the absence of violation of an independent duty arising from principles of tort law other than denial of the existence of, or liability under, the breached contract.").

118. Computrol, Inc. v. Newtrend, L.P., 203 F.3d 1064, 1070 (8th Cir. 2000) ("[There is a] strong public policy favoring freedom of contract.").

119. See Chapter 1 at note 1, and accompanying text.

120. Medical Specialists, Inc. v. Sleweon, 652 N.E.2d 517, 527 (Ind. Ct. App. 1995) ("When determining whether or not a contract is against public policy, we must keep in mind that it is to the best interest of the public that persons should not be unnecessarily restricted in their freedom of contract.") (quoting Hodnick v. Fidelity Trust Co., 183 N.E. 488, 491 (Ind. Ct. App. 1932)); Stephens v. Southern Pac. Co., 41 P. 783, 784 (Cal. 1895) ("While contracts opposed to morality or law should not be allowed to show themselves in courts of justice, yet public policy requires and encourages the making of contracts by competent parties upon all valid and lawful considerations, and courts, recognizing this, have allowed parties the widest latitude in this regard; and, unless it is entirely plain that a contract is violative of sound public policy, the court will never so declare.").

121. Black's Law Dictionary 588 (7th ed. 1999) ("A contractual provision relieving a party from any liability re-

owner of a ski resort may disclaim liability for injuries suffered by skiers. The UCC allows sellers to disclaim implied warranties.[122] Without hesitation, however, courts strike terms that attempt to absolve a party from liability for intentional or reckless conduct.[123] Contract law, along with other instrumentalities of the law, seeks to deter such anti-social conduct. The more challenging issue here is whether public policy disfavors the enforcement of exculpatory clauses that insulate a party, such as a landlord, seller, or property owner, from negligent behavior.

Generally, the following factors interest courts deciding whether to overturn an exculpatory clause on the grounds of public policy: The exculpatory clause must "contravene[] long established common law rules" of liability, such as a landlord's duty to maintain common areas; the clause must absolve a party in total (meaning that the clause precludes liability in any context for any type of conduct); and the state must have an interest in protecting a large class of citizens who cannot protect themselves (for example, tenants in substandard housing).[124]

A common response to public policy concerns by proponents of the enforceability of exculpatory clauses is to focus on the negative incentives created by striking such clauses. Critics of the public-policy defense argue that, instead of protecting people, decisions striking terms based on public policy will increase costs and reduce choices for the class of parties supposedly being protected.[125] For example, landlords will increase rents to cover their additional liability or decide to go out of business, thereby diminishing housing. Manufacturers will stop making products, such as small airplanes or vaccines, that could lead to potentially large liability claims. These are serious concerns, but whether the net benefit of enforcing exculpatory clauses exceeds the net benefit of striking them challenges courts, and, for that matter, legislators.[126] Now is not the time to get into all of the hurdles that make empirical studies of the effects of laws so difficult for lawmakers and analysts

---

sulting from a negligent or wrongful act.")

122. UCC § 2–316.

123. John E. Gregory & Son, Inc. v. A. Guenther & Sons Co., 432 N.W.2d 584, 586 (Wis. 1988) ("[An exculpatory clause] is not enforceable in such cases of abuse as intentional wrongdoing or gross negligence, on the part of the party seeking to be protected."); Mankap Enters., Inc. v. Wells Fargo Alarm Services, 427 So.2d 332, 333–334 (Fla. Dist. Ct. App. 1983) ("The law is settled that a party cannot contract against liability for his own fraud in order to exempt him from liability for an intentional tort, and any such exculpatory clauses are

void as against public policy."); Kalisch–Jarcho, Inc. v. City of New York, 448 N.E.2d 413, 416 (N.Y. 1983) ("[A]n exculpatory clause is unenforceable when, in contravention of acceptable notions of morality, the misconduct for which it would grant immunity smacks of intentional wrongdoing.").

124. McCutcheon v. United Homes Corp., 486 P.2d 1093,1097 (Wash. 1971).

125. See generally Richard A. Epstein, Unconscionability: A Critical Reappraisal, 18 J. L. & Econ. 293 (1975).

126. See generally Robert A. Hillman, The Rhetoric of Legal Backfire, 43 B.C. L. Rev. 819 (2002).

or to opine on the ramifications of this uncertainty.[127] (You can do so at your next law school party.) Suffice it to say that the clash between the public policy of striking clauses that insulate parties from their own negligence and the public policy of freedom of contract remains unresolved. Judicial decisions mirror this uncertainty, with some courts enforcing such exculpatory clauses and some courts striking them.[128]

2. Covenants not to compete. Employers often include a covenant not to compete in their employment contracts. Such a term protects an employer, who may have revealed to its employee its private methods of doing business or other secrets, from the employee's direct competition when the employment ends.[129] Courts enforce reasonable restriction on competition on the grounds of freedom of contract[130] and the employer's right to earn a livelihood.[131]

On the other hand, lots of case reports make clear that employers sometimes become greedy in defining the duration, geographical area, and subject matter of the covenant not to compete.[132] Courts police such activity by striking overbroad covenants that unfairly

---

127. For such a discussion, see id.

128. Valhal Corp. v. Sullivan Assocs., 44 F.3d 195, 202 (3d Cir. 1995) ("The law recognizes different methods by which a party can limit his/her exposure to damages resulting from his/her negligent performance of a contractual obligation. An exculpatory clause immunizes a person from the consequences of his/her negligence."); Scott v. Pacific West Mountain Resort, 834 P.2d 6, 10 (Wash. 1992) ("The general rule in Washington is that exculpatory clauses are enforceable unless ... the negligent act falls greatly below the standard established by law for protection of others."); O'Connell v. Walt Disney World Co., 413 So.2d 444, 446 (Fla. Dist. Ct. App. 1982) ("While exculpatory clauses are enforceable, they are looked upon with disfavor; and any attempt to limit one's liability for his own negligent act will not be inferred from an agreement unless such intention is expressed in clear and unequivocal terms.").

129. Hopper v. All Pet Animal Clinic, Inc., 861 P.2d 531, 539 (Wyo. 1993) ("There is general recognition that while an employer may seek protection from improper and unfair competition of a former employee, the employer is not entitled to protection against ordinary competition."); Allen v. Rose Park Pharmacy, 237 P.2d 823, 826 (Utah 1951)

("Restrictive covenants are generally upheld by the courts where they are necessary for the protection of the business....").

130. Gomez v. Chua Medical Corp., 510 N.E.2d 191, 195 (Ind. Ct. App. 1987) ("[W]e respect and believe in individual freedom to contract. That freedom, if it is to be real, must necessarily include the freedom to enter into enforceable contracts that are unwise or even foolish.... If an individual agrees to be bound by a covenant against competition under circumstances where he is terminated at will, we see no compelling reason to deny enforcement of his promise.").

131. Intelus Corp. v. Barton, 7 F.Supp.2d 635, 641 (D. Md. 1998) ("A covenant not to compete is enforceable if its duration and geographic area are only so broad as is reasonably necessary to protect the employer's business....").

132. Tandy Brands, Inc. v. Harper, 760 F.2d 648 (5th Cir. 1985) (striking a covenant not to compete for being "unreasonable as to territorial scope"); Static Control Components, Inc. v. Darkprint Imaging, Inc., 240 F.Supp.2d 465 (M.D.N.C. 2002) (striking a covenant not to compete for overreaching).

inhibit an employee from earning a living and that diminish competition.[133] For example, in one case, Ingrasci, an oral surgeon fresh out of dental school, took a job with Karpinski, an oral surgeon practicing in five counties in central New York.[134] In the three-year employment contract, Ingrasci promised never to practice oral surgery or dentistry in the five counties except as Karpinski's employee. The contract ended and Ingrasci began practicing oral surgery in the restricted area. The court reported that "about 90% of [Ingrasci's] present practice comes from referrals from dentists in the counties specified in the restrictive covenant, the very same dentists who had been referring patients to [Karpinski's] Ithaca office when [Ingrasci] was working there."[135]

Karpinski sought an injunction to enforce the covenant not to compete. The court held that the clause was reasonable as to area and time, but narrowed its subject matter to allow Ingrasci to practice dentistry in the restricted area.[136] By focusing on the situations in which Ingrasci actually would be competing with Karpinski, the court attempted to find a reasonable middle-ground between the contradictory policies at work in the cases. It is somewhat curious, however, why the court enforced the time duration (the contract literally says "forever").[137] What happens if Karpinski retires or dies? Perhaps, the court interpreted "forever" to mean for as long as Ingrasci remains a competitor of Karpiniski. On the other hand, if Ingrasci could practice oral surgery upon Karpinski's retirement or death, perhaps the value of the latter's practice would be unfairly diminished and Karpinski or his estate would receive less value for selling his practice.

3. Illegal contracts. Not surprisingly, contracts to perform illegal acts under a state's criminal law, such as prostitution or embezzlement, are not enforceable.[138] This principle sometimes makes courts uncomfortable because defendants, who have willingly engaged in an illegal scheme and gained from it, can then use the

---

133. Stunfence, Inc. v. Gallagher Sec. (USA), Inc., 2002 WL 1838128, 6 (N.D. Ill. 2002) ("Because covenants not to compete at their heart restrain trade, they warrant careful scrutiny. If the covenant is reasonably calculated to safeguard the interests of one party without overburdening the other's ability to effectively do business or impeding the benefit to the public of a competitive market, courts will enforce these agreements according to their terms."); Petrzilka v. Gorscak, 556 N.E.2d 1265, 1269 (Ill. App. Ct. 1990) ("Noncompetition clauses should be limited in time so that the agreement is no more restric-

tive than necessary to accomplish this goal so as to prevent injury to the public from a restraint on trade.").

134. Karpinski v. Ingrasci, 268 N.E.2d 751 (N.Y 1971).

135. Id. at 752

136. Id. at 754–56.

137. Id. at 752.

138. United States Nursing Corp. v. Saint Joseph Medical Ctr., 39 F.3d 790, 792 (7th Cir. 1994) ("[W]hen a statute makes an act illegal, contracts for the performance of the illegal act are deemed void and unenforceable."); Lloyd Capital Corp. v. Pat Henchar, Inc., 603

illegality as a shield against contractual liability.[139] Nonetheless, most courts follow the admonition to "leave the parties where it finds them," meaning that courts will not enforce illegal contracts even if defendants have already gained from them.[140]

D. Unconscionability

For you to get a good handle on the doctrine of unconscionability, think first of our earlier historical discussion of specific performance.[141] Recall that the English courts of equity stood side-by-side with the English law courts.[142] The two courts differed in many ways, including the substantive rules they applied.[143] In fact, courts of equity arose in part because of the inflexibility of the substantive legal rules, and the Chancellor and deputies developed various equitable doctrines to alleviate the harsh results in the law courts.[144] One of these doctrines was unconscionability.

Now, in lightning speed, let's complete the history of unconscionability.[145] English equity courts often employed unconscionability as a defense to specific performance of land-sale contracts, for example, when a party procured the contract unfairly.[146] Courts in the United States followed this practice and began to expand the

N.E.2d 246, 247 (N.Y. 1992) ("Illegal contracts are, as a general rule, unenforceable.").

139. Early Detection Center, Inc. v. Wilson, 811 P.2d 860, 867 (Kan. 1991) ("While it may not always seem an honorable thing to do, a party to an illegal agreement is permitted to set up the illegality as a defense even though the party may be alleging his or her own turpitude."); United Calendar Mfg. Corp. v. Huang, 94 A.D.2d 176, 180 (N.Y. App. Div. 1983) (" '[A] party to an illegal contract . . . cannot ask a court of law to help him carry out his illegal object. . . . The denial of relief to the plaintiff in such a case is not based on any desire of the courts to benefit the particular defendant. That the defendant may profit from the court's refusal to intervene is irrelevant.' ") (quoting Stone v. Freeman, 82 N.E.2d 571, 572 (N.Y. 1948)).

140. Marathon Petroleum Co. v. Chronister Oil Co., 687 F.Supp. 437, 442 (C.D. Ill. 1988) ("It is a well established rule in Illinois that when the parties to an illegal bargain are *in pari delicto*, 'the law will not stoop to inquire whether one has gained an advantage over the other.' ") (quoting Arter v. Byington, 44 Ill. 468, 469 (1867)); Grant v. Grant, 286

S.W. 647, 650 (Tex. Civ. App. 1926) ("[W]hile a court of equity will on swift wings fly to relieve the innocent from wrong and injury, it travels with leaded feet and turns a deaf ear, when called on to furnish a cloak of righteousness to cover sin, and, where both parties are equally guilty, neither can be said to come with clean hands, and the court will relieve neither, but leave the parties where they are found.").

141. See Chapter 5 at notes 289–296, and accompanying text.

142. See id.

143. See id.

144. Id.; see also Robert A. Hillman, Debunking Some Myths About Unconscionability: A New Framework for U.C.C. Section 2–302, 67 Cornell L. Rev. 1 (1981) (hereinafter Hillman, Debunking).

145. For a more complete discussion, see Arthur Allen Leff, Unconscionability and the Code–The Emperor's New Clause, 115 U. Pa. L. Rev. 485 (1967).

146. Id., see also Robert A. Hillman, The Richness of Contract 131 (Kluwer 1997) (hereinafter Hillman, Richness).

use of the principle to other cases involving unfair bargaining or the substantive unfairness of terms.[147] UCC section 2–302 codified unconscionability as a defense in sale-of-goods cases, and the Restatement (Second) of Contracts promotes its use in other kinds of cases as well.[148]

Section 2–302 provides in part:

> If the court as a matter of law finds the contract or any clause of the contract to have been unconscionable at the time it was made the court may refuse to enforce the contract, or it may enforce the remainder of the contract without the unconscionable clause, or it may so limit the application of any unconscionable clause as to avoid any unconscionable result.[149]

The section is clear on a couple of things. Courts are supposed to determine whether a contract or term is unconscionable "as a matter of law," and they are supposed to do so "at the time" the parties make the contract.[150] Section 2–302 is no help, however, in determining *which* contracts or terms are unconscionable. The section's official comments add little: The goal of the section is to prevent "oppression and unfair surprise."[151] Actual decisions offer more guidance. Generally, courts look at whether the bargaining process is deficient (called "procedural unconscionability") and whether the substantive terms are oppressive ("substantive unconscionability").[152] Further, courts are most willing to strike a contract or provision when the case involves both procedural and substantive unconscionability.[153] For example, when a contract con-

147. Campbell Soup Co. v. Wentz, 172 F.2d 80, 83 (3d Cir. 1948) ("[A contract may be] too hard a bargain and too one-sided an agreement to entitle the plaintiff to relief in a court of conscience."); see also Brunsman v. DeKalb Swine Breeders, Inc., 138 F.3d 358, 360 (8th Cir. 1998) ("[A] court considering a claim of unconscionability should consider the factors of assent, unfair surprise, notice, disparity of bargaining power, and substantive unfairness.").

148. See Restatement (Second) of Contracts § 208.

149. UCC § 2–302(1).

150. American Software, Inc. v. Ali, 54 Cal.Rptr.2d 477, 479 (Cal. Ct. App. 1996).

151. UCC § 2–302, cmt. 1; See generally Hillman, Richness, supra note 146, at 129–143.

152. See, e.g., American Stone Diamond, Inc. v. Lloyds of London, 934 F.Supp. 839, 844 (S.D. Tex. 1996)

("[T]he party asserting unconscionability of contract bears the burden of proving both the substantive unconscionability and the procedural unconscionability of the contract at issue."); Leff, supra note 145, at 487–488.

153. See Bischoff v. DirecTV, Inc., 180 F.Supp.2d 1097, 1107 (C.D. Cal. 2002) ("[A] contract is unconscionable when both procedural unconscionability, meaning surprise or distress stemming from unequal bargaining power, and substantive unconscionability, meaning overly harsh or one-sided terms are present."); American Stone Diamond, Inc. v. Lloyds of London, 934 F.Supp. 839, 844 (S.D. Tex. 1996) ("[T]he party asserting unconscionability of contract bears the burden of proving both the substantive unconscionability and the procedural unconscionability of the contract at issue."); Hillman, Debunking, supra note 144, at 30.

tains confusing language, or hidden terms (procedural unconscionability) that undermine a party's reasons for agreeing to the contract and the other party cannot justify the terms because of its own needs (substantive unconscionability), the contract or term is ripe for a finding of unconscionability.[154] A few courts have also found that either substantive or procedural unconscionability alone are sufficient to strike a contract or term.[155] Let's investigate further the meaning of procedural and substantive unconscionability.

1. Procedural unconscionability. Cases in this category involve bargaining unfairness (although most also contain a sprinkling of substantive unconscionability too).[156] Often the kinds of bargaining infirmities that trigger a finding of procedural unconscionability could also constitute duress, fraud, undue influence, or another policing doctrine.[157] For example, in one case, the court found unconscionable a timber deed after the purchaser misrepresented both his experience and knowledge of the value of the timber and the seller relied on the purchaser's inaccurate estimate of the value of the timber.[158] In another case, the court found unconscionable a contract for the sale of carvings after the seller, who knew the purchaser was unfamiliar with them, charged twice their market value.[159] These cases could also have been decided on the basis of fraudulent misrepresentation and duty to disclose, respectively.[160] Further, a definition of unconscionability widely quoted in the cases, "an absence of meaningful choice on the part of one of the parties together with contract terms which are

---

154. See, e.g., Ellis v. McKinnon Broadcasting Co., 23 Cal.Rptr.2d 80 (Cal. Dist. Ct. App. 1993); Hillman, Debunking, supra note 144, at 32.

155. See Hillman, Richness, supra note 146, at 131; Gillman v. Chase Manhattan Bank, N.A., 534 N.E.2d 824, 829 (N.Y. 1988) ("While determinations of unconscionability are ordinarily based on the court's conclusion that both the procedural and substantive components are present there have been exceptional cases where a provision of the contract is so outrageous as to warrant holding it unenforceable on the ground of substantive unconscionability alone."); Jones v. Star Credit, 298 N.Y.S.2d 264 (1969) (striking a term based on substantive unconscionability).

156. Rite Color Chemical Co. v. Velvet Textile Co., 411 S.E.2d 645, 648 (N.C. Ct. App. 1992) ("Procedural un-

conscionability involves 'bargaining naughtiness' in the formation of the contract.") (citing James J. White & Robert S. Summers, Uniform Commercial Code § 4–3 (3d ed. 1988)); Calamari & Perillo, supra note 11, at 373 ("More frequently elements of both [substantive and procedural unconscionability] are present.").

157. Hillman, Debunking, supra note 144, at 6.

158. Davis v. Kolb, 563 S.W.2d 438 (Ark. Sup. Ct. 1978).

159. Vom Lehn v. Astor Art Galleries, Ltd., 380 N.Y.S.2d 532 (Sup. Ct. 1976).

160. See also Industralease Automated & Scientific Equip. Corp. v. R.M.E. Enterprises, Inc., 396 N.Y.S.2d 427 (N.Y. App. Div. 1977) (unconscionability finding based on duress).

unreasonably favorable to the other party,"[161] sounds a lot like duress to me.

Another set of bargaining problems involves obtuse or hidden terms. Courts finding unconscionability on these grounds often could have decided against the drafter because a reasonable person would not have understood the meaning of the contract. For example, in the well-known case of *Williams v. Walker–Thomas Furniture Co.*,[162] a "cross collateral clause" in a sales contract, in almost incomprehensible language, authorized the seller, Walker–Thomas, to reclaim all of the goods sold to Williams if she defaulted on only one of the purchases.[163] O.k., you want to decide for yourself whether the language was understandable. Here's the language:

> "[T]he amount of each periodical installment payment to be made by [purchaser] to the Company under this present lease shall be inclusive of and not in addition to the amount of each installment payment to be made by [purchaser] under such prior leases, bills or accounts; and all payments now and hereafter made by [purchaser] shall be credited pro rata on all outstanding leases, bills and accounts due the Company by [purchaser] at the time each such payment is made."[164]

When Williams defaulted on the purchase of a stereo set in 1962, the seller sought the return of all the items Williams purchased since 1957.[165] The court sent the case back to the trial court for a determination of whether the term was unconscionable.[166] The court could have declined to enforce the term on the basis that a reasonable person would not have understood the poorly drafted clause. (Right?)

We'll return to procedural unconscionability during our discussion of standard forms, but you get the idea. A court will be inclined to find procedural unconscionability when defects in the bargaining process cast a shadow on the quality of a party's assent to a contract.[167] The various contexts in which such a shadow arises are similar to those that deny enforcement on the basis of any of the policing doctrines discussed earlier in this chapter.[168] Since many, if not most cases could be decided applying either unconscionability or another doctrine, you might ask why contract law bothered to introduce the concept of procedural unconscionability. At least in some cases, a policing defense may be more difficult to prove than the somewhat relaxed standard of procedural uncon-

---

161. Williams v. Walker–Thomas Furniture Company, 350 F.2d 445, 449 (D.C. Cir. 1965).

162. 350 F.2d 445 (D.C. Cir. 1965).

163. Id. at 447.

164. Id.

165. Id.

166. Id. at 450.

167. See generally Hillman, Debunking, supra note 144.

168. See supra notes 5–140, and accompanying text.

scionability.[169] In others, the contested conduct may not quite measure up to duress, misrepresentation, or the like, but the court may still believe that the sum-total of the conduct should not be condoned.[170] Cases in which a party takes advantage of the age, lack of sophistication or education, or emotional state of the other party may call out for relief, but still not quite constitute a policing defense.[171]

2. Substantive unconscionability. Substantive unconscionability focuses on the nature of a term or contract itself, not on how the parties made the contract.[172] Certainly immoral contracts (such as a contract for the sale of a child) or those that contravene public policy (for example, a contract that allows for corporal punishment for delay) are unconscionable.[173] In addition, a term is substantively unconscionable when it subverts a party's purpose for contracting and the other party cannot justify use of the term to protect its own needs.[174] Courts resolve the question of a party's purpose for contracting by examining the equivalency of the exchange. If it is too one-sided, the disfavored party cannot achieve its purpose.[175] Courts resolve the question of whether a party can justify a term based on its needs by determining whether a term performs a reasonable function in the context of the transaction.[176] For example, an excessive price may be enough to constitute substantive unconscionability.[177] The price may not be excessive, however, if the buyer is a large credit risk, the seller's net profit is reasonable, and similarly situated sellers charge a comparable

---

169. See Richard A. Epstein, Unconscionability: A Critical Reappraisal, 18 J. L. & Econ. 293, 303–305 (1975).

170. Hillman, Debunking, supra note 144.

171. See, e.g., Ryan v. Weiner, 610 A.2d 1377 (Del. Ch. 1992).

172. Harris v. Green Tree Fin. Corp., 183 F.3d 173, 181 (3d Cir. 1999) ("Substantive unconscionability refers to contractual terms that are unreasonably or grossly favorable to one side...."); Kinney v. United Health-Care Services, Inc., 83 Cal.Rptr.2d 348, 353 (Cal. Dist. Ct. App. 1999) ("Substantive unconscionability focuses on the terms of the agreement....").

173. Hillman, Debunking, supra note 144, at 31.

174. See supra notes 152–155, and accompanying text.

175. Monsanto Co. v. McFarling, 302 F.3d 1291, 1301 (Fed. Cir. 2002) ("[T]he one-sidedness of the [challenged provision's] substantive terms provides

strong evidence that the forum selection clause was imposed, rather than (even in the abstract sense) bargained for.") (Clevenger, J., dissenting).

176. Frank's Maintenance & Engineering, Inc. v. C. A. Roberts Co., 408 N.E.2d 403, 410 (Ill. App. Ct. 1980) ("Substantive unconscionability concerns the question whether the terms themselves are commercially reasonable.").

177. E.g., Ahern v. Knecht, 563 N.E.2d 787, 792 (Ill. App. Ct. 1990) ("Gross excessiveness of price alone can make an agreement unconscionable."); American Home Improvement, Inc. v. MacIver, 201 A.2d 886, 889 (N.H. 1964) ("Inasmuch as the defendants have received little or nothing of value and under the transaction they entered into they were paying $1,609 for goods and services valued at far less, the contract should not be enforced because of its unconscionable features."); Restatement (Second) of Contracts § 208 cmt. c.

amount.[178] A cross-collateral clause, such as the one in *Williams v. Walker–Thomas Furniture Co.*,[179] therefore may not be unconscionable if most sellers in comparable contexts use them,[180] at least if the clause is comprehensible and the purchaser is a large credit risk.

In general, cases finding what amounts to substantive unconscionability are pretty outrageous. For example, in *Weaver v. American Oil Co.*,[181] Weaver leased a gas station from American Oil Co.[182] The lease required Weaver to indemnify American Oil for its own negligence, so that when an American Oil employee sprayed gasoline on Weaver and he was burned, American Oil sought a declaratory judgment finding the amount of *Weaver's* liability.[183] Understandably, the court declined to enforce the provision, while indicating that the result might have been different if American Oil had explained the clause to Weaver.[184]

E. Special Problems of Standard Form Contracts

1. Paper standard forms. Most exchange transactions today involve paper standard forms.[185] We have all signed these forms many times and should be familiar with the nature of these transactions.[186] As a refresher, here's a typical scenario: You have just flown from Ithaca, New York to Memphis, Tennessee. (If you own a recording of "Memphis" by Chuck Berry, play it in the background while you read this section. Don't play the inferior version by Johnny Rivers.) In the Memphis airport, somewhat haggard, you wait on a long line at Cheapo Rental Cars. Finally, you reach the sales agent, who presents you with a detailed standard rental agreement in fine print. The agent asks you to initial a few terms and sign at the bottom. Others wait behind you impatiently. You are tired and wish to get to your destination. Bargaining over terms or proceeding to another rental car counter would prove fruitless because the agent has no authority to bargain[187] and

---

178. Hillman, Debunking, supra note 144, at 33.

179. 350 F.2d 445 (D.C. Cir. 1965).

180. Leff, supra note 145, at 555–56.

181. 276 N.E.2d 144 (Ind. 1971).

182. Id. at 145.

183. Id.

184. Id. at 148; See also Ahern, 563 N.E.2d 787 (Ill. App. Ct. 1990).

185. See W. David Slawson, Standard Form Contracts and Democratic Control of Lawmaking Power, 84 Harv L. Rev. 529 (1971).

186. See Friedrich Kessler, Contracts of Adhesion—Some Thoughts About Freedom of Contract, 43 Colum. L. Rev. 629 (l943); see also Arthur A. Leff, Contract as Thing, 19 Am. U. L. Rev. 131 (1970); Todd D. Rakoff, Contracts of Adhesion: An Essay in Reconstruction, 96 Harv. L. Rev. 1173 (1983).

187. Farnsworth, supra note 2, at 296 ("Sometimes basic terms relating to quality, quantity, and price are negotiable. But the *boilerplate*—the standard terms printed on the form—is not subject to bargain. It must simply be adhered to if the transaction is to go forward.").

competitors offer similar terms[188] (not to mention that competitors may have no car for you). In addition, you could not understand most of the language of the form if you decided to read it.[189] You don't think that anything will go wrong with your car or the rental anyway[190] and that Cheapo will help you if something does go awry.[191] You therefore sign and initial the form without reading it. In sum, the car rental agent presented you with a largely incomprehensible form on a take-it-or-leave-it basis and I just mentioned about ten reasons why you did not read the form.[192]

On the other hand, after spending big bucks perfecting its form, Cheapo understands it and finds it very useful.[193] By using the form for each transaction, Cheapo standardizes its risks, meaning that it will have the same rights and duties in each transaction, and can plan accordingly.[194] Cheapo also avoids the cost of bargaining over terms.[195] Further, most analysts believe that, because of its expertise and experience, Cheapo can best determine who should bear the risk of each of the various problems that may develop, such as mechanical trouble or accidents.[196] And there is something in all of this for you and me. At least in theory, Cheapo can pass

---

188. See Kessler, supra note 186, at 632 ("[A consumer] is frequently not in a position to shop around for better terms, either because the author of the standard contract has a monopoly (natural or artificial) or because all competitors use the same clauses."); Richard L. Hasen, Efficiency Under Informational Asymmetry: The Effect of Framing on Legal Rules, 38 UCLA L. Rev. 391, 126–27, 430–31 (1990); Alan Schwartz & Louis L. Wilde, Intervening in Markets on the Basis of Imperfect Information: A Legal and Economic Analysis, 127 U. Pa. L. Rev. 630, 661 (1979) ("[I]n the absence of formal analysis it cannot be said that term competition occurs in precisely the same way as price competition.").

189. See Michael I. Meyerson, The Reunification of Contract Law: The Objective Theory of Consumer Form Contracts, 47 U. Miami L. Rev. 1263, 1270 n. 33 (1993); Melvin Aron Eisenberg, Text Anxiety, 59 S. Cal. L. Rev. 305, 309 (1986).

190. See Robert A. Hillman & Jeffrey J. Rachlinski, Standard–Form Contracting in the Electronic Age, 77 N.Y.U. L. Rev. 429, 452–54 (2002); Rakoff, supra note 186, at 1221.

191. See Karl N. Llewellyn, The Common Law Tradition: Deciding Appeals 370 (Little, Brown & Co. 1960); see also John J. A. Burke, Contract as Commodity: A Nonfiction Approach, 24 Seton Hall Legis. J. 285, 293 (2000).

192. See Rakoff, supra note 186, at 1179 ("Virtually every scholar who has written about contracts of adhesion has accepted the truth [that consumers do not read their forms] and the few empirical studies that have been done have agreed."); id. at 1179 n.22.

193. Melvin Aron Eisenberg, The Limits of Cognition and the Limits of Contract, 47 Stan. L. Rev. 211, 243 (1995) ("For the form giver ... a form contract is a high-volume, repeat transaction. Thus, a rational form giver will spend a significant amount of time and money ... to prepare a form contract that is optimal from his perspective.").

194. See Kessler, supra note 186, at 631 ("[U]niformity of terms of contracts typically recurring in a business enterprise is an important factor in the exact calculation of risks."); Farnsworth, supra note 2, at 296 ("Because a judicial interpretation of one standard form serves as an interpretation of similar forms, standardization facilitates the accumulation of experience.").

195. See Kessler, supra note 186, at 631–32; Farnsworth, supra note 2, at 296.

196. But see Rakoff, *supra* note 186, at 1204.

along some of the savings that result from using its form to consumers in the form of lower prices.[197]

Standard forms obviously do not constitute typical "bargains," such as when you and Alice, enjoying equal bargaining power, hammer out the terms of an agreement for the sale of your piano. Remember you have had no say in what appears in Cheapo's form and you didn't even read the form. Nevertheless, at least in theory, competition with other car rental companies creates incentives for Cheapo to avoid drafting one-sided terms that place all of the risks and costs only on you. For example, Cheapo wants to establish a good reputation so that it will attract more customers than, say, Budget Rent-a-Car, and drafting unfair clauses in its standard form is obviously not the way to accomplish that.[198]

The drawback to this rosy picture, however, is the suspicion that competitors in an industry tend to draft comparable terms, so there may be no threat of competition to curtail Cheapo from overreaching.[199] Moreover, if you have a multitude of reasons not to bother to read your form (enumerated above), you obviously won't search for terms even if companies offered different terms.[200] Further, few believe that a small, but sufficient, number of "type A" personalities actually read their forms word-for-word, which might create an incentive for Cheapo to write reasonable terms.[201] Cheapo's reputation may remain largely intact no matter what it puts in its form.

---

197. Rakoff, supra note 186, at 1230 ("[C]osts saved by shifting risks to the customer via form terms may well be returned to the customer by means of lower prices....").

198. See Hasen, supra note 188, at 426–27 (citing Schwartz & Wilde, supra note 188, at 660).

199. See Arthur Alan Leff, The Leff Dictionary of Law: A Fragment, 94 Yale L. J. 1855, 1931–32 (1985).

200. See Michael I. Meyerson, The Efficient Consumer Form Contract: Law and Economics Meets the Real World, 24 Ga. L. Rev. 583, 596 (1990) ("Even though consumers may know many of the characteristics of frequently purchased products, they will remain ignorant of the characteristics of contract terms which typical experience does not reveal."); Rakoff, supra note 186, at 1231 ("Because customers generally neither are expected to nor do read, understand, or shop the form terms, market behavior gives no clue to their prefer-

ences."); Hasen, supra note 188, at 428 ("If consumers do not read the standardized terms, and are concerned only about price, they will be unaware that one firm's standard contract is better than another's.... Although consumers know that *some* contracts contain unfavorable terms, they cannot identify *which* contracts contain unfavorable terms and which contain favorable terms.").

201. See Meyerson, supra note 189, at 1270–71 ("Despite wishful commentary to the contrary, there is no evidence that a small cadre of type-A consumers ferrets out the most beneficial subordinate contract terms, permitting the market to protect the vast majority of consumers."); R. Ted Cruz and Jeffrey J. Hinck, Not My Brother's Keeper: The Inability of an Informed Minority to Correct for Imperfect Information, 47 Hastings L.J. 635, 636 (1996) (asserting that the "informed minority" argument is incorrect).

Obviously, then, businesses such as Cheapo have a considerable bargaining advantage over individuals such as you and me, and standard forms present too much of a temptation for some businesses.[202] This is an important reason why courts arm themselves with a large arsenal of policing doctrines, such as those discussed in this chapter. Karl Llewellyn, the principal drafter of Article 2 of the UCC, first synthesized the common policing strategy that each of these doctrines reflects.[203] The idea is that a court should presume that you have consented to all of the negotiated terms in your standard form, and that you have given your "blanket assent" to all additional "conscionable" terms, provided that you had a reasonable opportunity to read the standard form.[204] "Blanket assent" means that you have delegated to Cheapo the duty of drafting the non-negotiated terms of the contract.[205] But don't worry, you do lots of this kind of delegating. For example, the last time you bought a car or a computer you delegated to the manufacturer the responsibility of selecting appropriate parts.[206] Further, we have already discussed how market forces (to some extent) and the judicial power to strike any "unreasonable or indecent" standard terms protect you from unfair terms.[207]

202. See Eisenberg, supra note 193, at 242–43 (form contracts designed to hide rights); W. David Slawson, The New Meaning of Contract: The Transformation of Contracts Law by Standard Forms, 46 U. Pitt. L. Rev. 21, 44 (1984) (lawyers draft form contracts "as one-sidedly in the interests of the corporate client as possible").

203. Hillman & Rachlinski, supra note 190, at 454–63.

204. Llewellyn, supra note 191, at 370:

Instead of thinking about 'assent' to boiler-plate clauses, we can recognize that so far as concerns the specific, there is no assent at all. What has in fact been assented to, specifically, are the few dickered terms, and the broad type of transaction, and but one thing more. That one thing more is a blanket assent (not a specific assent) to any not unreasonable or indecent terms the seller may have on his form, which do not alter or eviscerate the reasonable meaning of the dickered terms. The fine print which has not been read has no business to cut under the reasonable meaning of those dickered terms which constitute the dominant and only real expression of agreement, but much of it commonly belongs in.

205. Id.

206. See Jeffrey E. Thomas, An Interdisciplinary Critique of the Reasonable Expectations Doctrine, 5 Conn. Ins. L.J. 295, 308 & n.63 (1998) (quoting Gordon R. Foxall & Ronald E. Goldsmith, Consumer Psychology for Marketing 31 (1994)):

"[N]umerous studies [indicate] that consumers drastically limit their search for information about durable products like furniture and cars, and services such as those of general practitioners.... [M]ost consumers for domestic appliances visit a single store, fail to consult advertising, use restricted price information, consider only one make, and employ perceptions of the manufacturer's reputation and packaging rather than make evaluations of the product/service attributes to arrive at judgments of quality."

But see Eisenberg, Text Anxiety, supra note 189, at 309 ("The same consumer who is willing to read simple narrative text that discloses a product attribute (such as a list of ingredients) is often unwilling to read the dense text that comprises a form contract.").

207. Llewellyn, supra note 191, at 370; see also Karl N. Llewellyn, Book Review, 52 Harv. L. Rev. 700, 704 (1939)

hand, the facts of the cases are often straightforward. The leading case, *Hill v. Gateway 2000*,[222] decided by a former law professor (therefore a very authoritative opinion), is typical and similar to your air conditioner hypo above.[223] Recall that the Hills called Gateway on the telephone and ordered a computer.[224] They gave their credit card information, and Gateway delivered the computer.[225] The container contained terms, including an agreement to arbitrate all disputes, and the Hills had thirty days to return the computer.[226] After thirty days, the Hills became dissatisfied with the computer, and brought an action in federal court. Gateway sought arbitration.[227]

The Hills argued that their credit card payment and Gateway's shipment constituted an offer and acceptance and that section 2–207(2) of the UCC excluded as "proposals" any "additional" terms that followed contract formation, including the arbitration provision.[228] The court did not agree and held that Gateway's shipment of the computer and terms with the proviso that the Hills could return the computer within thirty days constituted an offer and, by retaining the computer for more than thirty days, the Hills accepted.[229] The contract, formed at the end of the thirty days, therefore included the arbitration provision.[230]

The court may have erred about the time of formation of the contract. Section 2–206(1)(b) of the UCC states that

> "Unless otherwise unambiguously indicated by the language or the circumstances * * * an order or other offer to buy goods for prompt or current shipment shall be construed as inviting acceptance either by a prompt promise to ship or by the prompt or current shipment of conforming or non-conforming goods * * *."[231]

---

222. 105 F.3d 1147 (7th Cir. 1997).

223. See, e.g., The Gateway Thread–AALS Contracts Listserv, 16 Touro L. Rev. 1147 (2000) [hereinafter Gateway Thread]; For a recent case following Hill, see Bischoff v. DirecTV, 180 F.Supp.2d 1097, 1107 (C.D. Cal. 2002).

224. Hill, 105 F.3d at 1148.

225. Id.

226. Id. at 1148, 1150.

227. Id. at 1148.

228. UCC § 2–207(2) ("The additional terms are to be construed as proposals for addition to the contract."). The rest of the subsection would not apply because the Hills were not merchants. For discussion of UCC § 2–207,

see Chapter 2 at notes 262–278, and accompanying text.

229. 105 F.3d at 1150.

230. Id.; see also M.A. Mortenson Co. v. Timberline Software Corp., 998 P.2d 305 (Wash. 2000); Westendorf v. Gateway 2000, Inc., 763 A.2d 92 (Del. 2000); Brower v. Gateway 2000, Inc., 676 N.Y.S.2d 569 (N.Y. App. Div. 1998); Levy v. Gateway 2000, Inc., 1997 WL 823611 (N.Y. Sup. Ct. 1997).

231. UCC § 2–206(1)(b); Shubha Ghosh, Where's the Sense in Hill v. Gateway 2000?: Reflections on the Visible Hand of Norm Creation, 16 Touro L. Rev. 1125, 1132–33 (2000) (pointing out Section 2–206(1)(b)'s applicability).

The parties likely gave little thought to whether the contract technically was formed at the time of payment, on delivery of the goods, or thirty days after delivery.[232] The "unless" preamble of section 2–206(1)(b) was therefore not applicable to the Hills transaction.[233] Under these circumstances, the offer and acceptance (order and shipment) took place before the Hills received the terms. Therefore, the arbitration clause is only a proposal for an addition to the contract that would not become part of the contract under UCC section 2–207(2).

Unfortunately for the Hills, the court thought otherwise.[234] However, even if the Hills had prevailed on the time of formation, they still could have lost the case. Their use of the computer for more than thirty days could constitute an agreement to modify the contract to include Gateway's terms.[235] Recall that section 2–209(1) dispenses with the consideration requirement for modification agreements.[236] Gateway could argue that the Hills agreed to the new contract by keeping the computer without protest. Alternatively, Gateway could assert that the Hills, who knew that the package containing the computer would include terms (you knew there would be terms in the carton containing your air conditioner, right?), delegated to Gateway the right to ascribe those terms. Neither of these arguments are sure-fire winners for Gateway, but they tend to show the inconclusiveness of determining the rights of parties to rolling contracts based on when the contract was formed.

I guess I owe you an alternative theory for resolving rolling contracts cases, since I am being so critical of the *Hill v. Gateway* approach. I have already suggested in print (in a fabulous article) that courts should adopt Llewellyn's general approach to standard-form contracts in the rolling contracts setting.[237] We have seen that Llewellyn's approach entails enforcing any bargained-for terms (but obviously there are none in the carton) and any conscionable standard terms, and throwing out any unfair terms.[238] In other word, courts should dispense with the time-of-formation analysis, assume that the Hills gave blanket assent to the terms in the container, and strike any unconscionable terms.

If we apply unconscionability to the Hill–Gateway problem, for example, a court would determine whether the arbitration term was procedurally or substantively unconscionable. As to procedural

---

232. See Chapter 2 at notes 283–284, and accompanying text.

233. See UCC § 2–206(1)(b).

234. 105 F.3d at 1150.

235. See UCC § 2–209(1).

236. UCC § 2–209(1) ("An agreement modifying a contract within this

Article needs no consideration to be binding.").

237. Hillman, Symposium, supra note 220.

238. See supra notes 203–207, and accompanying text.

unconscionability, Gateway's "rolling contract" approach is very common[239] (think about the last time you purchased a major item from Wal–Mart or travel tickets or, for that matter, anything by phone or by the internet). Further, Gateway's rolling contract reduces the costs of doing business.[240] Requiring Gateway to read the terms over the phone or to send a contract ahead to a prospective purchaser would increase costs and would achieve little. Would people like the Hills even listen to or understand the recitation or read the form when it arrived? (The court in *Hill v. Gateway* thought not.[241]) In addition, Gateway's approach may even increase the chance that people will read their forms. Remember, a purchaser has thirty days to peruse the terms in her own home or workplace, free from a badgering sales clerk or other time pressures.[242] Gateway may hope that few purchasers will take the time and bear the expense of returning a computer based on adverse terms, assuming they discover them.[243] But if people who read their terms do not return the computer, they must believe that the costs of doing so, which should be relatively low, still outweigh the costs of living with the adverse terms.[244]

All of this suggests that rolling contracts should not be outlawed on the theory that they are procedurally unconscionable. But what about substantive unconscionability? Recall that the Hills were fighting the enforcement of an arbitration provision.[245] For a long time arbitration was the darling of lawyers and theorists because of its potential as a money- and time-saving alternative to litigation.[246] Further, federal law supports arbitration as a dispute-

239. Hill, 105 F.3d at 1149 ("Payment preceding the revelation of full terms is common for air transportation, insurance, and many other endeavors.")

240. See ProCD, Inc. v. Zeidenberg, 86 F.3d 1447, 1452 (7th Cir. 1996) ("[Eliminating rolling contracts] would drive prices through the ceiling or return transactions to the horse-and-buggy age."); Restatement (Second) of Contracts § 211, cmt. a ("Standardization of agreements serves many of the same functions as standardization of goods and services; both are essential to a system of mass production and distribution.").

241. Hill, 105 F.3d at 1149 ("If the staff at the other end of the phone for direct-sales operations such as Gateway's had to read the four-page statement of terms before taking the buyer's credit card number, the droning voice would anesthetize rather than enlighten many potential buyers. Others would hang up in a rage over the waste of their

time. And oral recitation would not avoid customers' assertions (whether true or feigned) that the clerk did not read term X to them, or that they did not remember or understand it.").

242. See generally Hillman and Rachlinski, supra note 190, at 447–50 (social pressures on consumers not to read and discuss terms).

243. See Comment: An Overview of the Uniform Computer Information Transactions Act: Warranties, Self–Help, and Contract Formation–Why UCITA Should be Renamed "The Licensors' Protection Act", 25 S. Ill. U. L. J. 389, 399 (2001).

244. James J. White, Autistic Contracts, 45 Wayne L. Rev. 1693, 1717 (2000).

245. Hill, 105 F.3d at 1148.

246. Gilmer v. Interstate/Johnson Lane Corp., 895 F.2d 195, 196 (4th Cir. 1990) ("[T]he Supreme Court has en-

resolution mechanism, so it would be hard for a court to declare arbitration terms substantively unconscionable.[247]

Recently, however, analysts have raised serious issues over whether businesses can use arbitration unfairly to their advantage.[248] Courts should therefore examine an arbitration clause in context to determine whether the particular facts show that the term is substantively unconscionable as applied. For example, in *Brower v. Gateway 2000, Inc.*,[249] the court held that the arbitration term was substantively unconscionable because it required Brower to pay "excessive costs" that "surely serves to deter the individual consumer from invoking the process."[250] Further,

> Barred from resorting to the courts by the arbitration clause in the first instance, the designation of a financially prohibitive forum effectively bars consumers from this forum as well; consumers are thus left with no forum at all in which to resolve a dispute.[251]

In sum, the main difference between rolling contracts and other standard-form transactions involves when purchasers have an opportunity to read their terms. Although some analysts worry about rolling contracts, ironically the opportunity for purchasers to read the terms at home at their leisure seems a good reason to *favor* rolling contracts as a method of contract formation.[252] On the other hand, if people do not read forms no matter when they receive them, contract law should not focus on when the seller makes the forms available.[253] Instead, courts should vigorously apply substantive unconscionability.

---

dorsed arbitration as an effective and efficient means of dispute resolution."); Zosky v. Boyer, 856 F.2d 554, 562 (3d Cir. 1988) ("Arbitration is an expeditious and inexpensive mode of alternative dispute resolution.").

247. Gateway Thread, supra note 223, at 1172 (statement of Franklin G. Snyder); see 9 U.S.C. § 2 ("[A] contract evidencing a transaction involving commerce to settle by arbitration a controversy thereafter arising out of such contract or transaction, or the refusal to perform the whole or any part thereof, or an agreement in writing to submit to arbitration an existing controversy arising out of such a contract, transaction, or refusal, shall be valid, irrevocable, and enforceable, save upon such grounds as exist at law or in equity for the revocation of any contract.").

248. See, e.g., Katherine Van Wezel Stone, Rustic Justice: Community and Coercion under the Federal Arbitration Act, 77 N.C.L Rev. 931 (1999).

249. 676 N.Y.S.2d 569 (N.Y. App. Div. 1998).

250. Id. at 574.

251. Id.

252. See Hillman & Rachlinski, supra note 190, at 480.

253. Gateway Thread, supra note 223, at 1165 (statement of Kenneth C. Kettering) ("The focus on the process by which the terms are communicated to the buyer before the buyer makes the final decision whether to consummate the purchase seems to me ultimately a red herring.... [I]n most cases 'buyers will not bother to read or fathom the significance of the terms.' ").

3.   Electronic standard forms. If you are a first-year law student or a young attorney (or even somewhat more advanced in years), you have purchased goods or services, such as a computer, airline tickets, or software, over the internet or while downloading software.[254] As you know, the atmosphere is quite different from the typical paper standard form transaction:

> "The harried traveler who faces a complex form after waiting in a long line at the car rental counter has been replaced by the impatient college student buying virus-protection software, delivered via the Internet. She sits comfortably in her dorm room as she searches the Internet for a product. After settling on a product, she might casually browse through some online reviews of the software she wants to purchase, posted by anonymous reviewers to an electronic bulletin board. Once deciding to purchase, she opens an online account with the vendor, using her credit card, and downloads the desired software. She quickly clicks 'I agree' to terms and conditions on the website or while installing the software, without scrolling down through several pages to read the boilerplate completely. At the same time, she is listening to a compact disk from her cd-rom drive and playing 'Minesweeper' (or she is perhaps sitting in a law school contracts class at a well-wired law school)."[255]

Lawmakers must decide whether electronic standard forms require a new set of policing (and other) rules, or whether the rules focusing on paper transactions will suffice in this new environment.

Despite the somewhat rosier picture of the process of electronic standard-form contracting depicted above (after all, our college student has time to look at the form free from distractions not of her own making), lots of the less encouraging realities of the paper world apply equally to electronic standard-form transactions.[256] Electronic standard forms are still non-negotiable (our student doesn't have anyone to talk to), difficult to understand, and comprised of the same substantively problematic terms (such as an agreement to arbitrate in a distant place).[257] At present, some evidence suggests e-business use lots of different terms,[258] but, before long, these businesses likely will start employing common terms, just as in the paper world.[259]

E-businesses can also experiment with methods of presentation of terms and produce standard forms most likely to induce accep-

---

254. See Hillman & Rachlinski, supra note 190, at 429–30.

255. Id. at 468–469.

256. Id. at 464.

257. Jane K. Winn, What Does a Chick Mean? Balancing Efficiency and Fairness Concerns in Internet Contracting (unpublished manuscript).

258. Hillman & Rachlinski, supra note 190, at 473.

259. Id.

tance (for example, by discouraging e-consumers to read through many pages of text and presenting the opportunity to click "I agree" on the first page).[260] In addition, e-businesses can gain information about their users and tailor terms to different classes of e-consumers.[261]

On the other hand, certain aspects of e-commerce offer e-consumers greater protection than in the paper world. E-businesses may worry more than other businesses about the content of their standard forms because of the capacity of e-consumers to spread the word electronically about particularly nasty forms or presentations. E-businesses understand that "with a few mouse clicks, disgruntled e-consumers can broadcast their dissatisfaction to thousands of potential customers. These companies also know that they have to distinguish themselves from the unreliable Internet businesses that are using the Internet to take advantage of e-consumers."[262]

Further, as the example of the college student e-purchaser suggests, e-consumers have the opportunity to study electronic standard forms without the pressure of impatient people standing in line behind them or sales clerks expecting them to show their trust by declining to read the terms.[263] However, although e-consumers probably have lots more time to decide whether to purchase, they may have good reason not to use the time to try to decipher the legalese.[264] E-consumers also may have come to expect instant gratification from their computers, and therefore be too impatient to try to read the standard form.[265] In the article constantly appearing in the footnotes to this discussion, we coined the phrase "click happy" to describe today's impatient e-consumer.[266]

Well, perhaps you are getting impatient to learn whether lawmakers have drafted new rules to account for electronic standard forms. For the most part, the answer is no. The cases that have spoken on the enforcement of electronic standard forms apply good old contract policing law, much as described already in this chapter.[267] Courts generally enforce what they call "clickwrap" standard-form contracts, in which the e-consumer must click on "I agree" or similar language to form the contract after presentation of the standard form on the screen.[268]

---

260. Id. at 481.

261. Id. at 482.

262. Id. at 470.

263. Id. at 448, 478.

264. Id. at 478.

265. Id. at 479.

266. Id. at 480.

267. See supra notes 185–219, and accompanying text.

268. See, e.g., Barnett v. Network Solutions, Inc., 38 S.W.3d 200, 204 (Tex. Ct. App. 2001) ("Parties to a written contract have the obligation to read what they sign; and, absent actual or constructive fraud . . . they are not excused from the consequences attendant

A more worrisome method of presentation of terms has not been as well received by the courts. "Browsewrap" contracts do not require the e-consumer to view and agree to a set of terms presented on the screen.[269] Instead, a screen may contain an optional "terms and conditions" hyperlink that takes the e-consumer to the terms.[270] For example, at one time Netscape included a hyperlink that stated, "please review and agree to the terms of the * * * licensing agreement before downloading and using the software."[271] Browsewrap presents the possibility that an e-consumer would never see the hyperlink and would not have the opportunity to view the terms before making a commitment.[272] Browsewrap presentations therefore have been less successful in the courts on the ground that e-consumers have not received adequate notice of standard terms.[273]

Case law thus does not appear to be making dramatic changes to accommodate e-commerce. Both the paper and electronic worlds look (1) for a reasonable presentation of terms so the consumer has an opportunity to review them; and (2) a manifestation of assent by the consumer.[274] To date, legislation governing electronic transactions has been rather narrow and unsuccessful. At this writing, only two states have adopted the Uniform Computer Information Transactions Act ("UCITA"), which applies to the transfer of computer information, such as software, and not to the sale of goods or services. Further, it has not been endorsed by the American Law Institute. UCITA parallels existing case law by enforcing standard-form contracts only when a person manifests assent after an "opportunity to review" the terms.[275] A person has an "opportunity to review" a term if it is "made available in a manner that ought to call it to the attention of a reasonable person and permit review."[276]

upon a failure to read the contract. The same rule applies to contracts which appear in an electronic format."); Caspi v. Microsoft Network, 732 A.2d 528 (N.J. Super. Ct. App. Div. 1999).

269. Specht v. Netscape Communs. Corp., 306 F.3d 17, 23 (2d Cir. 2002) ("[Readers] were required neither to express unambiguous assent to that program's license agreement nor even to view the license terms or become aware of their existence....").

270. See ACTONet, Ltd. v. Allou Health & Beauty Care, 219 F.3d 836, 839 (8th Cir. 2000); America Online, Inc. v. National Health Care Disc., Inc., 121 F.Supp.2d 1255, 1261 (N.D. Iowa 2000); Ticketmaster Corp. v. Tickets.Com, Inc., 2000 WL 525390, at *1 (C.D. Cal. 2000).

271. Specht v. Netscape Communs. Corp., 306 F.3d 17, 23 (2d Cir. 2002).

272. Id. at 23 ("[Readers] were required neither to express unambiguous assent to that program's license agreement nor even to view the license terms or become aware of their existence....").

273. Id. at 30 ("[A] consumer's clicking on a download button does not communicate assent to contractual terms if the offer did not make clear to the consumer that clicking on the download button would signify assent.").

274. UCITA § 105(d) (1999).

275. UCITA § 112(a).

276. UCITA § 112(e)(1).

Chapter Seven

THE PAROL EVIDENCE RULE AND CONTRACT INTERPRETATION

If you read the introduction to this book (Chapter 1) carefully, you already know that the spelling of "parol" in the title to this chapter is not a typo and that you will advance your career by understanding this. To review, there is no "e" at the end of the word parol. "Parol" means "expressed or evidenced by speech only; not expressed by writing."[1] The parol evidence rule serves as a filter that controls the evidence a party can introduce at trial to prove the terms of a contract, barring evidence of prior or contemporaneous oral agreements or promises that contradict or vary a term in a writing the parties intend to be complete with respect to that term.[2] Despite the definition of parol, the rule also precludes evidence of prior *written* agreements that contradict the parties' final written agreement.[3] Part A of this chapter discusses the tricky parol evidence rule, which will make the above more understandable.

Once we understand what evidence courts can use to interpret a contract, we shall look in Part B of this chapter at the rules of contract interpretation, which are the rules contract law uses to ascertain the meaning of the words in a contract. Part B also examines the process by which courts fill gaps in incomplete contracts.

A. Parol Evidence Rule

The illustration in Chapter 1 was pretty brilliant, so let's repeat it here in order to introduce the parol evidence rule. You and your neighbor, Alice Franklin, enter a written contract for the sale of your piano. You include all of the pertinent terms, including a price of $500. However, at the time of performance, Alice refuses to pay more than $300 for the piano. She claims that, prior to signing the written contract, you orally agreed to accept $300 for the piano. She asserts that the contract says $500 only because you thought that your mother would be angry with you for selling the piano for

---

1. Black's Law Dictionary 1273 (rev. 4th ed.1968).

2. See, e.g., James J. White & Robert S. Summers, Uniform Commercial Code 90–91 (5th ed. 2000).

3. See, e.g., 3 Arthur Linton Corbin, Corbin on Contracts 357 (1960).

so little. You sue Alice, and at trial she seeks to introduce evidence of your alleged oral agreement. The traditional parol evidence rule, defined in the introduction to this chapter, bars this evidence.[4] Alice's evidence is of a prior oral agreement that contradicts the written contract. Further, the contract is complete on its face with respect to the price of the piano.

The reason for the parol evidence rule should be clear from this example. The rule deters untruthful attacks on the terms of contracts. You can rest assured that you have a contract for the sale of your piano for $500, and that Alice cannot weasel her way to a lower price. Application of the parol evidence rule thus helps assure that contract law carries out the intentions of the parties.

Wait a minute, you say. My rendition of the facts does not make it clear whether you and Alice really did agree to $500 only to fool your mother. If she is telling the truth, the parol evidence rule subverts the parties' intentions, it does not assist in enforcing them. It should not be surprising to learn, then, that the rule is full of exceptions, created because courts sometimes believe that the party who offers evidence that contradicts the writing is telling the truth. Let's look at each of these exceptions. After we consider them, we'll return to our hypo to see if any of the exceptions apply.[5]

1. Collateral contract exception. Let's consider another problem to illustrate this exception. Suppose you agree to sell Alice your house. You and Alice further agree that the written sales contract is complete on the terms of the sale. (Contract law calls a writing the parties intend to be complete on all of the terms a "full integration" and on some of the terms a "partial integration." More on this shortly.[6]) Alice refuses to go through with the sale, claiming that, as part of the transaction, you had promised to remove an old tree on the property and you have not done so.[7] You sue Alice for breach of the land-sale contract and she defends by seeking to introduce evidence of your alleged broken promise to remove the tree.

Under the traditional parol evidence rule, a court would admit evidence of the tree-removal agreement only if it did not contradict or vary the written contract or if the parties did not intend the writing to be complete on that issue. The written contract says nothing about tree removal, so, at first blush, you might think that Alice can introduce her evidence without a problem. However, courts have also wrestled with the issue of whether parol evidence contradicts or varies an *implied* term of the written contract and

---

4. See supra note 2, and accompanying text.

5. See infra notes 55–56, and accompanying text.

6. See infra notes 20–22, and accompanying text.

7. See Mitchill v. Lath, 160 N.E. 646 (N.Y. 1928).

therefore should not be admitted for that reason.[8] For example, perhaps the parties' silence about tree removal in the written contract implies that you do not have to remove any trees. This implication would arise if reasonable parties who had made an agreement for tree removal ordinarily would have put such an agreement in the land-sale contract.[9] That, of course, depends on whether land-sale contracts generally include such agreements when made. If so, your contract with Alice would not require you to remove trees and Alice's evidence would contradict the contract. Therefore, a court would not receive Alice's evidence. But if land-sale contracts usually do not include agreements with respect to tree removal, the agreement for the tree-removal is called a "collateral contract" (a separate contract), and Alice's evidence is admissible.[10] Her evidence does not contradict the written contract, which is silent on tree removal.

Distinguishing between collateral contracts and agreements that parties would ordinarily include in the written contract is no easy task. Let's look at our example again. On the one hand, we can say that your promise to remove the tree helped induce Alice to enter the land-sale contract, so we would expect that she would insist on putting the promise in the written contract. On the other hand, tree removal is a task unrelated to the actual sale of the property, and such sale contracts ordinarily deal only with the subject matter of the sale.

A leading parol evidence rule case, *Mitchill v. Lath*,[11] contemplated just this problem (what a coincidence!). Prior to contracting, the sellers of land promised the prospective buyer to remove an ice house on adjacent land. When the sellers failed to keep their promise, the buyer sought specific performance. The court barred evidence of the promise on the theory that the promise, if made, would have been part of the written contract.[12] A strong dissent thought that an agreement for removal of the ice house would constitute a collateral contract. After all, the typical land-sale contract focuses on the terms of conveyance and does not include personal-services agreements. The dissent was also motivated in part by its belief (mentioned more than once) that the parties really had made an agreement for removal of the ice house.[13]

---

8. Id. at 647 ("Is it also implied that the defendants are not to do anything unexpressed in the writing?").

9. Id. ("Were such an agreement made it would seem most natural that the inquirer should find it in the contract.").

10. Marinelli v. Unisa Holdings, Inc., 655 N.Y.S.2d 495, 496 (App. Div. 1997) ("[T]he standard for the introduc-

tion of an oral promise was satisfied here. The ... agreements are collateral, they do not conflict with the [written] agreement and they would not reasonably be expected to be found there.").

11. 160 N.E. 646 (N.Y. 1928).

12. Id. at 647.

13. Id. at 649 (Lehman, J. dissenting) ("The plaintiff's assertion of a parol agreement by the defendants to remove

Courts employ different techniques in applying the collateral-contract exception. One approach, favored by those who believe the parol evidence rule serves a useful role, requires the judge to determine the admissibility of parol evidence simply by reading the contract, without resort to extrinsic evidence (evidence outside of the actual agreement).[14] Writers supporting this view reason that if courts admit extrinsic evidence, a party such as Alice or the purchaser in *Mitchill*, could prove that the parties did not intend the writing to be complete on the subject at issue simply by introducing evidence of the additional oral agreement.[15] If the evidence is credible, then the parties could not have intended the writing to be complete. For example, Alice's evidence of the tree-removal agreement would show that the parties did not intend the written contract to be complete with respect to the promises that induced the contract. Here's how Samuel Williston, one of the giants of contract law during the past century, described the problem and its solution:

> Even if the oral agreement is repugnant to the writing, what was orally agreed would be of equal importance with what was written, since its existence would prove that there was no complete integration of the contract in regard to the matter to which it related. * * * It is generally held that the contract must appear on its face to be incomplete in order to permit parol evidence of additional terms.[16]

As a potential contract drafter, however, you should know that not all courts follow Williston by determining whether a writing is complete (fully integrated) without the aid of extrinsic evidence. In fact, the tide is turning against Williston.[17] Arthur Corbin, another leading contract law figure of the twentieth century, and no fan of the parol evidence rule, disagreed with Williston.[18] Corbin pointed out that the parol evidence rule operates only when the parties intended a writing to be complete with respect to the contested subject matter. Further, a court should not preclude any evidence in determining whether the parties so intended: "The 'parol evidence rule' does not itself purport to establish the fact of 'integration'; and until that fact is established the 'rule' does not

---

the ice house was completely established by the great weight of evidence.").

14. 4 S. Williston and W. Jaeger, A Treatise on the Law of Contracts 1014 (4th ed. 1990).

15. Id. at 1015–16 (" 'If we may go outside of the instrument to prove that there was a stipulation not contained in it, and so that only part of the contract was put in writing, and, because of that fact, enforce the oral stipulation, there

will be little of value left in the rule itself.' ") (citation omitted).

16. Id. at 1014.

17. See, e.g., E. Allen Farnsworth, Contracts 435 (3d ed.1999).

18. See John D. Calamari & Joseph M. Perillo, A Plea for a Uniform Parol Evidence Rule and Principles of Contract Interpretation, 42 Ind. L. J. 333, 341 (1967).

purport to have any legal operation."[19] The only logical conclusion, then, is that the parol evidence rule cannot preclude the admissibility of evidence of an oral agreement to show that the writing was not complete.[20]

If you are thinking that Corbin's approach emasculates the parol evidence rule, I would have to agree. But here's what you can do as a contract drafter to help protect your client who wants to be able to rely on her written contract and to fight off evidence of additional promises or agreements: Draft a term in the contract that provides that the writing is complete and is the only agreement between the parties. (If your client wants the writing to be complete on only certain subjects, you can make that clear as well.) Such a provision is often called a "full integration clause" (or "partial integration clause" if your client wants the writing to be complete only on certain subjects) because it demonstrates that the parties intend to "integrate" all of the terms of their agreement in their writing. Language such as "the parties intend this writing to be the full, complete, and only statement of the agreement between them" should do. Faced with such a clause, even courts otherwise inclined to follow Corbin's reasoning may be hard-pressed to admit evidence on whether the contract is fully integrated.[21] Of course, you should never be too content with your drafting prowess, and this area is no exception. Some courts resist the parol evidence rule even in the face of a full integration clause.[22]

2. Ambiguity exception. The idea behind the ambiguity exception is that a court must admit parol evidence if a writing is unclear, even if the parties intended the writing to be complete.[23] In case the meaning of "ambiguous" is itself ambiguous, let's explain it: The ambiguity exception applies when the language in the contract is reasonably susceptible to more than one meaning.[24]

As you might expect, courts disagree about the appropriate process for deciding whether language is reasonably susceptible to more than one meaning. For example, some courts have held that the judge must determine the issue simply by reading the contract, without the aid of extrinsic evidence.[25] Determining ambiguity

---

19. 3 Corbin, supra note 3, at 442.

20. "[I]t can never be determined by mere interpretation of the words of a writing whether it is an 'integration' of anything * * *." Id. at 441.

21. See Harrison v. Fred S. James, P.A., Inc., 558 F.Supp. 438, 442 (E.D. Pa. 1983) ("[W]hen a writing contains an integration clause which expressly provides that the written instrument contains the entire agreement of the

parties, it is conclusively presumed to do so . . . .").

22. See, e.g., Farnsworth, supra note 17, at 436 & n. 36 (citing cases).

23. See, e.g., Gold Kist, Inc. v. Carr, 886 S.W.2d 425, 429 (Tex. App. 1994).

24. See, e.g., Coker v. Coker, 650 S.W.2d 391, 393 (Tex. 1983).

25. See Gold Kist, Inc., 886 S.W.2d at 429.

without the aid of extrinsic evidence is, of course, consistent with Williston's approach for determining whether the parties intended a writing to be complete.[26] Not surprisingly, critics do not like this method of determining ambiguity any better than they liked Williston's treatment of integration, and many courts have adopted a more expansive view.

Consider, for example, *Pacific Gas and Electric Co. v. G. W. Thomas Drayage & Rigging Co.,*[27] decided by Justice Traynor, an influential judge during the middle of the last century. The parties disagreed over the meaning of the word "indemnify" in a contract calling for the defendant, Thomas Drayage & Rigging Co., to replace a portion of the plaintiff, PG & E's, steam turbine. The clause in contention stated that defendant agreed to perform the work "at [its] own risk and expense" and to "indemnify [plaintiff] against all loss, damage, expense and liability resulting from injury to property, arising out of or in any way connected with the performance of this contract."[28] During the work, plaintiff's turbine was damaged and plaintiff sought damages based on the indemnification provision. Defendant offered parol evidence, including PG & E's admissions and the parties' previous dealings, to prove that the parties intended the indemnification provision to cover only property owned by third parties, not the plaintiff's property.

According to the traditional approach, a court should determine whether to admit defendant's evidence of the meaning of "indemnify" simply by reading the clause and determining whether it is ambiguous on its face. In fact, Justice Traynor determined that the word "indemnify" was ambiguous on its face because people use the word, not only to refer to protection against third party liability, but also to describe protection against their own loss.[29] But Justice Traynor then went further.

Justice Traynor hesitated to determine ambiguity without resort to contextual evidence. He reasoned that, because of the inherent imprecision of language, what appears clear to one judge might seem ambiguous to another.[30] Justice Traynor's objections, although long, are worth quoting directly:

> A rule that would limit the determination of the meaning of a written instrument to its four-corners merely because it seems to the court to be clear and unambiguous, would either deny the relevance of the intention of the parties or presuppose

26. See supra notes 16–17, and accompanying text.

27. 442 P.2d 641 (Cal. 1968).

28. Id. at 642.

29. Id. at 646 n.8.

30. Id. at 644.

a degree of verbal precision and stability our language has not attained.

* * *

* * * A court must ascertain and give effect to [the intention of the parties] by determining what the parties meant by the words they used. Accordingly, the exclusion of relevant, extrinsic evidence to explain the meaning of a written instrument could be justified only if it were feasible to determine the meaning the parties gave to the words from the instrument alone.

If words had absolute and constant referents, it might be possible to discover contractual intention in the words themselves and in the manner in which they were arranged. Words, however, do not have absolute and constant referents. "A word is a symbol of thought but has no arbitrary and fixed meaning like a symbol of algebra or chemistry * * *." The meaning of particular words or groups of words varies with the "verbal context and surrounding circumstances and purposes in view of the linguistic education and experience of their users and their hearers or readers (not excluding judges). * * * A word has no meaning apart from these factors; much less does it have an objective meaning, one true meaning." Accordingly, the meaning of a writing "can only be found by interpretation in the light of all the circumstances that reveal the sense in which the writer used the words. The exclusion of parol evidence regarding such circumstances merely because the words do not appear ambiguous to the reader can easily lead to the attribution to a written instrument of a meaning that was never intended. * * * ."

Although extrinsic evidence is not admissible to add to, detract from, or vary the terms of a written contract, these terms must first be determined before it can be decided whether or not extrinsic evidence is being offered for a prohibited purpose.[31]

Justice Traynor's approach was bound to alarm proponents of the parol evidence rule, who saw in his language the implication that there should be no restrictions whatsoever on evidence offered to show that contract language was ambiguous.[32] This approach, of course, would completely circumvent the parol evidence rule. For example, recall the example from the beginning of this chapter in which Alice wants to prove that $500 meant $300 in her purchase

---

31. Id. at 644–45.

32. See, e.g., Trident Center v. Connecticut General Life Ins. Co., 847 F.2d 564, 569 (9th Cir. 1988).

of your piano.[33] Under Traynor's reasoning, would Alice's evidence be admissible? Some people thought so, and basically concluded that Traynor's decision portended the end of the world (well, almost):

> "*Pacific Gas* casts a long shadow of uncertainty over all trans-
> actions * * *. It also chips away at the foundation of our legal
> system. By giving credence to the idea that words are inade-
> quate to express concepts, *Pacific Gas* undermines the basic
> principle that language proves a meaningful constrain on pub-
> lic and private conduct."[34]

In actuality, Justice Traynor's opinion is not too clear on how he would handle Alice's offer of evidence, proving, I guess, his point about the limitations of language. (Maybe you're saying the same thing right now about my prose.) On the one hand, he says that the parties' intentions control and that courts cannot determine the meaning of language "from the instrument alone."[35] On the other hand, he says that the parol evidence must be relevant to prove a meaning to which the language of the instrument is "*reasonably* susceptible."[36] Further, he thinks courts should look preliminarily at all "*credible* evidence" to determine the parties' intentions.[37] Perhaps $500 is not "reasonably susceptible" to the meaning $300, or perhaps Alice's evidence is not "credible." But if Alice's evidence is true, the parties' intentions will not control.

One thing that is clear from *Pacific Gas and Electric Co.* is that Justice Traynor did not support a plain-meaning approach to the issue of ambiguity. Many courts have followed Traynor's lead, and some have explicitly defined the kinds of evidence a party can offer to prove ambiguity. For example, one court allowed objective evidence, including course of performance, usage of trade, and course of dealing, at a formal preliminary hearing.[38] We take up these kinds of evidence shortly.[39] Suffice it to say here that course of performance, usage of trade, and course of dealing are reliable sources of contextual evidence involving respectively: earlier performances under the same contract, the customary meaning of terms within the same area or trade, and conduct of the same parties under earlier contracts or arrangements. Most important for now is that you understand that the court would not allow testimony of the parties' private understanding of a term inconsis-

---

33. See supra note 4, and accompanying text.

34. Id.

35. Pacific Gas and Electric Co.,
442 P.2d at 644.

36. Id. (emphasis supplied).

37. Id. at 645 (emphasis supplied).

38. Eskimo Pie Corp. v. Whitelawn
Dairies, Inc., 284 F.Supp. 987 (S.D.N.Y.
1968).

39. See infra notes 73–99, and accompanying text.

tent with general usage (such as "we intended $500 to mean $300").

3. Proof of fraud, duress, or mistake. Think back to Chapter 6 and the example in which Alice claims that she is selling you 5.5 acres of land when she knows the property contains only 3.5 acres.[40] Assume further that she tells you to ignore the written contract, which lists the property as 3.5 acres. Can you introduce parol evidence of Alice's fraudulent misrepresentation? Remember, the evidence is of a prior oral representation that contradicts the written contract.

Most courts allow you to introduce such evidence on the theory that the fraud preceding the contract induced you to make the deal.[41] If the parol evidence is true, there is no enforceable contract and no role for the parol evidence rule. Thus, prior to considering the application of the parol evidence rule, courts admit evidence to prove the misrepresentation. This approach should deter fraud. If the parol evidence rule barred evidence of fraud, victims would not be able to prove it, and nasty people would feel free to engage in it. For the same reason, evidence should be admissible to prove fraud notwithstanding the presence of a full integration clause in the alleged contract.[42] Of course, just because a court will admit your evidence of Alice's fraud, doesn't mean you win the case. Recall that you must show reasonable reliance on her misrepresentation of the acreage. This may be difficult because the contract states that Alice is selling you 3.5 acres of land.[43]

All of what has been said, about fraud also should apply to related policing defenses, such as duress and mistake. Chapters 6 and 9 contain discussions of the substantive grounds for these theories. The point here is that evidence of duress or mistake should be admissible notwithstanding the parol evidence rule. Although not all courts agree, as with fraud, if the grounds for these defenses exists, there is no enforceable contract and no role for the parol evidence rule.[44]

---

40. See Chapter 6 at notes 66–67, and accompanying text.

41. See, e.g., Culbreth v. Simone, 511 F.Supp. 906, 915 (E.D. Pa. 1981) ("Exceptions to the parol evidence rule exist to explain essential written terms in instances of fraud. . . .").

42. Farnsworth, supra note 17, at 442–43.

43. See Chapter 6 at notes 66–67, and accompanying text. See also Harrison v. Fred S. James, P.A., Inc., 558 F.Supp. 438 (E.D. Pa. 1983).

44. See Hynansky v. Vietri, 2003 WL 21976031, at *2 (Del. Ch. August 7, 2003) ("The operation of the parol evidence rule is premised upon a showing of the existence of an enforceable written contract. '[P]arol evidence may be available to show that the agreement was rendered invalid, void, or voidable by such causes as fraud, illegality, duress, mutual mistake, lack or failure of consideration, and incapacity.' ") (quoting Rodgers v. Erickson Air–Crane Co., 2000 WL 1211157, at *4 (Del.Super.2000)); Krossa v. All Alaskan Seafoods, Inc., 37 P.3d 411, 417 (Alaska

4. Parol evidence and promissory estoppel. Can a party introduce parol evidence to establish a claim of promissory estoppel when a court has already barred the evidence for purposes of interpreting a contract? Think once again of your written agreement to sell Alice your piano for $500. She sues you for failing to deliver the piano. As you now are beginning to suspect, the parol evidence rule may preclude Alice from proving that the true purchase price was $300. Can she nonetheless proffer the evidence on the alternative ground of promissory estoppel?[45]

You may first ask, what is the detriment to Alice to support her promissory estoppel claim? You are forgetting that I am a law teacher and can make up hypos at the spur of the moment to help illustrate a point. So, assume that Alice is a piano teacher and, due to her reliance on you, she cannot get another piano for a few weeks and therefore loses profits from the time you should have delivered your piano until she receives a substitute. Can she succeed in showing that you broke your promise to deliver the piano for $300 even though the written contract says $500, and recover on a promissory estoppel claim?

Most courts would say no and would extend the parol evidence rule to promissory estoppel cases.[46] Decisions that utilize the parol evidence rule in promissory estoppel cases worry that any other approach would circumvent the parol evidence rule and jeopardize people's confidence in contract law. After all, if Alice collects lost profits based on a claim of promissory estoppel, you will find little solace in the fact that your written contract says $500 and that Alice could not prove otherwise in her breach of contract case.

People who are not enamored of the parol evidence rule can point out that the remedy for a successful promissory estoppel claim may be smaller than the remedy for breach of contract, and so the parol evidence rule, in barring the contract claim, would still play a role. In our example, Alice's lost expectancy damages under a breach of contract claim (assuming she could prove the true contract price was $300) would be the market price-contract price

2001) ("The parol evidence rule does not apply where a contract has been formed as a result of misrepresentation or mutual mistake."). But see Harrison v. Fred S. James, P.A., Inc., 558 F.Supp. 438 (E.D.Pa.1983) ("In order for evidence of the prior negotiations to be admissible, plaintiff must first prove mistake.").

45. For a discussion of promissory estoppel, see Chapter 3 at notes 1–64, and accompanying text.

46. E.g., Kinn v. Coast Catamaran Corp., 582 F.Supp. 682 (E.D. Wis. 1984); see also Farnsworth, supra note 17, at 438.

differential, plus consequential damages (here, lost profits from teaching piano). If the market price of the piano is $500, Alice would recover $200, plus lost profits. Alice's recovery for promissory estoppel, however, would not include the $200. She did not sustain the $200 loss by relying on your contract and forgoing a chance to buy a piano elsewhere, because she would have had to pay market value for an equivalent piano, namely $500.

5. UCC section 2–202. Section 2–202 of the UCC sets forth the sale-of-goods parol evidence rule. The section provides that "confirmatory memoranda" or other writings intended by the parties to be the "final expression of their agreement with respect to such terms as are included therein," cannot be contradicted by parol evidence. On the other hand, such agreements can be "explained or supplemented" by evidence of a course of dealing, usage of trade, or course of performance.[47] Remember, we'll get to these sources of evidence in detail soon.[48] And we'll also touch upon how to distinguish contradictory evidence from evidence that explains or supplements.[49] For now, it is clear that, by allowing these evidentiary supplements, section 2–202 authorizes parties to introduce evidence of the commercial context, even without a finding that the contract language is ambiguous. Under section 2–202, a party can also introduce evidence of "consistent additional terms" unless the parties intended the entire writing to be a full integration.[50]

As at common law, the Code approach recognizes the possibility of a partially integrated contract, so that a court can find that the writing is complete on some subjects, but not others.[51] The test for precluding contradictory evidence is similar to the collateral contract methodology of common law:[52] "If the additional terms are such that, if agreed upon, they would certainly have been included in the document in the view of the court, then evidence of their alleged making must be kept from the trier of fact."[53] Section 2–202 does not speak to the controversy over whether courts should decide, without the benefit of extrinsic evidence, the parties's intentions as to the completeness of a writing.[54]

47. UCC § 2–202(a).

48. See infra notes 73–99, and accompanying text.

49. See infra notes 98–99, and accompanying text.

50. UCC § 2–202 (b).

51. UCC § 2–202, cmt. 1.

52. See supra notes 6–22, and accompanying text.

53. UCC § 2–202, cmt. 3.

54. See supra notes 14–22, and accompanying text.

6. Conclusion. Finally, let's decide whether any of the exceptions discussed above apply to your piano sale.[55] Remember, Alice wants to introduce evidence that you promised to sell your piano for $300, but the contract says $500. Certainly, the collateral contract exception is of little help. Reasonable parties who made an agreement for $300 would have put that in the contract. The price term also is not ambiguous. You have not committed fraud, and the problem is not one of a mistake. Alice's best hope is to maintain that the court should follow Corbin and admit the evidence of the $300 deal to show the parties did not intend the writing to be complete. Alice can also argue along the lines of Justice Traynor that all "credible" evidence is admissible preliminarily and that the reason for the $300 oral deal (to fool your Mother) are credible.

But we can't leave the parol evidence rule just yet. I believe that no matter how outlandish the issue, a good researcher can find a highly relevant case. Incredibly, there is a case in which a court admitted evidence that the parties intended the purchase price of $15,000 in a contract for the sale of a business to mean $50,000. The parties set forth the lower price in order to defraud the Small Business Administration into making the purchaser a loan. The court admitted the evidence, but came up with a rather unique way of dealing with the parol evidence rule. In short, the court required the seller to prove the oral agreement by clear and convincing evidence, a higher burden of proof than the normal preponderance of the evidence.[56]

B. Contract Interpretation

In this part, we assume that any battles over the admissibility of evidence are over. One question for discussion is how does contract law use admissible evidence to determine the meaning of contract language?[57] In addition, how does contract law fill gaps in contracts.

1. Objective contract interpretation. How does a court determine the meaning of an agreement? Not surprisingly, the answer is consistent with the objective test of assent, discussed in Chapter 2.[58] Courts generally determine the meaning of language by ascertaining what a reasonable person would believe the language means, not what either of the parties actually thought the language

---

55. See supra notes 4–5, and accompanying text.

56. Hield v. Thyberg, 347 N.W.2d 503 (Minn. 1984).

57. "What is interpretation? It is the process of endeavoring to ascertain the meaning or meanings of symbolic

expressions used by the parties to a contract * * * ." Edwin W. Patterson, The Interpretation and Construction of Contracts, 64 Colum L. Rev. 833, 833 (1964).

58. See Chapter 2 at notes 108–125, and accompanying text.

meant.[59]

Of course, we will see that if both parties intended a particular meaning, contract law enforces that meaning, even if it is inconsistent with the reasonable person test.[60] However, relatively few judicial decisions reflect this observation. In most cases, courts enforce apparent, not necessarily real, intentions.[61] Judge Learned Hand's famous observation makes the point succinctly:

> A contract has, strictly speaking, nothing to do with the personal, or individual, intent of the parties.... If ... it were proved by twenty bishops that either party, when he used the words, intended something else than the usual meaning which the law imposes on them, he would still be held, unless there were some mutual mistake, or something else of the sort.[62]

So don't be fooled by language you find in numerous judicial decisions that refers to the parties' intentions.[63] We have learned that one of contract law's important goals is to facilitate freely-made private agreements.[64] It is therefore not surprising to find language in opinions that is consistent with this goal, even when courts are giving lip service to the idea when interpreting language.

Contract law's objective approach to interpretation (the reasonable person test) is a logical extension of its objective test of contract formation.[65] Both processes protect a party's reasonable reliance on the other party's manifestation of intent.[66] If you promise in writing to sell your piano to Alice for $500, contract law will enforce what a reasonable person would believe the terms mean, namely the sale of your piano for $500. It doesn't matter if you unreasonably thought that "piano" meant your toy electric

59. See, e.g., Zell v. American Seating Co., 138 F.2d 641, 647 (2d Cir. l943) (Frank, J.), rev'd, 322 U.S. 709 (1944) (per curiam) ("We ask judges or juries to discover that 'objective viewpoint'— through their own subjective processes."); Hotchkiss v. National City Bank, 200 F. 287, 293 (S.D.N.Y. l911), aff'd, 201 F. 664 (2d Cir. 1912), aff'd, 231 U.S. 50 (1913); see also Robert A. Hillman, Contract Lore, 27 J. Corp. L. 505, 510–12 (2002).

60. Restatement (Second) of Contracts § 201(1) (1981). See infra notes 108–110, and accompanying text.

61. Farnsworth, supra note 17, at 116–17.

62. Hotchkiss, 200 F. at 293.

63. See, e.g., Haber v. St. Paul Guardian Ins. Co., 137 F.3d 691, 702 (2d Cir. 1998) (Parker, J., dissenting) ("[I]t is the intent of the parties which controls the interpretation of contracts."); Philadelphia Eagles Football Club, Inc. v. City of Philadelphia, 823 A.2d 108, 125 n.25 (Pa. 2003) ("A fundamental rule in construing a contract is to ascertain and give effect to the intent of the contracting parties").

64. See Chapter 2 at notes 41–43, and accompanying text.

65. See Chapter 2 at notes 108–125, and accompanying text.

66. See Hillman, supra note 59, at 511–512; McDonald v. Mobil Coal Producing, Inc., 820 P.2d 986, 990 (Wyo. 1991) ("Under the 'objective theory' of contract formation, contractual obligation is imposed not on the basis of the subjective intent of the parties, but rather upon the outward manifestations of a party's assent sufficient to create reasonable reliance by the other party.").

keyboard or that $500 meant $300 (unless, as we will see, Alice knew what you thought.[67]).

Under the objective approach, contract law commonly incorporates multiple sources of evidence. This should not be surprising in light of the overall goal to determine what a reasonable person would believe the language means under the circumstances.[68] (I use to say "surrounding circumstances," but a student told me that's redundant). The circumstances include "all writings, oral statements, and other conduct by which the parties manifested their assent, together with any prior negotiations between them and any applicable course of dealing, course of performance, or usage."[69] Let's consider the most important sources.

a. Purposive interpretation. Evidence of the parties' purpose in making the contract is probative of a reasonable person's understanding of language.[70] For example, suppose an installment sales contract sets forth a schedule for the delivery of 7500 humidifiers and then provides that "the above release schedule [is] to be reviewed quarterly."[71] After accepting a number of humidifiers, the purchaser refuses to accept any more and claims that the provision requiring review allowed it to cancel after any quarter. Evidence of preliminary negotiations, drafts, and other conversations show that the purpose of the clause was to allow the parties to change the delivery schedule, not to give the purchaser the right to cancel after each quarter. A court therefore should have little trouble interpreting the language in this way and finding the purchaser in breach.[72]

b. Usage of trade, course of dealing, and course of performance. A second source of evidence is any applicable usage of trade (also called a "trade custom"), course of dealing, or course of performance. I have grouped these sources together because they are equally important tools for finding the meaning of contract terms, and because most lawyers usually think of them as a group. All of them constitute objective evidence of the meaning of words because they go beyond the parties' own claims about their intentions. Usage of trade shows what other similarly situated parties mean when they use the language, while course of dealing and course of performance rely on the parties' prior conduct to show the meaning of their language.

The UCC defines each of these sources of evidence, and I will use the UCC definitions for purpose of discussion. But you should

---

67. See infra notes 111–112, and accompanying text.

68. Farnsworth, supra note 17, at 467.

69. Id.

70. See Farnsworth, supra note 17, at 468–69; Restatement (Second) of Contracts § 202(1).

71. Leslie v. Pennco, Inc., 470 A.2d 110, 112 (Pa. Super. Ct. 1983).

72. Id. at 114; Keating v. Stadium Mgmt. Corp., 508 N.E.2d 121, 124–25

understand that courts utilize this evidence in a wide variety of cases outside sales of goods.[73]

According to the UCC, "[a] usage of trade is any practice or method of dealing having such a regularity of observance in a place, vocation or trade as to justify an expectation that it will be observed with respect to the transaction in question."[74] Notice that the definition is broad enough to allow for the possibility that a party will be bound to a usage of trade even though she is not a member of the trade, if she should reasonably expect the trade meaning to apply because it is regularly observed in the *place* she is doing business.[75] Further, a usage of trade does not have to be "ancient or immemorial," or practiced by literally everyone in the trade, but only "regularly observed" over a reasonable period of time by "the great majority of decent dealers."[76]

A footnote in *Pacific Gas and Electric Co. v. G.W. Thomas Drayage & Rigging Co.* supplies lots of examples of trade usage:

> Extrinsic evidence of trade usage or custom has been admitted to show that the term "United Kingdom" in a motion picture distribution contract included Ireland (Ermolieff v. R.K.O. Radio Pictures (1942) 19 Cal.2d 543, 549–552, 122 P.2d 3); that the word "ton" in a lease meant a long ton or 2,240 pounds and not the statutory ton of 2,000 pounds (Higgins v. Cal. Petroleum, etc., Co. (1898) 120 Cal. 629, 630–632, 52 P. 1080); that the word "stubble" in a lease included not only stumps left in the ground but everything "left on the ground after the harvest time" (Callahan v. Stanley (1881) 57 Cal. 476, 477–479); that the term "north" in a contract dividing mining claims indicated a boundary line running along the "magnetic and not the true meridian" (Jenny Lind Co. v. Bower & Co. (1858) 11 Cal. 194, 197–199) and that a form contract for purchase and sale was actually an agency contract (Body-Steffner Co. v. Flotill Products (1944) 63 Cal.App.2d 555, 558–562, 147 P.2d 84).[77]

(Mass. App. Ct. 1987) ("[T]he construction which ... we approve, 'is the one which appears to be in accord with justice and common sense and the probable intention of the parties. It [interprets the Agreement] as a business transaction entered into by practical men to accomplish an honest and straightforward end ... ' ") (quoting Clark v. State St. Trust Co., 169 N.E. 897, 903 (Mass 1930)).

73. See, e.g. Restatement (Second) of Contracts § 202(4).

74. UCC § 1–205(2); see also Restatement (Second) of Contracts § 222.

75. Nanakuli Paving and Rock Co. v. Shell Oil Co., 664 F.2d 772, 791 (9th Cir.1981) ("[A] usage need not necessarily be one practiced by members of the party's own trade or vocation to be binding *if* it is so commonly practiced in a locality that a party should be aware of it.") (emphasis added).

76. UCC § 1–205, cmt. 5, quoted in Nanakuli Paving and Rock Co., 664 F.2d at 792.

77. 442 P.2d at 645 n.6.

You can see from these examples that evidence of trade usage may trump any different dictionary definition in ascertaining the meaning of contract language. This is appropriate when a party reasonably should expect the trade meaning to control: "[O]ne cannot understand accurately the language of * * * trades without knowing the peculiar meaning attached to the words which they use."[78]

The UCC also defines a course of dealing: It is a "sequence of previous conduct between the parties to a particular transaction which is fairly to be regarded as establishing a common basis of understanding for interpreting their expressions and other conduct."[79] Suppose in previous contracts for the delivery of a "ton" of coal, the seller has always delivered a long ton of 2,240 pounds and not a statutory ton of 2,000 pounds. This "course of dealing" evidence would be relevant to show that the purchaser reasonably expected the seller to deliver 2,240 pounds under the present contract.

Finally, a course of performance involves "repeated occasions for performance by either party" where the other party has "knowledge of the nature of the performance and opportunity for objection to it * * *."[80] If the other party does not object, the course of performance is "relevant to determine the meaning of the agreement."[81] The main difference between a course of dealing and a course of performance lies in when the conduct takes place. If the conduct occurred as part of a particular contract it is called a course of performance. If the conduct occurred prior to the contract at issue it is called a course of dealing.

Course of performance evidence is relevant in at least two ways. First, the evidence may help prove a contract modification or waiver of express terms. If you agree to mow Alice's lawn every Saturday during the summer, but during the month of July you actually mowed every Sunday without Alice's objection, you can persuasively argue that your course of performance establishes a modification agreement allowing Sunday mowing (there are no peaceful days in my neighborhood either). Second, course of performance evidence may help determine what a reasonable person would believe an ambiguous agreement means. If your contract to mow Alice's lawn says only that mowing shall take place at a reasonable time and you show up repeatedly without Alice's objection on Sundays at 9 a.m., a court likely will find that this time is reasonable.

---

78. Hurst v. W. J. Lake & Co., 16 P.2d 627, 629 (Or. 1932).

79. UCC § 1–205(1); see also Restatement (Second) of Contracts § 223.

80. UCC § 2–208(1); see also Restatement (Second) of Contracts § 202(4).

81. Id.

Some analysts object to use of course of performance as an interpretive tool. They claim that incorporating parties' previous conduct as a mode of interpretation has the perverse effect of making the parties more inflexible and uncooperative.[82] Critics argue that parties who act cooperatively lose the right in the future to insist on performance according to the express contract. For example, when Alice lets you mow her lawn on a few successive Sundays, although the contract calls for mowing on Saturdays, she may lose the right to insist that you mow on Saturdays.[83] Therefore, to avoid losing her rights, she must rigidly insist on Saturday performance at all times. If contract law did not consider course of performance evidence, obviously Alice would not have this concern about losing contract rights, and she could afford to be more flexible.

What these critics miss, however, is that Alice can preserve her contract rights at a very low cost.[84] Remember, to establish a course of performance, you must prove that there have been "repeated occasions for performance," that Alice has actual "knowledge of the nature" of those performances, *and* that she has had an opportunity to object.[85] With such stringent standards, Alice does not have to expend resources monitoring (checking up on) your performance for fear of losing rights. Further, under UCC section 2–208(1), a course of performance must be "accepted or acquiesced in *without objection* * * *."[86] Therefore, Alice can accept performance on Sunday, but reserve her right to performance on Saturdays in the future,[87] and a verbal reservation should suffice.[88] With these ground rules, a

82. See Omri Ben–Shahar, The Tentative Case Against Flexibility in Commercial Law, 66 U. Chi. L. Rev. 781, 784 (1999); Lisa Bernstein, Merchant Law in a Merchant Court: Rethinking the Code's Search for Immanent Business Norms, 144 U. Pa. L. R. 1765, 1812–1813 (1996).

83. Dixie Aluminum Prods. Co. v. Mitsubishi Int'l Corp., 785 F.Supp. 157, 160 (N.D. Ga. 1992) ("Where, as here, there are repeated opportunities for performance by either party and repeated opportunities for objection, and where no objection is made, that course of dealing is relevant to the meaning and terms of the written agreement...."); Bernstein, supra note 82, at 1812 ("The Code's course of performance provision ... increases the cost of agreeing to forgiving adjustments. It creates a significant risk that a series of such adjustments will be found to constitute a course of performance....").

84. Schulze and Burch Biscuit Co. v. Tree Top, Inc., 831 F.2d 709, 715 (7th Cir. 1987) ("[Defendant] had sent a confirmation form containing the same arbitration provision to [plaintiff] in each of the previous nine transactions he brokered between the two parties.... To prevent the clause from becoming part of the contract, [plaintiff] needed only to give notice of objection within a reasonable time.").

85. See supra notes 80–81, and accompanying text.

86. UCC section 2–208(1) (emphasis added).

87. See Schulze and Burch Biscuit Co., 831 F.2d at 715. See also UCC § 1–207.

88. Ben–Shahar, supra note 82, at 808. ("[T]he cost of verbal objections— may often be trivial."). But see Bernstein, supra note 82, at 1813 (It will be "difficult" for parties to "negate the influence" of their conduct on how courts interpret contracts).

party should not have to worry too much about inadvertently losing contract rights.

Courts have had little trouble determining when the parties have established a course of performance and whether a party has reserved rights.[89] Many cases finding a course of performance require repeated performances without any form of protest at all. For example, in *Margolin v. Franklin*,[90] purchasers of a car agreed to pay in installments. The seller accepted payment at least eight days late for seven months and then repossessed the car the following month.[91] Although the seller claimed to have sent "reminder notices," the court accepted one of the purchaser's testimony that the seller sent only one notice and then told the purchaser it sent the notice by mistake. The court found that "the testimony and exhibits indicate a pattern of conduct on the part of [the seller] to accept payments from the [purchasers] on or before the 27th day of each month."[92] In *Oregon Bank v. Nautilus Crane & Equipment Corp.*,[93] the seller of equipment authorized certain repair work and promised to credit the buyer's account for the cost of the repairs, despite a warranty disclaimer in the contract. Further, the seller met with the buyer "on the average of three times per week" for over a year without mentioning the warranty disclaimer.[94] The court therefore denied seller's motion for summary judgment to determine whether the course of performance overrode the warranty disclaimer.

Before we leave trade usage, course of dealing, and course of performance, you may be wondering what happens if these sources of evidence contradict each other or contradict express terms in the contract. Both the second Restatement of Contracts and the UCC establish the same hierarchy for resolving such matters. Specifically, express terms trump the other sources of evidence.[95] Course of performance prevails over course of dealing and trade usage, and course of dealing defeats trade usage.[96] Contract law bases this

---

89. See Lancaster Glass Corp. v. Philips ECG, Inc., 835 F.2d 652, 659–60 (6th Cir. 1987); Ben–Shahar, supra note 82, at 808 ("Courts have ... consistently held that rights are waived only when the breached-against party did not protest the violation."). But see Jason Scott Johnston, Should the Law Ignore Commercial Norms? A Comment on the Bernstein Conjecture and Its Relevance for Contract Law Theory and Reform, 99 Mich. L. Rev. 1791, 1803 (2001) ("[T]here is much too high a probability that courts will err in determining what the parties have actually done or said in their prior dealings.").

90. 270 N.E.2d 140 (Ill. App. Ct. 1971).

91. Id. at 142.

92. Id.

93. 683 P.2d 95 (Or. Ct. App. 1984).

94. Id. at 102.

95. Restatement (Second) of Contracts § 203(b); UCC §§ 2–208(2), 1–205(4). For a criticism of this hierarchy, see Eyal Zamir, The Inverted Hierarchy of Contract Interpretation and Supplementation, 97 Colum. L. rev. 1710

96. Restatement (Second) of Contracts § 203(b); UCC §§ 2–208(2), 1–205(4)

hierarchy on the degree of likelihood that each kind of evidence reveals the parties' real intentions (with express terms being the most likely).

Recall that the UCC's parol evidence rule allows evidence of a course of dealing, usage of trade, or course of performance to explain or supplement express terms, but not to contradict them.[97] This, of course, is consistent with the UCC's preference for express terms discussed here. Courts have not been consistent, however, differentiating between evidence that explains or supplements and evidence that contradicts.[98] As with other issues involving the parol evidence rule, the trend here seems towards admissibility of evidence, with courts increasingly finding that the evidence "explains or supplements," even when it seems otherwise.[99]

c. Other rules of interpretation. Courts often set forth many additional aids for interpreting contracts. For example, one common rule is that courts construe ambiguous language against the drafter.[100] Suppose a nine-hole golf course holds a tournament in which each player is to play eighteen holes (two times around the course). The golf course promises $1000 to anyone who makes a hole-in-one on the eighth hole. Taylor Plantations scores a hole-in-one on the eighth hole, but the second time around so that it is his seventeenth hole of the tournament. Should he win the $1000? Many courts would find for Taylor because the golf course created an ambiguity about whether it required a hole-in-one on the eighth hole of the tournament or the eighth hole of the golf course.

Here are some additional rules of interpretation that almost speak for themselves. Parties intend to incorporate the common meaning of language, not an unusual definition.[101] Specific language

---

97. UCC § 2–202(a); see supra notes 47–50, and accompanying text.

98. Farnsworth, supra note 17, at 486–89.

99. See, e.g., Nanakuli Paving & Rock Co. v. Shell Oil Co., 664 F.2d 772, 805 (9th Cir. 1981) (evidence admitted that "all suppliers to the asphaltic paving trade price protected customers" even though the express contract set "the price at seller's posted price, with no mention of price protection...."); Columbia Nitrogen Corp. v. Royster Co., 451 F.2d 3 (4th Cir. 1971).

100. State ex rel. Dept. of Transp. v. Delta Inn, Inc. , 3 P.3d 180, 186 (Or. Ct. App. 2000) ("In resolving that ambiguity, we resort, necessarily, to the 'construe against the drafter' principle."). But see Joyner v. Adams, 361 S.E.2d

902, 905–06 (N.C. Ct. App. 1987) ("[The] rule [of construction against the drafter] is usually applied in cases involving an adhesion contract or where one party is in a stronger bargaining position.... In this case, where the parties were at arms length and were equally sophisticated, we believe the rule was improvidently invoked.").

101. Southgate Recreation & Park Dist. v. California Assn. for Park & Recreation Ins., 130 Cal.Rptr.2d 728, 730 (Cal. Ct. App. 2003) ("The basic rule of contract interpretation is to effectuate the parties' intent as expressed in the contract's terms, which are given their common meaning."); see also Restatement (Second) of Contracts § 202(3)(a).

trumps general language.[102] Courts favor an interpretation that upholds a contract instead of defeats it.[103] An interpretation that furthers the public interest trumps a different interpretation.[104] Terms should be interpreted with the meaning of the whole contract in mind.[105] Maybe you think I'm not spending enough time on these rules. But the rules are of limited importance. The problem with these and other rules of interpretation of this nature is that courts often trot them out to support a decision that they have made on other grounds and ignore them when they don't serve the court's purpose.[106] In fact, these rules may have little clout at all, except as after-the-fact rationalizations of results.[107]

2. Exceptions to the objective interpretation of contracts. Several rules of interpretation constitute exceptions to the objective interpretation of contract language. We take them up here.

a. Restatement (Second) section 201. If both parties intend a particular meaning, contract law enforces that meaning, even if it contradicts the objective interpretation of the language.[108] Recall that Alice offered evidence that you and she meant $300, not $500, in your contract for the sale of your piano.[109] If that evidence survives the parol evidence rule, contract law will interpret the language in the manner you both intended, even though to us reasonable people $500 means $500.[110] This rule should be no

---

102. Genunzio v. Genunzio 598 So.2d 129, 132 (Fla. Dist. Ct. App. 1992) ("'[G]eneral language of a contract must yield to specific language which deals with the matter at issue ....'").

103. Torncello v. United States, 681 F.2d 756, 761 (Ct. Cl. 1982) ("[W]e assume that the parties intended that a binding contract be formed. Thus, any choice of alternative interpretations, with one interpretation saving the contract and the other voiding it, should be resolved in favor of the interpretation that saves the contract.)."

104. Beck Park Apartments v. United States Dept. of Hous. and Urban Dev., 695 F.2d 366, 370 (9th Cir. 1982) ("Where, as here, a public interest is involved, 'an interpretation is preferred which favors the public.'") (quoting Restatement (First) of Contracts § 236(f) (1932)); Patterson, supra note 57, at 855.

105. Hilman v. Hilman, 2003 WL 21766254, *2 (Tenn. Ct. App. July 31,

2003) ("The cardinal rule for contract interpretation is to ascertain the parties' intentions from the contract as a whole and to give effect to that intention consistent with legal principals."); Robert W. Carlstrom Co. v. German Evangelical Lutheran St. Paul's Congregation of Unaltered Augsburg Confession at Jordan, 662 N.W.2d 168, 173 (Minn. Ct. App. 2003) ("Phrases found in the contract should not be interpreted out of context, but rather given meaning in accordance with the obvious purpose of the contract as a whole."); Patterson, supra note 57, at 854.

106. Patterson, supra note 57, at 852.

107. Id. at 853.

108. Restatement (Second) of Contracts § 201(1).

109. See supra note 4, and accompanying text.

110. Berke Moore Co. v. Phoenix Bridge Co., 98 A.2d 150, 156 (N.H. 1953)

surprise. It is consistent with freedom of contract and supports all of the "intentions of the parties" and "meeting of the mind" flag waving in the opinions. The problem is that courts rarely receive cases where they can enforce parties' mutual, but unreasonable, interpretations of language. In the usual litigated case, each party is trying to prove that her interpretation of the language is the reasonable one. You can comfortably think of the "both parties intend the same unusual meaning" rule as an *exception* to the objective interpretation of language.

Now suppose you know or have reason to know that Alice believes the meaning of $500 is $300, and she does not know nor have reason to know that you believe she must pay you $500. Alice's meaning prevails.[111] The Restatement (Second) states the rule, which is easier to understand if we plug in our heroes:

> Where the parties have attached different meanings to a promise or agreement or a term thereof, it is interpreted in accordance with the meaning attached by one of them [Alice] if at the time the agreement was made
>
> (a) that party [Alice] did not know of any different meaning attached by the other [you], and the other [you] knew the meaning attached by the first party [Alice]; or
>
> (b) that party [Alice] had no reason to know of any different meaning attached by the other [you], and the other [you] had reason to know the meaning attached by the first party [Alice].[112]

b. Misunderstanding. What approach if the contractual language is ambiguous and the parties have assigned different meanings to the language? This problem first came up in the wonderful case of *Raffles v. Wichelhaus*,[113] which appears in virtually every contracts casebook.

In *Raffles*, the contract called for the plaintiff to sell cotton scheduled to arrive on a ship called the "Peerless." The buyers refused to take the cotton, claiming that the cotton arrived on a

("[W]hen it appears that the understanding of one is the understanding of both, no violation of the rule results from determination of the mutual understanding according to that of one alone.").

111. Restatement (Second) of Contracts 201(2); Joyner v. Adams, 361 S.E.2d 902, 905 (N.C. Ct. App. 1987) ("[W]here one party knows or has rea-

son to know what the other party means by certain language and the other party does not know or have reason to know of the meaning attached to the disputed language by the first party, the court will enforce the contract in accordance with the innocent party's meaning.").

112. Restatement (Second) of Contracts 201(2).

113. 159 Eng. Rep. 375 (Ex. 1864).

ship called the Peerless that sailed from Bombay in December and that the buyers had intended to buy cotton arriving on another ship called the Peerless that sailed from Bombay in October. The seller tested the legal sufficiency of the buyers' defense by demurring. The issue before the English Court of Exchequer, therefore, was whether to excuse the buyers, assuming there was more than one ship called "Peerless" and the seller and buyers were thinking of different ships.

The report of the case consists of interchanges between the lawyers and judges during the oral argument of the case, to the endless entertainment of law students trying to figure out what is going on. In fact, the actual decision consists of one line from the judges declaring *per curium* that the buyers' defense was legally sufficient. The court issued this decision after the buyers' lawyer argued that the existence of two ships named Peerless created latent ambiguity and that the court should admit evidence to show that the seller and buyers were thinking of different ships.

From this case we can glean the law of misunderstanding. A misunderstanding exists when (1) the parties' contract is ambiguous, meaning that it is reasonably susceptible to more than one meaning; (2) the parties actually had in mind different interpretations of the language, and (3) the misunderstanding is material (or important). When all of these elements are satisfied, the contract is unenforceable. [114]

In *Raffles* (where we can assume the facts most favorable to the buyers for purpose of the seller's demurrer), the contract was ambiguous because two ships sailed under the name Peerless. A reasonable person reading the contract would not have known which Peerless was the subject matter of the contract. Further, the parties actually were thinking of different ships. (You have just learned that if the buyers actually knew that the seller was thinking of the December Peerless, the seller's meaning would prevail.[115]) Finally, the misunderstanding was material (important) because one Peerless sailed in October and one in December.

Suppose there was only one Peerless and the contract called for delivery on that ship. But for reasons that are hard to explain (just

---

114. Id.; see also First United Leasing Corp. v. Campagnie Nationale Air France, 1995 WL 560918, *5 (N.D.Ill. 1995) ("When parties attach different meanings to a contract term, a situation best understood as a 'misunderstanding' or a 'mistake,' there is ... technically no meeting of the minds and, consequently, no contract.").

115. Restatement (Second) of Contracts, § 201(2)(a); see also Trinidad v.

King, 1998 WL 823653, *6 (S.D.N.Y. Nov. 24, 1998) ("If the 'parties had conflicting understandings as to the meaning of a material term, there is contract based on the meaning of the party who is unaware of the ambiguity if the other party knows or has reason to know of the ambiguity.'") (quoting John D. Calamari & Joseph M. Perillo, The Law of Contracts 169 (3d ed. 1987)).

go with the hypo), the seller believes he is supposed to deliver the cotton on a ship called the Intrepid and the buyers believe they are supposed to purchase cotton from a ship called the Inferno. According to the rules of objective interpretation, the parties are bound to buy and sell using the Peerless even though neither party intended that result. Contract law can't be this obtuse, and I doubt that a court would use objective interpretation, but a comment in the first Restatement suggests otherwise.[116]

3. Rules of gap filling

If contracting parties leave so many gaps in a contract that a court simply doesn't know what to enforce, the court will declare the contract unenforceable for indefiniteness.[117] Short of this extreme, courts are inclined to fill gaps for the parties, rather than give up on the contract.

Parties may leave gaps for many reasons. A problem may be unforeseeable at the time they contract, or, at least, may have been unforeseen by them. You agree to mow Alice's lawn on Saturdays, but you and Alice do not foresee that it would rain every Saturday in June and July. Do you have to mow on an another day? Which day? Alternatively, parties may understand the existence of an issue, but choose not to deal with it in their contract because they believe they cannot resolve it or that it is too remote to worry about. You and Alice understand the unpredictability of weather, but c'mon, what are the chances it is going to rain *every* Saturday? (Unfortunately, the chances are high in Ithaca, N.Y., where I live.)

Determining exactly when a court is filling a gap or simply interpreting a contract sometimes challenges lawyers. Suppose that in previous summers, you always mowed on the next clear day if it rained on Saturday. A court may find that this year's contract requires you to mow on the next clear day. But is the court supplying a term for the parties or interpreting contractual language and the circumstances to determine the term the parties intended for themselves?

116. See Restatement (First) of Contracts, § 230, Cmt. b and illustration 1 ("In an integrated agreement A promises to sell, and B promises to buy certain patents. A intends to sell only English patents on a certain invention. B understands that A promises to sell the English, French, and American patents on the invention. If a reasonably intelligent person at the time when the integration is made and at the place as of which the standard of interpretation is applicable, under the circumstances accompanying its making, would understand the agreement to state a promise to sell the English and American patents, but not the French patents, there is a contract and A and B are bound by that meaning.").

117. Champaign Nat'l Bank v. Landers Seed Co., 519 N.E.2d 957, 959–60 (Ill. App. Ct. 1988) ("The terms of a contract must be reasonably certain. Some terms may be missing or left to be agreed upon, but if the essential term or terms are so uncertain that there is no basis for deciding whether the agreement has been kept or broken, there is no contract.").

Bear in mind also that the objective-interpretation strategy of courts is similar to gap filling because the court enforces what a reasonable person would believe a contract means, not necessarily what the parties actually intended. Notwithstanding the ambiguous line between interpretation and gap filling, the following discussion focuses on judicial solutions after the court concludes that the parties failed to include an important term, meaning that they have left a gap in their contract.

We now look at several "sources of gap filling," which constitute the various justifications for the terms courts supply to fill gaps in agreements. For example, a court may fill a gap in a certain way, believing that the parties would have contracted that way had they thought about the matter. Alternatively, a court may decide that a particular gap filler creates appropriate incentives for future parties. Or a court may fill a gap in a manner that the court believes is fair to the contracting parties or that protects third parties. And so on. This subsection takes up the most common judicial gap-filling approaches.

a. What the parties would have done. Courts that fill gaps based on what the parties would have done had they contracted on the issue can support their decision by invoking freedom of contract.[118] By asking what you and Alice would have done about the miserable Saturday weather had you thought about the issue, a court reasons that it is simply facilitating the parties' own contractual arrangements. Of course, this is largely a fiction, especially to the extent that it is difficult to determine what you would have done.

This strategy of gap filling also appeals to analysts who apply economic reasoning to legal problems. We already have discussed the economic perspective on gap filling in *Hadley v. Baxendale*.[119] Recall that a contract between the miller and carrier for the carrier to transport the miller's broken crank shaft said nothing about what happens if the carrier delays and the miller suffers lost profits as a result. How should contract law fill the gap? One answer is with the term the parties would have wanted.[120] Why? Because this

---

118. See Richard A. Posner, Economic Analysis of Law 96–97 (6th ed. 2003); National Distillers & Chem. Corp. v. First Nat'l Bank of Highland Park, 804 F.2d 978, 982 (7th Cir. 1986) ("Ambiguities and gaps in contracts should be resolved by finding what the parties would have bargained for had they addressed the matter explicitly at the time.").

119. 156 Eng. Rep. 145 (Ex. 1854). See Chapter 5 at notes 149–165, and accompanying text.

120. See Binder v. Aetna Life Ins. Co., 89 Cal.Rptr.2d 540, 553 (Cal. Ct. App. 1999) (" 'Sometimes it is said that the search [for an omitted term or omitted meaning] is for the term the parties would have agreed to if the question had been brought to their attention.' ") (quoting Restatement (Second) of Contracts § 204, cmts. a, b & d.); Richard A.

strategy serves economic efficiency. Private exchange is efficient because each party gains more than the party gives up. Carriage of the crankshaft was worth more to the miller than the price of carriage and the price was worth more to the carrier than its cost of carriage. The miller-carrier contract therefore moves resources to "higher valued uses."[121] Contract law's goal should be to reduce the costs of transactions, such as the cost of bargaining to reach an agreement, because this will increase the gains from contracting. By filling gaps with the terms the parties would have wanted, future parties do not have to invest resources bargaining over terms, such as whether carriers are liable for lost profits if they delay.[122]

But what term would the parties have wanted in *Hadley*? We have learned that economic analysts reason that the parties would have allocated the risk of lost profits to the party who can deal with the problem most inexpensively. This is either the "superior risk bearer," the party better able to accept the risk, such as by purchasing insurance, or the "superior risk avoider," the party who can better prevent the loss from occurring in the first place.[123] Such reasoning is consistent with the idea that the goal of the parties is to maximize their gains from the transaction. In *Hadley*, for example, the superior risk bearer may be the miller, who can insure most cheaply against the risk of a broken crank shaft. The miller therefore should bear the risk of the carrier's delay.

We have already pointed out the shortcomings of this analysis.[124] One can argue that the carrier should be liable for the lost profits because it can take precautions to ensure delivery of the crank shaft on time more cheaply than the miller can insure against the risk of a broken shaft.[125] On the other hand, the miller can avoid the problem by owning a spare crank shaft, which should not be very expensive. But all of this is pretty speculative in most cases and, ultimately, not a very convincing method of filling gaps.

b. Creating incentives. A court filling a gap may feel free to try to create incentives for future contracting parties. We have

Posner & Andrew M. Rosenfield, Impossibility and Related Doctrines in Contract Law: An Economic Analysis, 6 J. Legal Stud. 83, 88–90 (1977).

121. See, e.g., Farnsworth, supra note 17, at 762.

122. Posner, supra, note 118, at 96–98; see also United States v. Westlands Water Dist., 134 F.Supp.2d 1111, 1137 (E.D. Cal. 2001) ("[I]f no other method can adequately interpret the contractual provision in question, the court allocates the risk of the unforeseeable loss to the more efficient risk bearer.").

123. See Chapter 5 at note 149, and accompanying text.

124. See Chapter 5 at note 150, and accompanying text.

125. See Ian Ayres & Robert Gertner, Filling Gaps in Incomplete Contracts: An Economic Theory of Default Rules, 99 Yale L.J. 87, 101 (1989).

already discussed what may be the best example of this process, and again *Hadley* served as our illustration.[126] We saw that commentators treat *Hadley* as an example of a "penalty default," which penalizes the miller for failing to reveal the ramifications of tardy delivery (the loss of profits). The miller's penalty is that it cannot recover the lost profits.[127] Further, were it not for the *Hadley* rule, the miller would have an incentive not to disclose. The information would lead the carrier to raise its price of carriage because it would be taking a greater risk (assuming that most millers do not suffer lost profits due to a carrier delay).[128] In sum, penalty-default theorists assert that *Hadley* creates incentives for the miller to reveal information and for the carrier to select the appropriate level of precaution.[129]

We also saw that the "penalty default" gap-filling strategy is controversial. Specifically, the cost of revealing information may outweigh the gain even for the miller.[130] Still, courts may find very alluring the idea of crafting substantive gap-filling provisions for the purpose of creating positive incentives to disclose information.

c. Fairness concerns. Courts also fill gaps based on their view of what is fair in the circumstances. For example, a court may consider a particular gap filler's effect on the potential gains and losses of each party.[131] Lets revisit our lawn-mowing contract. What are the ramifications of requiring you to mow Alice's lawn on the first dry day if it rains on Saturday? Perhaps you have counted on working only on Saturdays and took another job on other days. A court may consider whether filling the gap by requiring you to work on the next dry day would cause you considerable harm. On the other hand, perhaps Alice has relied on you to mow as soon as possible after a rainy Saturday because she is trying to sell her house and wants the yard to look presentable. You can see that the potential gains and losses analysis only helps a court select the appropriate gap filler if one party's needs greatly outweighs the other's.

Now let's look at an example from the business context. Suppose a domestic oil supplier seeks relief from a fixed-price, long-

---

126. See Chapter 5 at notes 152–156, and accompanying text.

127. See Chapter 5 at note 153, and accompanying text.

128. See Jason Scott Johnston, Strategic Bargaining and the Economic Theory of Contract Default Rules, 100 Yale L.J. 615, 622 (1990).

129. Ayres & Gertner, supra note 125, at 104.

130. See Chapter 5 at note 157, and accompanying text.

131. See Robert A. Hillman, An Analysis of the Cessation of Contractual Relations, 68 Cornell L. Rev. 617, 629–634 (1983); see also Dato v. Mascarello, 557 N.E.2d 181, 184 (Ill. App. Ct. 1989)

term supply contract with an electric utility after an international disruption in oil supply causes the price of oil to skyrocket. The supplier claims that the parties did not contract about performance in the face of a catastrophic disruption and that, if forced to perform, it will go bankrupt. We will see in Chapter 9 that some courts will entertain such an argument even though the supply contract contains an unconditional promise by the supplier to perform.[132] The usual explanation is that the court believes the parties reasonably failed to foresee a disruption of such proportions and, hence, left a gap with respect to it. If the supplier will go bankrupt by performing, and the utility can raise the price it charges customers (me and you), a court may fill the gap by placing the risk of the international disruption on the utility (which means excusing the supplier). In doing so, the court averts disproportional harm to the supplier, without harming the utility. We consumers bear the loss, but remember, we are only going to pay fair market value for our electricity; it's just that the market value takes into account world events.

Courts also fill gaps to try to assure that each party enjoys the fruits of her contract.[133] Obviously, this does not mean that contract law assures each party of making a profit on every contract. Circumstances change and one party may be disappointed with how the exchange turns out. Nevertheless, courts avoid using gap fillers that would be catastrophic to one party and a windfall for the other. Instead they prefer solutions that would roughly preserve the benefit of the bargain for each party.

O.k., you are thirsting for an example of this point too. Suppose Alice promises to supply water to your rural vacation home through a well on her nearby property. You promise to pay her $10 on Monday of each week. After months of successful performance on both sides, you show up to pay on a Tuesday instead of Monday. Alice claims you have materially breached the contract and she is relieved of her duty to supply any water in the future. The contract says nothing about what happens if you are a day late in tendering payment. You cannot get another water supply for your home.

This problem involves the law of implied conditions and material breach, subjects we treat in Chapter 8.[134] For our purposes here, all we have to know is that the court has a choice of filling the gap

---

("[I]t was proper for the trial court to supply terms which it determined to be reasonable, either by construing the expressed terms together with the circumstances surrounding and occurring subsequent to the formation of the contract, or on the basis of fundamental principles of fairness, or both.").

132. See Chapter 9 at notes 64–82, and accompanying text.

133. Hillman, supra note 131, at 638–9.

134. See Chapter 8 at notes 76–88, and accompanying text.

in your contract by finding that Alice can cancel the contract because you are late, or by finding that Alice must perform notwithstanding your broken promise to pay on Mondays. You are probably not surprised to learn that courts likely will choose the latter provision (and force you to pay Alice any damages she sustains because of the delay in payment).

Fairness also takes into account the reasonableness of the parties actions.[135] Courts tend to select gap filling terms that favor a party who acts reasonably. Conversely, of course, courts frown on unreasonable behavior in selecting gap fillers. Determining what is reasonable involves comparing a contracting party's conduct with that of similarly situated parties or against community standards.[136]

Suppose, for example, a supplier of molasses to a manufacturer promises to deliver approximately "1,500,000 wine gallons * * * of the usual run from the National Sugar Refinery."[137] The supplier does not contract with National Sugar for the molasses, but assumes that the latter will produce a sufficient quantity. The refinery produces only about 344,000 gallons for the supplier, which it delivers to the manufacturer. The manufacturer sues the supplier for breach of contract. The supplier claims that the contract says nothing about what happens if National Sugar does not produce enough molasses. However, if similarly situated suppliers would have contracted with National Sugar to assure that it produced the necessary amount of molasses, and our supplier failed to do so, it is unlikely that a court would excuse the supplier. In fact, a court considering almost identical facts held that the supplier acted unreasonably in failing to secure a contract with National Sugar.[138]

4. Good-faith performance. You have already encountered the obligation of good faith. For example, we saw that UCC section 2–209 authorizes courts to strike a contract modification agreement made in bad faith.[139] The concept of good faith purchase, beyond the

---

135. Hillman, supra note 131, at 637; see also Marshall Constr. Co. v. Forsyth, 57 A.2d 902 (Pa. 1948) (holding that a reasonable time should be implied where no time was specified in the contract, and that the exercise of an option three months after contract date was reasonable and timely performance).

136. Hillman, supra note 131, at 637; see also Howell v. United States, 51 Fed.Cl. 516, 523 (Fed. Cl. 2002) ("[W]here parties to a binding agreement have not agreed to an essential term, 'a term which is reasonable in the circumstances' may be supplied by the court. In supplying a term, [Restatement] comment d of § 204 says that 'the court should supply a term which comports with community standards of fairness and policy rather than analyze a hypothetical model of the bargaining process.'") (quoting Restatement (Second) of Contracts § 204, and cmt. d).

137. Canadian Indus. Alcohol Co. v. Dunbar Molasses Co., 179 N.E. 383, 384 (N.Y. 1932).

138. Id. at 384–85.

139. See Chapter 2 at notes 72–83, and accompanying text; Chapter 6 at notes 29–40, and accompanying text.

scope of this book, is another use of the good-faith principle.[140] Courts also impose an obligation of good faith *performance*, which is the subject matter for discussion here. Actually, we have already discussed good faith performance in Chapter 2, in the context of the mutuality-of-obligation problem.[141] We now look further at the question of what it takes for a party to be in good faith or bad faith. We study the subject here because courts decide the question through the processes of interpretation and gap filling.

The best way to understand good faith performance is to think of the principle as excluding various forms of bad faith performance.[142] Restatement (Second) section 205 uses this model:

> "[t]he phrase 'good faith' is used in a variety of contexts, and its meaning varies somewhat with the context. Good faith performance or enforcement of a contract ... excludes a variety of types of conduct characterized as involving 'bad faith' because they violate community standards of decency, fairness or reasonableness.[143]

But how do courts determine the kinds of conduct that "violate community standards" in the context before them? To find out, we now take up two examples of conduct that courts have ruled out, namely asserting an overreaching interpretation of contract language and failing to cooperate.

a. Overreaching interpretation. Suppose a written employment contract grants a salesperson commissions on sales in excess of certain minimum sales requirements. The contract also grants the employer the right to raise the sales quota retroactively without prior notice or reason in the employer's "sole discretion" and therefore to reduce the employee's commissions. The employer raises the sales quota. The employee claims the employer did so in bad faith, solely to deprive the employee of earned compensation.[144] To determine whether the employer's actions were in bad faith, the

---

140. See, e.g., UCC § 2–403.

141. See Chapter 2 at notes 65–71, and accompanying text.

142. Mahan v. Avera St. Luke's 621 N.W.2d 150, 159 (S.D. 2001) ("The term 'good faith' generally indicates an absence of bad faith on behalf of a party to a contract."); see Robert S. Summers, "Good Faith" in General Contract Law and the Sales Provisions of the Uniform Commercial Code, 54 Va. L. Rev. 195 (1968).

143. Restatement (Second) of Contracts, § 205, cmt. a; see also Mahan, 621 N.W.2d at 159–160 ("Examples of bad faith performance include depriving the other party of a negotiated right

under the contract, preventing the aggrieved party from receiving the benefits of the bargain, or interfering in the other party's performance of the contract.").

144. See Tymshare, Inc. v. Covell, 727 F.2d 1145 (D.C. Cir. l984) (employer contracted for right to modify or terminate employee's compensation plan in its "sole discretion"); Nolan v. Control Data Corp., 579 A.2d 1252, 1254 (N.J. Super. Ct. 1990) (employer reserved the right to "make any retroactive, current and/or prospective adjustments or revisions to salaries, bonuses, [or] incentive compensation levels. . . .").

court must interpret the contract to determine whether the employer had the right to raise the quota in order to diminish the employee's compensation. If through interpretation or gap filling, the court concludes that the employer did not have such a right, then the court would find bad faith, assuming, of course, that the employee proved that the employer's motive was solely to reduce the employee's compensation.

At first blush, it looks like the employer simply exercised an express contract right and so motives are irrelevant. Remember, the contract expressly says that the employer has the right to raise the sales quota retroactively without prior notice or reason. How can an employer's conduct constitute bad faith when the contract expressly authorized the employer's actions?[145] We have learned that courts find the meaning of contract terms by looking at the circumstances in which the parties used them. Further, courts interpret language objectively, meaning according to a reasonable party's understanding of the words. So, the question in the sales-quota scenario is whether, under all of the facts, the employee should reasonably have understood the contract to allow the employer retroactively to increase the sales quota solely to reduce the employee's compensation.

Courts have recognized that terms that appear to allow a party sole discretion do not necessarily allow the party to exercise the discretion in an "arbitrary or unreasonable" manner.[146] In *Tymshare, Inc. v. Covell,* a case involving a sales quotas very similar to our hypothetical, then Judge Scalia described the concept:

> [A]greeing to such a provision would require a degree of folly on the part of these sales representatives we are not inclined to posit where another plausible interpretation of the language is available. It seems to us that the 'sole discretion' intended was discretion to determine the existence or nonexistence of the various factors that would reasonably justify alteration of the sales quota. Those factors would include ... an unanticipated volume of business from a particular customer unconnected with the extra sales efforts of the employee assigned to that account; and ... a poor overall sales year for the company,

145. Carma Developers, Inc. v. Marathon Dev. Cal., Inc., 826 P.2d 710, 728 (Cal. 1992) ("We are aware of no reported case in which a court has held the covenant of good faith may be read to prohibit a party from doing that which is expressly permitted by an agreement."); Storek & Storek, Inc. v. Citicorp Real Estate, Inc., 122 Cal. Rptr.2d 267, 277 n.10 (Cal. Ct. App. 2002) ("[T]he implied covenant of good faith and fair dealing does not impose an affirmative duty on a party to forbear from enforcing rights expressly given under the contract.").

146. Tymshare, Inc., 727 F.2d at 1154 (holding "sole discretion" is not equivalent of "for any reason whatsoever, no matter how arbitrary or unreasonable."); see, e.g., Patterson, supra note 57, at 838–842; Restatement (Second) of Contracts § 212(1) and cmt. b.

leaving less gross income to be expended on commissions.... But the language need not (and therefore can not reasonably) be read to confer discretion to [increase] the quota for any reason whatever—including ... a simple desire to deprive an employee of the fairly agreed benefit of his labors.[147]

This reasoning is typical in cases involving good faith performance and shows that the source of good faith lies on the border between contract interpretation and gap filling. Judge Scalia thought that the parties probably did not intend to allow the employer to reduce the employee's compensation retroactively and arbitrarily because a reasonable employee would not agree to such an arrangement and a reasonable employer would not seek it.[148] Reasonable parties, in other words, intend to incorporate the meaning of terms society would find fair and just.

Suppose the quota provision expressly permitted the employer to change the sales quota at any time "for the sole purpose of reducing or eliminating the employee's earned commissions?" Such a term would leave little room for the kind of argument made by Justice Scalia. In short, the employer would not be asserting an overreaching interpretation of contract language and use of the term would not be bad faith. Recall, however, that such a provision might be unconscionable under the tests we developed in Chapter 6.[149]

b. Failing to cooperate. Contracting parties often know each other, having dealt with each other repeatedly during the performance of a long-term contract or over a series of contracts.[150] Parties to such contracts should not expect their counterparts to act as fiduciaries (meaning to place the interests of the other party above their own), but they do reasonably expect cooperation and flexibility.[151] In light of these expectations, good faith performance may rule out uncooperative conduct even when the express contract terms do not.

The issue comes up, for example, when one party fails to share important information with the other party. Suppose a landlord has been sending notices to a tenant reminding her of her obligations,

---

147. Tymshare, Inc., 727 F.2d at 1154.

148. Id.

149. See Chapter 6 at notes 141–184, and accompanying text.

150. See Robert A. Hillman, Court Adjustment of Long–Term Contracts: An Analysis Under Modern Contract Law, 1987 Duke L. J. 1, 4–6.

151. Benefit Mgmt. of Maine, Inc. v. Allstate Life Ins. Co., 993 F.2d 1530,

1993 WL 177120, **8 (1st Cir.1993) (" '[B]ad faith' has been described as 'opportunistic advantage-taking or lack of cooperation depriving the other contracting party of his reasonable expectations'....") (quoting Hentze v. Unverfehrt, 604 N.E.2d 536, 538 (Ill. App. Ct. 1992)); Best v. United States Nat'l Bank of Oregon, 739 P.2d 554, 558 (Or. 1987) ("[D]iscretion had to be exercised within the confines of the reasonable expectations of the depositors.").

such as paying taxes or utility bills. The landlord knows that the time for exercising an option to renew the lease will expire in three days and that the tenant is not aware of this. The landlord wants to deter the tenant from exercising the option to renew because the landlord can charge a higher rent on the open market. Despite notifying the tenant about other legal duties, the landlord does not alert the tenant about the option to renew.

The landlord does not have a fiduciary duty here and the parties' lease does not expressly require the landlord to send a notice about the option to renew. The tenant only has rights if the landlord had a good-faith performance obligation to notify the tenant.

In circumstances similar to these, Judge Posner found a good-faith obligation to cooperate, which he characterized as "halfway between a fiduciary duty . . . and the duty merely to refrain from active fraud."[152] Posner justified his findings not based on fairness or justice, but by considering what the parties would have intended had they contracted with respect to the issue: Good faith performance "is a stab at approximating the terms the parties would have negotiated had they foreseen the circumstances that have given rise to their dispute."[153] Posner concluded that the parties would have agreed to cooperate, and would not have allowed the landlord to lull the tenant into losing her right to renew the lease.

Posner's effort to define good-faith performance by finding "what the parties would have intended" should not surprise you. We have seen that his general formula for filling gaps follows this approach. In his view, good-faith performance is simply what the parties would have wanted.

---

152. Market Street Associates Ltd. Partnership v. Frey, 941 F.2d 588, 595 (7th Cir. 1991).

153. Id.

Chapter Eight

CONDITIONS AND BREACH

After parties agree to an exchange, if everything goes smoothly, they will have little need to seek the assistance of a court. You promise to mow your neighbor, Alice's, lawn on Saturday and Alice promises to pay $40 on condition that you mow on Saturday. You mow, she pays. You complete the deal. Unfortunately, however, lots of things can go wrong, even between fine people such as you and Alice. You fail to mow, or mow poorly or only partially. She fails to pay or offers only some of the money. A dispute arises over whether you are supposed to mow first, or she is supposed to pay before you mow, or if you have a duty to mow even if it is raining.

You and Alice may have provided for all these contingencies in your agreement. But I doubt it. People rarely foresee all that can go wrong, and, for that matter, rarely provide in their contract for all of the contingencies they do foresee.[1] This is true not only for neighbors making an informal, personal agreement, but for large corporate titans engaged in exchanges worth millions of dollars.

Contract law supplies rules to resolve all of the issues between you and Alice, whether you have expressly addressed them or not. We call these rules the law of conditions and breach. Many students find this material daunting, but, after careful analysis, I have concluded that this material is really very easy. (Aren't you relieved?) What holds students back is their lack of familiarity with lots of new terminology. You will learn about express and constructive (implied) pure conditions, express and constructive promissory conditions, independent and dependent promises, substantial performance, material breach, divisible contracts, and more.

Let's introduce the new principles so you can familiarize yourself with the terminology, then return to them in detail in the body of this chapter. Chapter 8 concerns things that can go wrong during contract performance and explains how to draft terms in advance to take care of these exigencies. Generally, mishaps fall into two categories, problems with the order of performance (who must perform first) and with the quality of performance (was the performance good enough). Let's begin with order-of-performance issues. Consider again your contract with Alice to mow her lawn.

---

1. See Chapter 9 at notes 74–76, and accompanying text.

Notice that Alice promised to pay you $40 *on condition* that you mow her lawn on Saturday, a job you have promised to do. Contract law says your mowing is an "express promissory condition precedent" (pronounced preceedent if you want to impress your teacher) to Alice's duty to pay. You have promised to mow, hence the "promissory" part of the name of what you are to do. Further, Alice agreed to pay on condition that you mow, hence your mowing constitutes a "condition precedent" that must occur before she must pay.[2] The promissory condition precedent is "express" because you and Alice used the language of a condition in your contract—she agreed to pay "on condition" that you mow.[3]

Reread the previous paragraph a few times. Got it? Now more terminology that means the same thing as above. Older cases often used the terminology of "dependent" and "independent" promises.[4] Alice's promise to pay you is a dependent promise because her promise *depends* on your mowing. On the other hand, your promise to mow is an independent promise because you have promised to mow with no conditions attached.

Notice that you and Alice have set the order of performance of your contract by making your promise to mow an express promissory condition precedent to Alice's duty to pay, and by failing to make Alice's promise to pay a promissory condition precedent to your duty to mow. You have to mow first. Further, you have guided a

2. Northern Heel Corp. v. Compo Indus., 851 F.2d 456, 461 (1st Cir. 1988) ("A condition is customarily an undertaking on one side to do something (Thing One) which, by its terms, is made a condition to the performance of some corresponding obligation (Thing Two) by the other party, as where the latter agrees to do Thing Two if the former shall carry out Thing One.") (citing Dr. Seuss [pseud.], The Cat in the Hat 33–54 (Random House ed. 1957)); Merritt Hill Vineyards Inc. v. Windy Heights Vineyard, Inc., 460 N.E.2d 1077, 1081 (N.Y. Ct. App. 1984) ("A condition ... is 'an event, not certain to occur, which must occur, unless its non-occurrence is excused, before performance under a contract becomes due.'") (quoting Restatement (Second) of Contracts § 224 (1981)).

3. Oppenheimer & Co. v. Oppenheim, Appel, Dixon & Co., 660 N.E.2d 415, 418 (N.Y. 1995) ("Express conditions are those agreed to and imposed by the parties themselves."); Merritt Hill, 460 N.E.2d 1077; see also Smeader v. Mason, 67 N.W.2d 131, 133 (Mich. 1954) ("No liability can be predicated upon an agreement which the parties by express and unambiguous terms declared shall be void upon the failure of a condition. The language of the agreement being controlling, it is unnecessary to discuss the other questions raised by appellant.").

4. See, e.g., K & G Const. Co. v. Harris, 164 A.2d 451, 454 (Md. 1960) ("Promises and counter-promises made by the respective parties to a contract have certain relations to one another, which determine many of the rights and liabilities of the parties. Broadly speaking, they are (1) independent of each other, or (2) mutually dependent, one upon the other. They are independent of each other if the parties intend that performance by each of them is in no way conditioned upon performance by the other.... Promises are mutually dependent if the parties intend performance by one to be conditioned upon performance by the other....") (emphasis omitted).

court on what happens if you don't mow and Alice sues. If you weasel out and go body surfing instead (yes, you live near the ocean), you have broken your promise to mow. Alice can sue you for breach of contract and recover damages. You have also failed to do what is necessary to mature her duty to perform her promise to pay you. Alice gets damages and doesn't have to pay you anything. The court's role here is pretty straightforward because you and Alice were good drafters. You expressly allocated both parties' respective duties of performance in the contract.

But now let's suppose your agreement with Alice states that you promise to mow and she promises to pay, and contains no express promissory conditions precedent. In this situation, a court dealing with a dispute between you and Alice cannot simply enforce the contract as written. Using the tools of interpretation and gap filling that we discussed in Chapter 7, the court must determine the "implied" or "constructive" promissory conditions in your contract. Did you agree to mow on condition that Alice performs her promise to pay, or is it the other way around? We shall study in detail how courts resolve such issues by looking at the evidence to see whether your agreement contains an implied-in-fact promissory condition precedent and, if not, which judicial gap fillers can be used to settle the issue.

Besides the order of performance, the other major kind of contract breakdown involves the quality of performance. Courts also analyze these disputes using the principles of express and implied promissory conditions. In Chapter 1, we posited the example in which Alice promises to pay you for mowing her lawn on condition that she is satisfied with the quality of your mowing. Your mower drips gasoline on several areas of Alice's lawn, which kills the grass in those areas. (Would you please get rid of that mower!) If Alice is not satisfied with your mowing, she does not have to pay (and it looks like she has sufficient grounds for being dissatisfied).

Suppose, however, your contract says nothing about the quality of performance necessary before Alice must pay you. You demand payment, notwithstanding the many burned-out sections of Alice's lawn. She refuses to pay and you sue. The court must determine whether your contract contains any *implied* conditions precedent to Alice's duty to pay based on the quality of your performance. Contract law's general answer is that Alice must pay only if you have "substantially performed."[5] The difficult issue, of course, is just what entails substantial performance in a given situation.

5. See infra notes 61–75, and accompanying text.

Still more terminology: A court that finds that you have not substantially performed also may say that you have "materially breached" the contract. But the result is the same whether the court decides you have failed to satisfy an implied promissory condition precedent, that you have not substantially performed, or that you have materially breached. Alice does not have to pay, and you owe her damages for breaking your promise to mow competently. If you substantially, but not fully, perform your promise to mow, you have immaterially breached. Alice must pay you because you have fulfilled the implied promissory condition precedent of substantial performance, but she can deduct the amount of damages she sustains because you didn't fully perform.[6]

Even if you have materially breached, you may still get something for your efforts. Remember, if you have conferred a benefit over and above the damages you have caused, you might me able to recover under the theory of unjust enrichment.[7] This is an important point to bear in mind as you read through the materials and wonder whether it is fair to allow one party to avoid her contract obligations even in the face of a material breach by the other party.

Just a little more terminology before we can look at all of this stuff in detail. Suppose you promise to mow Alice's lawn on condition that the weather is sunny on Saturday. Alice promises to pay for the services. It is very cloudy on Saturday and you refuse to mow. You do not have to perform because of the failure of what is called a "pure" condition precedent to your duty to perform, namely a sunny day. Notice that you don't have to perform, but you also have no cause of action against Alice. She didn't promise you beautiful weather. Hence a sunny day is a "pure" not a "promissory" condition precedent.

Pure conditions do not always involve the occurrence of an event beyond the parties' control (like the weather). In the previous examples, you promised to mow Alice's lawn for $40 on Saturday. Suppose you made no promise to mow. Instead, Alice simply promised you $40 if you mow her lawn. In this situation, mowing her lawn is a pure condition precedent to Alice's obligation to pay. Mowing is not a *promissory* condition precedent because you didn't promise to mow. Of course, you and Alice haven't even made an enforceable contract in this example because you haven't furnished any consideration. You don't have to do anything (so the "agreement" lacks mutuality of obligation).[8] Alice has made an offer for a unilateral contract.[9]

---

6. See infra notes 76–88, and accompanying text.

7. See Chapter 3 at notes 91–100, and accompanying text.

8. See Chapter 2 at notes 55–71, and accompanying text.

9. See Chapter 2 at notes 166–174, and accompanying text.

A. Express Conditions

1. Creation of an express condition. The introduction to this chapter has already described how an express condition operates. You promise to mow Alice's lawn. Alice agrees to pay you $40 on condition that you mow. If you do not mow, she does not owe you anything.[10] You failed to satisfy an express promissory condition precedent to her obligation to pay you. (She can also sue you for damages for breaking your promise to mow.) Parties don't always draft their express conditions so clearly, however. Further, circumstances do not always reveal the parties' intentions very well, so contract law sets forth rules of interpretation to determine whether contract language creates an express condition. Not surprisingly, many of these rules of interpretation coincide with the general rules of interpretation described in Chapter 7.[11]

For example, contract law directs courts to look at the language of the alleged express condition on its face.[12] A manufacturer of blank compact disks makes arrangements with Freight Express to ship the disks to your local music store. The shipping contract states "Freight Express to deliver on or before June 4." Is delivery by June 4 a condition precedent to the manufacturer's duty to pay for shipping? One ancient case involving shipment by sea stated that "[t]he very words themselves, '*to sail* on or before a given day' do, by common usage, import the same as the words '*conditioned* to sail' * * *."[13] A court may therefore conclude that the parties to the blank-disk shipping contract intended "to deliver on or before June 4" to be a condition precedent to the manufacturer's obligation to pay.

Courts also compare the language at issue with other language in the agreement. For example, if an agreement contains a list of express conditions, a court may assume that other terms omitted from the list are *not* conditions. *Howard v. Federal Crop Ins. Corp.*[14] illustrates the point. The Howards sought to recover on an insur-

---

10. Brown–Marx Assocs. v. Emigrant Sav. Bank, 703 F.2d 1361, 1367 (11th Cir. 1983) (" 'As a general rule, conditions which are either expressed or implied in fact must be exactly fulfilled or no liability can arise on the promise which such conditions qualify.' ") (quoting 5 Samuel Williston and Walter H.E. Jaeger, A Treatise on the Law of Contracts 184 (3d ed. 1961)); Della Ratta, Inc. v. American Better Cmty. Developers, Inc., 380 A.2d 627, 638 (Md. Ct. Spec. App. 1977) ("The express condition precedent to [plaintiff's] performance not having been performed or excused, there was no duty of performance by [plaintiff] nor could there have been a breach for nonperformance.").

11. See Chapter 7 at notes 57–138, and accompanying text.

12. Glaholm v. Hays, 133 Eng. Rep. 743, 747 (C.P. 1841).

13. Id.; Star of Detroit Line, Inc. v. Comerica Bank, 1999 WL 33454888, at *4 ("[I]n determining whether an express condition precedent has been fulfilled or satisfied, Michigan courts look to the plain language of the contract in light of the surrounding circumstances.").

14. 540 F.2d 695 (4th Cir. 1976).

ance policy after excessive rain damaged their tobacco crop. One of the provisions of the policy stated that "[i]t *shall be a condition precedent* to the payment of any loss" that the Howards establish that the contract protected them against the hazard that occurred.[15] Another provision stated only that "[t]he tobacco stalks * * * *shall not be destroyed until*" the insurance company inspected them.[16] The Howards plowed the tobacco fields before an adjuster could inspect them. The insurance company claimed that the second provision established a condition precedent to their obligation to pay, namely that the Howards had not destroyed the stalks before an inspection. But the court held that the provision was not a condition precedent, largely because the contract used the language of condition in the first clause, but not the second.[17]

The purpose of an agreement also influences courts in determining whether a term is a condition precedent.[18] For example, courts usually assume that in the business world the time for delivery of a shipment of goods is very important.[19] Money is going to exchange hands, retailers need inventory to sell, such as blank disks (and you need the disks to rip off music companies by downloading music from the internet), etc. If Freight Express doesn't deliver the disks to the music store until, say, June 10, the manufacturer therefore has a good argument that Freight Express has failed to satisfy an express promissory condition precedent to the manufacturer's obligation to pay, namely delivery by June 4.[20]

---

15. Id. at 696.

16. Id.

17. Id. at 698; Glaholm, 133 Eng. Rep. at 746 ("[S]ome distinction must have been intended by the contracting parties, between [a] particular clause and those which precede and follow it, as to the nature of the obligations thereby respectively created."); see also Cedar Point Apartments, Ltd. v. Cedar Point Inv. Corp., 693 F.2d 748, 755 n.9 (8th Cir. 1982) ("[C]ourts will not construe contract provisions to be conditions precedent to another party's duty under the contract unless 'required to do so by plain, unambiguous language or by necessary implication.'") (quoting Kansas City S. Ry. Co. v. St. Louis–San Francisco Ry. Co., 509 S.W.2d 457, 460 (Mo. 1974)).

18. See Chapter 7 at notes 70–72, and accompanying text.

19. John Morrell & Co. v. Burlington N., Inc., 560 F.2d 277, 280 (7th Cir. 1977) (upholding lower court's finding that "defendant knew or should have known that timely delivery of a shipment of meat is essential to its value."); Chronister Oil Co. v. Elleron Chems. Corp., 1986 WL 13445 (S.D. Tex. 1986) ("The price of gas was dropping so precipitously by late December 1985, with each days' delay frustrating [buyer's] chances of profitably reselling the cargo, that [supplier] must have known [buyer] intended timely delivery. Where it is clear that there is a reason for timely performance (e.g., when delay causes the goods to depreciate) limits will be regarded as an essential part of the contract.").

20. See McFadden & Bro. v. Henderson, 29 So. 640, 642 (Ala. 1900) (" 'If any time be agreed upon and the vendor fails to comply with the agreement, the vendee will not be bound to accept, if a compliance with the terms in respect of the time be an essential consideration of the bargain.' ") (quoting Story on Sales, § 310); Glaholm, 133 Eng. Rep. 743.")

Courts also may consider usage of trade, course of dealing, and course of performance in determining whether contract language creates an express condition.[21] Consider the Freight Express example and suppose the contract says that "time is of the essence." The manufacturer may show that in the freight trade this language means that the time of delivery is a condition precedent.[22] Evidence of a course of dealing or course of performance may play a similar role. For example, if the manufacturer and Freight Express treated the time of delivery as a condition precedent in many previous contracts that used the language "Freight Express to deliver on or before June 4," a court should find that the language creates a condition precedent in the current contract.

If you have been following the discussion up to this point, you are probably aware that the ramifications of a judicial finding of a condition precedent can be pretty tough on a party. Freight Express doesn't get paid. You mowed Alice's lawn with your leaky mower for nothing. However, you may have a claim for unjust enrichment.[23] And we will soon consider several other vehicles for judicial avoidance of express conditions.[24] For now, I want to point out one principle used to avoid them. Contract law generally assumes that the parties did *not* intend an express condition and makes the party asserting one prove the condition.[25] For example, if the manufacturer cannot prove delivery on time was an express promissory condition precedent to its obligation to pay Freight Express, the manufacturer will have to pay Freight Express even for a late delivery (at least if it is not too late).

2. The content of an express condition. In the introduction to this chapter, we discussed what happens when an express

---

21. See Chapter 7 at notes 73–107, and accompanying text for a discussion of these sources of evidence.

22. Cf. Gaskill v. Jeanette Ent., Inc., 554 S.E.2d 10, 13 (N.C. App. 2001).

23. See Chapter 3 at notes 91–100, and accompanying text.

24. See infra notes 36–49, and accompanying text.

25. Standard Oil Co. v. Perkins, 347 F.2d 379, 383 (9th Cir. 1965) ("Nowhere in the agreement is notice made an express condition precedent to suit. And a court will not imply that a covenant is a condition unless it clearly appears the parties so intended it...."); K & K Pharmacy, Inc. v. Barta, 382 N.W.2d 363, 365 (Neb. 1986) ("The party seeking to enforce a contract containing a condition precedent bears the burden of proof as to the occurrence of the condition, and if there is no evidence of the occurrence of the condition, the contract is not binding and cannot be enforced."); Jacob & Youngs, Inc. v. Kent, 129 N.E. 889, 891 (N.Y. 1921) ("We must weigh the purpose to be served, the desire to be gratified, the excuse for deviation from the letter, the cruelty of enforced adherence. Then only can we tell whether literal fulfilment is to be implied by law as a condition.... [T]he law will be slow to impute the purpose, in the silence of the parties, where the significance of the default is grievously out of proportion to the oppression of the forfeiture.").

condition precedent is not satisfied. In the preceding subsection, we looked at how courts determine the existence of an express condition. Another important question involving express conditions is just what is required to satisfy an express condition.

The question often comes up in "satisfaction" cases (no, not what the Rolling Stones were complaining about, but what we studied in Chapter 2).[26] If you have a good memory, you can recall the example in which you promise to purchase a water-color picture of your house "if you are satisfied with the picture." Courts generally interpret your satisfaction to be an express condition precedent to your obligation to purchase the picture. But that is not the end of the matter. What exactly is the test of your satisfaction? We saw that courts often interpret satisfaction clauses to require "good faith" on your part.[27]

Further, we saw that, for you to be in good faith, your decision must meet either a standard of reasonableness or honesty.[28] Reasonableness means that you cannot refuse to take the picture if the content and price compare favorably with other pictures of the same type.[29] Honesty means that you are actually dissatisfied with the picture, and that you did not have some other motive for rejecting the picture, such as that the painter's mother was rude to you.[30] Generally, if a satisfaction clause concerns "commercial value

26. See Chapter 2 at notes 65–69, and accompanying text.

27. See, e.g., Mattei v. Hopper, 330 P.2d 625, 627 (Cal. 1958) ("Where the question is one of judgment, the promisor's determination that he is not satisfied, when made in good faith, has been held to be a defense to an action on the contract."); Brack v. Brownlee, 273 S.E.2d 390, 393 (Ga. 1980) ("[T]he purchaser may be entitled to a refund of his earnest money because the condition precedent of obtaining the loan was not fulfilled after the purchaser's good faith efforts to do so.... As a general rule, however, if a purchaser fails to make a good faith effort to obtain financing after agreeing to the contract, he would forfeit his earnest money.").

28. Mattei, 330 P.2d at 626–27; Royal Bank of Can. v. Beneficial Fin. Leasing Corp., 1992 WL 167339, at *6 (S.D.N.Y. 1992) ("[A] satisfaction clause may require objective or subjective dissatisfaction with the tendered performance, depending on the subject matter of the contract.").

29. Davidson & Jones Dev. Co. v. Elmore Dev. Co., 921 F.2d 1343, 1354 (6th Cir. 1991) ("[S]atisfaction of conditions contained in the Assignment Agreement must be viewed from the perspective of a reasonable man, and not [plaintiff's] subjective beliefs concerning their satisfaction."); Mattei, 330 P.2d at 626–27 ("[I]n those contracts where the condition calls for satisfaction as to commercial value or quality, operative fitness, or mechanical utility, dissatisfaction cannot be claimed arbitrarily, unreasonably, or capriciously, and the standard of a reasonable person is used in determining whether satisfaction has been received.").

30. Forman v. Benson, 446 N.E.2d 535, 540 (Ill. App. Ct. 1983) ("Both plaintiff and defendant testified that an increased purchase price was discussed.... [W]e hold that while defendant may have had a basis in his personal judgment for rejecting plaintiff's credit (i.e., outstanding debts and a $2,000 loss reflected in an income tax return), his attempted renegotiation

or quality, operative fitness, or mechanical utility" courts apply a reasonableness test.[31] On the other hand, when satisfaction involves "fancy, taste, or judgment," courts usually apply an honesty test.[32] Because your picture contract involves art work, courts likely will determine good faith based on the honesty test.[33]

Putting all of this together, an express condition precedent to your obligation to take the artist's picture is that you are satisfied with the picture. You must decide whether you are satisfied honestly. Contract law reaches these conclusions because they are the best estimate of what you and the painter intended. You each believed that you would decide whether you were satisfied with the picture based on its quality and not because of some extraneous factor.

Of course, courts must utilize their interpretation tools to determine the content of express conditions in other contexts as well. For example, suppose you agree to purchase Alice's house for $150,000 on condition that you can obtain financing "from a bank or other lending institution* * * at an interest rate which does not exceed 8½ percent per annum."[34] You cannot obtain a better rate than 9 percent, but Alice offers to lend you the money at 8½ percent herself. Must you accept Alice's offer? The answer depends on the meaning of the express condition precedent. Is the condition precedent that you obtain financing at the agreed rate, or that you do so "from a bank or other lending institution." The purpose of the clause might suggest the former. After all, why should you care if you borrow money from a bank or from Alice. In fact, these days you might prefer to borrow money from your seller, with banks finding no shortage of reasons for charging extra "fees" that you may not have considered. But a careful reading of the language indicates that only a bank loan will do. In fact, a court interpreted similar language literally and found that a "bank or other lending

---

demonstrates that his rejection was based on reasons other than plaintiff's credit rating and was, therefore, in bad faith."); Nebraska Panhandle Cmty. Action Agency, Inc. v. Strange, 200 N.W.2d 23, 25 (Neb. 1972) ("If the agreement leaves no doubt that honest satisfaction and no more is meant, the condition does not occur if the obligor is honestly, even though unreasonably, dissatisfied.") (citing Restatement (Second) Contracts § 254 (1972)).

31. Mattei, 330 P.2d at 626–27; see also Nebraska Panhandle Cmty. Action Agency, 200 N.W.2d at 25 ("If a condition of an obligor's duty is that he be satisfied with the obligee's performance, an interpretation is preferred under which the condition occurs, provided a

reasonable man in the position of the obligor would be satisfied and such a test is practicable.").

32. Mattei, 330 P.2d at 627; K & K Pharmacy, Inc. v. Barta, 382 N.W.2d 363, 365 (Neb. 1986) ("'[T]he evidence need only show honest dissatisfaction and no more.").

33. See Gibson v. Cranage, 39 Mich. 49, 50 (Mich. 1878) ("Artists or third parties might consider a portrait an excellent one, and yet it prove very unsatisfactory to the person who had ordered it and who might be unable to point out with clearness or certainty the defects or objections.").

34. Luttinger v. Rosen, 316 A.2d 757, 757–58 (Conn. 1972).

institution" had to make the loan to satisfy the condition precedent.[35]

3. Avoiding express conditions. We've already mentioned (several times, sorry) that enforcing express conditions can lead to rather harsh results. We've also seen that courts utilize the tools of unjust enrichment and judicial interpretation to avoid harsh results. Here we introduce a few more judicial vehicles for avoiding express conditions.

a. Impossibility. Suppose you agree to purchase Alice's house for $100,000. You also agree to pay an additional $10,000 if, after living there for one year, you have not had to make repairs to the house totaling more than $100. But six months after you purchase the house, Taylor Plantations makes you an offer you can't refuse and you sell him the house. At the end of the year, Alice claims that you owe her $10,000. Obviously, the condition precedent to your obligation to pay the $10,000 has not been satisfied because you did not keep the house for a year.

A court could hold that you don't owe Alice anything, since the express condition precedent remains unfulfilled. But a court might find, instead, that a reasonable person would believe that you promised to keep the house for a year, so that Alice would have a fair chance of earning the $10,000.[36] The court also could find that, by breaking your promise, the condition became impossible to satisfy. The court therefore could refuse to enforce the condition and make you pay $ 10,000.[37]

Sometimes conditions become impossible not because of anything a contracting party does, but because of events beyond the

35. Id. at 758 ("In this case the language of the contract is unambiguous and clearly indicates that the parties intended that the purchase of the defendants' premises be conditioned on the obtaining by the plaintiffs of a mortgage as specified in the contract."); see also Reagan v. Bankers Trust Co., 863 F.Supp. 1511, 1513 (D. Utah 1994) ("If the occurrence of a condition is required by the agreement of the parties, rather than as a matter of law, a rule of strict compliance traditionally applies.") (quoting E. Allan Farnsworth, Contracts 571 (2d ed. 1990)).

36. E.I. Du Pont De Nemours Powder Co. v. Schlottman, 218 Fed. 353, 354–55 (2d Cir. 1914); see also, E.B. Harper & Co. v. Nortek, Inc., 104 F.3d 913, 919 (7th Cir. 1997) ("Good faith

and fair dealing requires that parties use reasonable efforts to bring about the occurrence of conditions precedent within their control. The duty is an implied promise between the parties that they will not do anything to injure the other party's right to enjoy the benefits of the contract.").

37. Du Pont, 218 F. at 355 ("Because the defendant has made the performance of this test impossible, the plaintiff should not be remediless."); Canyon Land Park, Inc. v. Riley, 575 F.2d 550, 552 (5th Cir. 1978) ("It is generally agreed that one who unjustly prevents the performance or the happening of a condition of his own promissory duty thereby eliminates it as such a condition.").

parties' control. For example, an insured motorist disappears and his beneficiary cannot provide the "affirmative proof of death or injury" that the life insurance contract requires within six months of the accident. Years later, proof emerges that the insured accidentally drove his car into a river and drowned. Courts have split on whether to excuse the beneficiary from the condition of providing the proof on time, when it was impossible to do so.[38]

b. Waiver. A waiver is an "intentional relinquishment of a known right."[39] The waiving party can do so expressly or by her conduct.[40] A waiver effectively defeats an express condition. Suppose the insurance company in the above disappearing-driver example tells the beneficiary that she does not have to file a proof of death. If the statement constitutes an enforceable waiver, the insurance company cannot avoid the contract because the beneficiary failed to file the proof.

Obviously, then, the crucial issue is what constitutes an enforceable waiver? Must it be in writing? No.[41] Must consideration support the waiver? No again.[42] Surely a waiver must at least require reliance, you say. No, a court may enforce a waiver even if

38. Compare Trippe v. Provident Fund Soc'y, 35 N.E. 316, 317 (N.Y. 1893) ("The condition must . . . receive a liberal and reasonable construction in favor of the beneficiaries under the contract. The provision requires not only notice of the death, but 'full particulars of the accident and injury.' It is quite conceivable that in many cases of death by accident the fact cannot be and is not known until days or even weeks after it has occurred. Such conditions in a policy of insurance must be considered as inserted for some reasonable and practical purpose, and not with a view of defeating a recovery in case of loss by requiring the parties interested to do something manifestly impossible.") and Hanna v. Commercial Travelers' Mut. Accident Ass'n, 204 A.D. 258, 259 (N.Y. App. Div. 1922) aff'd 142 N.E. 288 (N.Y. 1923) ("[W]hen a person by express contract engages absolutely to do an act not impossible or unlawful at the time, neither inevitable accident nor other unforeseen contingency not within his control will excuse him, for the reason that he might have provided against them by his contract.").

39. Irvin Water Dist. No. 6 v. Jackson Partnership, 34 P.3d 840, 847 (Wash. Ct. App. 2001); see also Wagner v. Wagner, 621 P.2d 1279, 1283–84

(Wash. 1980) ("It is necessary that the person against whom waiver is claimed have intended to relinquish the right, advantage, or benefit and his action must be inconsistent with any other intent than to waive it.").

40. Ryder v. Bank of Hickory Hills, 585 N.E.2d 46, 49 (Ill. 1991) ("Waiver may be made by an express agreement or it may be implied from the conduct of the party who is alleged to have waived a right."); Wagner, 621 P.2d at 1284 ("[T]o constitute a waiver, other than by express agreement, there must be unequivocal acts or conduct evincing an intent to waive. Intent cannot be inferred from doubtful or ambiguous factors.").

41. Becker v. HSA/Wexford Bancgroup, 157 F.Supp.2d 1243, 1252 n.2 (D. Utah 2001) ("The parties to a contract may . . . make oral waivers of contract conditions."); E.A. Farnsworth, Contracts 542 (3d ed. 1999).

42. Koedding v. Slaughter, 481 F.Supp. 1233, 1239 (E.D. Mo. 1979) ("It is clear that a party may waive a condition. . . . It is also clear that consideration is not a prerequisite to the validity of such a waiver."); Farnsworth, supra note 41, at 542.

there was no reliance. For example, if an insurance company waives a filing requirement after the time for filing has passed, such as a proof of loss, a court may enforce the waiver. [43]

You can see that waivers are, as Johnny Carson used to say, "some crazy stuff," and they represent a significant exception to the rule requiring that promises must be supported by consideration or be relied on to be legally enforceable. One significant limitation on all of this is that courts tend to restrict waivers without consideration or reliance to non-material relinquishments of a right, such as a waiver of an insured's duty to file proofs of loss within a particular time period.[44] Parties generally cannot waive material terms without consideration or reliance. For example, suppose Champ's Sporting Goods promises to pay $2000 to Ron D. Jockefeller, a manufacturer of sports apparel, for 1000 athletic supporters. Contract law would not recognize Champ's waiver if, after paying, it released Jockefeller from its duty to deliver the goods.

Another limiting factor with respect to waivers is that a party can retract a waiver if the other party has a reasonable time to perform according to the original terms of the contract.[45] Suppose, for example, immediately after the death of an insured, the insurance company waives a condition that the beneficiary file a proof of death within six months, notwithstanding the fact that the beneficiary has the proof and could comply. One month later, the insurance company retracts the waiver, before the beneficiary has relied in any way and while the beneficiary still has ample time to comply with the proof of death deadline. The insured would have to fulfill the condition.

43. Connecticut Fire Insurance Co. v. Fox, 361 F.2d 1, 8 (10th Cir. 1966) (favoring the rule that "allow[s] the insurer to waive or extend the [time] requirement even though the original time requirement had expired."). But see Globe Mut. Life Ins. Co. of New York v. Wolff, 95 U.S. 326, 333 (1877) ("The doctrine of waiver, as asserted against insurance companies to avoid the strict enforcement of conditions contained in their policies, is only another name for the doctrine of estoppel. It can only be invoked were the conduct of the companies has been such as to induce action in reliance upon it, and where it would operate as a fraud upon the assured if they were afterwards allowed to disavow their conduct and enforce the conditions.").

44. Cole Taylor Bank v. Truck Ins. Exch., 51 F.3d 736, 739 (7th Cir. 1995) ("Unless the right waived is a minor one ... why would someone give it up in exchange for nothing?"); Farnsworth, supra note 41, at 544.

45. Computer Strategies, Inc. v. Commodore Bus. Mach., Inc., 483 N.Y.S.2d 716, 722 (App. Div. 1984) ("Commodore could not retract the waiver as it did not give Computer reasonable notice or time to alleviate the prejudice created thereby."); Restatement (Second) of Contracts § 84(2) ("[T]he promisor can make [the promisee's] duty again subject to the condition by notifying the promisee or beneficiary of his intention to do so if (a) the notification is received while there is still a reasonable time to cause the condition to occur....").

c. Forfeiture. Some courts refuse to enforce an express condition simply because enforcement would cause excessive harm to one of the parties. A party seeking to avoid the condition does not have to show a waiver, impossibility, or unjust enrichment, just harm.[46] This judicial tactic is similar to the policing doctrine of substantive unconscionability that courts use to throw out offensive contracts and terms.[47] But, whereas courts generally evaluate whether a term is substantively unconscionable by examining the situation at the time the parties made the contract, courts focus on the *results* of enforcing a condition in forfeiture cases: "[Forfeiture] is intended to deal with a term that does not appear to be unconscionable at the time the contract is made but that would, because of ensuing events, cause forfeiture."[48]

A leading case illustrating the harm or forfeiture principle is *J.N.A. Realty Corp. v. Cross Bay Chelsea, Inc.*[49] Reduced to its essentials, JNA leased a restaurant building to Chelsea. Chelsea had a right to renew the lease for a twenty-four year period, subject to a condition precedent that Chelsea request a renewal in writing at least six months before the original lease ended. Through negligence, Chelsea missed the deadline and did not notify JNA that it wanted to renew until about six weeks before the lease terminated. Chelsea had operated its restaurant for about five years and had invested a total of $55,000 improving it.

Chelsea sought to retain possession of the premises by asking the court to relieve it from a forfeiture. The court noted that Chelsea would forfeit its $55,000 investment and much of the restaurant's good will if it could not renew the lease. Further, Chelsea's delay in notifying JNA was not willful, the result of gross negligence, or part of a strategy to take advantage of a fluctuating real estate market. In addition, JNA had "regularly informed" Chelsea about its other obligations, such as paying taxes and insurance, but had waited until the renewal notice deadline had passed before reminding Chelsea of that condition. The court therefore decided that Chelsea was entitled to relief from the express condition, so long as JNA had not relied on Chelsea's failure to satisfy the condition, for example, by committing the premises to

---

46. See, e.g., Holiday Inns of Am., Inc. v. Knight, 450 P.2d 42, 44 (Cal. 1969) (" 'Whenever, by the terms of an obligation a party thereto incurs a forfeiture, or a loss in the nature of a forfeiture, by reason of his failure to comply with its provisions, he may be relieved therefrom, upon making full compensation to the other party, except in the case of a grossly negligent, willful, or fraudulent breach of duty.' ") (quoting Cal. Civ. Code § 3275).

47. See Chapter 6 at notes 172–184, and accompanying text.

48. Restatement (Second) of Contracts § 229, cmt. b.

49. 366 N.E.2d 1313 (N.Y.1977).

another tenant. The court remanded the case for a new trial to determine the latter issue.

J.N.A. Realty Corp. helps us isolate several factors that support a finding of forfeiture. Where a tenant significantly invests in its leasehold, its failure to satisfy a condition is pardonable (not strategic or really stupid), the landlord lulls the tenant into failing to satisfy the condition, and the landlord has not relied on the condition, a court is very likely to refuse to enforce the condition against the tenant. Of course, these factors would apply to other types of contracts as well.

4. Condition subsequent. Before we leave express conditions, I should introduce one additional wrinkle. So far we have been dealing with the interpretation and avoidance of express conditions precedent. There is another form of condition called a "condition subsequent."[50] Whether a condition is precedent or subsequent depends on the language used by the drafter. We have seen that "Alice promises to pay you $40 on condition that you mow her lawn" is a condition precedent. The drafter could have drafted the same agreement as a condition subsequent: "Alice promises to pay you $40, but if you don't mow her lawn on Saturday, she doesn't have to pay." All of what we have said so far concerning conditions precedent also applies to conditions subsequent such as this one. So why even make the distinction? Drafting a condition as subsequent rather than precedent may have some affect on allocations of burdens of proof.

If your agreement with Alice includes a condition precedent ("Alice promises to pay you $40 on condition that you mow her lawn"), you must mow before her obligation to pay matures. If you sue Alice for failing to pay, you will have to prove that you mowed. However, if your agreement includes a condition subsequent ("Alice promises to pay you $40, but if you don't mow her lawn on Saturday, she doesn't have to pay"), Alice already has the duty to pay, but she is excused if you don't mow. Alice therefore may have to prove that you didn't mow. In many states, procedural rules may trump this simple drafting strategy, further diminishing the significance of drafting a condition precedent or subsequent.

B. Implied Conditions

Now let's look more systematically at how courts resolve order and quality of performance issues when the parties have not drafted express conditions to deal with these matters.

50. See, e.g., Detels v. Detels, 830 A.2d 381, 385 (Conn. App. 2003).

1. Order of performance. In the introduction to this chapter, we considered what happens if you promise to mow Alice's lawn and she promises to pay, but your agreement contains no express language dealing with who must perform first. Courts must use the tools of interpretation and gap filling to determine the "implied" or "constructive" conditions in your contract that dictate the order of performance. Did you agree to mow on condition that Alice pays you first, or must you mow before she pays you?

Assuming the absence of evidence showing who you and Alice intended to perform first, contract law must supply the term. Contract law generally requires that the party whose performance will take longer go first.[51] This gap filler makes sense because it reflects the general practice of paying people after they perform services, not before.[52] We can assume you and Alice would have agreed to follow the general practice had you thought about the matter.

One famous case, *Stewart v. Newbury,*[53] presents an order-of-performance problem in the context of a construction contract. Through a series of letters, Stewart agreed to do the excavation and concrete work on Newbury Manufacturing Company's new building. The agreement omitted any reference to pay periods, although Stewart contended that the parties agreed on the phone that Newbury would make payments "in the usual manner."[54] Stewart also claimed that the custom was to pay 85% of work done every thirty days, with 15% to be paid when the work was completed. After Stewart sent a bill for three months' work and Newbury refused to pay it, Stewart stopped working and sued Newbury. At trial, the judge charged the jury that if the parties did not agree to a payment plan, and no custom on payment existed to fill the gap, Newbury had to make payments "at reasonable times."[55] On appeal, the New York Court of Appeals held that the jury charge was in error. The correct rule was that Newbury had to pay only after Stewart had substantially performed the contract.

51. International Ass'n of Firefighters Local 1596 v. City of Lawrence, 798 P.2d 960, 969 (Kan. Ct. App. 1990) ("Under a contract of service, the employee must render the service before payment is due.") (citing 6 Samuel Williston and Walter H. E. Jaeger, Treatise on the Law of Contracts 85 (3d ed. 1962)); Restatement (Second) of Contracts § 234(2).

52. El Dorado Hotel Props. v. Mortensen, 665 P.2d 1014, 1017 (Ariz. Ct. App. 1983) (discussing Restatement (Second) of Contracts § 234; Edwin W. Patterson, Constructive Conditions in Contracts, 42 Colum. L. Rev. 903, 919 (1942) ("The policy of the law, here as in the tendency to construct concurrent conditions, is to minimize credit risks. If employers usually present less credit risks than employees, the rule of construction effectuates this end. That colleges and theaters ordinarily require payment in advance for the services which they furnish merely exemplifies the operation of the principle.").

53. 115 N.E. 984 (N.Y. 1917).

54. Id.

55. Id. at 985.

Stewart v. Newbury supports the rule that the party whose performance takes longer must perform first. But performance does not have to be perfect. Substantial performance is enough. More about substantial performance shortly.[56]

Sometimes one performance does not take longer than the other. Contract law requires parties to such contracts to perform concurrently (at the same time). For example, Alice agrees to purchase your house. You and Alice can sit at a table across from each other and you can give her the deed to the property at the same time she slides a check in your direction. Remember, however, that you and Alice can fix the order of performance in any way you want. You can agree that you will pay for the property, and she will convey the deed two weeks later. You can agree that she will convey the land and you will pay after inspecting it. However, if you and Alice do not expressly fix the order of performance, contract law fills the gap by requiring concurrent performances.[57]

Requiring concurrent performances makes sense when each party's performance takes about the same amount of time. Neither party must take the risk that the other will not perform. For this reason, concurrent performances is what most parties would have adopted had they dictated the order of performance. In cases of concurrent performances, each performance is an implied promissory condition precedent to the other performance.[58] Your duty to convey is conditioned on Alice's paying and vice versa. If Alice balks, you can sue her for breach of her promise to purchase, but only if you show you were ready, willing, and able to perform (in other words, you "tender" performance). If you fail to perform, Alice must tender performance before she can recover.[59]

---

56. See infra notes 61–75, and accompanying text.

57. El Dorado Hotel Props., 665 P.2d at 1017 ("[W]here a time is fixed for the performance of one of the parties (the payment of $400,000.00 on March 1) and no time is fixed for the other (the approval and delivery of the release) simultaneous performance is possible and will be required unless the language or the circumstances indicate the contrary."); Restatement (Second) of Contracts § 234(1).

58. Northern Heel Corp. v. Compo Indus., 851 F.2d 456, 461 (1st Cir. 1988) ("[T]he term 'concurrent condition' is merely 'an elliptical expression for a condition precedent where performances are due at the same time.'") (quoting 3A Arthur Linton Corbin, Corbin on Contracts 19, n.21); Southern Nat'l Bank v. Crateo, Inc., 458 F.2d 688, 695

(5th Cir. 1972) ("Concurrent conditions ... do not differ from conditions precedent in the relation of time which the happening of the condition bears to the duty of immediate performance on the contract. They are, indeed, mutual conditions precedent.") (quoting 5 Samuel Williston and Walter H. E. Jaeger, Treatise on the Law of Contracts 144 (3d ed. 1961)).

59. Southern Nat'l Bank, 458 F.2d at 695 ("If two persons are bound to give concurrently, one a book and the other the price, neither party will be liable until performance has either been made or tendered by the other. But though the tender may be absolute, it need be only conditional, that is, subject to receiving concurrent performance from the other side.") (citing 5 Williston and Jaeger, supra note 58, at 144).

The UCC provides comparable gap-filling provisions for sales of goods, and it, too, favors concurrent performances. Section 2–507(1) provides in part that "[t]ender of delivery is a condition to the buyer's duty to accept the goods and, unless otherwise agreed, to his duty to pay for them." Conversely, section 2–511(1) provides that "tender of payment is a condition to the seller's duty to tender and complete any delivery."

2. Quality of performance. The introduction to Chapter 8 posited the following problem: Alice promises to pay you for mowing her lawn, the mower drips gasoline on several areas, and Alice refuses to pay. We said that your substantial performance was an implied condition precedent to Alice's duty to pay. Now it is time to learn more about the meaning of substantial performance. We discuss the related doctrine of material breach in the next subsection.[60]

a. Substantial performance. *Jacob & Youngs, Inc. v. Kent*[61] is a leading Cardozo opinion often used to teach substantial performance. Jacob & Youngs ("J & Y") built a $77,000 house for Kent. The contract stated that "all wrought iron pipe must be well galvanized, lap welded pipe of the grade known as 'standard pipe' of Reading manufacture."[62] Kent moved in, but failed to pay the balance due of over $3000 after he learned that most of the pipe in the house was not manufactured by Reading. J & Y's subcontractor simply had not paid attention to this specification when installing the pipe. J & Y sued for the balance due and offered evidence at trial that the brands of pipe used in the house were of the same quality as Reading pipe and that the only difference was the name stamped on the pipe and where it was manufactured. The trial court excluded this evidence and directed a verdict for Kent.

If you carefully perused the introduction to this chapter, you know that the trial court should have excused Kent from the final payment only if the use of Reading pipe was a condition precedent to Kent's obligation to pay. It follows that the trial court erred in excluding evidence that the pipe used was just as good as Reading pipe if the evidence could help determine whether Reading pipe was a condition. This is just what Cardozo found. He concluded that "the evidence, if admitted, would have supplied some basis for the inference that the defect was insignificant in its relation to the project."[63] Further, he thought that the insignificance of the defect would show that (1) justice would be served by deciding that

---

60. See infra notes 76–88, and accompanying text.

61. 129 N.E. 889 (N.Y. 1921).

62. Id. at 890.

63. Id.

Reading pipe was not a condition precedent; and (2) the parties did not intend Reading pipe to be a condition precedent.

Cardozo observed the close relationship between a reasonable interpretation of the Reading pipe term and the parties' probable intentions: "Intention not otherwise revealed may be presumed to hold in contemplation the reasonable and probable."[64] Cardozo also elaborated on the various additional factors relevant in determining whether to treat the use of Reading pipe as a condition precedent: "We must weigh the purpose to be served, the desire to be gratified, the excuse for deviation from the letter, the cruelty of enforced adherence. Then only can we tell whether literal fulfillment is to be implied by law as a condition."[65] J & Y's evidence was certainly relevant to the first two factors mentioned by Cardozo. If the purpose of the Reading pipe provision was to have reliable pipe in the house, and J & Y's evidence was accurate, Kent got what he sought.[66] The first two factors therefore suggest that the use of Reading pipe was not a condition precedent.

The latter two factors focus on J & Y's situation, namely the reason for its breach and the consequences for J & Y if the court ruled that the use of Reading pipe was a condition precedent. Recall that the very same factors also influence whether a court will override an express condition on the grounds of forfeiture.[67] In fact, Cardozo's discussion of these factors suggests that he might not have enforced even a clearly written express condition precedent requiring Reading pipe. After all, J & Y's breach was not willful and J & Y would forfeit the remaining compensation for work done if the court found that Reading pipe was a condition precedent. On the other hand, Cardozo recognized the parties' freedom to draft an express condition precedent.[68] At any rate, what is clear is that in the absence of an express condition requiring Reading pipe, Cardozo, considering all of the factors, would not find that Reading pipe was a condition precedent. He believed that the pipe used satisfied Kent's purpose for requiring Reading pipe. J & Y's breach was inadvertent, and J & Y would suffer a forfeiture if Reading pipe was a condition.

64. Id. at 891.

65. Id.

66. See Richard Danzig, The Capability Problem in Contract Law: Further Readings on Well–Known Cases, 121–22 (1978) ("Jacob and Youngs were prepared to show equality of price, weight, size, appearance, composition, and durability for all four major brands of wrought iron pipe. Indeed, in addition to other witnesses, an employee of the Reading Company was prepared to testify to this effect.").

67. See supra notes 46–49, and accompanying text.

68. Jacob & Youngs, 129 N.E. at 891 ("This is not to say that the parties are not free by apt and certain words to effectuate a purpose that performance of every term shall be a condition of recovery.").

Jacob & Youngs thus stands for the proposition that, in the absence of an express promissory condition precedent requiring perfect performance, contract law usually does not require a perfect performance before the other party must perform. Although Cardozo did not use the terminology, contract law denominates what is required as "substantial performance."[69] Put another way, J & Y's substantial performance, not perfect performance, *is* the condition precedent to Kent's obligation to pay.[70] Assuming J & Y's evidence is credible that all wrought iron pipe is equal, Kent must pay the last installment, minus any damages for breach of its promise to use Reading pipe. With respect to damages, however, Cardozo thought that the appropriate measure was the difference in value between the house with Reading pipe and with other pipe, which was probably zero if the pipe used was just as good as Reading.

We now understand that substantial performance means less than perfect performance. And, of course, we can assume it requires more than doing nothing. Between these extremes, we should apply the parameters Cardozo suggested for determining the quality of performance needed to satisfy the substantiality test. *Plante v. Jacobs* is another helpful case elaborating on these factors.[71] The Jacobs hired Plante to build a new home. The Jacobs selected a stock floor plan, with standard specifications, and made few changes. They moved into the "completed" house, only to find that their patio walls and floor were defective, cracks had appeared in the living room and kitchen ceilings, and a misplaced wall between the kitchen and living room narrowed the living room by more than one foot. The cost of rebuilding the wall was $4000. Adding other assorted defects, the cost of completing the house as promised

69. Plante v. Jacobs, 103 N.W.2d 296, 298 (Wis. 1960) ("Substantial performance as applied to construction of a house does not mean that every detail must be in strict compliance with the specifications and the plans. Something less that perfection is the test of ... performance unless all details are made the essence of the contract."); Crouch v. Gutmann, 31 N.E. 271, 273 (N.Y. 1892) ("Since the rule of exact or literal performance has been relaxed and recovery may be founded upon substantial performance, that term, in its practical application to building contracts, has perhaps necessarily become somewhat indefinite otherwise than that the builder must have in good faith intended to comply with the contract, and shall substantially have done so in the sense that the defects are not pervasive, do not constitute a deviation from the general plan contemplated for the work,

and are not so essential that the object of the parties in making the contract and its purpose cannot, without difficulty, be accomplished by remedying them.").

70. Brown–Marx Assocs., Ltd, v. Emigrant Sav. Bank, 703 F.2d 1361, 1368 (11th Cir. 1983) (" 'It is not substantial performance of 'a condition' that must be rendered; 'substantial performance' *is* the condition—the fact that must exist before payment is due.' ") (quoting 3A Corbin, supra note 58, at 314); Brink v. Hayes Branch Drainage Dist., 376 N.E.2d 78, 81 (Ill. App. Ct. 1978) ("[S]ubstantial performance is a condition precedent 'not because it is so stated in words, but because justice requires it.' ") (quoting 3A Corbin, supra note 58, at 347).

71. 103 N.W.2d 296 (Wis. 1960).

would be about twenty-five to thirty percent above the purchase price. The Jacobs had already paid $20,000 for the $26,765 house. Do they have to pay the final installment of $6765?

Based on our discussion of *Jacob & Youngs*, we know that the issue here is whether Plante has substantially performed. If so, the Jacobs must pay the $6765, minus damages caused by the breach. The court focused on the fact that the Jacobs used a stock floor plan and held that Plante had substantially performed.[72] But the court did deduct the cost of repairing most of the defects from the $6765 due. The court was not moved, however, by the homeowner's complaint about the misplaced wall after evidence showed that the error did not diminish the market value of the house.[73] Therefore, Plante substantially performed notwithstanding the misplaced wall and Jacobs could not recover damages for it measured by the cost of moving the wall.

Are you outraged by this result? The Jacobs wanted a nice new home, and instead they received an assortment of headaches. You may be mumbling that you can accept that a homeowner may have to swallow non-Reading pipe (not literally, of course), but not a living room with the wrong dimensions. Don't forget, however, that construction headaches are unavoidable, and this appeared to influence the court: "Many of the problems that arose during the construction had to be solved on the basis of practical experience."[74] In addition, the Jacobs recovered damages measured by the cost of repairs for most of the defects. And the Jacobs must not have cared too much about the space in their living room, having selected a stock floor plan. The result probably would have been different if the Jacobs had painstakingly measured the size of the living room they desired and hired an architect to draw plans to realize their goal. Finally, you may be reassured to learn that, when considering a builder's substantial performance, some other decisions give greater weight to the homeowners' wishes.[75]

---

72. Id. at 298.

73. Id. at 299.

74. Id. at 298; see also Bernhardt v. McGuire & Pritchard, 607 S.W.2d 8, 12–13 (Tex. Civ. App. 1980) ("The Texas courts have applied the doctrine of 'substantial performance' to construction contracts since 1891. This doctrine recognizes that literal performance of each and every particular of such a contract is virtually impossible. Rather than require perfect performance of every particular, substantial performance is regarded as full performance.").

75. See, e.g., O.W. Grun Roofing and Constr. Co. v. Cope, 529 S.W.2d 258,

262 (Tex. Civ. App. 1975) ("In the matter of homes and their decoration ... mere taste or preference, almost approaching whimsy, may be controlling with the homeowner, so that variations which might, under other circumstances, be considered trifling, may be inconsistent with that 'substantial performance' on which liability to pay must be predicated."); Cf. Carter v. Quick, 563 S.W.2d 461, 465 (Ark. 1978) (the homeowner is interested "in having defective construction corrected so that he and his family may enjoy a properly constructed dwelling and he is not concerned with offsetting any loss on a possible resale of the property. In such a

b. Material breach. As we have seen, most construction-breach cases ask whether a contractor has substantially performed. In contracts involving some other subject matters, courts often use different terminology, although the issues are the same. Specifically, courts ask whether a party has materially breached the contract.[76] A material breach occurs when, in the parlance of construction cases, a party fails to substantially perform. As with the lack of substantial performance, a material breach means that the breaching party has failed to satisfy an implied promissory condition precedent to the other party's duty to perform.[77] The Restatement (Second) of Contracts, section 241, presents several factors for determining a material breach. These look very much like the factors for determining whether a contractor has substantially performed:

(a) the extent to which the injured party will be deprived of the benefit which he reasonably expected;

(b) the extent to which the injured party can be adequately compensated for the part of that benefit of which he will be deprived;

(c) the extent to which the party failing to perform or to offer to perform will suffer forfeiture;

(d) the likelihood that the party failing to perform or to offer to perform will cure his failure, taking account of all the circumstances including any reasonable assurances;

(e) the extent to which the behavior of the party failing to perform or to offer to perform comports with standards of good faith and fair dealing.

One way of summarizing factors (a) and (b) is to ask whether the aggrieved party will get substantially what she bargained for in making the contract. As with the inquiries into whether a party has substantially performed or whether the enforcement of an express

case, aesthetic values are properly involved.").

76. GMC v. New A.C. Chevrolet, Inc., 263 F.3d 296, 317 n.8 (3d Cir. 2001) (" 'The doctrine of material breach is simply the converse of the doctrine of substantial performance. Substantial performance is performance without a material breach, and a material breach results in performance that is not substantial.' ") (quoting Farnsworth, supra note 41, at 496); Walker & Co. v. Harrison, 81 N.W.2d 352, 355 (Mich. 1957) ("What is our criterion for determining whether or not a breach of contract is so fatal to the undertaking of the parties

that it is to be classed as 'material'? There is no single touchstone. Many factors are involved.").

77. Youell v. Grimes, 217 F. Supp. 2d 1167, 1174 (D. Kan. 2002) ("[A] material breach by either party relieves the other of its duty to perform under the contract."); Restatement (Second) of Contracts § 237 ("[I]t is a condition of each party's remaining duties to render performances to be exchanged under an exchange of promises that there be no uncured material failure by the other party to render any such performance due at an earlier time.").

condition will cause a forfeiture,[78] factors (c) through (e) focus on what will happen to the breaching party if the court finds a material breach and on the reasons for the breach.

Notwithstanding these rather facile generalizations about the Restatement factors, you should painstakingly apply each factor when dealing with a particular case. Consider again your leaky mower that spills gasoline on Alice's lawn.[79] Alice expected a nice, freshly cut lawn, not a lawn that looks like green Swiss cheese. Clearly, the more sections of the lawn that the gasoline kills, the more persuasive is the argument that Alice did not receive what she reasonably expected (factor (a)) and that money damages will not make her whole (factor (b)). With respect to factor (b), think also of the embarrassment that Alice will suffer as the result of your work, which generally is not compensable. On the other hand, you will not be paid for your efforts if the court finds that you materially breached, and this may deter the court from declaring a material breach (factor (c)). (By the way, now may be a good time to remind you that even if the court finds that you materially breached and therefore excuses Alice from paying you, you may be able to recover under unjust enrichment if the amount of benefit you conferred exceeds the damages you caused.[80])

Sorry, you can't cure the damage you've done to Alice's lawn very effectively (other than by seeding the bare spots, which will take time to grow), so factor (d) hurts your argument that your breach was immaterial. On the other hand, assuming you didn't know about the mower's defect, your breach was inadvertent and not in bad faith, so factor (e) helps your cause.[81]

You can see that applying the factors of section 241 doesn't give an easy answer. Each factor is important, but not conclusive. None of the factors necessarily clearly favors one party or the other. Factors often contradict each other. Fortunately, section 241 is not the only guidance for lawyers and courts in litigating material breach cases. In addition, they can look at how other courts have dealt with breaches comparable to the one at hand. And chances are that they will find a nice analogous case, because the case

---

78. See supra notes 47–49, 61–75, and accompanying text.

79. See supra note 5, and accompanying text.

80. See supra note 7, and accompanying text.

81. See Restatement (Second) § 241(e) and cmt. f ("The extent to which the behavior of the party failing to perform or to offer to perform comports with standards of good faith and fair dealing is ... a significant circum-

stance in determining whether the failure is material...."); see also Intervisual Communications, Inc. v. Volkert, 975 F.Supp. 1092, 1102 (N.D. Ill. 1997) ("The single incident of inadvertent omission does not rise to the level of a material breach of contract...."); Sackett v. Spindler, 56 Cal.Rptr. 435, 441 (Cal. Ct. App. 1967) (breaching party's "failure to perform could certainly not be characterized as innocent; rather it could be but ascribed to gross negligence or wilful conduct on his part.").

reports are filled with breach cases of all stripes and colors. Here are only two more examples: One court held that a sign maker's two-month delay in cleaning a large sign leased for three years to a dry cleaner was not a material breach, even though the sign had been hit by a tomato (seriously).[82] Another court held that a subcontractor materially breached a contract to perform excavation work when he crashed a bulldozer into a house the contractor was building, destroying a wall and causing damages of $3400.[83]

One thing is certain. Clients will call on lawyers for advice at the time of a contract breakdown. For example, what would you tell the contractor in the latter example if he called at the time of the mishap and asked whether he must pay the subcontractor for work done on the project. Suppose the value of the house was $20,000? $50,000? (The case arose in the late 1950s, so these are realistic numbers.) Not to put pressure on you, but if you give the wrong advice to the contractor, you may be doing your client a great disservice. Suppose you tell the contractor that the subcontractor has materially breached and, in response to that advice, the contractor refuses to pay the subcontractor and hires another subcontractor to do the excavation work. If your advice was wrong, you have induced your client to become the first materially breaching party, and he might have to pay large expectancy damages.[84] If you advise the contractor to pay the subcontractor and keep him on, and this advice is wrong, you have needlessly led your client into further dealings with a materially breaching party.

In fact, the second Restatement increases the challenge for lawyers advising at the contract-breakdown stage. The Restatement (Second) does not always excuse an aggrieved party from performing after the other party's material breach. In some instances, the injured party initially may only *suspend* performance and wait for the other party to cure the default.[85] Under the second Restatement, therefore, a lawyer must predict whether the subcontractor's collision with the wall constituted an immaterial or material

82. Walker & Co. v. Harrison, 81 N.W.2d 352 (Mich. 1957).

83. K & G Const. Co. v. Harris, 164 A.2d 451 (Ct. App. Md. 1960).

84. Walker & Co., 81 N.W.2d at 355 ("[T]he injured party's determination that there has been a material breach, justifying his own repudiation, is fraught with peril, for should such determination, as viewed by a later court in the calm of its contemplation, be unwarranted, the repudiator himself will have been guilty of material breach and himself have become the aggressor, not an innocent victim.").

85. Restatement (Second) of Contracts § 242; see also id. at §§ 237, 241; RW Power Partners v. Virginia Elec. and Power Co., 899 F.Supp. 1490, 1496 (E.D. Va. 1995) (" 'Although a material breach justifies the injured party in suspending performance, it does not of itself justify the injured party in terminating the contract. Fairness ordinarily dictates that the party in breach be allowed a period of time—even if only a short one—to cure the breach if it can.' ") (quoting 2 E. Allan Farnsworth, Farnsworth on Contracts 447 (1990)).

breach, *and*, if material, whether the breach allows the contractor to suspend performance or to cancel the contract. In sorting out whether an injured party can suspend or cancel, the Restatement first refers to the factors in section 241 for determining the materiality of the breach.[86] Needless to say, the more definitive the factors are towards a finding of material breach, the more likely a court will excuse the injured party. (Why only suspend the contractor's performance if the subcontractor completely knocked down the house due to gross negligence?) The Restatement (Second) also directs lawyers to consider whether the injured party needs to make substitute arrangements quickly and whether the agreement called for timely performance.[87] It is also important to consider whether the injured party gave reasonable notice of his grievance.[88]

    c. Divisible contracts. While driving across the interstate in South Dakota on a family vacation a few years ago, we saw a curious sign advertising a drug store in western South Dakota, called "Wall Drug" (at least that's the name I remember—write me if you are from South Dakota and I have made a mistake). I have to admit that I became a bit annoyed at the intrusion of commercialism into what otherwise was a beautiful environment. Then we came across another sign, then another. To make a long story short, the signs appeared intermittently across the entire state, and by the time we saw the tenth sign or so, I was curious enough about this establishment to stop at what turned out to be a real tourist trap.

    You are probably wondering whether I have turned this handy book about contract law into my own personal travelogue. You are about to see the wisdom of my ways. Suppose Wall Drug paid Simon's Sign Company to build ten signs for $5000 each. Simon's builds only five signs. Is Simon's entitled to payment on the contract?[89] (Let's not worry about Article 2 of the UCC for now, and focus on the common law treatment of this problem. We'll see how the UCC treats problems relating to the quality of performance shortly.[90])

    Contract law analyzes this problem by asking whether the contract between Wall Drug and Simon's was "entire" or "divisi-

---

86. Restatement (Second) of Contracts § 242(a); see also Ragnar Enters. v. Tapley, 110 Wash. App. 1033, 2002 WL 234841, at *3 (Wash. App. Div. 1 2002) ("The materiality of a breach is an issue of fact that depends upon the circumstances of each particular case.").

87. Restatement (Second) of Contracts § 242(b) & (c); see also Bailie Communications, Ltd. v. Trend Business Systems, 765 P.2d 339, 343 (Wash. Ct. App. 1988) ("[T]he early character of [defendant's] breach made a cure unlikely.").

88. Restatement (Second) of Contracts § 242, cmt. b.

89. See John v. United Adver., Inc., 439 P.2d 53 (Colo. 1968).

90. See infra notes 94–101, and accompanying text.

ble." In an entire contract, the parties agree to a " 'single whole, so that there would have been no bargain whatever, if any promise or set of promises were struck out.' "[91] In a divisible contract (also called a "severable" contract), the parties' promises "can be apportioned into corresponding pairs of part performances so that the parts of each pair are properly regarded as agreed equivalents * * *."[92] Here are the ramifications of this new classification: In determining whether Wall Drug must pay for the five signs, if the Wall Drug contract is entire, we ask the now familiar question of whether Simon's breach was material. If the contract is divisible, however, Wall Drug must pay for each divisible portion of the contract that Simon's successfully performed, meaning that Wall Drug must pay for five signs.[93] Contract law determines whether a contract is entire or divisible based on the parties' intentions. In the absence of express drafting on the matter, did the parties intend the building of each sign to be a condition precedent to payment for that sign (a divisible contract) or did they intend substantial performance of all the signs to be a condition precedent to payment (an entire contract)? If the parties did not think about the matter, what would they have decided if they had dealt with it?

Wall Drug has a legitimate argument that the parties intended an entire contract if a sucker like me would have to read a minimum of ten signs before being lured into stopping at Wall Drug. If so, Simon's probably has materially breached by producing only five signs. Contract law excuses Wall Drug from the contract because Simon's has failed to satisfy a promissory condition precedent to payment. On the other hand, if each sign has value to Wall Drug, and that value is not diminished by having fewer total signs, the court may find that the parties intended a divisible contract. In that case, Wall Drug must pay for each of the five signs. Simon's

---

91. United States v. Bethlehem Steel Corp., 315 U.S. 289, 298 (1942) (quoting Samuel Williston and George J. Thompson, A Treatise on the Law of Contracts 2422 (rev. ed. 1936)); see also Municipal Capital Appreciation Partners, I v. Page, 181 F.Supp.2d 379, 394 (S.D.N.Y. 2002) ("A contract is generally considered to be entire when, by its terms and purposes, it contemplates that all of its parts are interdependent and common to one another. A contract is severable when its nature and purpose are susceptible to division and apportionment.").

92. Restatement (Second) of Contracts § 240; see also id., cmt. e; Mun. Capital, 181 F. Supp. 2d at 394 (" '[A] contract will not be regarded as severa-

ble' unless '(1) the parties' performances can be apportioned unto corresponding pairs of partial performances, and (2) the parts of each pair can be treated as agreed equivalents.") (quoting Ginett v. Computer Task Group, Inc., 962 F.2d 1085, 1091 (2d Cir.1992)).

93. Restatement (Second) of Contracts § 240; see also John v. United Adver., Inc., 439 P.2d 53, 55 (Colo. 1968) ("So, if the contract be *severable* or *divisible*, then the plaintiff is *only* entitled to recover those monies paid defendant for signs No. 4 and 5, which sum is $120. But if the contract be deemed entire in nature, the plaintiff would be entitled to recover *all* of the monies paid by him to the defendant, which would be the sum of $680.").

has satisfied an implied promissory condition precedent to payment for each of those signs.

d. Uniform Commercial Code.

Let's continue the analysis of the Wall Drug matter assuming that the building of the signs is a sale of goods and that UCC Article 2 applies.[94] Section 2–601 sets forth a perfect tender rule (although we will see that there are several noteworthy exceptions). Perfect tender means what it says: "if the goods or the tender of delivery fail in any respect to conform to the contract, the buyer may * * * reject the whole * * *."[95] So, if the contract between Simon's and Wall Drug called for one sign of 20 square feet, and Simon's tendered a sign of 19.5 square feet, Wall Drug could reject the sign, unless an exception applies.

Section 2–601 requires perfect tender only when the parties have not contracted for a different result.[96] For example, if the contract expressly allowed small deviations in the size of the sign, Simon's would not have to make a perfect tender in order to be paid. A further mitigating factor is the UCC's emphasis on trade custom, course of dealing, and course of performance in determining the meaning of contracts.[97] For example, suppose sign manufacturers and their customers observe a custom that allows for certain deviations in the size of signs. A court would presume that Wall Drug and Simon's intended to incorporate the trade custom into their contract. Simon's would not have to tender a sign of exactly 20 feet.

Sticking with the "one sign" hypo for a moment, let's consider another UCC section that also modifies the perfect tender rule. Under section 2–508, a seller can cure a deficiency in performance if the time for performance has not passed or the seller reasonably believed the tender would be acceptable.[98] If Simon's tendered the

---

94. For a discussion of the scope of Article 2, see Chapter 1 at note 4, and accompanying text.

95. UCC § 2–601.

96. UCC 1–102(3) ("The effect of provisions of this Act may be varied by agreement....").

97. See Chapter 7 at notes 73–99, and accompanying text; see also T. J. Stevenson & Co., Inc. v. 81,193 Bags of Flour, 629 F.2d 338, 356 n.33 (5th Cir. 1980) ("In practice the harsh edges of the perfect tender rule have been smoothed down in cases where the goods themselves are tendered: either a clause in the contract or trade custom or the past practice of the parties will be construed to permit minor discrepancies and an innocent delay of a day or two will not necessarily be fatal.").

98. UCC § 2–508 provides:

(1) Where any tender or delivery by the seller is rejected because non-conforming and the time for performance has not yet expired, the seller may seasonably notify the buyer of his intention to cure and may then within the contract time make a conforming delivery.

(2) Where the buyer rejects a non-conforming tender which the seller had reasonable grounds to believe would be acceptable with or without money allowance the seller may if he seasonably notifies the buyer have a further reasonable time to substitute a conforming tender.

See also Extrusion Painting, Inc. v. Awnings Unlimited, Inc., 37 F.Supp.2d

19.5 foot sign on July 11, but delivery was not due until July 18, and Wall Drug rejected the sign, Simon's would have the right to cure the defect by building another sign the right size or, if possible, repairing the existing one.[99]

In our original problem, of course, Simon's agreed to build ten signs. Section 2–612, involving "installment contracts" (which are basically equivalent to divisible contracts),[100] addresses such a problem by codifying the entire-divisible contract framework discussed above.[101] Indeed, section 2–601 expressly refers to section 2–612 as an exception to the perfect tender rule. Section 2–612(2) states that "[t]he buyer may reject any installment which is non-conforming if the non-conformity substantially impairs the value of that installment and cannot be cured * * *." The buyer must accept the non-conforming installment if "the seller gives adequate assurance of its cure * * *." If Simon's agrees to deliver ten signs at different times, but the second sign is 19.5, instead of 20 feet, Wall Drug can reject that sign only if the deficiency "substantially impairs" the value of that sign. Even if it does, Wall Drug cannot reject the installment if Simon gives adequate assurance that it will cure the deficiency. Thus, section 2–612(2) does not require perfect tender of individual installments of installment contracts.

Section 2–612(3) provides in part that "[w]henever non-conformity or default with respect to one or more installments substantially impairs the value of the whole contract there is a breach of the whole." If Simon's delivers only five signs in installments, Wall Drug can reject all of them if having only five signs "substantially impairs the value of the whole contract." Substantial impairment will depend, as before, on whether Wall Drug needed a minimum of ten signs to induce people to stop at the store or whether each of the signs had an independent value to Wall Drug.

985, 995 (E.D. Mich. 1999) ("[T]he Code mitigates the harsh effects that would otherwise result from [the perfect tender] rule by providing the [seller] with a correlative 'right to cure'. . . .").

99. See Bodine Sewer, Inc. v. Eastern Illinois Precast, Inc., 493 N.E.2d 705, 712 (Ill. App. Ct. 1986) ("[T]he time for performance had not expired at the time of [seller's] attempted August 25, 1984, cure. We therefore conclude that the August 25, 1984, delivery of class V pipe constituted a perfect tender in cure of [seller's] August 24, 1984, delivery of defective 30–inch class III pipe."); see also Wilson v. Scampoli, 228 A.2d 848, 850 (D.C. Cir. 1967) (" 'The seller . . . should be able to cure (the

defect) under subsection 2–508(2) in those cases in which he can do so without subjecting the buyer to any great inconvenience, risk or loss.' ") (quoting William D. Hawkland, Curing an Improper Tender of Title to Chattels: Past, Present and Commercial Code, 46 Minn. L. Rev. 697, 724 (1962)).

100. UCC § 2–612(1) ("An 'installment contract' is one which requires or authorizes the delivery of goods in separate lots to be separately accepted, even though the contract contains a clause 'each delivery is a separate contract' or its equivalent.").

101. See supra notes 89–93, and accompanying text.

In other words, substantial impairment occurs when the seller commits what would be called a material breach at common law.

C. Anticipatory Repudiation

Up to now, we have considered things that go wrong at the time of performance. Simon's doesn't deliver ten signs; you don't show up on Saturday to mow Alice's lawn; Alice refuses to pay you after you mow her lawn. This section deals with problems that develop after the parties make their contract, but *before* performance is due. The name "anticipatory repudiation" gives the subject matter away. Simon's sends Wall Drug a letter months before delivery of the signs is due, stating that it will not build the signs; you tell Alice on Thursday that you have decided to go surfing on Saturday instead of mowing her lawn; Alice tells you on Wednesday that she will not pay you for mowing the lawn. The anticipatory repudiation doctrine presents many new issues. We'll focus on two crucial ones: What constitutes a repudiation and what can the aggrieved party do after one?

Every casebook worth its salt (or worth the exorbitant price you paid for it) includes the great English case, *Hochster v. De La Tour*.[102] In April of 1852, defendant engaged a courier to accompany defendant on a trip starting June 1. On May 11, defendant sent a letter to the courier saying he had changed his mind and did not want the courier's services. The courier sued on May 22. Sometime after that, but before June 1, the courier accepted a substitute job starting July 4. The issues before the court were whether the courier could sue before the time for performance and whether the court should sustain the action even though the courier, having entered a substitute arrangement, could no longer perform the agreement.

The court answered both questions affirmatively. The court relied in part on the mitigation of damages principle: "[I]nstead of remaining idle and laying out money in preparations which must be useless, [plaintiff] is at liberty to seek service under another employer, which would go in mitigation of the damages to which he would otherwise be entitled for a breach of contract."[103] Further, the court was not swayed by the courier's inability to perform the June 1 contract, which made it impossible for the defendant to change his mind: "It seems strange that the defendant, after

---

102. 118 Eng. Rep. 922 (Q. B. 1853).

103. Id. at 926. For more on mitigation of damages, see Chapter 5 at notes 67–78; 114–132, and accompanying text; see also Saewitz v. Epstein, 6 F.Supp.2d 151, 156 (N.D.N.Y. 1998) ("'[The] princi-

ple, known as the doctrine of anticipatory repudiation, provides that when there has been a repudiation of the contract by one party before the time for his performance has arrived, the other party may treat the entire contract as breached . . . .'").

renouncing the contract, and absolutely declaring that he will never act under it, should be permitted to object that faith is given to his assertion, and that an opportunity is not left to him of changing his mind."[104] Finally, the court rejected the argument that damages calculations will be too speculative if people can sue before the time for performance: "An argument against the action before the 1st of June is urged from the difficulty of calculating the damages: but this argument is equally strong against an action before the 1st of September, when the three months would expire."[105] The court felt that if the jury could ascertain damages during the time for performance, it could do so before that time. This argument would not be very persuasive, however, if the contract was long-term and the repudiation was months or even years before performance would begin.

Hochster establishes the right of an aggrieved party to treat an anticipatory repudiation as a breach of contract. Although the court relied in large part on the mitigation principle, the court offered the aggrieved party an election, either to sue immediately, as the courier did, or to wait until performance. In modern sale-of-goods cases, UCC section 2–610 limits the latter option, allowing an aggrieved party to wait only a "commercially reasonable time" for performance.[106]

Although the defendant in *Hochster* clearly repudiated the contract, the court also laid down an approach for determining, in less obvious cases, whether a party has repudiated. Suppose, for example, that the defendant's letter to the courier said that the defendant "did not want to go on the trip after all." According to the court, a party must "utterly renounce[] the contract, or [do] some act which render[s] it impossible for him to perform it."[107] Under this test, this last letter would not be a repudiation.

---

104. Hochster, 118 Eng. Rep. at 926; see also Franconia Assocs. v. United States, 536 U.S. 129, 143 (2002) ("Such a repudiation ripens into a breach prior to the time for performance only if the promisee 'elects to treat it as such.'") (citing Roehm v. Horst, 178 U.S. 1, 13 (1900)); Saewitz, 6 F.Supp.2d at 156 ("It is firmly established that one who wrongfully renounces an obligation in contract should not be heard to complain when he is immediately sued by the non-breaching party.").

105. Hochster, 118 Eng. Rep. at 927.

106. Trinidad Bean & Elevator Co. v. Frosh, 494 N.W.2d 347, 353 (Neb. Ct. App. 1992) ("Under the common law, a buyer in anticipatory repudiation cases was privileged to await a seller's performance until the date performance was scheduled under the contract.... However, prior law was changed by § 2–610(a), which allows an aggrieved party to await performance only 'for a commercially reasonable time.'").

107. Hochster, 118 Eng. Rep. at 926; see also Trinidad Bean, 494 N.W.2d at 350 ("Anticipatory repudiation centers upon an overt communication of intention or an action which renders performance impossible or demonstrates a clear determination not to continue with performance.").

The Restatement (Second) of Contracts has adopted an objective test for determining a repudiation. A statement must "indicat[e]" that the party will not perform.[108] An act must be "voluntary" and it must make the party "unable" or "apparently unable" to perform.[109] The defendant's letter stating that he does not want to go on the trip probably is not a repudiation because a reasonable person would believe that the defendant was merely unsure of his plans. On the other hand, a definitive statement that a party will not perform unless the other party agrees to new significant terms should constitute a repudiation. For example, if the defendant in *Hochster* wrote that he would not go on the trip unless the courier accepted a material pay cut, the defendant's letter would constitute a repudiation.[110]

The Restatement and UCC provide tools for parties faced with equivocal language or conduct. For example, the courier who receives a worrisome letter from the defendant about the prospect of performance can ask for "adequate assurance of due performance," because the courier has "reasonable grounds for insecurity."[111] If the courier doesn't receive such assurances, he can treat the situation as a repudiation.[112] Of course, what constitutes "reason-

108. Restatement (Second) of Contracts § 250; see also cmt. b ("In order to constitute a repudiation, a party's language must be sufficiently positive to be reasonably interpreted to mean that the party will not or cannot perform."); Gilman v. Pedersen, 438 A.2d 780, 781 (Conn. 1981) ("Repudiation can occur either by a statement that the promisor will not perform or by a voluntary, affirmative act that indicates inability, or apparent inability, substantially to perform."); Wallace v. Kuehner, 46 P.3d 823, 828 (Wash. Ct. App. 2002) ("An anticipatory repudiation must be a positive statement or action indicating distinctly and unequivocally that a party cannot or will not perform its obligations.").

109. Restatement (Second) of Contracts § 250; see also Kasarsky v. Merit Sys. Protection Bd., 296 F.3d 1331, 1337 (Fed. Cir. 2002) ("The [defendant's] silence did not amount to a 'statement or voluntary affirmative act.' Thus, its delay in paying the attorney fees could not amount to a breach of the fee agreement, until it communicated its refusal to pay.").

110. Restatement (Second) of Contracts § 250, cmt. b ("[L]anguage that under a fair reading 'amounts to a statement of intention not to perform except on conditions which go beyond the con-

tract' constitutes a repudiation.") (quoting UCC § 2–610, cmt. 2); see also Truman L. Flatt & Sons Co. v. Schupf, 649 N.E.2d 990, 994 (Ill. App. Ct. 1995).

111. Restatement (Second) § 251, cmt. a; UCC 2–609, cmt. 1 (The goal of the section is to provide "a continuing sense of reliance and security" on the contract); see also Diskmakers, Inc. v. DeWitt Equip. Corp., 555 F.2d 1177, 1179 (3d Cir. 1977) (" 'Any facts which should indicate to a reasonable merchant that the promised performance might not be forthcoming when due should be considered reasonable grounds for insecurity....' ") (citing New Jersey Study Comment on N.J.Stat, Ann. § 12A:2–609); Koch Materials Co. v. Shore Slurry Seal, Inc., 205 F.Supp.2d 324, 330 (D. N. J. 2002) ("When, in a contract for the sale of goods, one party has reasonable grounds to doubt that the other party will be able to perform, the doubting party may demand of its counterpart assurance that performance will occur.... A party need not wait for an actual material breach to demand assurances; it need only show that it reasonably believed that such an event might be in the offing.").

112. Koch Materials, 205 F.Supp.2d at 330 ("If no adequate assurance is forthcoming within a commercially rea-

able grounds for insecurity" and what constitutes "adequate assurance of due performance" suffer from the same lack of clarity as questions of material breach and the right to suspend or cancel.[113] For example, are a distributor's poor history of making punctual payments and bounced checks enough to constitute "reasonable grounds for insecurity?" At least one court thought so.[114] Is a statement by the debtor that he will honor the contract in the future sufficient to constitute "adequate assurance of due performance," or must the debtor prove that his financial situation has improved?[115] Obviously, the nature of the insecurity has a huge influence on what kind of assurances are necessary.

A party can retract an anticipatory repudiation before the other party has relied on it or indicates acceptance of the repudiation as final.[116] This suggests that an aggrieved party should notify the party repudiating the contract if the aggrieved party intends to treat the repudiation as final.[117]

sonable time, or in any event within 30 days, the doubting party may treat its counter party as having repudiated the contract.").

113. See supra notes 85–88, and accompanying text.

114. Hornell Brewing Co. v. Spry, 664 N.Y.S.2d 698, 702–703 (S. Ct. 1997) ("[P]laintiff had reasonable grounds to be insecure.... Defendants were substantially in arrears almost from the outset of their relationship with plaintiff, had no financing in place, bounced checks, and had failed to sell even a small fraction of the product defendants ... originally projected."); see also Coral Bay, Inc. v. Zakaspace Corp., 1999 WL 446823, at *4 (N.D. Ill. June 24, 1999) ("[Defendant] never gave [plaintiff] assurance of payment, only continuous requests for [plaintiff] to 'be patient.' Since [plaintiff] had already been told by [defendant] to hold delivery on several Piccadilly invoices, and then [defendant] fell behind in its payments, [plaintiff] had reasonable grounds for insecurity and thus withholding performance.").

115. See UCC § 2–609, cmt. 4 (whether verbal assurances are adequate depends on the circumstances); Cherwell–Ralli, Inc. v. Rytman Grain Co., 433 A.2d 984, 987 (Conn. 1980) (finding inadequate grounds for insecurity where "presidents of the parties had exchanged

adequate verbal assurances only eight days before" buyer's refusal to perform).

116. See, e.g., Anderson Excavating & Wrecking Co. v. Sanitary Improvement Dist., 654 N.W.2d 376, 383 (Neb. 2002) ("A repudiation can be nullified by a retraction of the statement before the injured party materially changes his or her position in reliance on the repudiation or indicates to the other party that he or she considers the repudiation to be final."); Truman L. Flatt & Sons Co., 649 N.E.2d at 994–95 (" 'The effect of a statement as constituting a repudiation under Restatement (Second) § 250 or the basis for a repudiation under § 251 is nullified by a retraction of the statement if notification of the retraction comes to the attention of the injured party before he materially changes his position in reliance on the repudiation or indicates to the other party that he considers the repudiation to be final.' ") (quoting Restatement (Second) of Contracts § 256(1)); see also UCC § 2–611.

117. Restatement (Second) of Contracts § 256; see also Kinesoft Dev. Corp. v. Softbank Holdings Inc., 139 F.Supp.2d 869, 898 (N.D. Ill. 2001) ("If the injured party notifies the repudiating party that it considers the repudiation final, either by statements to that effect or by filing a lawsuit, then it need not show reliance on the repudiation to prevent revocation.").

*

Chapter Nine

GROUNDS FOR EXCUSING PERFORMANCE

In the last chapter, we saw that a party can cease performance and cancel a contract when, among other things, the other party fails to satisfy an express promissory condition or commits an uncured material breach. Chapter 9 also concerns grounds for releasing a party from the duty to perform a contract, but these new grounds are not based on the other party's failure to perform. Instead, Chapter 9 focuses on various grounds for excusing a party from performance because both parties have a mistaken view of the facts existing at the time of contracting or, at that time, they reasonably fail to foresee a "supervening" event (an event that takes place after contract formation) that makes performance very different from what they expected. Chapter 9 also covers mistakes by only one party that excuse performance.

Contract law calls an excuse based on both parties' mistaken view of existing facts a "mutual mistake." (Surprise!) Recall an example of a mutual mistake from Chapter 1, in which both parties to a sale of jewelry reasonably thought the seller was selling a worthless stone for $1, but the stone turned out to be a diamond worth $50,000.[1] The seller may claim a mutual mistake and seek a return of the diamond.

Contract law labels excuses based on a supervening event either "impossibility," "impracticability," or "frustration of purpose" depending on the context. We will discuss examples of each of these excuses shortly.[2] For now, consider the following example of an impracticability claim: After an international disruption in oil supply causes the price of oil to skyrocket, an oil supplier seeks relief from a long-term, fixed-price contract to supply oil to an electric utility. The oil supplier may claim relief from performance on the basis of impracticability.[3]

In our discussion of legal excuses, you will see that, although these doctrines introduce new terminology and strategies of analysis, in the end they amount to nothing more than judicial interpre-

---

1. See Chapter 1; cf. Wood v. Boynton, 25 N.W. 42, 44 (Wis. 1885).

2. See infra notes 40–90, and accompanying text.

3. See infra notes 63–82, and accompanying text.

tation of a contract to determine whether the parties assigned the risk of the mistake or of the supervening event. If the court concludes the parties did not assign the risk themselves, the court may engage in judicial gap filling. For example, did the parties in the oil supply contract intend to condition the supplier's performance on the absence of international disruptions? If the parties did not foresee the disruption, should the court construct such a condition for the parties? By keeping in mind what courts are really doing, you may be able to take some of the mystery out of the excuse cases.

As mentioned in Chapter 1, the excuse doctrines are controversial because they allow a party to avoid duties under an otherwise enforceable contract. Obviously, if too generous, the excuse doctrines discourage people from entering contracts or relying on them. For example, what company will want to make or rely on a fixed-price contract to purchase oil if the supplier can avoid the deal simply because the market price goes up? Purchasers of oil enter such contracts precisely because they want to assign the risk of price increases to the supplier. On the other hand, if the supplier must obtain oil at astronomical prices because of an unforeseeable world crisis, relieving the supplier seems more palatable, both on grounds of freedom of contract (arguably, the supplier never agreed to perform under such circumstances) and of fundamental fairness. Further, because circumstances such as world crises disrupting oil supplies are thankfully rare, people can justifiably rely on their contracts secure in the knowledge that the supplier will not easily wiggle out of the deal. Let's investigate the excuse doctrines more closely.

A. Mistake

I would be remiss (and I hate being remiss), if I didn't begin our discussion of mistake with the famous case of *Sherwood v. Walker*.[4] The Walkers contracted to sell a cow named Rose 2d of Aberlone to Sherwood for $80. According to the majority opinion, both parties thought that Rose was barren. Rose turned out to be pregnant and worth at least $750. The Walkers refused to deliver Rose to Sherwood and he sued. The trial court instructed the jury that Rose's sterility or lack thereof was inconsequential and the jury decided in favor of Sherwood. The Michigan Supreme Court reversed and remanded the case for a new trial. The court stated that the jury should have been instructed that "if they found that the cow was sold, or contracted to be sold, upon the understanding of both parties that she was barren * * * and that in fact she was

---

4.   33 N.W. 919 (Mich. 1887).

not barren * * * then [the Walkers] had a right to rescind * * * and the verdict should be in their favor."[5]

The majority based its holding on the "mutual mistake" excuse: Contract law excuses a party from its contract when the parties are mutually mistaken about a material fact.[6] Notice how easy it will be for you to remember the elements of the rule. Each element starts with the letter "m." In order for the Walkers to avoid the contract there must be a mutual, material, mistake. Let's analyze each of these elements.

1. Mutual. The mistake must be mutual, meaning, of course, that both parties must believe the mistaken assumption. The jury charge required by the *Sherwood* majority incorporates the mutuality requirement by directing the jury to find for the Walkers only if *both* parties believed that Rose was barren. The dissent thought that because Sherwood had seen Rose with a bull, he believed she might not be barren.[7] If the dissent was correct, Sherwood did not share the Walkers' mistake and the mistake was not mutual.[8] The dissent therefore disagreed with the majority's decision to grant a new trial.

Contract law recognizes some exceptions to the mutuality requirement. Recall in Chapter 6 our discussion of fraudulent concealment.[9] You might wonder, if the dissent is correct on the facts, whether Sherwood had a duty to disclose his view about Rose's breeding capability and whether the Walkers therefore had a right to rescind for fraudulent concealment. Relief for the Walkers is not likely on this ground because, even under the dissent's view of the facts, Sherwood only thought that Rose could be made to breed and did not have any hard facts about her condition. Even if Sherwood had such facts, Sherwood probably did not have a disclosure duty because the Walkers, as owners of Rose, reasonably should have ascertained the facts for themselves.[10]

---

5. Id. at 924.

6. Id. at 923. See Restatement (Second) of Contracts § 152 (1981); see also Renner v. Kehl, 722 P.2d 262, 265 (Ariz. 1986) ("'[A] contract may be rescinded when there is a mutual mistake of material fact which constitutes 'an essential part and condition of the contract.' ") (quoting Mortensen v. Berzell Inv. Co., 429 P.2d 945, 947 (Ariz. 1967)); Dover Pool & Racquet Club, Inc. v. Brooking, 322 N.E.2d 168, 170 (Mass. 1975) ("We have long recognized that land contracts may be rescinded for mutual mistake.").

7. Sherwood, 33 N.W. at 925 (Sherwood, J., dissenting).

8. See George E. Palmer, Mistake and Unjust Enrichment 95 (1962) ("Sherwood was a banker who also had a stock farm on which he raised purebred cattle. The whole sense of the matter suggested that he was not buying the purebred cattle . . . to fatten and sell for beef; rather . . . he thought there was a chance Rose 2d would breed.").

9. See Chapter 6 at notes 73–84, and accompanying text.

10. See Chapter 6 at notes 74–82, and accompanying text.

I don't mean to suggest that the duty to disclose can never arise in unilateral mistake situations. Consider a variation of the facts of *Johnson v. Healy*,[11] a case first discussed in Chapter 6.[12] Suppose Healy sells a new home to Johnson, knowing that the house is defective because of improper fill supporting the foundation.[13] Johnson reasonably does not know about the defect. Healy says nothing about the quality of the home to Johnson. If Johnson claimed a mutual mistake, asserting that both parties mistakenly believed the house's foundation was solid, he would be unsuccessful. Healy, of course, was not mistaken about the quality of the foundation, so the mistake was not mutual. However, Healy had a duty to disclose the defect and Johnson can avoid the contract on this basis.[14]

The case is even stronger for rescission when one party knows or should know of the other party's mistake.[15] Suppose Healy not only knew that the house had a defective foundation, but also knew or reasonably should have known that Johnson was unaware of the defect. Again, Johnson's mutual mistake claim would be unsuccessful. Healy was not mistaken about the quality of the foundation, so the mistake was not mutual. However, contract law allows Johnson to rescind the contract because Healy knew or should have known about Johnson's mistake. One party cannot take advantage of the other's unilateral mistake.[16]

Here is one more example of a unilateral mistake that can lead to rescission: Suppose you have a garage sale and place several

11.   405 A.2d 54 (Conn. 1978).

12.   See Chapter 6 at notes 55–59, and accompanying text.

13.   Johnson, 405 A.2d at 55–56.

14.   See, e.g., Hill v. Jones, 725 P.2d 1115, 1118–19 (Ariz. Ct. App. 1986) ("[U]nder certain circumstances there may be a 'duty to speak.' ... [N]ondisclosure of a fact known to one party may be equivalent to the assertion that the fact does not exist.... Thus, nondisclosure may be equated with and given the same legal effect as fraud and misrepresentation."); Johnson v. Davis, 480 So.2d 625, 629 (Fla. 1985) (holding that "where the seller of a home knows of facts materially affecting the value of the property which are not readily observable and are not known to the buyer, the seller is under a duty to disclose them to the buyer.").

15.   Restatement (First) of Contracts § 503 (1932); Restatement (Second) of Contracts § 153, 154; see also Aviation Sales, Inc. v. Select Mobile Homes, 548 N.E.2d 307, 310 (Ohio Ct. App. 1988) ("[A] contract is voidable if one party made a mistake at the time that contract was entered into, the mistake had a material effect on the agreed exchange of performances that was adverse to the mistaken party, and the other party had reason to know of the mistake."); Elsinore Union Elementary School Dist. v. Kastorff, 353 P.2d 713, 717 (Cal. 1960) ("Relief from mistaken bids is consistently allowed where one party knows or has reason to know of the other's error and the requirements for rescission are fulfilled.").

16.   See Powder Horn Constructors, Inc. v. City of Florence, 754 P.2d 356, 364 (Colo. 1988) ("Here, [defendant] did not act upon any reasonable expectations, but rather sought to take advantage of [plaintiff's] mistake and gain a windfall profit."); see also Jackson Enters., Inc. v. Maguire, 355 P.2d 540, 543 (Colo. 1960) ("[O]ne party can not knowingly take advantage of the mistake of the other party to the contract.").

items on your driveway for your customers' perusal. Alice asks to purchase your set of 45 r.p.m. records (the kind with the big hole in the middle), your ten-year-old Dell Computer, and your old set of golf clubs. You decide to sell the records for $12, the computer for $100, and the golf clubs for $15, but you don't tell Alice the individual prices. You draw up a bill of sale listing the three items, but not their individual prices. You use your portable adding machine to add up the total because you were not good at arithmetic in school. Unfortunately, you're not too good at using the adding machine either, and you enter $10 for the computer instead of $100. You write $37 instead of $127 beside the three items, Alice pays you that amount, and carts off the junk.

Let's assume that Alice reasonably is unaware of your clerical error. (Perhaps she was distracted by looking through the records and by finding Nancy Sinatra's, "These Boots Are Made for Walking," one of the most insipid, yet memorable, songs ever recorded.) You can rescind the deal. Contract law generally grants rescission for unilateral clerical errors.[17] Of course, the clerical error must be readily provable. If the real reason a party seeks relief is that she realizes the price was too high or low, an error of judgment, contract law should not grant her relief.[18] Remember, people will not be very enthusiastic about making and relying on contracts if the other party can exit from them too easily.[19]

On the other hand, if you can prove that you made a clerical error, your negligence in making the error should be irrelevant, unless extreme.[20] Contract law is not in the business of punishing parties for their harmless errors, even if the errors are pretty

---

17. Kenneth E. Curran, Inc. v. State, 215 A.2d 702, 704 (N.H. 1965) ("[E]quity recognizes that honest, sincere men, even in the exercise of ordinary care, under such pressure can make mistakes of such a fundamental character that enforcement of the apparently resulting agreement would be unconscionable. In such a situation . . . equitable relief will be granted."). But see Triple A Contractors, Inc. v. Rural Water District No. 4, 603 P.2d 184, 186 (Kan. 1979) ("We see no occasion to make a distinction between a clerical error and an error in judgment. . . . [I]n the absence of fraud a unilateral mistake does not excuse the nonperformance of a contract.").

18. See Berg v. Hessey, 256 N.W. 562, 564 (Mich. 1934) ("Rescission is not a vent for bad bargains unless induced by fraud."); Wood v. Boynton, 25 N.W.

42, 44 (Wis. 1885) ("[Plaintiff] cannot repudiate the sale because it is afterwards ascertained that she made a bad bargain.").

19. See supra notes 3–4, and accompanying text.

20. Florida Ins. Guar. Ass'n v. Love, 732 So.2d 456, 457 (Fla. Dist. Ct. App. 1999) (granting recission because while defendant's "error certainly involved some degree of negligence, the evidence was not sufficient to support a finding of an inexcusable lack of due care."); White v. Berrenda Mesa Water Dist., 87 Cal.Rptr. 338, 343 (Cal. Ct. App. 1970) ("[P]laintiff will not be denied rescission or reformation because of lack of care unless his conduct amounts to gross negligence or the neglect of a legal duty.") (citing Van Meter v. Bent Constr. Co., 297 P.2d 644, 647 (Cal. 1956)).

stupid. "Harmless" is a key word here, however. If Alice reasonably relies on your deal at the $37 price, you would not be able to rescind.[21]

Incidentally, you can obtain judicial relief of another kind if you and Alice had agreed on a price of $127 before you committed your arithmetical error, but she now insists on holding you to the $37 contract. Contract law seeks to enforce the contract the parties intended to make, not the one that results from a failure to record the terms correctly on paper.[22] So you can ask the court to reform (rewrite) your contract to reflect the true price.[23]

From this discussion, it may appear that the exceptions to the mutuality requirement swallow up the rule. The exceptions infrequently apply, however. Most cases involve situations similar to the dissent's description of *Sherwood v. Walker*, in which Sherwood had no hard facts about Rose's condition. None of the exceptions apply to this scenario. Sherwood would not have a duty to disclose. Walker could not claim a clerical error or that Sherwood was aware of Walker's error. So, in most cases, contract law affords no relief when the contract proves to be a losing one for one of the parties.

2. Material. The mutual mistake must also be material, meaning it must be large or serious.[24] This "m" caused some confusion because early decisions sought to distinguish between mistakes pertaining to the "substance" of a transaction, in which contract law would grant relief, and mistakes as to "quality" or "value" in which contract law would not grant relief. In *Sherwood,* for example, the majority based its decision in part on the fact that

---

21. Maryland Cas. Co. v. Krasnek, 174 So.2d 541, 543 (Fla. 1965) (stating that rescission is inappropriate where "respondent so changed his position in reliance upon petitioner's undertaking that it would be unconscionable to rescind the contract or that it would be impossible to restore him to the status quo."); see also John Price Assocs., Inc. v. Warner Elec., Inc., 723 F.2d 755, 757 (10th Cir. 1983) ("[Defendant] submitted a bid ... with the expectation that companies bidding on the general contract would rely on its bid in making their bids. [Plaintiff] relied on [defendant's] bid.... In this situation promissory estoppel should apply to prevent Warner from withdrawing its bid.").

22. Metropolitan Prop. & Cas. Ins. Co. v. Dillard, 487 S.E.2d 157, 159 (N.C. Ct. App. 1997) (where by mutual mistake home insurance policy includes wrong address reformation "is proper to give effect to the terms of the contract the parties originally agreed upon."); Morton v. Park View Apartments, 868 S.W.2d 448, 451 (Ark. 1993) ("Courts of equity have the authority to reform deeds when the evidence is clear, convincing, and decisive that there is ... a mutual mistake in the drafting of the instrument....").

23. See, e.g., E. Allan Farnsworth, Contracts 443–45 (3d ed. 1999).

24. Palumbo v. Ewing, 540 F.Supp. 388, 393 (D. Del. 1982) (Land sale rescinded in light of "evidence adduced at trial as to the potentially adverse health, safety and aesthetic ramifications of the location of [a previously unknown] sewer line and manhole, ... constitut[ing] a material fact as to which the parties were mutually mistaken.").

the mistake concerning Rose's condition was one of substance.[25] But the dissent argued that the parties' mistake, if any, was over one of the qualities of Rose, namely whether she could breed. Because substance and quality are not concise terms and courts manipulated them based on whether they thought that a mistake was material, the modern approach is to dispense with the substance and quality distinction and to ask directly whether the mistake was material (important).[26] The Walkers originally purchased Rose for $850, and she turned out to be worth at least $750,[27] so the sale of Rose to Sherwood for about one tenth of her true value, which is the value of a barren cow, certainly seems to satisfy the materiality requirement.

3. Mistake. The third requirement focuses on whether the parties made a "mistake." By mistake, courts are not talking about the dictionary meaning of the word. The parties would be mistaken in the dictionary sense if they thought that Rose was barren, but understood the possibility that she was not. But that would not be enough for a legal mistake, legal in the sense that it would give the Walkers the legal ground to avoid the contract. A useful way of thinking about a legal mistake is to ask whether the parties contracted on the basis of a set of facts that they took as true (Rose is barren) or whether they contracted on the basis of some conjecture as to the facts (Rose is probably barren). Contract law excuses the Walkers from their contract only in the former case.[28]

The requirement of a legal mistake makes sense. Parties who make contracts value what they are getting more than what they are giving up, but they know that circumstances may be different than assumed and that they ultimately may be disappointed with their contract. Sherwood valued Rose more than $80, the purchase price, and the Walkers valued the money more than Rose. But each knew, at the time they struck the deal, that Rose might be worth a bit more or less than $80. In effect, they gambled over whether the deal would turn out to be beneficial. Contract law should not upset

25. Sherwood v. Walker, 33 N.W. 919, 923 (Mich. 1887) ("[T]he mistake or misapprehension of the parties went to the whole substance of the agreement. If the cow was a breeder, she was worth at least $750; if barren, she was worth not over $80.").

26. See, e.g., Lenawee County Bd. of Health v. Messerly, 331 N.W.2d 203, 209 (Mich. 1982) ("We find that the inexact and confusing distinction between contractual mistakes running to value and those touching the substance of the consideration serves only as an impediment to a clear and helpful analysis....").

27. Sherwood, 33 N.W. at 920.

28. Restatement (Second) of Contracts § 296 ("A party bears the risk of a mistake when ... he is aware, at the time the contract is made, that he has only limited knowledge with respect to the facts to which the mistake relates, but treats his limited knowledge as sufficient...."); Bennett v. Shinoda Floral, Inc., 739 P.2d 648, 654 (Wash.1987) (when parties contract on the basis of a conjecture "there is no mistake. Instead, there is an awareness of uncertainty or conscious ignorance of the future.").

these wagers just because one or the other's gamble proves to be wrong.[29] Otherwise, people could not rely on their contracts and their would be little reason to make them. Why would you enter a contract to sell your neighbor, Alice, your piano for $400 if she could rescind the deal if she learns that the market value of the piano was only $350? If both parties in *Sherwood* "knew" that they were selling and buying a barren cow and did not believe they were gambling over this quality of Rose, however, then affording relief to the Walkers when Rose turned out to be pregnant makes some sense. If the court required the Walkers to sell, it would be enforcing a contract the parties did not make and Sherwood would receive an undeserved windfall.

Another way of analyzing the mistake factor in *Sherwood v. Walker* is through the law of implied conditions.[30] If the contract expressly stated that the Walkers promised to sell Rose "on condition that Rose is barren," the Walkers would not have to perform when Rose turned out to be pregnant.[31] Of course, contract language is often unclear about whether the parties allocated such a risk. For example, lots of courts agonize over whether the parties meant an "as is" clause or the like to allocate the risk of defects that are not easy to discover. Consider a clause that states that a purchaser of real property "has examined this property and agrees to accept same in its present condition."[32] The court presented with this language held that the parties intended to allocate the risk of a defective septic system to the purchaser of the property, even though the purchaser failed to discover the defect after an inspection and the defect made the property uninhabitable. Another reasonable interpretation of the language is that the parties intended the purchaser to assume the risk only of those defects that a reasonable inspection would uncover. But this argument has not been very successful.[33] The message for the contract drafter (maybe you, some day) is to draft risk allocation clauses clearly. A general "as is" clause will not do.

Because the parties did not expressly allocate the risk of the mistake in *Sherwood v. Walker*, the issue for the court was whether a condition should be implied in fact or law. If Sherwood had

---

29. Covich v. Chambers, 397 N.E.2d 1115, 1121 (Mass. App. Ct.1979) ("Avoidance is not permitted just because one party is disappointed in the hope that the facts accord with his wishes."); Aldrich v. Travelers Ins. Co., 56 N.E.2d 888, 889 (Mass. 1944) ("Neither side can rescind the contract merely because the known and assumed risk turned out to be greater than either or both expected it to be.").

30. See Chapter 8 at notes 51–93, and accompanying text.

31. See, e.g., Lenawee County Bd. of Health v. Messerly, 331 N.W.2d 203 (Mich. 1982); Restatement (Second) of Contracts § 154(a).

32. Lenawee, 331 N.W.2d at 205.

33. See id; cf. UCC § 2–316(3)(a) (1989) ("as is" clause disclaims implied warranties in the sale of goods).

specifically asked for a barren cow (destined for Wendy's, let's say), and the Walkers offered Rose for $80, with neither party suspecting Rose's true nature, a good case could be made that the parties meant to condition the sale on Rose being what they thought she was—barren. On the other hand, if Sherwood had stated that he was interested in purchasing breeding cows, and thought that Rose could be made to breed, while the Walkers assumed otherwise, the parties obviously did not intend such a condition. We can understand the disagreement between the majority and dissent in *Sherwood* based on these alternative views of the facts. The majority clearly believed the facts were closer to the Wendy's example, but the dissent favored the interpretation that Sherwood wanted to purchase a breeder.

Suppose the parties never discussed Rose's qualities and, in fact, never even thought about this issue. The court must then wrestle with the question of whether to imply a condition precedent of Rose's infertility as a matter of law. We saw in Chapter 7 the several sources of gap fillers available to the court, including economic analysis, fairness, and other instrumental reasons.[34] On fairness grounds, for example, a court would have to compare the parties' positions if the court enforces the contract with their positions if it does not. If the court enforces the contract, Sherwood gets a cow worth at least $750 for $80. The Walkers lose at least $670, or more if you consider that they paid $850 for Rose. If the court refuses to enforce the contract, Sherwood loses a windfall of $670. The $670 is a windfall because, under the assumption that the parties never thought about Rose's attributes, Sherwood's skill in evaluating Rose or his bargaining prowess did not contribute to his achieving the large gain. If the court rescinds the contract, the Walkers continue to own an asset that is worth about what they paid for it. A good argument can therefore be made that the fair result is to find an implied-in-law condition precedent of Rose's infertility and to grant the Walkers relief. (We will look at how economic analysis helps fill gaps shortly.)[35]

The question of whether contracting parties made what we are calling a "legal mistake" comes up in lots of different contexts. Each calls for a difficult determination of whether the parties contracted on the basis of the perceived truth of certain facts or whether the parties were gambling over them. For example, people suing for injuries in auto or other accidents often agree to releases after the defendant's insurance company pays them a sum of money.[36] Suppose Alice is in an auto accident and breaks her arm.

34. See Chapter 7 at notes 118–138, and accompanying text.

35. See infra notes 49–51, and accompanying text.

36. E.g. McWaters v. Parker, 995 F.2d 1366, 1370 (7th Cir. 1993) ("A valid release bars a claimant from bringing a subsequent cause of action on the claim he released."); see also Matlock v.

She agrees to a release after the insurance company pays her $1000. Complications then develop and Alice's arm falls off. Medical costs alone amount to over $100,000. Is Alice entitled to relief under the doctrine of mutual material mistake?

At first blush you might say (at least I would) that, although both parties thought she had only a $1000 injury (mutuality requirement satisfied) and that the difference between her apparent and actual injuries were material (more than 100 times as large), contract law should not excuse Alice from her release because the parties were not legally mistaken. Everyone knows that complications can develop after an injury and that a release allocates the risk of additional complications to Alice. Put another way, the parties gambled over whether the injury was worth more or less than $1000 and Alice lost the gamble.

This is the approach most courts have taken.[37] However, when new injuries come to light that are sufficiently catastrophic and unforeseeable, some courts have been more receptive to a mistake argument.[38] The following reasoning supports such a result. Alice and the insurance company gambled over some degree of unknown risk, for example, the amount of time for her arm to heal, but they did not intend for Alice to take the risk of unknowable and catastrophic injuries. Granting relief to Alice in this situation should not threaten the reliability of releases because the reasoning would apply only in rare instances.

There is one situation in which a person who has sustained personal injuries has been quite successful in avoiding releases. I'm

National Union Fire Ins. Co., 925 F.Supp. 468, 475 (E. D. Tex. 1996) (doubting validity of release because it was "unlikely that a plaintiff who was seeking $25,000 and who agreed to settle the claim for $2,500 intended to foreclose her option to seek a judicial remedy for any subsequent noncompliance.").

37. See, e.g., Christensen v. Oshkosh Truck Corp., 12 F.3d 980, 989 (10th Cir. 1993) (holding that a release showed defendant "assumed the risk of all consequences arising from the known injury to his head, including any unforeseen consequences of that injury."); Gumberts v. Greenberg, 115 N.E.2d 504, 507 (Ind. Ct. App. 1953) ("[A]s a general rule, where the intention to settle for unknown injuries is clearly expressed, and there is no fraud or over-reaching involved, the release is a bar to recovery for injuries subsequently discovered.");

Anderson v. Oregon Short Line R. Co., 155 P. 446, 448 (Utah 1916) ("a release include[s] all the consequences of that accident. If such were not the law, a single cause of action could be split up into a number of actions.").

38. Reynolds v. Merrill, 460 P.2d 323, 324 (Utah 1969) (holding court must "distinguish between an unknown injury and unknown consequences of a known injury. The former can be the basis of a mutual mistake of fact, while the latter would be only a mistake of opinion."); Nygard v. Minneapolis St. Ry. Co., 179 N.W. 642, 643 (Minn. 1920) ("[P]arties in settling had in mind only the superficial bruises received in the accident and of which they had knowledge, and that the amount paid was to compensate merely for the loss of wages likely to result therefrom. There was no compromise of a disputed claim or of unknown injuries.").

thinking of the unfortunate situation where the injured party does not know she is injured at all at the time of signing the release. Later, she learns the truth and seeks compensation for her injuries. Courts may grant relief under the theory of mutual, material, mistake.[39]

B.   Impossibility of Performance

1.   Objective impossibility. First we study "objective" impossibility, meaning that the promisor literally cannot perform because of circumstances beyond the promisor's control. Then we will turn to "subjective" impossibility, where performance is impossible, but the promisor is somehow responsible for her plight.[40] Sorry, no relief to the silly promisor in the latter case.

Suppose on January 2, the owner of a music hall rents the hall to Eminem for a performance on April 2, for a rental fee of $5000. The contract says nothing about what happens if the music hall burns down. On March 30—you guessed it—the hall does burn down.[41] Is the music hall owner liable to Eminem for breach of contract when she cannot provide the hall for his singing (if that is what I should call what Eminem does)?

The parties wrongly assumed that the music hall would be in existence on April 2. When a supervening event, like the fire, makes performance impossible, contract law may excuse performance under the doctrine of "impossibility of performance." But just as not every mistake excuses performance, not every event that makes performance impossible brings relief. The court first asks whether the parties allocated the risk of the event, like the fire, either expressly or impliedly in the contract. Further, if they didn't contemplate the occurrence of the event at all, courts must fill the gap for the parties. This set of inquiries is no different than the implied-terms analysis discussed previously under the mutual mistake rubric.[42]

---

39. Bennett v. Shinoda Floral, Inc., 739 P.2d 648, 653 (Wash. 1987) (en banc) ("When a person signs a release of all claims and has no knowledge that he has any personal injury ... it is supportable to permit avoidance of the release once it is found that the release was not executed fairly and knowingly."); Denton v. Utley, 86 N.W.2d 537, 542 (Mich. 1957) ("A releasor who believes he is without personal injuries, or that he has certain minor injuries only, and who, secure in his belief, executes a general release, will not be bound by it if other and more serious injuries are discovered later.").

40. See Columbian Nat. Title Ins. Co. v. Township Title Services, Inc., 659 F.Supp. 796, 802 (D. Kan. 1987) ("A distinction is drawn between impracticability that is 'subjective' and 'objective.' This has been described as the difference, respectively, between 'I cannot do it' and 'the thing cannot be done.' Only objective impracticability will relieve a party of its contractual obligation.").

41. See Taylor v. Caldwell, 122 Eng. Rep. 309, 311, 3 B & S 826, 830 (Q.B. 1863).

42. See supra notes 30–39, and accompanying text.

a. Express risk allocation. I've already told you that the music-hall contract did not contain an express allocation of the risk of the music hall burning down. Of course, resolution of the case would be easy if it did. If the contract stated that "music hall promises to furnish the hall to Eminem on April 2, but if the music hall burns down before that date, music hall has no liability to Eminem," a court should enforce this condition subsequent.[43] The music hall owner would not be liable to Mr. Eminem.

Express clauses such as above are often called *"force majeure"* clauses. Such terms excuse promisors in case of natural catastrophes, such as fires, earthquakes, or hurricanes—you get the picture. *Force majeure* clauses often also excuse promisors in case of war, governmental regulation, or labor strikes. For that matter, parties can condition a promisor's performance on the non-occurrence of any event they choose. One caveat, however. Courts construe *force majeure* terms rather narrowly, meaning that if the disruption is not within the meaning of the clause, a court is not likely to include it by analogy.[44]

b. Implied-in-fact risk allocation. In the absence of an express allocation of the risk of a fire, the court will look for factual evidence to determine whether the parties nonetheless intended to release the music hall owner if fire destroyed the hall.[45] Sources of interpretation discussed in Chapter 7, such as the parties' negotiations and purposes, trade custom, and course of dealing, are helpful in determining the parties' intentions.[46] Remember also that courts prefer to decide cases based on the parties' intentions and may

---

43. For a discussion of conditions subsequent, see Chapter 8 at note 50, and accompanying text.

44. Kel Kim Corp. v. Central Markets, Inc., 519 N.E.2d 295, 296 (N.Y. 1987) ("Ordinarily, only if the *force majeure* clause specifically includes the event that actually prevents a party's performance will that party be excused."); see also Seitz v. Mark–O–Lite Sign Contractors, Inc., 510 A.2d 319, 321 (N.J. Super Ct. Law Div. 1986) ("[T]he catch-all language of the force *majeure* clause relied upon by defendant is not to be construed to its widest extent; rather, such language is to be narrowly interpreted as contemplating only events or things of the same general nature or class as those specifically enumerated.").

45. See Taylor v. Caldwell, 122 Eng. Rep. 309, 312, 3 B & S 826, 834 (Q. B. 1863) ("There seems little doubt that [excusing performance when the foundation of the contract becomes impossible] tends to further the great object of making the legal construction such as to fulfil the intention of those who entered into the contract."); see also McGhee v. Arabian American Oil Co., 871 F.2d 1412, 1419 (9th Cir. 1989) ("A court looks to the contract for an express or implied allocation of risks where circumstances beyond a party's control cause it to breach a contract.").

46. See Chapter 7 at notes 70–99, and accompanying text; see also Trans-

strain to find them, because they feel uncomfortable filling gaps. After all, the parties, not the courts are supposed to draft contracts. Courts therefore may speak of the parties' intentions even when the evidence is far from clear that the parties even thought about the matter.

c.   Implied-in-law risk allocation. In *Taylor v. Caldwell*, an old classic closely resembling my Eminem hypo, the court observed that the parties did not consider the possibility of the hall burning down when they wrote the agreement: "The parties when framing their agreement evidently had not present to their minds the possibility of such a disaster * * *."[47] Instead of finding the parties' intentions, the court filled the gap by asking how the parties *would have* allocated the risk of the fire had they thought about the issue. Specifically, the court thought that the parties would have excused the music hall owner. In language that some courts still use today, the court labeled the existence of the music hall the "foundation" of the contract, and held that the parties would have excused the music hall owner if the "foundation" was destroyed.[48]

Thus, the "foundation" inquiry requires courts to fill gaps first by finding the purpose of the contract and then by presuming the parties would call off the contract if that purpose (foundation) was destroyed. This approach, which requires the court to determine what the parties would have wanted, leaves much to the court's discretion and makes the results hard to predict. Courts therefore may turn to other sources of gap filling.

We have seen that another source of judicial gap filling is based on economic efficiency.[49] Some lawyer-economists assert that courts should fill gaps by supplying the rule the parties would have wanted. Unlike the court's analysis in *Taylor*, however, the economic approach seeks to place the risk of unanticipated events more scientifically on the "superior risk bearer" or the "superior risk avoider" because that is what the parties would have wanted.[50] For example, the "superior risk bearer" is the party better able to

atlantic Fin. Corp. v. United States, 363 F.2d 312, 316 (D.C. Cir. 1966) ("Proof that the risk of a contingency's occurrence has been allocated may be expressed in or implied from the agreement. Such proof may also be found in the surrounding circumstances, including custom and usages of the trade.").

47. Taylor v. Caldwell, 122 Eng. Rep. 309, 312, 3 B & S 826, 833 (Q.B. 1863).

48. Id.

49. See Chapter 7 at notes 119–125, and accompanying text.

50. See Richard Posner and Andrew M. Rosenfield, Impossibility and Related Doctrines in Contract Law: An Economic Analysis, 6 J. Legal Stud. 83, 97–104 (1977).

bear the risk, such as by purchasing insurance.[51] Because the music hall owner can purchase fire insurance, this source of gap filling suggests the music hall owner should bear the risk of the hall's demise. Impossibility therefore would not be a defense for the music hall under this approach.

d. The Restatement (Second) and the Uniform Commercial Code. The Restatement (Second) of Contracts and the UCC contain impossibility provisions.[52] The Restatement excuses a promisor when a person "necessary for the performance of a duty" dies or is so incapacitated that performance is impracticable.[53] In such cases, the Restatement declares that the death or incapacity "is an event the non-occurrence of which was a basic assumption" of the contract.[54] This rule constitutes a default or gap-filling rule that assigns the risk of the necessary person's death or incapacity to the promisee. The Restatement (Second) also excuses a promisor when a "thing" necessary for performance fails "to come into existence," is destroyed, or deteriorates sufficiently to make performance impracticable.[55] The UCC section 2–613 excuses a seller of goods when the goods are identified to the contract at the time of

51. In re Brame, 23 B.R. 196, 201 (Bankr. W.D. Ky. 1982) ("Economic analysis of loss-shifting suggests that losses should be borne by the 'superior risk-bearer'—a designation given, in the esoteric parlance of economics, to the party to a transaction who is in the best position to appraise the nature and extent of risks contractually assumed and the possibility of losses resulting from their occurrence."); Transatlantic, 363 F.2d at 319 ("[Plaintiff] Transatlantic was no less able than the [defendant] to purchase insurance to cover the contingency's occurrence. If anything, it is more reasonable to expect owner-operators of vessels to insure against the hazards of war.").

52. Restatement (Second) of Contracts §§ 262, 263; UCC § 2–613.

53. Restatement (Second) of Contracts § 262; see also Cazares v. Saenz, 256 Cal.Rptr. 209, 212 (Cal. Ct. App. 1989) ("Where a contract contemplates the personal services of a party, performance is excused when that party dies or becomes otherwise incapable of performing.").

54. Restatement (Second) of Contracts § 262; see also Seitz v. Mark–O–Lite Sign Contractors, Inc., 510 A.2d 319, 322 (N.J. Super. Ct.1986) ("[T]he

primary application of the impossibility defense in the form asserted by defendant is in the area of personal service contracts, that is, contracts which contemplate the peculiar skill or discretion of a particular person.").

55. Restatement (Second) of Contracts § 263; see also Opera Co. of Boston, Inc. v. Wolf Trap Foundation for the Performing Arts, 817 F.2d 1094, 1102 (4th Cir. 1987) ("[T]he existence of electric power was necessary for the satisfactory performance by the Opera Company.... Such findings meet the requirement of Restatement (Second) on Contracts § 263 for an event, the 'non-occurrence of which was a basic assumption on which the contract was made ... ' "); Bissell v. L. W. Edison Co., 156 N.W.2d 623, 626 (Mich. Ct. App. 1967) ("[T]he essence of the modern defense of impossibility is that the promised performance was at the making of the contract, or thereafter became, impracticable owing to some extreme or unreasonable difficulty, expense, injury, or loss involved, rather than that it is scientifically or actually impossible.") (citing 6 Samuel Williston & George Thompson, A Treatise on the Law of Contracts § 1931 (rev. ed 1936)).

contracting and then, before the risk passes to the buyer,[56] they "suffer casualty" through no fault of the parties.[57] Consider, for example, a grower who has agreed to sell certain wheat to a grain elevator, but a violent flood destroys the wheat before harvesting. Under section 2–613, a court could excuse the grower. However, if the contract does not specify which wheat crop the grower will sell, the UCC does not protect the grower (because the goods are not identified to the contract).[58]

2. Subjective impossibility. Here's a kind of impossibility that will *not* excuse a promisor. Suppose a supplier of molasses promises to deliver "1,500,000 wine gallons * * * of the usual run from the National Sugar Refinery."[59] National fails to produce a sufficient quantity of molasses and the purchaser sues when the supplier delivers only about 344,000 gallons. The supplier claims impossibility of performance because National Sugar fell down on the job!

If the supplier could have assured a sufficient quantity of molasses by contracting with National Sugar and failed to do so, the supplier's impossibility claim will fail even though it is literally impossible for the supplier to perform.[60] This is because the shortfall was the "fault" of the supplier, who did not secure the contract with National Sugar. Because other suppliers, acting reasonably, would have obtained a contract with National Sugar and therefore could have performed, contract law calls our supplier's impossibility "subjective" rather than "objective."[61]

The supplier's failed impossibility defense can also be seen as interpretation of an implied condition. The parties impliedly conditioned the supplier's performance on National Sugar producing enough molasses, provided that the supplier did everything reason-

---

56. See UCC §§ 2–509, 2–510 (risk of loss).

57. UCC § 2–613; see also Windows, Inc. v. Jordan Panel Sys. Corp., 177 F.3d 114, 116 (2d Cir. 1999) ("Because the goods suffered casualty 'without fault of either party,' Section 2–613(b) was found to bar [purchaser's] suit...."); Red River Commodities v. Eidsness, 459 N.W.2d 805, 807 (N.D. 1990) ("Impossibility caused by casualty or commercial impracticability caused by failure of presupposed conditions excuses performance of contracts for sale of goods."); Conway v. Larsen Jewelers, Inc., 429 N.Y.S.2d 378, 380 (N.Y. Civ. Ct. 1980) ("When the subject matter of a contract is destroyed (or, as in this case, stolen) through no fault of the seller, the contract is deemed avoided.").

58. Clark v. Wallace County Co-op. Equity Exch., 986 P.2d 391, 393 (Kan. Ct. App. 1999) ("[A] seller of grain is not excused by [UCC provisions] from the delivery performance specified in an agreement of this nature when the grain is not identified by a specific tract of land on which it is to be grown."); Bunge Corp. v. Recker, 519 F.2d 449, 451 (8th Cir. 1975) ("[A]ppellee could have fulfilled its contractual obligation by acquiring the beans from any place or source as long as they were grown within the United States.").

59. Canadian Industrial Alcohol Co. v. Dunbar Molasses Co., 179 N.E. 383, 384 (N.Y. 1932).

60. Id. at 384.

61. Farnsworth, supra note 23, at 651.

able to assure that National Sugar would produce a sufficient supply. This implication arises because of the purpose of the contract between the purchaser and the supplier. After all, why contract with a supplier if the supplier is not going to try to get a commitment for the product?[62] Alternatively, the court could justify the holding as gap-filling, finding that the parties would have constructed such a condition had they bargained over the matter.

C. Impracticability of Performance

Suppose a supervening event does not make performance impossible, but it dramatically increases the promisor's cost of performance. Contract law also recognizes an excuse in this situation. Early cases recognized that absolute impossibility was too narrow a ground for relief: " 'A thing is impossible in legal contemplation when it is not practicable; and a thing is impracticable when it can only be done at an excessive and unreasonable cost.' "[63]

Consider again the example with which we opened this chapter: An oil supplier seeks relief from a long-term, fixed-price contract to supply oil to an electric utility after an international disruption in oil supply causes the price of oil to skyrocket. Assume, for example, that oil becomes ten times more expensive for the supplier to import. Because this contract involves the sale of goods, the UCC would apply. Section 2–615(a) sets forth the standard of impracticability, and also serves as a model in non-sale of goods cases.[64] The section provides in part:

> Delay in delivery or non-delivery in whole or in part by a seller * * * is not a breach of his duty under a contract for sale if performance as agreed has been made impracticable by the occurrence of a contingency the non-occurrence of which was a basic assumption on which the contract was made * * *.[65]

You can see that section 2–615 requires that performance is "impracticable" and that the parties erred over their "basic assumption" that a contingency causing the impracticability would

62. Canadian Industrial Alcohol, 179 N.E. at 384 ("If the plaintiff had been so informed, it would very likely have preferred to deal with the refinery directly, instead of dealing with a middleman.").

63. Mineral Park Land Co. v. Howard, 156 P. 458, 460 (Cal. 1916) (quoting 1 Charles Fisk Beach, A Treatise on the Modern Law of Contracts, § 216 (1897)); Natus Corp. v. United States, 371 F.2d 450, 456 (Ct. Cl. 1967) ("[S]omething is impracticable when it can only be done

at an excessive and unreasonable cost."); see also Restatement (Second) of Contracts §§ 262, 263.

64. See Restatement (Second) of Contracts § 261; Moyer v. Little Falls, 510 N.Y.S.2d 813, 814 (N.Y. Sup. Ct. 1986) ("[UCC 2–615] has been applied in non-commercial cases.... [S]uch a provision suggests an underlying policy of the law to protect a contracting party from unforeseeable hardships.").

65. UCC § 2–615(a).

not occur.[66] Comment 4 to the section nicely fills out the meaning of these requirements:

> Increased cost alone does not excuse performance unless the rise in cost is due to some unforeseen contingency which alters the essential nature of the performance. Neither is a rise or a collapse in the market in itself a justification, for that is exactly the type of business risk which business contracts made at fixed prices are intended to cover. But a severe shortage of raw materials or of supplies due to a contingency such as war, embargo, local crop failure, unforeseen shutdown of major sources of supply or the like, which either causes a marked increase in cost or altogether prevents the seller form securing supplies necessary to his performance is within the contemplation of this section.[67]

Let's look further at the elements of impracticability of performance both in sale-of-goods and other contexts.

1. Impracticability. Together section 2–615 and comment 4 suggest that a very serious disruption must occur ("alters the essential nature;" "severe shortage;" "prevents the seller from securing supplies necessary to performance").[68] Foreseeable moderate changes in market prices or in the promisor's financial situation alone should not be enough for a finding of impracticability because these are precisely the kinds of risks that parties expect to take when they enter contracts.[69] In our problem, the price of oil inflates

---

66. See Aluminum Co. of America v. Essex Group, Inc., 499 F.Supp. 53, 71 n.11 (W.D. Pa. 1980) ("Where, after a contract is made, a party's performance is made impracticable without his fault by the occurrence of an event the non-occurrence of which was a basic assumption on which the contract was made, his duty to render that performance is discharged, unless the language or the circumstances indicate the contrary."); Mishara Constr. Co., Inc. v. Transit–Mixed Concrete Corp., 310 N.E.2d 363, 367 (Mass. 1974) (" 'The important question is whether an unanticipated circumstance has made performance of the promise vitally different from what should reasonably have been within the contemplation of both parties when they entered into the contract. If so, the risk should not fairly be thrown upon the promisor.' ") (quoting 6 Samuel Williston & George Thompson, A Treatise on the Law of Contracts § 1931 (rev. ed. 1936)).

67. UCC § 2–615, cmt. 4.

68. See Karl Wendt Farm Equip. Co. v. International Harvester Co., 931 F.2d 1112 (6th Cir. 1991) ("unreasonable and extreme" downturn in market required); Lawrance v. Elmore Bean Warehouse, Inc., 702 P.2d 930, 933 (Idaho Ct. App. 1985) ("The language of [UCC 2–615] comment 4 makes it incumbent upon [defendant] to show it can operate only at a loss and that loss will be so severe and unreasonable that failure to excuse performance would result in a grave injustice.").

69. Karl Wendt Farm Equip., 931 F.2d at 1117–18 (quoting Restatement (Second) of Contracts § 261, cmt. b); Columbian Nat'l. Title Ins. Co. v. Township Title Servs., Inc., 659 F.Supp. 796, 803 (D. Kan. 1987) ("When the contingency in question is sufficiently foreshadowed at the time of contracting, the contingency may be considered among the business risks that are regarded as

by a factor of ten, which courts usually find sufficient to satisfy the impracticability test.[70]

2. Basic assumption. For a court to find impracticability, the parties' basic assumption must be that the major disruption would not occur. This second requirement, as applied to our problem, boils down to the issue of whether the parties allocated the risk of the oil shortage expressly or impliedly in fact to the supplier, or whether they contracted on the assumption that such an oil disruption would not happen. If the facts support a finding that the parties intended to place the risk on the supplier, the court will not excuse the supplier on the basis of impracticability.[71] If the court believes a basic assumption of the parties was that there would be no such disruption (and the disruption is severe enough), the court will grant relief.[72] In the latter case, courts recognize that "[i]t is implicit * * * that certain risks are so unusual and have such severe consequences that they must have been beyond the scope of the assignment of risks inherent in the contract, that is, beyond the agreement made by the parties."[73]

What are the sources of evidence that would suggest that the parties did in fact allocate the risk of the disruption to the supplier? Foreseeability of the risk plays a large role in lots of cases.[74] If the parties reasonably should foresee a coming major disruption in oil supply and the supplier did not protect itself in the contract, many courts would say that the supplier must have intended to accept

part of the negotiated terms of the contract, either consciously or as a matter of reasonable, commercial interpretation from the circumstances.").

70. Mineral Park Land Co. v. Howard, 156 P. 458, 459 (Cal. 1916) ("[Complete performance would be possible] only at a prohibitive cost, that is, at an expense of 10 or 12 times as much as the usual cost per yard."); see also American Trading & Prod. Corp. v. Shell Int'l Marine, Ltd, 453 F.2d 939, 942–43 (2d Cir. 1972) ("[The] additional expense involved ... an increase of less than one third ... is not sufficient to constitute commercial impracticability....").

71. Cf. Agriculture Revolving Loan Fund v. Carpenter, 869 P.2d 1181,1184 (Alaska 1994) ("The disclaimers in the land sale contracts disclaim any warranty as to the soil condition or profitability of the land purchased by [defendant].... [Defendant] assumed the risk of the condition of the land that he purchased."); City of Littleton v. Employers Fire Ins. Co., 453 P.2d 810, 814–15 (Colo. 1969) ("The exception to the defense of impossibility is applicable

where, on an interpretation of the contract in the light of accompanying circumstances and usages, the risk of impossibility due to presently unknown facts is clearly assumed by the promisor.").

72. Restatement (Second) of Contracts § 261, cmt. b.

73. Mishara Constr. Co. v. Transit–Mixed Concrete Corp., 310 N.E.2d 363, 367 (Mass. 1974).

74. E.g., Roy v. Stephen Pontiac–Cadillac, Inc., 543 A.2d 775, 778 (Conn. App. Ct. 1988) ("If the risk of the occurrence of the contingency was unforeseeable, the seller cannot be said to have assumed that risk. If the risk of the occurrence of the contingency was foreseeable, that risk is tacitly assigned to the seller."); Waldinger Corp. v. CRS Group Engineers, Inc., 775 F.2d 781, 785 (7th Cir. 1985) ("Because the purpose of a contract is to place the reasonable risk of performance upon the promisor, however, it is presumed to have agreed to bear any loss occasioned by an event that was foreseeable at the time of contracting.").

that risk,[75] or at least that the supplier should have protected itself. Thus, the court might draw on a fault-based reason for holding the supplier to the contract.

A caveat is in order with respect to the foreseeability factor, however. As nicely stated in *Transatlantic Financing Corp. v. United States,* "[f]oreseeability or even recognition of a risk does not necessarily prove its allocation. * * * Parties to a contract are not always able to provide for all the possibilities of which they are aware, sometimes because they cannot agree, often simply because they are too busy."[76] Note that the court is saying that, even if a risk is foreseeable or foreseen, the parties did not necessarily intend to place that risk on the promisor. In short, the foreseeability of an event, or the fact that a risk was foreseen, should be probative factors in the risk allocation puzzle, perhaps heavily-weighted ones, but foreseeability should not preclude other inquiries.

What other facts are probative of the parties' actual risk allocation? Perhaps to support the conclusion that the supplier accepted the risk of world events, the purchaser of the oil could prove that it paid a premium (extra) for the oil due to the risk the supplier was accepting. Some courts also believe that the type of contract is probative of risk allocation. For example, courts reason that a fixed-price contract shows that the supplier intended to accept the risk of price increases and the purchaser intended to accept the risk of falling prices.[77] (But the possibility always exists, and this is the maddening thing about impracticability analysis, that the parties did not allocate the risk of *calamitous* rising or falling prices.) Further, the purchaser might try to show that the custom in the trade or the parties' course of dealing prove that suppliers ordinarily accept the risk of disruptions (at least to the extent experienced by the parties).[78]

---

75. Roy, 543 A.2d at 778 ("The seller's failure to provide a contractual excuse against the occurrence of a foreseeable contingency may be deemed to be an assumption of an unconditional obligation to perform."); see also Kel Kim Corp. v. Central Markets, Inc., 519 N.E.2d 295, 296 (N.Y. 1987) ("[T]he impossibility must be produced by an unanticipated event that could not have been foreseen or guarded against in the contract.").

76. Transatlantic Fin. Corp. v. United States, 363 F.2d 312, 318 (D.C. Cir 1966).

77. Golsen v. ONG Western, Inc., 756 P.2d 1209, 1213 (Okla. 1988) ("The defendant acquires a contractually-as-sured supply while the plaintiffs are assured a market; both parties doing so at a price which is an agreed part of the bargain."); see also Northern Indiana Pub. Serv. Co. v. Carbon County Coal Co., 799 F.2d 265, 267 (7th Cir. 1986) ("[Buyer] was eager to have an assured supply of low-sulphur coal and was therefore willing to guarantee both price and quantity.").

78. Cf. Colley v. Bi–State, Inc., 586 P.2d 908, 911 (Wash. Ct. App. 1978) ("Here, the agreement was supplemented by evidence of trade usage that parties to this type of agreement intend to be bound regardless of the success of the seller's crop. . . .").

Thus far we have focused on our supplier's plight and, therefore, the rights of sellers of goods to claim impracticability. But as should be clear, impracticability applies to other kinds of contracts,[79] and, for that matter, to purchasers of goods.[80] For an example of the latter, a buyer might claim impracticability when it agreed to excavate and purchase gravel from a landowner, only to find out that a large part of the gravel was under water and would be more than ten times the expected cost to excavate.[81] I know, I know, this is really a mistake example. The location of the gravel, underwater or not, was a situation that existed at the time of contracting, not a supervening event. But the court entertaining these facts treated the problem as one of impracticability (showing that these doctrines overlap).[82] In fact, the case is often cited as an early authority supporting the impracticability excuse.

D.   Frustration of Purpose

Impracticability cases involve grounds for excusing performance because an unanticipated event dramatically increases the cost of performance. What happens if the cost of performance does not change, but the value of what a party is going to receive drastically decreases? The famous case of *Krell v. Henry*[83] deals with this issue. Henry saw Krell's advertisement to rent his suite to view the King's coronation procession and entered an agreement with Krell to use the suite for two days during the coronation. The King became ill and the procession did not take place. Did Henry have to honor his contract nonetheless?

Notice that Henry's duty under the contract did not become more expensive due to the King's illness and the lack of a coronation procession. However, what Henry was to receive, the value of the rooms, dramatically decreased for that reason. Although the contract did not expressly state that Henry's purpose in renting the rooms was to view the procession, the court admitted parol evidence showing that purpose and found that viewing the procession was the "foundation" of the contract.[84] Further, the court excused Henry because "a state of things * * * essential to [contract]

79. See, e.g., Cape–France Enters. v. Estate of Peed, 29 P.3d 1011 (Mont. 2001) (sale of land); Marcovich Land Co. v. J.J. Newberry Co., 413 N.E.2d 935 (Ind. Ct. App. 1980) (lease); Bissell v. L. W. Edison Co., 156 N.W.2d 623 (Mich. Ct. App. 1967) (construction contract).

80. UCC § 2–615, cmt. 9; Lawrance v. Elmore Bean Warehouse, 702 P.2d 930, 933 (Idaho Ct. App. 1985) (purchaser not excused).

81. Mineral Park Land Co. v. Howard, 156 P. 458, 459 (Cal. 1916).

82. Id. at 460 ("But, where the difference in cost is so great as here, and has the effect, as found, of making performance impracticable, the situation is not different from that of a total absence of earth and gravel.").

83. Krell v. Henry, 2 K.B. 740 (Eng. C.A. 1903).

84. 2 K.B. at 749 ("[I]t is said that the condition or state of things need not be expressly specified, but that it is sufficient if that condition or state of things clearly appears by extrinsic evidence to

performance perishe[d] or fail[ed] to be in existence," and this failure "cannot reasonably be said to have been the contemplation of the parties at the date of the contract."[85] This analysis once again is reminiscent of the other excuse doctrines in that it asks whether the parties' allocated the risk of the supervening event, here the King's illness and cancellation of the procession. All of the usual suspects come into play in answering this question. Was such an illness and cancellation foreseeable? Should Henry have "guard[ed] against" it?[86] Did Henry have other use for the rooms, or was viewing the procession the only purpose? In fact, the court cites *Taylor v. Caldwell*, an impossibility case (you remember, the music hall burned down and the court declared performance impossible), as authority for granting Henry relief.[87]

The challenge in frustration cases (as well as in the other excuse domains) is drawing the line between events sufficiently unforeseeable and serious to justify granting relief and events not meeting these criteria. Contrast *Krell v. Henry*, for example, with another venerable case, *Lloyd v. Murphy*.[88] Murphy received no relief even though his five-year lease of a location "for the sole purpose of conducting thereon the business of displaying and selling new automobiles * * * and for no other purpose whatsoever" (except for an "occasional sale of a used automobile") was impaired by a federal government order that first halted and then restricted the sale of new automobiles.[89] The court thought that Murphy's hardship was insufficiently extreme because, with restrictions, he could continue to sell new cars. Further, the regulation restricting cars sales during World War II was foreseeable, even anticipated, at the time the parties contracted. In fact, at that time "[a]utomobile sales were soaring because the public anticipated that production would soon be restricted."[90] Clearly Henry's frustration claim was therefore more compelling, both in terms of the magnitude of the disruption and the lack of foreseeability of the supervening event. The latter observation, of course, requires the belief that the parties reasonably could not anticipate that the King could become so ill he would postpone the coronation.

E. Remedies After a Finding of Excuse

Now we look at the question of what relief, if any, a court should grant to a party after the court has excused the other party

have been assumed by the parties to be the foundation or basis of the contract, and the event which causes the impossibility is of such a character that it cannot reasonably be supposed to have been in the contemplation of the contracting parties when the contract was made. In such a case the contracting parties will not be held bound. . . .").

85. Id. at 751, 754.

86. Id. at 752.

87. Id. at 752, 753, see supra notes 47–51, and accompanying text.

88. 153 P.2d 47 (Cal. 1944).

89. Id. at 48–49.

90. Id. at 51.

from performing a contract. Suppose for example, you contract to construct a screen porch on the back of Alice's house for $10,000. You purchase all of the materials for the construction, spending $1000 before new zoning regulations prohibit the construction of such porches. (This is unusual, but just go with the hypo.) You are a litigious sort and you sue Alice for breach of contract after she refuses to pay you anything. The court excuses Alice from the contract on the basis of impossibility (it would be illegal for you to build the porch.).[91] This means that you cannot recover your lost profit on the porch project. But what about your $1000 reliance loss?

1. Judicial approach. Courts have not decided this remedial issue uniformly. Some courts simply "leave the parties where they find them" after declaring an excuse, meaning neither party gets anything once the court calls off the contract.[92] Under this approach, you can not recover the $1000. Other courts allow restitution claims, but your $1000 of expenses did not benefit Alice so you're out of luck in those jurisdictions as well.[93] Some courts do allow reliance recoveries, but the grounds for recovery may vary. Some of the possibilities: You can recover, but only for the work and supplies "wrought into" (incorporated in) the structure.[94] Al-

---

91. Quagliana v. Exquisite Home Builders, Inc., 538 P.2d 301, 306–07 (Utah 1975) ("Since the performance for which the parties had bargained—the construction of a house with a view of the valley, in accordance with the plans and specifications and in conformity with all zoning ordinances and restrictive covenants—was impossible from its inception, the sole remedy available to Exquisite for reimbursement was restitution.").

92. 20th Century Lites, Inc. v. Goodman, 149 P.2d 88, 92 (Cal. App. Dep't Super. Ct. 1944) ("[B]oth parties thereto were excused from further performance."); Butterfield v. Byron, 27 N.E. 667, 667 (Mass. 1891) ("destruction of [house] without the fault of either of the parties will excuse performance of the contract, and leave no right of recovery of damages in favor of either against the other.") (citing Taylor v. Caldwell, 122 Eng. Rep. 309 (Q.B. 1863)); see also Andrew Kull, Mistake, Frustration, and the Windfall Principle of Contract Remedies, 43 Hastings L. Rev. 1, 1 ("A sub-

stantial body of case law supports an important but unacknowledged rule of contract doctrine: that the proper legal response to certain problems resulting from contracts that are 'incomplete' ... is to leave the parties alone.").

93. Lichtenfels v. Bridgeview Coal Co., 531 A.2d 22, 26 (Pa. Super. Ct. 1987) ("'[A] party whose duty of performance is discharged due to impracticability 'is entitled to restitution for any benefit that he has conferred on the other party by way of part performance or reliance....'") (quoting Restatement (Second) of Contracts § 377); Quagliana, 538 P.2d 301, 307 ("Where a loss is caused by impossibility or frustration neither party can be compelled to pay for the other's disappointed expectations, but neither can be allowed to profit from the situation; one must pay for what one has received.").

94. Albre Marble and Tile Co. v. John Bowen Co., 155 N.E.2d 437, 439–40 (Mass. 1959) (citing Young v. Chicopee, 72 N.E. 63 (Mass. 1904)); see also Angus v. Scully, 57 N.E. 674, 674 (Mass. 1900) ("[W]here one is to make repairs

ternatively, you can recover for any *essential reliance*, meaning reliance "made pursuant to the specific request" of the party being excused "as set forth" in the contract.[95] Finally, you can recover, but only if Alice was somehow at fault in causing the event that excuses performance.[96] This, of course, is not the case in our hypo. But in another case where a general contractor's bid was irregular and the general contractor therefore lost the main contract, a court held that the subcontractor could recover for its reliance loss even though the court declared the contract impossible to perform.[97]

The Restatement (Second) of Contracts grants court lots of flexibility in determining remedial issues after an excuse finding. Restatement sections 158 and 272 provide that:

Relief Including Restitution

(1) In any case governed by the rules [of mistake, impracticability and frustration], either party may have a claim for relief including restitution * * *.

(2) * * * [I]f those rules * * * will not avoid injustice, the court may grant relief on such terms as justice requires including protection of the parties' reliance interests.

Under the Restatement, you have a fighting chance to recover your $1000, but the court has lots of discretion to decide one way or the other. In terms of "justice," you can argue that you spent the $1000 in a good faith belief that the contract would go through and, since you cannot recover your profit, awarding $1,000 to you is a fair compromise. On the other hand, Alice can assert that you accepted the risk of supervening zoning regulations that would make performance impossible.

---

or do any other work on the house of another under a special contract, and his contract becomes impossible of performance on account of the destruction of the house without any fault on his part, then he may recover for what he has done.").

95. Albre Marble, 155 N.E.2d at 440; M. Ahern Co. v. John Bowen Co., 133 N.E.2d 484, 487 (Mass. 1956) (" 'It is enough that [a party] has actually received in part performance of the contract something for which when completed he had agreed to pay a price.' ") (citing 6 Samuel Williston & Geroge

Thompson, A Treatise on the Law of Contracts § 1976 (rev. ed. 1936).

96. Boston Plate & Window Glass Co. v. John Bowen Co., 141 N.E.2d 715, 718 (Mass. 1957) ("In order for the plaintiff to recover for breach of the subcontracts, it must appear not only that the impossibility was caused by the defendant but also that, except for the defendant's conduct, there would have been in existence valid and enforceable contracts.").

97. Albre Marble, 155 N.E.2d at 441.

2. Judicial reformation after an unanticipated event.
We have now seen that courts sometimes excuse a party from
performance and give limited relief or no relief to the other party,
even when that other party is severely disappointed by recognition
of the excuse. For example, you will not be very happy when a court
declares your screen-porch construction contract unenforceable if
you stood to make a handsome profit from its completion. While
reading this chapter, perhaps the thought entered your head that
courts should reform (rewrite) contracts, not only because of a
mistake in setting down the terms of the agreement,[98] but because
of unanticipated circumstances. Indeed, in a crude way that is what
courts do when they award restitution or reliance to a disappointed
party. But why won't courts reform contracts, such as by adjusting
the price of Rose 2d, instead of allowing the Walkers to rescind,[99] or
by requiring the U.S. to pay some, but not all of Transatlantic's
extra expenses for transporting goods along a longer route because
of war?[100]

One now infamous case tried a judicial reformation strategy
with results more calamitous than most of the disruptions in the
cases we have discussed (at least in terms of feedback in the law
reviews and by other courts). *Aluminum Co. of America v. Essex
Group*[101] involved complex facts, but, boiled down, the case amounted to a promise by ALCOA to process aluminum and a promise by
Essex to pay according to a price formula dependent on the whole-
sale price index (WPI). Unexpected cost increases not reflected in
the WPI meant that ALCOA would lose over $75 million under the
contract. Among lots of other things, the court found that "the
shared objectives of the parties with respect to the use of the WPI
have been completely and totally frustrated," and reformed the
pricing provision to allow ALCOA to receive its costs of processing
plus a profit of one cent per pound.[102]

The reaction to this decision was brutal. One leading commen-
tator of the time called the court's decision "bizarre."[103] Most of the
criticism centered around the accusation that the court did not
have the expertise or the power to rewrite contracts for the parties.[104] Writers who favored court adjustment in some circumstances

98. See supra notes 22–23, and accompanying text.

99. See supra note 5, and accompanying text.

100. See supra note 76, and accompanying text.

101. 499 F.Supp. 53 (W.D. Pa.
1980).

102. Id. at 56.

103. John P. Dawson, Judicial Re-
vision of Frustrated Contracts: The

United States, 64 B.U. L. Rev. 1, 28
(1984).

104. Id. at 37 ("Nothing in their
prior training as lawyers or their experience in directing litigation and giving
coherence to its results will qualify them
to invent viable new designs for disrupt-
ed enterprises, now gone awry, that the
persons most concerned had tried to
construct but without success.").

(o.k., I was one of them[105]) thought that courts could accomplish the task of judicial reformation, at least in some circumstances, and that courts did have the power to do so.

With respect to whether judges were qualified to reform contracts, surely the parties could do a better job themselves. However, when parties cannot agree whether one of them has been excused, or cannot agree on an appropriate adjustment formula, judicial reformation, such as in *ALCOA*, doesn't seem that outlandish. For example, the parties' goals in entering the contract and the contract's express terms may offer guidance concerning how to adjust the contract. ALCOA bargained for a guaranteed market for its services, which it achieved by contracting with Essex Group. Obviously, it also desired to make a profit on the deal. Essex Group sought ALCOA's commitment to perform the processing of Essex Group's aluminum at a reasonable price.[106] Although these are rather broad parameters, and do not tell us very much about the allocation of risk of unanticipated increases in the cost of processing, these purposes do suggest that the parties did not expect one party to face massive losses in performing the contract.

Other guidance also may be available. A court could look to similar contracts made or modified by others under comparable conditions. A court could also investigate documents or statements concerning the purpose of the use of the WPI in the ALCOA contract. For example, if the parties intended the provision to assure that ALCOA made a profit, a court could adjust the contract to ensure such a result.

As a general matter, the argument against judicial reformation based on the lack of judicial competence seems unpersuasive because judges routinely involve themselves in complex cases, apparently with the approval of actors in the legal system. I'm thinking, for example, of the substantive and remedial complexities of securities, patent, and antitrust cases. (Don't worry, you'll get to these in upperclass courses.) Critics of judicial reformation overlook resources available to judges, including special masters, magistrates, and expert witnesses.

As mentioned, critics also claim that courts do not have the power (meaning authority) to adjust a contract for the parties because the strategy restricts the parties' freedom of contract.[107]

---

105. Robert A. Hillman, Court Adjustment of Long–Term Contracts: An Analysis Under Modern Contract Law, 1987 Duke L.J. 1.

106. ALCOA, 499 F.Supp. at 56 ("ALCOA contends that [the price] was intended by the parties to reflect actual changes in the cost of the non-labor items utilized by ALCOA in the production of aluminum ... and has in fact failed to so reflect such changes.").

107. Dawson, supra note 103, at 18 ("If the contract that was previously in force has through frustration ceased to exist, how can the parties to it be com-

But lots of evidence suggests that business parties expect flexibility and cooperation when things go awry in their contracts.[108] More concretely, they expect their contracting counterpart to agree to an adjustment when an unanticipated event means that one of them will suffer losses much greater than either imagined when they made the contract.[109] If the parties reasonably expect adjustment, judicial reformation is only a form of specific performance that supports parties' freedom of contract. Of course, this argument depends on a finding that each party reasonably believed that the other is under a legal duty to be flexible.[110]

If the court finds that the parties did not foresee the magnitude of the problem that has developed and did not allocate its risk, then court reformation does not impinge on the parties' freedom because the parties have left a gap in their agreement. Essex, of course, could have insisted that ALCOA promise to perform under *all* circumstances, in effect making ALCOA an insurer of the contract. In such a case, a court should hold ALCOA to its promise. But in the absence of such a promise, neither party is contractually entitled to any particular resolution of the contract breakdown. The parties' failure to allocate the risk themselves arguably constitutes implicit consent to allow the court to intervene to adjust the agreement for them.

Finally, the criticism of court reformation based on freedom of contract fails to recognize that courts often "make" portions of contracts for the parties. We have seen, for example, that the UCC authorizes courts to fill gaps in contracts based on reasonableness, instructs courts to excise unconscionable terms from contracts, and allows specific performance according to terms the court views as "just." In fact, a UCC comment expressly authorizes judicial reformation in excuse cases.[111] In addition, courts have long adjusted non-sale-of-goods contracts, including covenants not to compete, and land-sale contracts.[112]

Well, I have gotten my gripes about the reaction to judicial reformation off my chest. You should understand, however, that contract law has not, for the most part, taken this step. Remedies for mistake and disruptive supervening events remain limited.

pelled to accept a 'contract' that is manufactured by a court to replace it?").

108. Hillman, supra note 105, at 7–9.

109. See id. at 8, n. 43, citing Brief for Peabody Coal Co. at 21, Missouri Pub. Serv. Co. v. Peabody Coal Co., 583 S.W.2d 721 (Mo. Ct. App.) cert. denied, 444 U.S. 865 (1979) (only two utilities out of over forty refused to adjust after a coal supplier requested relief).

110. Id. at 9.

111. UCC § 2–615, cmt. 6. ("In situations in which neither sense nor justice is served by either answer when the issue is posed in flat terms of 'excuse' or 'no excuse,' adjustment under the various provisions of this Article is necessary....").

112. Hillman, supra note 105, at 29.

Chapter Ten

THIRD PARTIES

Up to now, we have devoted all of our efforts to analyzing the rights of the parties who make a contract (you know, often you and your neighbor, Alice). This chapter focuses on the rights of other parties, namely those who did not make the contract, called third parties. Part of the challenge of this topic is determining *which* third parties have rights under a contract made by others. In Chapter 1, I offered the example of a contract between a city and a manufacturer that regulated the amount of pollution emitted from the manufacturer's plant.[1] Third-party beneficiary law governs the issue of whether citizens, who were not a party to this contract, can sue the manufacturer directly if the manufacturer exceeds the pollution limits set in the contract. We will see that the answer depends on whether the city and manufacturer intended to give the citizens such a right.[2] Part A of this chapter discusses this and other questions about third-party beneficiary law.

Part B of this chapter discusses assignment of rights and delegation of duties under a contract. Again, Chapter 1 offers a helpful example of an assignment of rights (if I don't say so myself). A small local hardware store sells to True–Value the hardware store's contract right to the delivery of inventory from a wholesaler. In the terminology of assignment law, the hardware store has *assigned* its contract right to True–Value. Note that this is different from third-party beneficiary situations. True–Value's rights, if any, come about because of the assignment to it of the hardware store's rights under an existing contract between the hardware store and the wholesaler, not (as in third-party beneficiary law) because the hardware store and wholesaler made a contract to benefit True–Value. In assessing True–Value's rights, we ask whether requiring the wholesaler to deliver to True–Value instead of to the hardware store materially changes the wholesaler's duties, not whether the hardware store and wholesaler intended to benefit True–Value by making their contract. These distinctions are important and will become much clearer after reading the body of this chapter.

1. See Chapter 1.

2. See infra notes 18–39, and accompanying text.

Suppose True–Value purchases the local hardware store in its entirety, but the hardware store owed the wholesaler money. As part of the purchase of the hardware store, True–Value agrees to pay the debt. In the terminology of contract law, the hardware store has *delegated* to True–Value the hardware store's duty to pay the wholesaler. More on the respective rights and duties of the parties in this context in due time too.

A. Third–Party Beneficiaries

1. Introduction. Suppose you owe your friend, Taylor Plantations, $40. You agree to mow Alice's lawn. In exchange, she promises to pay Taylor directly the money you owe him, instead of paying you. Can Taylor sue Alice if you perform and Alice does not pay him?

A long time ago, the consensus was that Taylor could not sue. Taylor was not in "privity of contract" with Alice, meaning that he wasn't a party to your contract with Alice, so how could he sue for breach of that contract? The main exception to the privity barrier was for beneficiaries of trusts, who were allowed to sue the trustee, even though the beneficiary was not a party to the trust arrangement.[3] The last sentence is a lot to swallow if you are not familiar with trusts. Trusts are beyond the scope of this book (and first-year contracts courses), so a simple example will have to do. If parents set up a trust fund for their child at Perpetual Bank, the bank, as trustee, holds the money for the child, the beneficiary of the trust. Although the child was not a party to the contract between her parents and Perpetual Bank, the child can sue the bank for breach of the trust relationship, for example, if the bank breaches its fiduciary duty (duty of care) with respect to handling the trust fund.[4]

Apart from trusts, early contract law generally required a party to be in privity of contract in order to sue.[5] Reluctance to extend

3. See, e.g., Wickwire–Spencer Steel Corp. v. United Spring Mfg. Co., 142 N.E. 758, 759 (Mass. 1924) ("One for whose benefit a trust is established may avail himself of its advantages by instituting proceedings to enforce its terms."); Lawrence v. Fox, 20 N.Y. 268, 274 (1859) ("The principle ... so frequently quoted ... 'that a promise made to one for the benefit of another, he for whose benefit it is made may bring an action for its breach,' has been applied to trust cases....").

4. Restatement (Second) of Trusts § 200 (1959) ("No one except a beneficiary or one suing on his behalf can maintain a suit against the trustee to enforce the trust or to enjoin redress for a breach of trust.").

5. See, e.g., Verosol B.V. v. Hunter Douglas, Inc., 806 F.Supp. 582, 586 (E.D. Va. 1992) ("Under well-settled principles of contract law, a stranger to a contract ordinarily has no rights under the contract and cannot sue to enforce it."); Copiers Typewriters Calculators, Inc. v. Toshiba Corp., 576 F.Supp. 312, 322 (D. Md. 1983) ("Absent some recognized exception, it is hornbook law that only the parties to a contract can enforce it and that they may enforce it

the right to sue to non-parties was understandable because of the fear that over-extension of the right to sue on other people's contracts could deter promisors from entering contracts. For example, the manufacturer in our earlier example who agreed to pollution limits in a contract with the city may have thought twice about contracting if each and every citizen could sue it for breach of the agreement.[6] Further, over-extension could tax the courts. Think of the potential caseload if each citizen could sue over the pollution excesses of the manufacturer. Finally, contract law is supposed to be based on assent.[7] To be consistent with this principle, the manufacturer should be liable to individual citizens only if the manufacturer agreed to accept such liability.[8]

We now proceed to investigate two categories of third parties whose rights to sue have been recognized, namely *creditor* and *donee* beneficiaries. We will see that contract law recognized rights in these parties because many of the above concerns do not apply to them.

2. Creditor beneficiaries. In the opening problem in Section A, modern contract law allows Taylor to sue Alice for breach of her promise (made to you) to pay him. Taylor is a creditor beneficiary who can sue because you owed Taylor money and you made the contract with Alice in order to pay Taylor.

The court in the great case of *Lawrence v. Fox*[9] helped create the creditor-beneficiary category.[10] Holly owed Lawrence $300. Holly then loaned $300 to Fox in exchange for Fox's promise to pay $300 to Lawrence. The court had to decide whether Lawrence could sue Fox directly to enforce Fox's promise to pay Lawrence.

---

against only the parties to the contract.").

6. See, e.g., German Alliance Ins. Co. v. Home Water Supply Co., 226 U.S. 220, 231 (1912) (holding that allowing citizens to sue companies under contracts with the city "would unduly extend contract liability, would introduce new parties with new rights, and would subject those contracting with municipalities to suits by a multitude of persons for damages which were not, and ... could not have been, in contemplation of the parties."); H. R. Moch Co. v. Rensselaer Water Co., 247 N.Y. 160, 164 (1928) (the promisor must assume the "duty to make reparation directly to the individual members of the public.... The field of obligation would be expanded beyond reasonable limits if less than

this were to be demanded as a condition of liability.").

7. See Chapter 2 at notes 108–125, and accompanying text.

8. See, e.g., H. R. Moch Co., 247 N.Y. at 164; Rigney v. New York Cent. & H.R.R. Co., 111 N.E. 226, 228 (N.Y. 1916) (railroad company's contract with the city "can be read in no other light than as showing an intention on the part of the municipality that the railroad company should assume liability and pay the damage certain to accrue to the abutting owner from change of grade in the street.").

9. 20 N.Y. 268 (1859).

10. For an in-depth look at *Lawrence v. Fox*, see Anthony Jon Waters, The Property in the Promise: A Study of the Third Party Beneficiary Rule, 98 Harv. L. Rev. 1109 (1985).

First, the court noted the close analogy between the facts of the case and an actual trust arrangement, where a beneficiary could sue. The money Holly loaned Fox was not a trust fund because the money became Fox's property, meaning that Fox could use the money for whatever he wanted. Nevertheless, just as the nature of a trust implies a promise by the trustee to the beneficiary to pay the beneficiary, the arrangement between Holly and Fox implied a promise by Fox to Lawrence to pay him.[11] The logical step taken in the trust cases, of allowing a beneficiary to sue when the trustee breaches its duties, the court reasoned, therefore should also be taken in cases such as *Lawrence v. Fox.*

You may believe that the court's invocation of an implied promise from Fox to Lawrence was an unpersuasive legal fiction to avoid the problem of Lawrence's lack of privity of contract. But I hope to convince you that the policy reasons for extending the right to sue to Lawrence are strong. None of the concerns raised above about extending the category of who can sue too far seem very strong in *Lawrence.*[12] Creditor beneficiaries are a clear, finite category, minimizing the fear of overtaxing the courts or of discouraging promisors from contracting. Further, although finding an implied promise from Fox to Lawrence is a stretch, one can argue that Fox accepted the duty to pay Lawrence when Fox made his promise to Holly. After all, the contract specifically named Lawrence as the beneficiary. Not only do the policies against extending rights melt away, but strong positive policies in favor of extending rights exist. Contract law recognizes Lawrence's right to sue in order to decrease the likelihood of multiple lawsuits to resolve the parties' rights. (If Lawrence cannot sue Fox directly, Holly will have to sue Fox, then if Holly has second thoughts about paying Lawrence, Lawrence will have to sue Holly.) Contract law also recognizes Lawrence's standing to sue in order to place management of the lawsuit against Fox in the hands of the party with the greatest interest in pursuing the claim.

The *Lawrence* court considered another vexing issue: After their agreement, Holly and Fox had the right to change their minds and to release Fox from his obligation to pay Lawrence. In other words, Lawrence's rights are contingent on Holly and Fox *not* changing their minds. As a general matter, should the contingent nature of the third-party's rights mean that the third party should not be able to sue?[13] The court observed that Holly and Fox had not

---

11. 20 N.Y. at 274 ("[T]he consideration received and the promise to Holly made it as plainly his duty to pay [Lawrence] as if the money had been remitted to [Fox] for that purpose, and as well implied a promise to do so as if he had been made a trustee of property to be converted into cash with which to pay.").

12. See supra notes 6–8, and accompanying text.

13. 13 Samuel Williston & Richard A. Lord, A Treatise on the Law of Contracts 332 (4th ed. 2000) ("Contracting

changed their minds, so the court did not have to resolve the issue.[14] The court therefore left for later cases the question of *when* a third party's rights should vest (become non-changeable). We'll take up this issue shortly.[15]

As noted, third parties who can sue under the authority of *Lawrence v. Fox* became known as "creditor beneficiaries." The Restatement (First) of Contracts, section 133, defined creditor beneficiaries:

> (1) Where performance of a promise in a contract will benefit a person other than the promisee, that person is * * *
>
> (b) a creditor beneficiary if no purpose to make a gift appears from the terms of the promise in view of the accompanying circumstances and performance of the promise will satisfy an actual or supposed or asserted duty of the promisee to the beneficiary * * * .[16]

Note that the Restatement's definition of a creditor beneficiary encompassed a larger class than the one created by *Lawrence v. Fox*. Under the Restatement, the promisee did not have to owe the beneficiary a money debt. Further, the debt did not have to be real because a "supposed or asserted duty" would do.[17] This further expansion also should not be worrisome. If Holly tells Fox that Holly owes Lawrence money and extracts Fox's promise to pay Lawrence, what should it matter if Holly's obligation to Lawrence is only in Holly's mind? Fox should understand that, should Fox breach, Lawrence has the most to lose and that Holly intended to confer on Lawrence a right to performance. The class of potential plaintiffs still seems well within manageable bounds.

3. Donee beneficiaries. Donee beneficiaries also can sue. According to the first Restatement of Contracts, a party is a donee beneficiary if

> it appears from the terms of the promise in view of the accompanying circumstances that the purpose of the promisee

---

parties inherently possess the right to alter or even terminate their relationship by agreement. This power posed analytical problems during the development of the third party beneficiary doctrine.").

14. 20 N.Y. at 274 ("It is enough that the plaintiff did not release the defendant from his promise, and whether he could or not is a question not now necessarily involved. . . .").

15. See infra notes 42–43, and accompanying text.

16. Restatement (First) of Contracts § 133(1)(b) (1932).

17. See Hardware Ctr., Inc. v. Parkedge Corp., 618 S.W.2d 689, 693 (Mo. Ct. App. E.D. 1981) ("A person is a creditor beneficiary if performance of the promise will satisfy an actual, supposed, or asserted duty of the promisee to the beneficiary."); Northwest Airlines, Inc. v. Crosetti Bros., Inc., 483 P.2d 70, 73 (Or. 1971) ("To be a creditor beneficiary the performance of indemnity by [the promisor] must be to 'satisfy an actual or supposed or asserted duty of the promisee . . . to the beneficiary. . . .' ").

in obtaining the promise of all or part of the performance thereof is to make a gift to the beneficiary or to confer upon him a right against the promisor to some performance neither due nor supposed or asserted to be due from the promisee to the beneficiary * * *.[18]

As you can see, the first Restatement followed an objective approach to the interpretation of which third parties could sue as donee beneficiaries. It allowed a third party to sue when a reasonable person would believe that the promisee's "purpose" was to make a gift to the third party ("it *appears*" from the terms and context "that the purpose of the promisee"[19]). In just such a situation, a reasonable promisor would understand that, should she breach, the third party will be the primary aggrieved party because he was going to receive the gift. Some decisions have affirmed the view that a third party can sue when the promisor reasonably should know that the promisee's intent was to benefit the third party.[20]

The challenge, of course, is determining in a given case what a reasonable promisor should understand about the promisee's purpose in making a contract. In one early case, *Seaver v. Ransom*,[21] the court held that the plaintiff-niece was a third-party donee beneficiary of a promise by a husband to his wife (the plaintiff's aunt) to leave money to the niece in his will. The husband made the promise in exchange for his wife signing a will that gave the husband use of the wife's house during his life. As you can guess, the caddish husband left nothing to the niece in his will. The court emphasized the close relationship of the wife and her niece and the lack of interest of the representatives of the wife's estate in enforcing the husband's promise.[22] In just such a situation, a reasonable promisor should know the wife's purpose was to give her niece a gift.

Third parties have not always been successful, however, in establishing donee beneficiary status.[23] *H.R. Moch Co. v. Rensselaer*

---

18. Restatement (First) of Contracts § 133(1)(a).

19. Id (emphasis supplied).

20. See, e.g., Lucas v. Hamm, 364 P.2d 685, 689 (Cal. 1961) ("Insofar as intent to benefit a third person is important in determining his right to bring an action under a contract, it is sufficient that the promisor must have understood that the promisee had such intent.").

21. 120 N.E. 639 (N.Y. 1918).

22. Id. at 641 ("The desire of the childless aunt to make provision for a beloved and favorite niece differs imper-

ceptibly in law or in equity from the moral duty of the parent to make testamentary provision for a child.... The representatives of the wife's estate have no interest in enforcing it specifically.").

23. See, e.g., Isbrandtsen Co. v. Local 1291 of Int'l Longshoremen's Ass'n, 204 F.2d 495, 498 (3d Cir. 1953) ("We do not think ... that in ... this business setting any statement by the marine association that it intended its agreement with the labor union to benefit all the world who might be helped by the faithful performance of the contract would give these remote parties rights

Water Co.[24] helps us to understand appropriate line drawing. The city of Rensselaer entered a contract with a water company for the supply of water, including at fire hydrants. The court held that a citizen could not sue the water company when it failed to supply sufficient water to a fire hydrant to extinguish a fire that spread to the citizen's warehouse. Judge Cardozo reasoned that the citizen was not a creditor beneficiary because the city did not owe the citizen a duty to supply water at fire hydrants. Further, the citizen was not a donee beneficiary because, notwithstanding the citizen's obvious interest in the water company's performance, the contract did not evidence "an intention * * * that the promisor is to be answerable to individual members of the public as well as to the city for any loss ensuing from failure to fulfill the promise."[25] Judge Cardozo made no bones about the policy reason supporting his determination: "The field of obligation would be expanded beyond reasonable limits" if the citizen could sue under these circumstances.[26] Further, Cardozo thought that the water company would suffer a "crushing burden" by allowing citizens to sue.[27]

Cardozo's reasoning does not mean that a citizen can never sue as a third-party donee beneficiary of a contract between a governmental entity and a promisor. If a water company should know that the city contracted with the intention of granting the citizens a right to sue, the citizens would be donee beneficiaries.[28] For example, if the contract names citizens as the beneficiaries of the contract, they likely constitute donee beneficiaries.[29] Better still, if the contract expressly states that the parties intend to confer a cause of action on the citizens, they should be able to sue.

against one who broke it."); Davis v. Nelson–Deppe, Inc., 424 P.2d 733, 737 (Idaho 1967) ("Absent a manifested intent to the contrary, construction contracts between a contractor and a state or other public body for highway repair or construction of a new highway are generally not considered as being for the benefit of third persons . . . .").

24. 159 N.E. 896 (N.Y. 1928).

25. Id. at 897.

26. Id.

27. Id. at 897–98.

28. Id. at 897 (a member of the public can recover as a third party beneficiary under a contract between municipality and utility company when the benefit to the public is "primary and immediate in such a sense and to such a degree as to bespeak the assumption of a duty to make reparation directly to the individual members of the public if the benefit is lost."); see also La Mourea v.

Rhude, 295 N.W. 304, 306 (Minn. 1940) ("The city exacted from the [contractor] defendants a promise that they should be 'liable for any damages done to . . . private property' in connection with the work. . . . [Preventing injured citizens from suing as beneficiaries] would defeat obligation where obligation is not only intended but also expressed and paid for.").

29. See Keefer v. Lombardi, 102 A.2d 695, 696 (Pa. 1954) (holding that injured citizens could sue the contractor as third party beneficiary when the contract between the city and the contractor read, in part: "[Contractor] shall be alone liable and responsible for, and shall pay, any and all loss and damage sustained by any person or party either during the performance or subsequent to the completion of the work covered by this agreement. . . .").

Cardozo's approach places a lid on those who can sue, easing the concern about taxing the courts. Further, the approach extends rights only to those the water company should reasonably expect to have those rights. In case of any uncertainty, the water company can protect itself by refusing to contract unless the city agrees on a term barring third-party suits by citizens.

4. Restatement (Second) approach. The Restatement (Second) of Contracts dispenses with the "creditor" and "donee" terminology. But the issues remain the same.

Intended and Incidental Beneficiaries

(1) Unless otherwise agreed between promisor and promisee, a beneficiary of a promise is an intended beneficiary if recognition of a right to performance in the beneficiary is appropriate to effectuate the intention of the parties and either

(a) the performance of the promise will satisfy an obligation of the promisee to pay money to the beneficiary; or

(b) the circumstances indicate that the promisee intends to give the beneficiary the benefit of the promised performance.[30]

Under the Restatement (Second), only intended beneficiaries can sue.[31] A party is an intended beneficiary when (1) the parties intend to create "a right to performance in the beneficiary;" and (2) the promisee owes money to the beneficiary or the "circumstances indicate that the promisee intends to give the beneficiary the benefit of the promised performance."[32] The new rule omits any reference to creditor and donee beneficiaries, a supposed advance due to the technicalities of these terms. Nevertheless, you can see the strong resemblance of the new law to the old.[33] Parties heretofore called creditor beneficiaries can sue under section (1)(a) if the promisee owed the beneficiary money and parties formerly known as donee beneficiaries can sue under (1)(b) if the circumstances indicate that the promisee wanted to make a gift to the beneficiary. Section (1)(b) should also capture the first Restatement's category of creditor beneficiaries who the promisee wanted to benefit because the promisee believed that she owed the beneficiary an "actual or supposed or asserted duty."[34]

30. Restatement (Second) of Contracts § 302 (1981).

31. Id. § 304.

32. Id. § 302.

33. Harry G. Prince, Perfecting the Third Party Beneficiary Standing Rule Under Section 302 of the Restatement (Second) of Contracts, 25 B.C. L. Rev.

919, 990–97 (1984); cf. White v. General Motors Corp., 541 F.Supp. 190, 195 n.9 (D. Md. 1982). But see E. Allen Farnsworth, Contracts 678 (3d ed. 1999).

34. The quoted language is from Restatement (First) § 133(1)(b). See supra note 16, and accompanying text.

What is a bit unclear under the second Restatement is whether the rule requires *both* parties to intend to create a third-party right to performance. That, of course, is the way the rule reads.[35] But recall that the first Restatement applied an objective test of the promisee's intentions. What was important was what a reasonable promisor should know about the promisee's intentions, not what both parties actually intended.[36] An objective test is consistent with the general approach to contract formation and interpretation.[37] For my taste, therefore, the first Restatement approach is the better one. For you, the best thing to know is that there is more than one approach to the issue of what constitutes a donee or intended beneficiary.

Although line drawing between intended and incidental beneficiaries may be difficult in some instances,[38] a lawyer drafting a contract certainly can make the job easier by drafting appropriate language that reflects the parties' intentions. For example, if the contract expressly states that it is made for the benefit of certain third parties, those parties should have the right to sue. Conversely, if the contract restricts potential plaintiffs to the contracting parties, third parties should be out of luck.[39]

5. Defenses. Recall that one of the arguments against allowing *any* third parties to sue is based on the contingent nature of the third-party right.[40] For example, in *Lawrence v. Fox*,[41] Holly and Fox could modify their agreement to require Fox to pay Holly instead of Lawrence. Should the contingent nature of Lawrence's rights affect the court's conclusion that Lawrence can sue?

Modern contract law has taken care of this concern. First, suppose at the time of contracting Holly and Fox expressly agreed not to change Lawrence's rights. Contract law honors the parties'

---

35. See Hibbs v. K–Mart Corp., 870 F.2d 435, 441 (8th Cir. 1989) ("In order to be a third-party beneficiary of a contract, the contracting parties must intend that the third party receive a direct or primary benefit."); Grigerik v. Sharpe, 721 A.2d 526, 535 (Conn. 1998) ("[W]e conclude that the intent of both parties to a contract determines whether a third party has contract rights as a third party beneficiary.").

36. See supra notes 18–20, and accompanying text.

37. See Chapter 2 at notes 108–125, and accompanying text; Chapter 7 at notes 58–69, and accompanying text.

38. See, e.g., Kornblut v. Chevron Oil Co., 400 N.E.2d 368 (N.Y.1979) (finding that a motorist is not an intend-

ed beneficiary of a contract between the New York State Thruway Authority and Chevron Oil Co., in which Chevron promised to service cars on the thruway within thirty minutes).

39. See, e.g., Collins v. Morgan Stanley Dean Witter, 224 F.3d 496, 499 (5th Cir. 2000) ("Where a clause provides that the contracted-for services will run directly to and for the benefit of the other contracting party, any relevant third parties will be considered incidental rather than intended and immediate."); see also Edward B. Fitzpatrick, Jr. Const. Corp. v. County of Suffolk, 525 N.Y.S.2d 863, 866 (App. Div.1988).

40. See supra notes 13–15, and accompanying text.

41. 20 N.Y. 268 (1859).

intention not to discharge or modify the beneficiary's rights.[42] Second, the Restatement (Second) of Contracts enumerates several happenings that secure the third party's rights. If the beneficiary "materially changes his position" in reliance on his third-party rights, or brings a lawsuit based on the rights, or otherwise "manifests assent" to the creation of his rights "at the request" of one of the contracting parties, the contracting parties can no longer modify or discharge the beneficiary's rights.[43] Once the third party's rights have vested upon the happening of any of these events, a later modification or discharge by agreement of the contracting parties does not constitute a defense to a beneficiary's claim. A modification or discharge before the third party's rights have vested, of course, does constitute a defense.

The promisor can also assert defenses based on defects in the contract between the promisor and promisee. If the contract between Holly and Fox was invalid at the time of formation or becomes unenforceable because of "impracticability, public policy, non-occurrence of a condition," or a breach by the promisee, Fox can assert these defenses against Lawrence.[44]

6. Third parties under the UCC. Suppose you purchase a lawnmower from Sears. The lawnmower is defective and you are injured using it. We have learned that you can assert a breach of warranty claim against Sears.[45] (You may also have a claim under tort law.) But what are the rights of family members or others who use the mower and are injured? After all, they are not in privity of contract with the seller.

Section 2–318 of the UCC answers the question. It resolves the issue, not on the basis of the contracting parties' intentions, but on policy grounds. The drafters sought to create a balance between the protection of product users from shoddy products and the protec-

---

42. Restatement (Second) of Contracts § 311(1).

43. Id. § 311(3); see also Karo v. San Diego Symphony Orchestra Ass'n, 762 F.2d 819, 822 (9th Cir. 1985) ("The power to modify terminates when the beneficiary materially changes position in justifiable reliance on the promise before receiving notification of the modification."); Jardel Enters., Inc. v. Triconsultants, Inc., 770 P.2d 1301, 1303 (Colo. Ct. App. 1988) ("'[E]ach 'change of position' [the third-party beneficiary owners] assert was part of the normal progression on the restaurant project and was not related to reliance on the

subcontract [between the subcontractors and the contractor]. Therefore, the subcontractors and the contractor retained the power to discharge the duty to the owners.").

44. Restatement (Second) of Contracts § 309(2); see Rouse v. United States, 215 F.2d 872, 874 (D.C. Cir. 1954) ("[O]ne who promises to make a payment to the promisee's creditor can assert against the creditor any defense that the promisor could assert against the promisee.").

45. See Chapter 3 at notes 123–149, and accompanying text.

tion of sellers from unchecked liability. In fact, creating this balance proved so difficult and controversial that the drafters of the UCC offered three alternatives for the states. Alternative A is the most restrictive. Only "natural persons" (human beings, not the Terminator) who are in the buyer's family or in the family's household or are guests in the buyer's home and who have personal injuries can sue, and only if "it is reasonable to expect that such person may use, consume or be affected by the goods."[46] Alternative B extends the class of beneficiaries to any natural person if "it is reasonable to expect that such person may use, consume or be affected by the goods."[47] In other words, under Alternative B, a plaintiff does not have to be a family member, household member, or guest in the home. Alternative C goes still further by allowing "any person" (including organizations) to sue for economic loss as well as personal injury.[48]

The UCC doesn't expressly answer a related question—who can be sued for a defective product, meaning who are appropriate defendants. Can you (or a beneficiary under any of the alternatives to section 2–318) sue the manufacturer of the mower, Lawnboy, for breach of warranty, instead of Sears? Remember you are not in privity of contract with the manufacturer and you are not suing for negligence or strict tort liability, tort theories that would not require privity of contract.[49] Although the UCC does not expressly address the issue of who can be sued, commentary to section 2–318 invites courts to develop the issue.[50] Some courts have done just that, often allowing injured parties to sue the manufacturer directly.[51] As I mentioned in Chapter 1, the ALI recently adopted fairly extensive amendments to Article 2 (that previously were adopted by the ALI's sister organization for UCC purposes, NCCUSL).[52] Some

---

46. UCC § 2–318, Alternative A (1989); see, e.g., Armijo v. Ed Black's Chevrolet Ctr., Inc., 733 P.2d 870, 872 (N.M. Ct. App. 1987) ("[E]mployees of a purchaser are excluded from the manufacturer's warranty protections offered by provisions comparable to [section 2–318].").

47. UCC § 2–318, Alternative B.

48. UCC § 2–318, Alternative C. A "person" includes organizations. UCC § 1–201(30).

49. Restatement (Third) of Torts: Prod. Liab. § 1 (1998) ("One engaged in the business of selling or otherwise dis-

tributing products who sells or distributes a defective product is subject to liability for harm to persons or property caused by the defect.").

50. UCC § 2–318, cmt. 3.

51. See, e.g., Hadar v. Concordia Yacht Builders, Inc., 886 F.Supp. 1082, 1097 (S.D.N.Y. 1995) ("The doctrine of express and implied warranties, codified in the UCC, ... allows buyers to recover from manufacturers and sellers for [personal] injuries caused by defective products...").

52. See Chapter 1 at notes 5–6, and accompanying text.

of the amendments deal with the question of who can be sued for defective products (for personal injury or economic loss), so they require a paragraph or two here.

The amendments contain two new sections, sections 2–313A and B, that govern who can be sued for warranty-like obligations arising when the goods are defective. Section 2–313A applies to the problem of "terms in the box." For example, you purchase a computer at Best Buy, bring it home, and open the container, which contains the manufacturer's documentation. Section 2–313A requires that the goods live up to any "affirmation of fact or promise" about the quality of the goods, any description, or any promise relating to remedies for defects.[53] Under the section, any "remote purchaser," meaning a party who "buys or leases goods from" the first buyer "or other person in the normal chain of distribution," can assert the obligation against the manufacturer.[54] You qualify as a remote purchaser because you purchased from the immediate (first) buyer, Best Buy, who bought from the manufacturer-seller.[55] If the goods are defective, you will be successful against the manufacturer if a reasonable person would believe that the documentation creates an obligation.[56] You will lose if the language in the documentation is only "sales talk" or "puffing," meaning language, because of its generality or lack of verifiability, that does not rise to the level of an obligation.[57]

Section 313(B) governs advertising by the seller that reaches "remote purchasers" and that rises to the level of "an affirmation of fact or promise that relates to the goods, provides a description that relates to the goods, or makes a remedial promise."[58] For example, you see advertising about a Samsung computer and then purchase one at Best Buy. Again, you are a remote purchaser.[59] You must buy the goods with knowledge of the advertising and with the belief that the goods will conform to the advertising.[60] This section also sets forth the same defenses as section 2–313A. If a reasonable person would not believe the advertising created an obligation, you are out of luck.[61] Further, you lose if the advertising you read constituted only "sales talk."[62]

---

53. Amended UCC § 2–313A(3) (proposed final draft April 18, 2003).

54. Amended UCC § 2–313A.

55. Amended UCC § 2–313A(1) (" 'Immediate buyer' means a buyer that enters into a contract with the seller. 'Remote purchaser' means a person that buys or leases goods from an immediate buyer or other person in the normal chain of distribution.").

56. Amended UCC § 2–313A(3)(a).

57. Amended UCC § 2–313A(4).

58. Amended UCC § 2–313B(3).

59. Amended UCC § 2–313B(1)(b).

60. Amended UCC § 2–313B(3).

61. Amended UCC § 2–313B(3)(a).

62. Amended UCC § 2–313B(4).

B. Assignment of Rights and Delegation of Duties

1. Introduction. Now we turn to third-party rights and duties created *after* the formation of a contract. These third-party rights arise when a promisee *assigns* her rights under an existing contract to a third party. Third-party duties arise when a promisor *delegates* her duties under an existing contract to a third party.

As always, illustrations help to clarify the meaning of assignment and delegation. Suppose you mow Alice's lawn and she owes you $40 for the job. (This is the second half of our last chapter and I'm not about to abandon you and Alice at this point.) You can "assign" (transfer) your right to payment to Taylor Plantations, thereby conferring on Taylor the right to the money. You can do so as a gift,[63] or because you are obligated to Taylor. For an example of the latter, you agree to assign your right to payment of the $40 to Taylor in return for Taylor selling you his $35 baseball glove. Why would you take a $35 item in exchange for a $40 expectancy? Because the $40 is only an expectancy. Although Alice has been pretty reliable in our series of examples in this book, there is always the chance that she might not pay fully or at all. Even if Alice does pay, Taylor has to wait for payment and thus loses the time-value of money. Taylor therefore can buy your $40 contract right at a discount to take into account the risk of non-payment or delay in payment.

The law of assignment of rights governs much more complex and important transactions in our economy than the simple example above. Consider the assignment of contract rights by merchants or wholesalers to financial institutions. Suppose you and other consumers purchase hammers on credit from the local hardware store. Such stores usually are not in the business of financing such transactions. Instead, the hardware store sells (assigns) its rights to these payments (called "accounts") to a bank in exchange for immediate payment.[64] Wholesalers that supply the hardware store with inventory on credit may also assign their accounts to a bank in order to get cash up front. The law regulating the assignment of such rights facilitates business transactions and, hence, our economy. But regulating these transactions can be complex. For example, suppose the local hardware store wrongfully assigns its accounts to two different banks. The law must devise a system to enable banks to learn in advance if the accounts are already encumbered (assigned to someone else) and to determine who has priority between competing banks. Article 9 of the UCC deals with such issues. These and other interesting Article 9 issues are beyond the scope of most first-year contracts courses and, hence, this book.

63. Restatement (Second) of Contracts § 332.

64. UCC § 9–102(2) (2003).

Parties assign contract rights in additional types of transactions. For example, a bank may finance a construction company's building project in exchange for an assignment of the company's right to payment for the construction. For another example, the local hardware store may sell its business to a larger national chain, such as True–Value Hardware. As part of the transaction, the local hardware store may assign all of its contract rights to True–Value.

Let's stick with the latter example to illustrate the delegation of duties. The local hardware store may purchase inventory from a wholesaler on credit. As part of the sale of its business to True–Value, the latter may agree to pay all of the local hardware store's debts. We say that the local store has delegated the duty to pay to True–Value. Now let's look more closely at general contract law principles that apply to assignment and delegation (leaving for advanced courses the ins and outs of Article 9).

2. Assignment of rights. At the outset, you must understand the terminology courts often employ. Recall the example involving you, Alice, and Taylor.[65] You assign to Taylor your right to the $40 Alice owes you. You are the assignor, Alice is the obligor, and Taylor is the assignee.

As with third-party beneficiary law, a principle issue is whether Taylor can sue Alice directly if she doesn't pay him. Third-party beneficiary law resolves the question of who can sue by looking at the intent of the contracting parties. Assignment law asks whether the assignment materially changes Alice's obligation.[66] This depends on what you and Alice intended to get out of your contract. In our example, Alice wanted her lawn mowed and she should not care very much whether she pays you or Taylor. So it is likely that the parties did not intend to prohibit the assignment of your right to payment. Alice must pay Taylor and Taylor can sue her if she does not. Further, once you assign your right, you cannot sue Alice.[67] You have nothing left to sue on. The right belongs to Taylor.

A few more preliminaries. Suppose you have not yet secured your contract with Alice to mow her lawn. You cannot assign your future right to Taylor. You can make a contract promise to Taylor to assign your payment in the future (in exchange for Taylor's consideration), but you cannot presently assign what you don't yet have.[68] The legal ramification of making a contract promise to

65. See supra note 63, and accompanying text.

66. Restatement (Second) of Contracts § 317(2)(a).

67. Id. § 317(1).

68. See In re Richardson, 216 B.R. 206, 216–17 (Bankr. S.D. Ohio 1997) ("'A contract to assign a right in the future is not a valid assignment. A valid assignment contemplates no further action ... [by] the assignor to complete

Taylor instead of assigning a right is that Taylor may have a breach of contract claim against you if you don't secure the mowing contract and assign the right to payment to Taylor, but Taylor has no rights against Alice before you secure the contract with Alice (and none after, unless you and Alice make Taylor a third-party beneficiary of your mowing contract or you then assign your right to payment to Taylor).[69]

Crane Ice Cream Co. v. Terminal Freezing & Heating Co.[70] nicely illustrates a contract right that could not be assigned because it materially changed the obligor's duty. Reduced to its essentials, Frederick, was a local Baltimore ice cream manufacturer with one plant. Terminal promised to supply up to 250 tons of ice to Frederick per week at a fixed price, according to Frederick's requirements. Frederick promised to take the first 250 tons it needed from Terminal each week. Frederick sold its business to Crane, a large ice cream manufacturer doing business in Maryland and Pennsylvania. Did Terminal have to honor its commitment by delivering up to 250 tons of ice per week according to Crane's requirements?

The court held that Frederick's contract right to the ice was not assignable to Crane. The court pointed out that Terminal had already delivered ice to Frederick for three years before the parties made the current contract. Through its experience with Frederick and knowledge of the size and potential of Frederick's business, Terminal could easily calculate the likely amount of ice Frederick would need in a given week. The court reasoned that Terminal was willing to agree to a fixed-price contract because it could predict the amount of ice that Frederick would demand. Supplying Crane, however, would be a totally different matter. For example, Crane, doing business in a large geographic area, could demand the full 250 tons of ice from Terminal when the market price elsewhere was higher than the contract price and take no ice from Terminal when the reverse was true. The court therefore found that supplying Crane would materially change Terminal's duty, and held that Terminal did not have to supply Crane with ice.[71]

the ... assignee['s right]. A contract to assign involves a promise to do some future act in order to perfect ... the assignee['s right].' ") (quoting Morris v. Banning, 77 N.E.2d 372, 375 (Ohio Ct. App. 1947) (Wiseman, J., dissenting); see also Becker v. Godfrey Co., 324 N.W.2d 830, 1982 WL 172328, **2 (Wis. Ct. App. 1982) ("An agreement to make a future assignment is not an assignment.").

69. Restatement (Second) of Contracts § 330.

70. 128 A. 280 (Md.1925).

71. Id. at 283 ("[I]t is clear that the rights and duties of the contract under consideration were of so personal a character that the rights of Frederick cannot be assigned nor his duties be delegated without defeating the intention of the parties to the original contract.").

a. The obligor's defenses and claims. You assign to Taylor your right to the money Alice owes you for mowing her lawn. We have established that Taylor, as an assignee, has a cause of action against Alice if she does not pay him. But does Alice have any defenses against Taylor's claim? Suppose, for example, that you have done a miserable job mowing Alice's lawn and your performance constitutes a material breach. (Suppose you cut the lawn too low and Alice's lawn burned out.) If you had not assigned your right to payment, Alice could assert this defense against you. Because an assignee receives only what the assignor has to transfer, Alice can also assert your material breach as a defense against Taylor.[72] Similarly, if the contract between you and Alice is unenforceable because of impracticability (or another excuse doctrine[73]), the failure of a condition, or public policy (or another policing doctrine[74]), Alice can assert the defense against Taylor.[75]

Alice would not have a claim for an affirmative recovery of damages against Taylor, however, even if your performance constituted a material breach, and you destroyed Alice's lawn. Remember, Taylor received the right to payment from you and nothing more. He made no commitment with respect to your work for Alice. Nor did Taylor promise Alice directly to guarantee your performance. Alice has no theory for suing Taylor for your breach. (We will see shortly that the result would be different if, at the time of the assignment, you had not yet mowed Alice's lawn, and you not only assigned your right to payment, but also delegated your duty to Taylor. In this situation, Alice could sue Taylor if he did not mow Alice's lawn or did so poorly.[76])

---

72. Restatement (Second) of Contracts § 336(1) ("[A]ssignee acquires a right against the obligor only to the extent that the obligor is under a duty to the assignor...."); see also State v. Family Bank of Hallandale, 667 So.2d 257, 259 (Fla. Dist. Ct. App. 1995) ("The assignee steps into the shoes of the assignor and is subject to all equities and defenses that could have been asserted against the assignor had the assignment not been made."); Independent Nat'l Bank v. Westmoor Elec., Inc., 795 P.2d 210, 214 (Ariz. Ct. App. 1990) ("[A]n assignee of a chose in action acquires by virtue of his assignment nothing more than the assignor had and all equities and defenses which could have been raised by the debtor against the assignor are available to the debtor against the assignee.") (quoting Associates Loan Co.

v. Walker, 416 P.2d 529, 531 (N.M. 1966)).

73. See Chapter 9 for a discussion of the excuse doctrines.

74. See Chapter 6 for a discussion of the policing doctrines.

75. Restatement (Second) of Contracts § 336(3); see also Business Fin. Servs., Inc. v. Butler and Booth Dev. Co., Inc., 711 P.2d 649, 651 (Ariz. Ct. App. 1985) ("The assignee's right depends on the validity and enforceability of the contract creating the right, and is subject to limitations imposed by the terms of that contract and to defenses which would have been available against the obligee had there been no assignment.") (quoting Restatement (Second) of Contracts § 336, cmt. b).

76. See infra notes 108–109, and accompanying text.

Suppose after you mow Alice's lawn and after your assignment of the $40 to Taylor, but before Alice pays anything to anyone, you accidentally hit Alice's car while backing out of your driveway. Alice's car sustains $40 of damage. (As you know, this is a highly unrealistic example. Car manufacturers make cars so that the slightest impact causes a minimum of $10,000 of damage.) Alice could have asserted your tort liability as a "set off" (a claim unrelated to the contract) if you had not already assigned your right to payment and you were suing her for your $40. But can she assert the set off against Taylor under the actual facts?

The answer depends on when Taylor notified Alice of the assignment and when her tort claim against you "accrued."[77] If Taylor notified Alice before the tort claim accrued, Alice can not assert the set off against Taylor.[78] Conversely if the tort claim accrued first, Alice can assert the set off against Taylor.[79] You're probably wondering what "accrued" means. Basically, it is the time "when a cause of action comes into being."[80] This can be technical, but here the cause of action accrued when you hit Alice's car. A breach of contract cause of action accrues, not when the parties make a contract, but when a party repudiates or breaches it.[81] The moral of the story, of course, is that an assignee such as Taylor should notify the obligor of an assignment immediately to cut off potential set-off defenses.

There is another reason why an assignee should notify the obligor of the assignment immediately. Taylor's notification cuts off the right of you and Alice to modify your contract, for example, so that Alice must pay you instead of Taylor.[82] Without such a notification, Alice would be discharged from her obligation to Taylor if she pays you the $40.

77. Restatement (Second) of Contracts § 336(2) ("The right of an assignee is subject to any [set off] ... which accrues before the obligor receives notification of the assignment....").

78. See Heath v. Knutson, 698 P.2d 1015, 1017 (Or. Ct. App. 1985) ("[T]he evidence is undisputed that defendants received notice of the trustee's assignment of accounts to plaintiff before they acquired the claim on which they rely. Accordingly, they may not set off that claim against plaintiff's claims.").

79. Coplay Cement Co., Inc. v. Willis & Paul Group, 983 F.2d 1435, 1442 (7th Cir. 1993) ("The assignee ... stands in the shoes of the assignor and therefore takes the assignment subject to any defenses against the assignor's ... claim that arose before the assignment was made, and often after, provided it was before the [obligor] was notified of the assignment."); see also Bridgeport–City Trust Co. v. Niles–Bement–Pond Co., 20 A.2d 91, 94 (Conn. 1941) ("Ordinarily the assignee of a chose in action takes it subject to equities and defenses which could have been set up against it in the hands of the assignor, provided they have arisen before receipt of notice of the assignment.").

80. Seattle–First Nat'l Bank v. Oregon Pac. Indus., Inc., 500 P.2d 1033, 1035 (Or. 1972).

81. Id.

82. Restatement (Second) of Contracts § 338(1).

The rules that cut off defenses of obligors (including set offs, modifications, and discharges) after notification reflect contract law's attempt to protect obligors to the extent possible, without discouraging assignments. Taylor can accept the assignment with assurance that, after his notification to Alice, he is protected from new defenses Alice may accrue independent of her contract with you. After notification, Taylor also doesn't have to worry about you discharging Alice wholly or in part. For Alice's part, remember that she will have a cause of action against you for crashing into her car, she just can't use the crash as a defense against Taylor.

Now suppose that at the time of your assignment of rights to Taylor the contract in which you promise to mow Alice's lawn for $40 is executory (neither party has performed yet). Taylor notifies Alice of the assignment. If you and Alice later agree that Alice will pay you instead of Taylor, Alice can assert this defense against Taylor, even though Taylor has already notified Alice of the assignment.[83] With executory contracts, contract law weighs Alice's interest in being able to adjust her contract as circumstances dictate above Taylor's interest in being able to rely on payment. For example, suppose your lawnmower breaks down and you are short of funds. You and Alice can agree that she will pay you in advance instead of Taylor so that you can buy new parts for the mower. Consider also illustration 5 of section 338 of the Restatement (Second) of Contracts, which involves A's agreement to perform construction work for B.[84] A assigns its right to payments to C. C notifies B. If A becomes financially unable to perform, B can pay A instead of C so that the construction work can proceed. B's payment to A is a defense against C.

Finally, you may wonder whether contracting parties can prohibit an assignment of rights. With certain exceptions, especially under Article 9 of the UCC, the answer is yes.[85] The contracting parties must do so clearly, however.[86]

---

83. Id. § 338(2).

84. Id. § 338, cmt. f, illus. 5.

85. See Parkinson v. Caldwell, 272 P.2d 934, 937 (Cal. Ct. App. 1954) ("A contract right has its origin in the agreement of the parties and if the parties by their free agreement place a limitation on the right [of assignment] at the very time of its creation why they may not do so."); Allhusen v. Caristo Constr. Corp., 103 N.E.2d 891, 893 (N.Y. 1952) ("[W]hile the courts have striven to uphold freedom of assignability, they have not failed to recognize the concept of freedom to contract. In large measure they agree that, where appropriate language is used, assignments of money due under contracts may be prohibited.").

86. See Pro Cardiaco Pronto Socorro Cardiologica S.A. v. Trussell, 863 F.Supp. 135, 138 (S.D.N.Y. 1994) ("[A]ssignments are enforceable unless expressly made void, and not, as defendant apparently argues, void unless specified otherwise."); Owen v. CNA Ins./Cont'l Cas. Co., 771 A.2d 1208, 1214 (N.J. 2001) ("In the absence of such [clear] language, the provision limiting or prohibiting assignments will be interpreted merely as a covenant not to assign, [b]reach of [which] may render the [assignor] liable in damages to the [obli-

3. Delegation of duties. Again assume an executory contract in which you promise to mow Alice's lawn for $40. Suppose you "assign the contract" to Taylor. Contract law treats the assignment of the contract as both an assignment of your rights under the contract to the $40, and a delegation of your duty to mow Alice's lawn.[87] (This rule is only a "default" rule, meaning that it only applies in the absence of proof of other intentions. For example, if your "assignment of the contract" to Taylor clearly stated that it constitutes only an assignment of rights to the $40, but not a delegation of your duties to Taylor, contract law would enforce those intentions.)[88]

A party can delegate a duty in other contexts too. For example, assume you have a contractual obligation to mow Alice's lawn. Instead of assigning the contract to Taylor, you pay him $40 to mow the lawn instead of you. In each of these contexts, a delegation of duties means that Taylor, as delegatee, has agreed to perform your obligation, namely mowing Alice's lawn. This creates several issues.

Does Alice have to accept Taylor as the party who will mow her lawn or can she insist that you do it? Alternatively, does Taylor have a duty to mow Alice's lawn that Alice can enforce? Finally, after the delegation, do you still owe Alice a duty that she can enforce? Asked more generally, these questions are first, does an obligee (Alice) have to accept the delegatee's (Taylor's) performance; second, can the obligee enforce its rights against the delegatee; and third, does the obligee have a right against the delegator (you) even after the delegation?

a. Does an obligee have to accept the delegatee's performance? Does Alice have to accept Taylor as the party mowing her lawn or can she insist that you do the job? Alice has to accept Taylor's performance unless the contract is a "personal" one.[89] Under the second Restatement (and UCC section 2–210(1)), the test is whether "the obligee [Alice] has a substantial interest in having" the delegator (you) perform.[90] Another way of asking the same

---

gor], but the assignment, however, remains valid....").

87. Restatement (Second) of Contracts § 328(1).

88. See, e.g., Kunzman v. Thorsen, 740 P.2d 754, 760 (Or. 1987) ("Where the parties clearly intend otherwise (as evinced either by the terms of the assignment or by the surrounding circum-

stances ...), the implication that the assignee assumed the vendor's contractual duties is dispelled.").

89. See, e.g., Macke Co. v. Pizza of Gaithersburg, Inc., 270 A.2d 645 (Md. 1970). See also Janvey v. Loketz, 106 N.Y.S. 690, 692 (App. Div. 1907).

90. Restatement (Second) of Contracts § 318(2).

question is whether the delegation of performance would materially change Alice's rights under the contract.[91]

At first blush, you may be surprised by this analysis based on your love for freedom of contract. Alice contracted with you, why should she have to accept Taylor's lawn mowing prowess, regardless of how well he can do the job? Calm down, calm down. Consider the following. Alice could have protected herself in her contract with you by specifying that the lawn-mowing duty could not be delegated.[92] In the absence of such a term, contract law presumes that reasonable people in your and Alice's shoes would agree to allow a delegation, except when it would materially change Alice's rights. Again, this presumption is a "default" rule that applies when the parties have not contracted otherwise. Hence, no freedom-of-contract concern.

Some courts apply a rule that "personal services" contracts can never be delegated, thereby reversing the "substantial interest" default rule.[93] The idea is that, when a contract involves personal services, an obligee would always have a substantial interest in performance by the delegator. The challenge under this approach is to determine exactly what constitutes a personal services contract.[94] For example, perhaps your duty to mow Alice's lawn constitutes

---

91. See, e.g., Crane Ice Cream Co. v. Terminal Freezing & Heating Co., 128 A. 280, 283 (Md. 1925) ("[O]ne who is bound so as to bear an inescapable liability may delegate the performance of his obligation to another, if the liability be of such a nature that its performance by another will be substantially the same thing as performance by the promisor himself."); British Waggon Co. v. Lea & Co., 5 Q.B.D. 149, 153 (1880) ("[When p]ersonal performance is ... of the essence of the contract, [delegation] ... cannot ... be enforced against an unwilling party. But.... [a]ll that the hirers ... cared for in this stipulation was that the waggons should be kept in repair; it was indifferent to them by whom the repairs should be done.").

92. Restatement (Second) of Contracts § 322(1); see also UCC § 2–210(5).

93. See, e.g., Sally Beauty Co. v. Nexxus Prods. Co., Inc., 801 F.2d 1001, 1008 (7th Cir. 1986) ("When perform-

ance of personal services is delegated, the trier merely determines that it is a personal services contract. If so, the duty is per se nondelegable."); In re Rooster, Inc., 100 B.R. 228, 232 (Bankr. E.D. Pa. 1989) ("A contract for 'personal services' contemplates performance of contracted-for duties involving the exercise of special knowledge, judgment, taste, skill, or ability. These services are not assignable by the party under obligation to perform without the consent of the other contracting party.").

94. See, e.g., Sally Beauty, 801 F.2d at 1004–05 ("Although it might be 'reasonable to conclude' that [the original parties] had based their agreement on 'a relationship of personal trust and confidence,' ... this is a finding of fact."); In re Health Plan of Redwoods, 286 B.R. 407, 409 (Bankr. N.D. Cal. 2002) ("Whether or not a contract is a personal services contract is a question of fact to be made under state law after all facts and circumstances are considered.").

"personal services,"[95] but a court could also consider your work more akin to construction, which contract law typically finds can be delegated.[96]

Now let's consider the guidance offered by some of the cases that have wrestled with the question of whether an obligee must accept a contract delegation. Recall that the court in *Crane Ice Cream Co. v. Terminal Freezing & Heating Co.*,[97] held that Terminal's duties would materially change if it was required to supply Crane with ice instead of Frederick, and therefore barred the assignment from Frederick to Crane of the right to ice. The court also found that Terminal's *rights* would materially change if Frederick could substitute Crane as Terminal's debtor.[98] The court reasoned that Terminal had already tested the "character, credit, and resources" of Frederick.[99] The court therefore barred the delegation of Frederick's duties to Crane.

In *Macke Co. v. Pizza of Gaithersburg, Inc.*,[100] on the other hand, the court held that the owner of certain restaurants had to accept the performance of delegatee Macke to install, service, and maintain certain vending machines and to pay the owner a fee, even though the owner had chosen to deal with a different company, Virginia Coffee Service, Inc., for those services. The restaurant argued to no avail that Virginia paid commissions to the owner in cash and provided more personalized services.

Courts often frame the issue in cases such as *Crane* and *Macke* as boiling down to whether a promised performance was more like the work of a famous painter or author that involves "rare genius and extraordinary skill," which cannot be delegated, or was more like "digging down of a sand hill" or the "construction of brick sewers," which can.[101] The court in *Macke* concluded that Virginia's duties were more like the latter, so the delegation by Virginia to Macke would stand. But the right to delegate a duty is not as broad as the reference to "rare genius and extraordinary" skill suggests. For example, the test of whether you can delegate your duty to mow Alice's lawn should focus on whether you have special skills as a mower of lawns that Taylor lacks.[102]

---

95. Restatement (Second) of Contracts § 318, cmt. c, illus. 7.

96. Id. § 318, cmt. a, illus. 3.

97. 128 A. 280 (Md. 1925).

98. Id. at 282.

99. Id.

100. 270 A.2d 645 (Md. 1970).

101. Id. at 648 (citing Taylor v. Palmer, 31 Cal. 240, 247–48 (1866)).

102. See, e.g., In re Compass Van & Storage Corp., 65 B.R. 1007, 1011

In an interesting sale-of-goods context, *Sally Beauty Co. v. Nexxus Products Co., Inc.*[103] applies UCC section 2–210(1)'s "substantial interest" test for determining whether an obligee must accept a delegated performance. Best Barber & Beauty Supply Company agreed to be the exclusive distributor of Nexxus's hair care products. Sally purchased Best, but Nexxus refused to deal with Sally because Alberto–Culver Company, a major competitor of Nexxus, owned Sally. Sally sued Nexxus, but the court agreed with Nexxus. Nexxus had a substantial interest in avoiding having a competitor as its exclusive distributor.[104]

Judge Posner dissented because he believed that it was unlikely that Nexxus could be hurt by dealing with Sally. Alberto–Culver likely would not order Sally to "go slow" in distributing Nexxus's products because Alberto–Culver had no guarantee that buyers would then purchase its products instead of other competitors' products.[105] Sally might also lose other manufacturers' distribution contracts if it favored Alberto–Culver's products at Nexxus's expense, and this, of course, would be bad for Alberto–Culver. In addition, the distribution contract was only for one year, so it was unlikely that Sally could do much harm to Nexxus in that time. Finally, Sally would be liable to Nexxus for any harm caused by Sally's failure to use best efforts, an obligation Sally owed under UCC section 2–306(2).[106] Judge Posner concluded that "there is no principle of law that if something happens that trivially reduces the probability that a dealer will use his best efforts, the supplier can cancel the contract."[107]

(Bankr. E.D.N.Y. 1986) ("Ascertaining whether a contract is personal posits on close distinctions, *e.g.*, the nature and subject matter of the contract, the circumstances of the case placed in juxtaposition with the intention of the parties.") (citing In re Taylor Mfg., 6 B.R. 370 (Bankr. N.D.Ga.1980)); West Coast Cambridge, Inc. v. Rice, 584 S.E.2d 696, 2003 WL 21508232, *4 (Ga. Ct. App. 2003) ("[D]uties may not be delegated where performance by the delegate would materially vary from the performance required by the original obligor."); First Ill. Nat'l Bank v. Knapp, 615 N.E.2d 75, 78 (Ill. App. Ct. 1993) ("Where the party entitled to performance has placed trust and confidence in the performing party, the performing

party cannot unilaterally delegate his or her responsibilities.").

103. 801 F.2d 1001 (7th Cir. 1986).

104. Id. at 1008 ("Nexxus has a substantial interest in not seeing this contract performed by Sally Beauty, which is sufficient to bar the delegation....").

105. 801 F.2d at 1010.

106. UCC § 2–306(2) ("A lawful agreement by either the seller or the buyer for exclusive dealing in the kind of goods concerned imposes ... an obligation by the seller to use best efforts to supply the goods and by the buyer to use best efforts to promote their sale.").

107. Sally Beauty, 801 F.2d at 1011.

For my taste, the majority had the better argument in *Sally Beauty Co.* Judge Posner relies too heavily on market forces to deter Alberto–Culver from directing Sally not to use its best efforts in distributing Nexxus's products. If I was a stockholder in Nexxus, I wouldn't be too happy to learn that a major competitor controlled the distribution of my company's product. More important for you to understand, as a future lawyer who may have to draft an exclusive distributorship, is the strategy for avoiding litigation (and Posner's wrath) in the first place. It is simple. Draft a clause making the distributorship's duties non-delegable.

b. Can the obligee enforce its rights against the delegatee? Here we ask whether Alice has rights against Taylor if he doesn't mow. The answer is yes. Recall that an "assignment of contract" means both an assignment of rights and a delegation of duties, in the absence of evidence otherwise.[108] By an assignment of the contract, then, Taylor has promised you to mow Alice's lawn, a duty you owe Alice. Alice therefore has rights against Taylor based on third-party beneficiary law. Alice is a creditor beneficiary under the first Restatement and an intended beneficiary under the second Restatement.[109]

c. Does the obligee have a right against the delegator even after the delegation? Does Alice have a cause of action against you for delegating your performance? Let's assume first that your delegation to Taylor constitutes a material change in Alice's rights. Alice doesn't have to accept Taylor's performance and your attempt to cast off your duty would be a breach of contract.[110] Now let's assume that Alice does not have a substantial interest in your performance. Taylor does not perform, however, or performs poorly. Alice has a cause of action against you as well as Taylor because she never released you from your obligation to mow.[111] If she had released you, of course, she would have no rights against you.[112] When all three parties agree to a substitution of one

108. See supra notes 87–88, and accompanying text.

109. See supra notes 9–17; 30–39, and accompanying text.

110. See, e.g., Beck v. Mfrs. Hanover Trust Co., 481 N.Y.S.2d 211, 217 (N.Y. Sup. Ct. 1984) ("[A]ny transfer of contractual duty so as to discharge the original obligor, requires the obligee's assent where such transfer alters the substance of the contract or otherwise materially affects the obligee's rights.").

111. Restatement (Second) of Contracts § 318(3); see also Martinesi v. Tidmore, 760 P.2d 1102, 1104 (Ariz. Ct. App. 1988) ("Since Martinesi did not consent to release Tidmore from liability when he conveyed the property to Shallenberger, the court erred in determining as a matter of law that Tidmore had not breached the contract and in granting his motion to dismiss.").

112. See, e.g., F. Haag & Bro. v. Reichert, 134 S.W. 191, 193 (Ky. Ct. App. 1911) ("[I]n cases where the assignment is assented to by the other party to the contract, ... there is, in effect, a new contract. It is an agreed rescission of the old contract, and the substitution of a new one in which the same acts are to be performed by different parties."); see also Heaton v. Angier, 7 N.H. 397 (1835) ("The agreement of the plaintiff to take Chase as his debtor was clearly a discharge of the defendant.").

obligor (Taylor) for another (you) and to the release of the original obligor, the resulting contract is a special kind of contract, called a novation.[113]

113. See Security Benefit Life Ins. Co. v. F.D.I.C., 804 F.Supp. 217, 225 (D. Kan. 1992) ("An obligor is discharged by substitution of a new obligor only if the contract so provides or if the obligee makes a binding manifestation of assent to the substitution, forming a novation."); Harrington–Wiard Co. v. Blomstrom Mfg. Co., 131 N.W. 559, 563 (Mich. 1911) ("[T]he necessary legal elements to establish novation are: (1) Parties capable of contracting; (2) a valid prior obligation to be displaced; (3) the consent of all parties to the substitution, based upon sufficient consideration; and, (4) lastly, the extinction of the old obligation and the creation of a valid new one.").

Table of Cases

F

G

T

Y

Table of Citations to the Uniform Commercial Code

Table of Citations to Amended Article 2 of the Uniform Commercial Code

*

Table of Citations to Restatements of the Law

*

Index

371

†